Barcode in Back

Domestic Tourism in Asia

Domestic Tourism in Asia

Diversity and Divergence

Edited by Shalini Singh

earthscan

publishing for a sustainable future

London • Sterling, VA

First published by Earthscan in the UK and USA in 2009

Copyright © Shalini Singh, 2009

ISBN: 978-1-84407-660-4

Typeset by FiSH Books, Enfield
Cover design by Susanne Harris

For a full list of publications please contact:

Earthscan
Dunstan House
14a St Cross St
London, EC1N 8XA, UK
Tel: +44 (0)20 7841 1930
Fax: +44 (0)20 7242 1474
Email: earthinfo@earthscan.co.uk
Web: **www.earthscan.co.uk**

22883 Quicksilver Drive, Sterling, VA 20166-2012, USA

Earthscan publishes in association with the International Institute for
Environment and Development

A catalogue record for this book is available from the British Library
Library of Congress Cataloging-in-Publication Data
Domestic tourism in Asia : diversity and divergence / edited by Shalini Singh.
    p. cm.
  Includes bibliographical references and index.
  ISBN 978-1-84407-660-4 (hardback)
  1. Tourism—Asia. I. Singh, Shalini.
  G155.A74D66 2009
  338.4'7915–dc22
                                                        2008050076

At Earthscan we strive to minimize our environmental impacts and carbon footprint through reducing waste, recycling and offsetting our CO_2 emissions,
including those created through publication of this book. For more details of our
environmental policy, see www.earthscan.co.uk.

This book was printed in the UK by CPI Antony Rowe.
The paper used is FSC certified and the inks are
vegetable based.

Mixed Sources
Product group from well-managed
forests and other controlled sources
www.fsc.org Cert no. SGS-COC-2953
© 1996 Forest Stewardship Council

Contents

List of Figures, Tables and Boxes

Figures

Tables

Boxes

List of Contributors

Victor Alneng is a lecturer in the Department of Social Anthropology, Stockholm University, Sweden. His academic interests relate to issues concerning popular culture, travel, war and capitalism. Alneng is currently engaged with a project on current capitalist reformation of Vietnam. His study focuses on the former colonial hill station of Đà Lạt, where he conducts fieldwork for his doctoral degree.

Department of Social Anthropology
Stockholm University
SE-106 91 Stockholm, Sweden
Email: victor.alneng@socant.su.se; victor.alneng@gmail.com

Chan Yuk Wah is an assistant professor in the Department of Asian and International Studies, City University of Hong Kong, Hong Kong. Her research interests focus on gender, identity, tourism modernity, development and historical memories. Chan also studies ethnic Chinese in Vietnam, outbound Chinese tourism, ecotourism and Vietnamese diaspora.

Department of Asian and International Studies
City University of Hong Kong
Tat Chee Avenue, Kowloon Tong, Hong Kong
Email: yukchan@cityu.edu.hk

Janet Chang is a professor in the Department of Tourism Management, Chinese Culture University, Taipei. Her current academic interests focus on aspects of cultural tourism, particularly those associated with indigenous people. Chang also studies aspects of hospitality and marketing.

Department of Tourism Management
Chinese Culture University
Taipei, 111 Taiwan
Email: yukchan@cityu.edu.hk

Amartuvshin Dorjsuren is a PhD researcher at Sheffield Hallam University, UK. His continuing research focuses on issues in tourism development process and related impacts in rural areas of Mongolia. He has been involved with research on the social carrying capacity of nomadic peoples to tourism in the Gobi Desert region in southern Mongolia.

Centre for International Tourism Research (CITouR)
Faculty of Organization and Management, Sheffield Hallam University
City Campus, Howard Street
Sheffield S1 1WB, UK
Email: amara_phd@yahoo.com

Fung Yip Hing is an MA graduate in anthropology with the Department of Anthropology, Chinese University of Hong Kong, Hong Kong. His research interest focuses on nature and cultural tourism in Asian countries, particularly Hong Kong.

28B, Block 5, Villa Athena
600 Sai Sha Road,
Ma On Shan, NT, Hong Kong
Email: yhfung888@netvigator.com

Joan C. Henderson is an associate professor at Nanyang Technological University, Singapore. Her research interests focus on destination development and marketing within a South-East Asian context. Henderson's research publications also include work on heritage tourism and tourism crisis management.

Nanyang Business School
Nanyang Technological University
Nanyang Avenue, Singapore 639798
Email: ahenderson@ntu.edu.sg

Ranjith Ihalanayake is a lecturer at the School of Economics and Finance, Victoria University, Australia. His research interests include tourism taxation, computable general equilibrium modelling in tourism, tourism impact studies, and externalities in tourism and tourism-related issues in Sri Lanka, with specific reference to domestic tourism.

School of Economics and Finance
Centre for Tourism and Services Research
Victoria University, Footscray Park Campus
Ballarat Road, Footscray, PO Box 14428, Melbourne, Victoria 8001, Australia
Email: Ranjith.Ihalanayake@vu.edu.au

Cindia Ching-Chi Lam is a senior lecturer with the Institute for Tourism Studies, Colina de Mong-ha, Macau. Her research interests range from tourist behaviour, customer choice and quality of life to investor behaviour. She is the editor of the research notes for *Tourism and Hospitality e-Review* (Macau, China) and, as a certified accountant, she researches management accounting, accounting education and accounting history.

Institute for Tourism Studies
Colina de Mong-ha
Macau
Email: Cindia@ift.edu.mo

Nicola J. Palmer is a senior lecturer in the Faculty of Organization and Management, Sheffield Hallam University in Sheffield, UK. Her interest in the political, economic and social aspects of tourism development has kept her engaged with the destination of Kyrgyzstan, where she has been involved in a European Union-funded project and conducted field studies over the past decade. Palmer's publications relate to tourism policy, the involvement of external development agencies in an emerging post-Soviet economy, and issues of ethnic equality within the Kyrgyz Republic. In addition, she is actively researching the topical areas of national identity, destination image representation, corporate social responsibility and migrant workers and the visitor economy.

Centre for International Tourism Research (CITouR)
Faculty of Organization and Management, Sheffield Hallam University
City Campus, Howard Street
Sheffield S1 1WB, UK
Email: n.palmer@shu.ac.uk

Linda K. Richter has recently retired as professor emirata of political science at Kansas State University. She continues to write and lecture on the politics of tourism development. Richter's research interest focuses on public policy on tourism, gender and agrarian reform; public administration; and public policy in Asia, particularly in the Philippines, Pakistan and India. Some of her seminal publications include *Land Reform and Tourism Development: Policy-Making in the Philippines* (Schenkman Pub. Co.) and *The Politics of Tourism in Asia* (University of Hawaii Press).

Department of Political Science
Waters 226
Kansas State University
Manhattan, KS 66506, US
Email: lrichter@ksu.edu

Maria Cherry Lyn S. Rodolfo is programme director in the School of Economics at the University of Asia and the Pacific, the Philippines. She continues to align her research with government, private and academic projects related to tourism economy, destination development, tourism development strategies, and master plan and product development. Rodolfo also studies air transport and airport economics, logistics and trade-in services.

Master of Science in Industrial Economics
University of Asia and the Pacific
Pearl Drive, Ortigas Centre,
Pasig City 1605, The Philippines
Email: crodolfo@uap.edu.ph; cherrylyn.rodolfo@gmail.com

Shalini Singh is associate professor in the Department of Recreation and Leisure Studies, Brock University, Ontario, Canada. Her research in tourism is largely in the context of developing countries, in general, and India, in particular. Her areas of interest, in this regard, focus on tourism in destination communities, pilgrimages, community development, place and people synergies. Her recent field of interest concerns the role (and nature) of tourism as a reconciliatory agency. Singh is also the executive editor of *Tourism Recreation Research* (India).

Department of Recreation and Leisure Studies
Brock University
St Catharines, Ontario L2S 3A1, Canada
Email: ssingh@brocku.ca

Trevor H. B. Sofield is professor of tourism in the School of Management, University of Tasmania, Australia. He has recently completed a three-year term as team leader for the Mekong Tourism Development Project, which was based in Phnom Penh and Hanoi. Prior to this project, Sofield researched tourism planning in developing countries of the Asia Pacific for more than 30 years. As a prolific researcher, he is the author/editor of several books, monographs and reports, book chapters, and other publications. Some of his recent titles include *Empowerment for Sustainable Tourism Development* (Pergamon, 2003); *Tourism and Community Development: Asian Cases* (co-editor; UNWTO, 2008).

School of Management
University of Tasmania, Australia
Email: tsofield@postoffice.utas.edu.au

Christopher S. Thompson is associate professor of Japanese Language and Culture in the Linguistics Department of Ohio University, Ohio, US. As a cultural anthropologist, his teaching involves three study-abroad programmes that entail travelling to Japan twice a year to conduct long-term fieldwork at various sites in the country. Thompson's research interests include topics such as the intersection of tradition and modernity in specific regions of Japan. Having recently accomplished a co-authored work, *Wearing Cultural Styles in Japan: Concepts of Tradition and Modernity in Practice* (State University of New York Press, 2006), he is now working on a book on the social, political and cultural ramifications of municipal consolidation in Hanamaki, Iwate, Japan.

Department of Linguistics
Gordy Hall 351,
Ohio University
Athens, OH 45701, US
Email: thompsoc@ohio.edu

Christopher Vasantkumar is Luce junior professor of anthropology and asian studies at Hamilton College, New York. He is especially interested in studying cultural difference as both an impediment to and catalyst for development in economically backward minority regions in the People's Republic of China (PRC). For this he has conducted ethnographic fieldwork on ethnic diversity and economic development in north-west China on multiple occasions since 2003. Vasantkumar's work emerges from a larger project on the ambivalent relationship between Tibet and the Chinese nation state.

Hamilton College
198 College Hill Road
Clinton, NY 13323, US
Email: cvasantk@hamilton.edu

Louis Tze Ngai Vong is assistant professor in management with the Institute for Tourism Studies, Colina de Mong-ha, Macau. His area of research is leisure studies. Vong continues to study the roles of leisure in Chinese societies, with an emphasis on Macau.

Institute for Tourism Studies
Colina de Mong-ha, Macau
Email: louis@ift.edu.mo

Geoffrey Wall is a professor in the Department of Geography, University of Waterloo, Canada. He has extensive field-based research in many aspects of tourism in Asia, particularly in China, including Taiwan, as well as Indonesia. Wall is especially interested in studying the implications of tourism of different types for destinations with different characteristics, and the implications of the findings for tourism planning.

Department of Geography
University of Waterloo
Waterloo
Ontario N2L 5X4, Canada
Email: gwall@fesmail.uwaterloo.ca

John K. Walton is professor of social history in the Institute of Northern Studies, Leeds Metropolitan University, Leeds, UK. He conducts research on the social and cultural history of tourism since the 18th century, especially coastal resorts, and the relationships between tourism and regional identity, especially in the UK and Spain. Beyond these interests, he has worked on British regional history, the history of the British retail co-operative movement, and the influence of the British Victorian cultural critic John Ruskin. Walton's recent publications include, as editor, *Histories of Tourism* (Channel View, 2005); with Gary Cross, *The Playful Crowd: Pleasure Places in the Twentieth Century* (Columbia University Press, 2005); and *Riding on Rainbows: Blackpool Pleasure Beach and Its Place in British Popular Culture* (Skelter Publishing, 2007). He is the founding president of the International Commission for the History of Travel and Tourism and the editor of the new *Journal of Tourism History*.

Institute of Northern Studies, Leeds Metropolitan University
F Block, Civic Quarter,
Leeds LS1 3HE, UK
Email: johnkwalton@yahoo.co.uk

Audrey Yue is senior lecturer in the Cinema and Cultural Studies Programme, University of Melbourne, Australia. Her study of Asian media industries and diasporic cultures has been published as *Cultural Theory in Everyday Life* (Oxford University Press, 2008), *Between Home and the World: A Reader in Hong Kong Cinema* (Oxford University Press, 2004), *Asian Migrations: Sojourning, Displacement, Homecoming and Other Travels* (Asia Research Institute, 2005), *Chinese Films in Focus* (British Film Institute, 2003) and *Interpreting Everyday Cultures* (Arnold, 2003). Her work has also appeared in the following journals: *Datutop: Journal of Architectural Theory; Sexualities*; *GLQ*; *Studies in Australasian Cinema*; *Feminist Media Studies*; *Gay and Lesbian Issues; and Psychology Review*. Yue is the co-editor of *Mobile Cultures: New Media in Queer Asia* (Duke University Press, 2003) and *AsiaPacifiQueer: Rethinking Gender and Sexuality* (The University of Illinois Press, 2008).

School of Culture and Communication
University of Melbourne
Victoria 3010, Australia
Email: aisy@unimelb.edu.au

Foreword

Shalini Singh's research has always sought to fill in the gaps in academic work on tourism. In this eclectic collection, she has edited a volume of amazing variety. This time her focus is on the neglected area of domestic tourism, in general, and Asian domestic tourism, in particular.

Tourism as a field of academic enquiry blossomed with mass international tourism in the 1960s when wide-bodied jets made travel affordable for millions. Overlooked even then was the fact that for countries as different as the US and India most of the tourism was domestic. Moreover, the issues surrounding international tourism were primarily economic: the impact on the balance of trade; foreign exchange leakage; the ability of international tourists to make viable the attractions of the host country; and, of course, the multiplier effect and the impact of international travelers on employment.

While disciplines other than economics would take up the study of tourism and come to recognize its more problematic impacts, the focus remained on what international tourists were doing to, and for, the host nation and the impact of policy. Although pilgrimages, business travel and special events are acknowledged to have their share of domestic tourists, government planning and academic study have remained fixed on the international traveler. This is especially the case of Asian tourism, where attention is focused on tourists from European and North American countries.

This collection not only explicitly concentrates on domestic tourism in Asia, it also explores in breathtaking complexity the variety of motivations and types of forms this travel has assumed.

Undoubtedly, domestic tourism has been facilitated by the growing affluence in the region; but as these chapters demonstrate, domestic tourism in Asia has been neglected and overlooked in poorer nations because of the narrow stereotypical notions of what constitutes tourism and how even the impoverished may participate as visitors. Even ten years ago most researchers could not have imagined domestic tourism in Mongolia or Cambodia. The tiny land masses of Hong Kong or Singapore would have made us doubt the feasibility of their citizens escaping their urban environments by 'hill-walking' or the construction of artificial retreats from the city. This volume illustrates the incredible richness and variety that domestic tourism can take.

Singh has brought together an impressive array of scholars who use a wide range of methodologies to probe these divergences. This book is certain to encourage greater research into this overlooked and rapidly developing phenomenon. One can expect further research in Asia, as well as the use of many of the techniques employed in this work to be employed in studies of other regions.

Moreover, future research – in part thanks to this book – can be expected to go beyond domestic tourism to the study of the increasing numbers of tourists who will be both domestic travelers and international tourists.

Ultimately, a healthy global tourism industry in the 21st century will be one that affords the citizen an opportunity to explore the sacred and the secular attractions within their own country, and the affluence to put those experiences in context through travel abroad.

Linda K. Richter
Professor Emerita in Political Science
Kansas State University, US
January 2009

Preface

Reflections of my school days enliven a sense of excited impatience. As the seasonal two-month closure drew nigh, the hot and dusty Indian summers would make it unbearable to follow the disciplining regimens of school schedules. But the weather could not detract from family travel plans or dampen our spirits. Almost everyone was 'going somewhere' – and if not, then they must be staying behind to host their visitors. Some had cleverly intertwined hosting with guest-ships in an itinerary ideally suited to their kind of extended 'family' of friends and relatives who need to be 'touched', if not rounded up at a single rendezvous.

My early-age travels were invariably consecrated to family holidays – journeying with family to relatives and friends or joining relatives on their homeward journeys. Their everyday locales converted into my tourism periphery, endowed with a seasonal second home and local-area amenities and attractions – iconic and commonplace, and relished by residents and visitors alike. Travelling to these places was no less a delight: the Indian railways served up a recreational travel and sightseeing itinerary. In particular, I nostalgically remember the 'toy' trains that would chug visitors and locals to and from Himalayan towns. Off we went to meet, visit, picnic and savour the change of place, make new friends and partake in the life and living of our hosts. These childhood travels are so vividly etched that I am perpetually grateful to my parents and our gamut of friends and relatives for all the fun we had back then.

Our early schooling years graduated into university life, during which family travels began to space out. Occasionally, these were interspersed with student group travels and tours. Now we travelled in larger numbers and farther away from friends and relatives. Despite the large group size, responsibilities and accountabilities imperceptibly crept into our experiences in strange ways. In the company of same-age fellow travellers, there is a tendency to negotiate and re-negotiate mutual compatibilities, both within and outside the collective. A brief list of warnings (actually 'don'ts' and penalties) formed our guiding principles. Straying away from these was an individual choice and brought potential disrepute for the trespasser. I am grateful to my springtime mentors for such precious learning opportunities.

Ironically, my quest for 'life' brought me to the Centre for Tourism Research and Development in Lucknow, India – a literal waterhole for tourism students. Here, I could acquaint myself with the wisdom of subject experts.

While, for the most part, I fell in line with their assertions, I often wondered what the 'fuss' over tourists and tourism was all about. In my minimal travel experiences, I could not recall any explicit commotion over places and people. It had been so simple. A sense of mutual respect and responsibility had always been my travel mantra, and I wore this talisman to academic conferences, nationally and internationally. The centre became my Mecca, where I was fulfilled by the exchanges on our own travels as well as by the readings. I continue to cherish those times and bonds established.

Budget, more than time, permitted international travel to conferences in Asian countries with relative affordability. On these occasions, I began to real-ize the *raison d'être* of the fuss over the 'make-believe' world of tourists and tourism. Reflecting back on my own travel experiences in my home country (India), I wondered if I had really been a 'tourist' in the literal sense of the word. I realize that although my in-country travels and visits were 'ordinary' trips, the getaways were not only a refreshing change, but also economically budgeted enriching times, which were spatially and temporally suited to my needs.

Now I live and work far from home and country, in Canada. During the summer months, I make my annual pilgrimage to my home in India. My stay in India (approximately three months) is interspersed with research-related travel and work, conference travel, and visits to friends and relatives, besides some family time. All of these engagements are recreative and enjoyable. It is always nice to return home after being away for some time.

On my recent return to Canada, the immigration official enquired after my destination and purpose for leaving the country, while scrutinizing my travel documents. My spontaneous response was: 'I was in India – I was "visiting" home.' Immediately, the officer demanded to know what I was doing in Canada. I paused before replying: 'I live and work in Canada – I have a home here too!' My Indian passport and my Canadian residency card validated my claims of dual residency. This makes me wonder if I qualify as a domestic tourist in both or either countries.

ᴄᴊᴇᴠ

This book is inspired by my continuing bewilderment with the phenomenon of tourism. Despite the wealth of literature available on the subject, we seem to be missing a critical link – that of resident travels in one's own country. Two separate events have prompted this title. First, having completed an edited volume on *Tourism in Destination Communities* (CAB International, 2003), I realized that although the book strongly pleads and argues for a community orientation, specifically in regard to resident in-country leisure migrations, its purpose is defeated by the lack of our understanding of this aspect of tourism. Second, while co-editing a special issue of *Tourism Recreation Research* on domestic tourism in Asia in 2004, we were confronted with problems that could dampen the spirits of even the most impassioned. These crises led me to question whether there is any such thing as domestic tourism. However, having made a contribution to this themed edition, I realized that this arena was an un-traversed 'goldfield' – in want of attention from courageous explorers.

Since then the idea for an edited book on the theme began to grow upon me. Before taking the plunge, I sought the advice of professors T. V. Singh and Erik Cohen, who helped me to chisel the concepts further. The first call attracted some collaborators and strong appreciation for the proposal. I owe much to these early responses for strengthening my resolve. Headhunting fetched better outcomes. Although the soliciting and editing processes have been trying, there is no room for any complaints. Perhaps it behoves me to confess my obstinacy on certain accounts: I insisted on adhering to the conventional definition of domestic tourism – the 'in-country' travels of 'resident populations'. This overly simplistic criterion excluded 'diasporic' citizens and expatriates, regional tourists and other non-resident groups as these could blur the salience of native tourism. Readers may be disappointed by the absence of any contributions on or from Middle Eastern and Eurasian countries. Here was my second subjectivity – that of putting the United Nations World Tourism Organization (UNWTO) classification to use in order to limit the study region and, hence, the omission of many of the so-called Asian countries. All possible measures were made to incorporate as many Asian nations within this book as possible. Despite all sincere efforts, some 'legitimate' countries such as Thailand, North and South Korea, Pakistan, Indonesia, Fiji, Afghanistan, Bangladesh, Bhutan, Nepal and Maldives sorely failed to be included here.

Throughout this book I intended to explore domestic leisure travel and holidaying in Asia, asking how different or similar are the vernacular travel styles and patterns from tourism, in general, and in what ways, if at all, does domestic tourism and its modern/international counterpart interface in Asian countries? These queries forced us to dig through historical-geographic records to generate scenarios from the past. Such a premise posed a genuine problem as many existing Asian countries have reconfigured political boundaries (generating new place names), let alone revolutionized cultures and economies. Changes such as these altered my hypothesis to acknowledge that present-day tourism within Asia constitutes native and nativized elements. The contents of the book have been arranged in approximate compliance with this proposition.

This anthology describes our journey amongst the native peoples of Asian countries. As a result, an exhaustive itinerary must not be expected. But the volume certainly leads us along some untried paths that open into unchartered avenues for scholarly pursuit. I look forward to the furtherance of this initiative. For my part, I remain an inveterate sojourning domestic tourist in India.

Acknowledgements

The writing of this book has initiated fresh and fostered familiar acquaintances from Asia and beyond. This confluence of academics from within and outside tourism studies has been a source of encouragement and delight throughout the process. Together we formed a small and interesting bunch – to whom I extend my sincere gratitude.

A few named gurus have been influential in giving shape to my fragmentary ideas on the theme. Thanks are extended to Erik Cohen and T. V. Singh, both of whom examined my fuzzy ideas with patience and helped me to refine these into focus. T.V. Singh's consistent encouragement was particularly endearing. I am fortunate to have Linda Richter and John Walton join in to contribute their expertise. Linda's steadfastness, despite her calamitous circumstances, and the critical acuteness of John were heartening. At my workplace, Ann Marie Guilmette's long sufferance of my obsessions with this project deserves accolade – was it her fascination of my indulgence or that of the theme?

My earnest indebtedness is to the contributors: their belief in the theme and the book as a whole, alongside their patience, has made this publication a reality. I am especially enriched by the works of these researchers, many of whom I would never have known if it were not for this book. I would be remiss not to mention the role of TRINET (the Tourism Research Information Network) in bringing us together. Special thanks go to Margaret Swain and Jaap Lengkeek, whose attention to the introduction (Chapter 1) helped to bring out the nuances of the theme in the context of the region.

I am grateful for the small grant awarded to me by the Social Sciences and Humanities Research Council (SSHRC institutional) at Brock University, Canada, that went a long way in aiding the preparation of the manuscript. Loris Gasparrato deserves acknowledgement for lending cartographic assistance. Many thanks go to Ronald D'Souza for copyediting with assurance. Finally, I am pleased that Earthscan agreed to publish this work, for which I acknowledge Tim Hardwick and his team for their professional chaperonage.

I dedicate this collection to all holiday-seekers who journey near and far – much wisdom awaits those who sojourn their country: my respect for their quests.

List of Acronyms and Abbreviations

AFCD	Agricultural, Fishery and Conservation Department
AMRY	Association of Mongolian Revolutionary Youth
APSARA	Authority for the Protection of the Sites and Administration of Angkor
ASEAN	Association of Southeast Asian Nations
ATA	Asuke Tourism Association
BTMICE	business travel meetings, incentives, conventions and exhibitions
CBT	community-based tourism
CECD	*Creative Economy Cultural Development Strategy*
CIS	Commonwealth of Independent States
CITouR	Centre for International Tourism Research
DC-CAM	Documentation Centre of Cambodia
DOT	Philippine Department of Tourism
EMA	ecological mitigation area
EU	European Union
FSS	Film-in-Singapore Scheme
FUNCINPEC	Front Uni National pour un Cambodge Indépendant, Neutre, Pacifique et Coopératif
GDP	gross domestic product
GNH	gross national happiness
GNI	gross national income
GNP	gross national product
ha	hectare
HKFCA	Hong Kong Federation of Countryside Activities
HKHAC	Hong Kong Hiking Association China
HKTA	Hong Kong Tourist Association
HKWP	Hong Kong Wetland Park
HSDV	*Household Survey on Domestic Visitors*
km	kilometre
lb	pound
LTC	leave travel concession
m	metre
m^2	square metre
MAFF	Ministry of Agriculture Forestry and Fisheries (Japan)

MCM	money–commodity–money
MRTT	Ministry of Road, Transport and Tourism (Mongolia)
MTPDP	*Medium-Term Philippine Development Plan*
NCR	National Capital Region (the Philippines)
NGO	non-governmental organization
NRI	non-resident Indian
PAP	People's Action Party
PAS	Parti Islam SeMalaysia
PRC	People's Republic of China
RORO	Roll-On Roll-Off programme
S$	Singapore dollar
SARS	severe acute respiratory syndrome
SCC	social carrying capacity
SLR	single-lens reflex (camera)
SSHRC	Social Sciences and Humanities Research Council
STB	Singapore Tourism Board
STPB	Singapore Tourist Promotion Board
TAR	Tibetan Autonomous Region
TW$	Taiwan dollar
TPO	Transcultural Psychosocial Organization
UK	United Kingdom
UN	United Nations
UNESCO	United Nations Educational, Scientific and Cultural Organization
UNHCR	United Nations Commission on Human Rights
UNMO	United Malays National Organization
UNTAC	United Nations Transitional Authority of Cambodia
UNWTO	United Nations World Tourism Organization
US	United States
VFR	visit(ing) friends and relatives
VNAT	Vietnam National Administration of Tourism
WTO	World Tourism Organization
WTTC	World Travel and Tourism Council

Domestic Tourism: Searching for an Asianic Perspective

Shalini Singh

Introduction

Before tourism emerged as an international phenomenon, leisure jaunts and recreational travel were invariable adjuncts to people's way of life and living (Adler, 1989; Enzensberger, 1996). Most home-grown modes of travel and tours have more or less retained their popularity. Leisure migrations of pilgrims and other budget travellers, such as those visiting friends and relatives (VFR) and the culture, as well as health-seekers, are acknowledged illustrations of in-country travel practices. In this regard, therefore, the leisure travels of ordinary natives[1] within their own country have perpetuated strands of tradition into the New Millennium. Today, even as new traditions in travel and tourism are being formed, adopted or adapted, the *genius loci* continues to modify and determine suitable genres of tourism that withstand the test of time.

In the language of contemporary tourism, journeys and visits within a person's home country are discussed under domestic tourism. Given this simplistic criterion, and despite the absence of supportive data, domestic tourism can be assumed to far exceed its international counterpart in most countries of the world. Yet, from an academic and policy-making perspective, holiday and leisure travel in one's own country is, at best, a poor and under-valued cousin to international tourism – an established fact of all aspiring economies, and particularly true in the Asian region (Richter, 1989). Indeed, this is unfortunate since despite the apparent infrastructural and economic backwardness, domestic tourism is a ubiquitous feature of these countries, with ample economic and cultural significance. Its lack of visibility to researchers is questionable and raises a genuine concern for the disciplinary credibility of tourism (see Michaud, 1991; Hughes, 1992; Alneng, 2002; Aramberri, 2004; Gladstone, 2005; Young et al, 2007).

Not many scholars in tourism studies have engaged themselves in the theme of domestic tourism, whereas relatively more social anthropologists, social historians and urban planners have all contributed to the field of domestic holiday-making and leisure travel, especially in Western Europe and the US. The reasons for such a dearth of literature on this subject are usually ascribed to a paucity of hard and reliable data, which, in turn, reflects deeper issues – namely, disagreement on a standard set of criteria, complex colloquial terminology and incongruent socio-cultural contexts (see Brown, 1935; Crick, 1989). In essence, diverse cultural entities may present variegated representations of domestic holidaying and travel. Nonetheless, despite awareness of scholarly neglect, few tourism academics have 'braved' an initiative into this arena. Some of the earlier known studies on domestic tourism present a genuine concern for the lacunae (Richter and Richter, 1985; Jafari, 1986; Hughes, 1992; Pearce, 1996). The few known studies on the topic of domestic tourism are reported in conjunction with international tourism (see, for example, Williams, 1979; Helleiner, 1990), while others may be considered to be need serving (by way of market studies or to inform policy) (Mitchell, 1969; Rian, 1969; Williams, 1979; Canadian Tourism Commission, 1996) or regionally based (Christaller, 1963; Clawson and Knetsch, 1963; Pigram, 1983; Verbeke, 1988; Williams and Balaz, 2001). More recently, some tourism journals have published special issues that have addressed the theme directly (*Annals of Tourism Research*, vol 13, 1986; *Tourism Recreation Research*, vol 29, 2004) or tangentially (e.g. the special issues of the *Journal of Tourism Studies* on VFR, *Tourism* on sacred and spiritual travel, and *Tourism Recreation Research* on tourism in developing countries – International Geographical Union 1988 papers). A few publications, such as the edited works of Harrison (2001) and Ghimire (2001), are peripheral attempts on the theme since they typically focus on the 'less developed world' and 'developing countries', respectively. A recent treatise, entitled *From Pilgrimage to Package Tour* by David Gladstone (2005) is an acclaimed contribution to the theme – in which the author justifies the title in his investigation of the 'much, much larger universe of *(domestic)* tourists' (Gladstone, 2005, p130) in low-income (also developing world) countries – namely, India and Mexico. Gladstone's selection of the two locales identifies suitable exemplars for the theme. Likewise, any comprehensive study on domestic tourism would be considered inconclusive without a substantial, if not major, examination of Asian native holidaying and travel – a critically salient aspect of Asian tourism. Richter's exploration of *The Politics of Tourism in Asia* (1989) is, indeed, a seminal work in this regard, as it brings into focus the unique circumstances that characterize the Asian countries. On a smaller canvas, two separate studies (Kaur, 1985; Singh, 1989) on the Indian Himalaya are legitimately professed claims on the topic. Most of these studies, particularly Gladstone's, open up fresh avenues for exploration, as they challenge existing stagnant discourses in international tourism research.

Hence, two postulations prompt a comprehensive study on the theme of domestic tourism in Asia: first, the fact that native tourism in the non-Western world scarcely abides by the tenets or the language of international tourism (see Helleiner, 1990; Gladstone, 2005). Second, domestic tourism, particularly in Asia, is understood to constitute the largest, and most unaddressed, proportion of the tourism 'iceberg'. The following is an elaboration, however provisional, on some potential fields for investigation.

Making the case: Domestic tourism in Asia

Travel is one of the most ancient and common aspects of human life ... how do we justify historically isolating something called tourism from something that has always existed, as if it were something unique. (Enzensberger, 1996, p122)

The basic premise to be explored here is that domestic tourism requires an Asian perspective, which acknowledges that it is typically fulfilled through the established practices and settings. Furthermore, quite unlike international/ modern tourism that relies heavily on global systems, where researchers refer to super- and supra-structures as being crucial to its rituals, Asian domestic tourism seems to have evolved and sustained itself in the absence of heavy investments and commercialization as being vital to its rituals. Although domestic tourists require transport and safe shelter, their experience often emerges from the everyday environment of the place visited. Such settings tend to be the unpretentious by-product of the physical, economic, socio-cultural and political environment in which people conduct their everyday lives in intuitive ways. Jafari (1979, p4) refers to such *naturally charming, tourismagnetic gifts* as *background tourism elements* that are 'plentiful' and almost 'free' because they are founded on the distinctive character and flavour of place and people.

The 'natural charms' of ordinariness is, then, a visible expression and valuable source for developing an understanding of the character of the tourism phenomenon, as expressed through place (location attributes) and the resident community (community identity and values), together with the impact of the visitors in their interactions with these dimensions of a place, or vice versa. Furthermore, not only do the native visitors have the freedom to choose their leisure style, but the native hosts, too, have the necessary empowerment to partake of (instead of merely offering) their hospitality in their own terms. Often, residents can both offer and partake of the hospitality provided for tourists. For instance, residents and visitors eat in the same restaurants and enjoy the same space or events and festivities. Mongolia's *Naadam* festival celebration is an interesting example of such sharing (Thompson and

Matheson, 2008). Such informal exchanges are alien to large-scale international tourism and are worth scholarly exploration.

Systems of domestic tourism develop under the influence of various political regimes that impart their own quirks, affecting the commercial and collective provisioning of tours and travelling inhabitants of those countries (e.g. Lee, 2006; Michaud and Turner, 2006). Native holidaying may oscillate between or constitute a combination of self-provisioning by way of privately owned second homes and/or the homes of relatives and friends, and collective facilities in the public and quasi-public sectors, and the commercial sector, whether large or small scale. The 'big picture' of the range of provisioning and facilitation brings to light the purpose and approach with which governments envisage and embrace the phenomenon, both for its nationals and for those from other countries. Frequently, the quality gap between the provisions for resident hosts and native guests tends to be lesser than that between the national hosts and international guests, as envisaged by the governance. Admittedly, such combinations are all too common regionally and globally.

Another distinguishing feature of domestic tourism is that it displays people's ability to negotiate interchanges based on their own value judgements without getting trapped in the formalized tourism system. This negotiation not only enables an understanding of the aspirations and traditions of hosts, but also delineates the changes and continuities in value systems that impart character to social groups. Involvement and participation of locals in tourism processes provide the most desirable contexts for the sustainable progress of people and places.

Finally, the economic viability of holidays and travels among natives is often more appealing than that of international tourism. Frequently, these not only eschew mega-investments; more importantly, the monetary exchanges, however small, occur directly at the grassroots level with the local provider. These and other socio-cultural, environmental and politico-economic potentials of domestic tourism justify academic investments in this particular topic.

The Asian context

While it must be acknowledged that studying 'conventionally stylized ways' (Adler, 1989, p1366) of domestic tourism across continents is acknowledged to be a Herculean venture of encyclopaedic proportion, a pragmatic approach dictates a continent-wise handling of the theme. Cochrane's (2008, pxix) personal experience of the marvellously complex, challenging and charming 'way of life in Asia' is a fair assertion, albeit inconclusive for the purpose. Subsequently, the choice of the Asian region as a starting point can be argued for specific reasons, providing as it does an opportunity both for an introductory overview and for a comparison and contrast between countries.

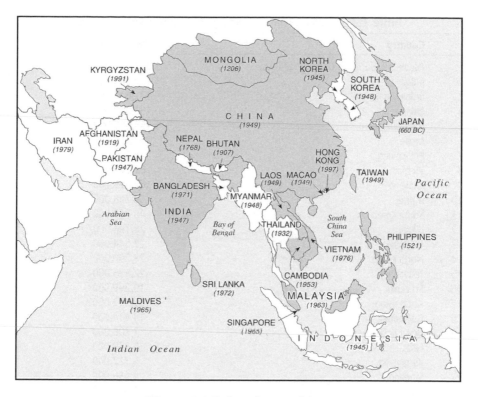

Figure 1.1 *Political map of Asia*

Note: shaded areas indicate countries discussed in this book. Figures in parentheses indicate year of enstatement to current political status.

Source: Shalini Singh

First, the region is home to the largest proportion of the world's population (60 per cent) (see Table 1.1). With more than 4 billion Asians, the difficulty is not in justifying the importance of resident travel within their respective countries, but in ascertaining travel data with precision. A large proportion of this population constitutes the 'broad and stable middle class' (Gilley, cited in Li, 2006, p80), who are reckoned as a major force in the socio-cultural, economic and political evolution of the Asian nations. In China, this category accounts for almost 68 per cent of the population, while in India they constitute nearly one third of the total population. The Asian middle class are professionals, intellectuals and salaried workers who uphold values and goals that are founded on rationality, so that these equip them with strong material as well as cultural interests (Rose, 1997). These qualities prod them to question both capitalism and arbitrary authority as they strive for meaningful, fair, orderly and justified social norms that are made public through various social movement initiatives, and as such bring hope for the future.

Table 1.1 *Selected Asian countries: Current population size*

	Country	Population
1	People's Republic of China (mainland)	1,322,597,000
2	India	1,131,043,000
3	Indonesia	231,627,000
4	Pakistan	161,998,000
5	Bangladesh	158,665,000
6	Japan	127,718,000
7	Philippines	88,706,300
8	Vietnam	87,375,000
9	Thailand	62,828,706
10	Burma	48,798,000
11	South Korea	48,512,000
12	Nepal	28,196,000
13	Malaysia	27,544,000
14	North Korea	23,790,000
15	Taiwan	22,935,000
16	Sri Lanka	19,299,000
17	Kazakhstan	15,422,000
18	Cambodia	14,444,000
19	Hong Kong	7,206,000
20	Laos	5,859,000
21	Kyrgyzstan	5,317,000
22	Singapore	4,436,000
23	Mongolia	2,629,000
24	Bhutan	658,000
25	Macau	481,000
26	Maldives	306,000

Source: Population and Development in the UN System, www.un.org/esa/population/index.html

Second, the region enjoys a distinctive reputation for its geophysical, socio-cultural, economic, historical and political attributes. Geographically, Asia is not only the largest continent, but is also endowed with the highest peaks, coldest deserts, broadest mountain ranges and a very extensive coastline (see Figure 1.2). More important still is the exuberance of Asia's historical and cultural diversity, socio-political mosaic and economic heterogeneity. Each of its countries is a compendium of numerous languages, dialects and ways of life. Although the Asian region is home to the two oldest civilizations – Indus Valley and Huang He – many of its countries share a common political history of European colonialism. The region's colonial history is a significant benchmark in its tourism history, especially in regard to the hill stations of the British Raj, the seaside/beach resorts of Cambodia, Vietnam, Japan and even China. The entire region thus boasts of ancient and recent patrimonies of living and historic significance (see Tables 1.2 to 1.4).

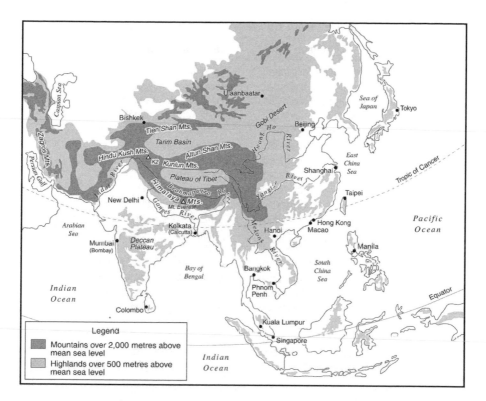

Figure 1.2 *Asia: Major physiographic features*

Source: Shalini Singh

Table 1.2 *Selected Asian countries: Glossary of former names with year of change*

Previous name	Year	Current name
Persian Empire	1935	Republic of Iran
Siam	1939	Kingdom of Thailand
Republic of Formosa	1945	Taiwan
Dutch East Indies	1949	Republic of Indonesia
French Indo-China	1949	Socialist Republic of Vietnam
Malaya, Sabah, Sarawak and Singapore	1963	Malaysia
East Pakistan	1971	People's Republic of Bangladesh
West Pakistan	1971	Republic of Pakistan
Ceylon	1972	Democratic Socialist Republic of Sri Lanka
Democratic Kampuchea	1975	Kingdom of Cambodia
Burma	1989	Union of Myanmar
Kirghizia (USSR)	1991	Republic of Kyrgyzstan

Source: http://en.wikipedia.org/wiki/Asia#Country_name_changes

Table 1.3 *Selected Asian countries: Glossary of vernacular names*

Common name	Vernacular name
People's Republic of Bangladesh	*Gônoprojatontri Bangladesh*
Kingdom of Bhutan	*Druk Yul or Dru Gäkhap*
Burma (also Union of Myanmar)	*Pyi-daung-zu Myan-ma Naing-ngan-daw*
Kingdom of Cambodia	*Preăh Réachéanachâkr Kâmpŭchea*
People's Republic of China	*Zhōnghuá Rénmín Gònghéguó*
Republic of India	*Bhārat Gaṇarājya*
Indonesia	*Republik Indonesia*
Japan	*Nihon-koku*
Kazakhastan	*Qazaqstan Respublïkası*
Kyrgyzstan	*Kyrgyz Respublikasi*
Laos, PDR	*Sathalanalat Paxathipatai Paxaxon Lao*
Maldives	*Divehi Rājje ge Jumhuriyyā*
Mongolia	*Mongol uls*
Federal Democratic Republic of Nepal	*Sanghiya Loktāntrik Ganatantra Nepāl*
North Korea	*Chosŏn Minjujuŭi Inmin Konghwaguk*
Islamic Republic of Pakistan	*Islāmī Jumhūrīyah Pākistān*
Republic of the Philippines	*Republika ng Pilipinas*
South Korea	*Daehanminguk*
Taiwan (also Republic of China)	*Jhonghuá Mínguó*
Kingdom of Thailand	*Ratcha Anachak Thai*
Socialist Republic of Vietnam	*Cộng hòa xã hội chủ nghĩa Việt Nam*

Note: some countries such as the Democratic Socialist Republic of Sri Lanka, Malaysia, Macau (SAR), Hong Kong (SAR) and Singapore are not distinctly identified in their vernacular language.

Source: http://en.wikipedia.org/wiki/Asia

Table 1.4 *Selected Asian countries: Current political status*

Country	Since	Country	Since
Japan	660 BC	Macau	1949
Mongolia	1206	India	1950
The Philippines	1521	Cambodia	1953
Nepal	1768	Malaysia	1963
Bhutan	1907	Maldives	1965
Indonesia	1945	Singapore	1965
Pakistan	1947	Bangladesh	1971
Korea	1948	Sri Lanka	1972
Laos	1949	Kyrgyzstan	1991
People's Republic of China	1949	Kazakhastan	1991
Taiwan	1949	Hong Kong	1997

Source: http://en.wikipedia.org/wiki/Asia

Table 1.5 *Selected Asian countries: Human Development Index*

Country	HDI	Country	HDI
Japan	0.953	Maldives	0.741
Hong Kong	0.937	Vietnam	0.733
Taiwan	0.932	Indonesia	0.728
Singapore	0.922	Mongolia	0.700
South Korea	0.921	Kyrgyzstan	0.696
Macau	0.909	India	0.619
Malaysia	0.811	Laos	0.601
Kazakhastan	0.794	Cambodia	0.598
Thailand	0.781	Bhutan	0.579
China	0.777	Pakistan	0.551
Philippines	0.771	Bangladesh	0.547
Sri Lanka	0.743	Nepal	0.534

Source: Human Development Reports, accessed from http://hdr.undp.org/en/statistics/

Third, Asia enjoys a distinct reputation as having strong religious and cultural traditions that emanate primarily from Hindu and Chinese mythologies, which convey deep-seated philosophical traditions as well. Although Islam is a relatively later introduction to the region, its presence in, and influence on, the cultural politics is unmistakable. Asian cultures exude a unique intertwining of religion and philosophy. In fact, faith journeys in the region constitute a major proportion of domestic sojourns. The region is the acknowledged birthplace of most of the world's mainstream religions, including Hinduism, Islam, Buddhism, Sikhism, Confucianism and Taoism (see Figure 1.3). Through the centuries, its people have maintained and endowed places, events and people with conceptions of the sacred, perpetuating their beliefs through a consciously cultivated way of life evincing a nature–culture interface. Eastern cultures – namely, Indian, Japanese and Chinese – attach pious sentiments to locations, landscapes and people. This aspect of geo-piety (pious emotion or sense of reverence) has transformed the high Himalaya into the Gods' cosmogony and earthy domiciles of Hindu Gods; the wonder retreats of Japanese wilderness into a complex of some 66 Kannon temples throughout the Kinai and Kanto regions; the relics of Buddhist into monumental *stupas* all over India, Tibet, Nepal, Indonesia and Thailand; and the slopes of Mount Emei into extraordinary (*qi*) Daoist landscapes in China. These and many other scenic sites and historical-cultural artefacts today constitute sacred centres, many of which have been woven into route-based pilgrimages and circuits, commonly found in practically every Asian country today. Despite intermittent efforts to alienate people from their convictions or to eliminate religion from the state (such as the propagation of conflicting ideologies and beliefs; see Martin, 2004), the overarching religious sentiment has been sustained in the travel propensities, patterns and behaviours. This is especially true in the case of India, Bhutan, Tibet and Bangladesh, where the distinction between sacred and secular in the behaviours of the Asian masses can still be quite difficult to establish. In recent times, religious resurgence in Asia has initiated contemporary spiritual and nationalist movements that have added to the repertoire of the region's spiritual retreats/centres and sites of patriotic patrimonies that continue to reaffirm conventional spiritual rigour.

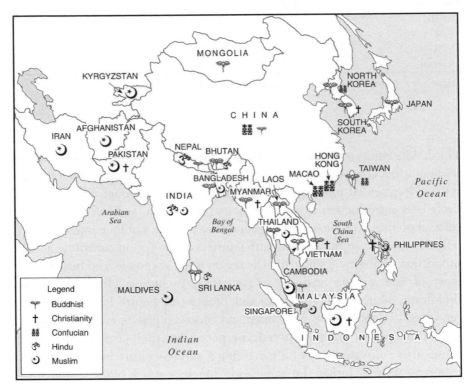

Figure 1.3 *Asia: Major religions*

Note: two religions have been identified for most countries; the larger of the two symbols indicates majority adherents in the population.

Source: Shalini Singh

Fourth, modern or contemporary tourism is often posited as a manifestation of early European colonization in Asia at best and Western industrialization in the recent past. Since the non-Western economies, especially the Asian region, were more or less distanced from the latter process, they remained for a long time oblivious of the social, political and commercial agenda of international leisure travel (or 'new' tourism). With time, however, and ever since the popularity of alternative forms of global tourism – namely, community/eco/green tourism – hypotheses concerning tourism as a new type of colonialism and appropriate forms of tourism have surfaced (Mowforth and Munt, 1998; Wang, 2000). Tourism, therefore, serves as a modernizing agency, especially for depressed economies such as Thailand, India, Nepal and the like. This 'new' opportunity assists these countries to participate in the international stage (Porananond and Robinson, 2008, p320).

Finally, as a corollary to the previous point, it is an opportune time not only to explore the unique vernacular forms of tourism in the Asian countries, but also to document and understand adapted and domesticated versions of 'new' tourism. Given that contemporary international tourism in the Asian region is on a 'firm growth path'[2] (UNWTO, 2007; see also Cochrane, 2008), the older system of native holidaying and travel has come under challenge.

This book sets out to explore domestic leisure travel and holidaying in Asia, asking such questions as how different or similar are the vernacular styles and patterns from the normative domestic tourism and what are the salient features of the domestic tourism practices of Asians?

Asian domestic tourism: The problematic

More often than not, Asian native travellers and visitors, including pilgrims, are reluctant to accept the label of 'tourists'. Their self-professed separation, and a concomitant alienation, from a system (tourism) formally designated for 'outside visitors' (international tourists) reflects an assertion of their identity as nationals. In the capacity of nationals, they are not complete strangers to the place, even if it is a first-time visit. Most travelling/visiting residents make conscious efforts to distance themselves from the tourist 'traps' or 'ghettos' and mobilize their leisure in ways familiar, howsoever peripheral, to themselves – in terms of their land, its people and their ethos – that are presumably grounded in the paradigm of native milieu (Helleiner, 1990). This makes the Asian context of domestic tourism somewhat distinctive. In this regard, two interdependent generic issues that are critical to the subject matter arise: definitional and contextual issues.

Definitional discord

Since translation is a difficult and tricky art, the terms of reference can be a major barrier to squarely situating the phenomenon of domestic tourism within various cultural settings. For example, Alneng's (2002) exposition on the 'tourist' (based on MacCannell's definition) implies a modern individual who is, by and large, culturally differentiated from the host. Would nationals and locals, then, be interpreted in terms of 'foreigners' or 'strangers'? In a parallel strain, the word 'holiday' may raise several doubts. Culturally, too, colloquial terms that could resonate with the phenomenon of travel and tourism may be rejected on the basis of their translation into the English language (see Srivastava, 2005). For instance, Singh and Singh (2009) use 'journey' and 'pilgrimage' as synonyms, while in the literal Hindi translation the two are distinct in that the former is typically secular travel and the latter essentially religious. Events such as holidays, celebrations and leisure travel are, indeed, localized affairs, and when compatriots participate and perform as visitors, travellers or leisure-seekers, the praxis is regarded as community tourism and/or domestic tourism. However, the fact that such indigenous events are differently perceived and classified by various social groups will tend to further complicate the terms of reference.

Various tourism dictionaries leave most generic terms open to interpretation (see Medlik, 1996; Beaver, 2002). Medlik, for example, includes domestic tourist and domestic same-day visitor under the rubric of domestic visitor (Medlik, 1996, p85), while making the definition of trip exclusive of tourism (Medlik, 1996, p262). Likewise, 'holiday forms/terms/types' (Medlik, 1996, p129) are divergent from 'travel/tourism forms/terms/types' (Medlik, 1996, p260). As more terms, such as recreation, leisure, outdoors and the like are added to the tourism vocabulary, the universality of tourism studies becomes debatable (Ogilvie, 1933; Brown, 1935). The blurred and overlapping boundaries of travel, holidaying, vacationing, visiting and hospitality engender ambivalence in the 'terms of reference' for domestic tourism. However, since the language of tourism continues to evolve, it may be acceptable to collapse all unique types of native holidaying and leisure travel into one rubric – domestic tourism.

Contextual discord

Tourism is commonly referred to as a Western phenomenon. There seems to be a visible bias in favour of the 'white' Westerner who is enabled by his/her mobile lifestyle and circumstantially endowed to be the 'tourist', thereby rendering other cultural groups incompatible with this designation. Dulles (1966) places this divide in the 'New World–Old World' dichotomy. However, Hughes (1992, p85) puts this difference aside in asserting that contemporary understanding of tourism is 'but another social construction' among others. This construct, however, is derived from consumerism of the industrial era (Moeran, 1983) within Western economies. Domestic holiday-seekers are usually not estranged from their native land and its people – in that the everyday life of individuals is largely conditioned by native norms and local settings. As a consequence, domestic holiday-makers do not necessarily abide by the tenets of standard/global tourism. In this regard, the geopolitical tensions between Western and non-Western positions have often surfaced in tourism studies (Cohen, 1995; Edensor, 1998; Alneng, 2002).

In terms of its structuring, tourism is generally perceived as supra-institutionalized or formalized provisioning. Such a formal or structured arrangement of the travel and hospitality sector is more difficult to identify in the domestic sector, whose institutions tend to be compatible with the country's politics, culture and economy. In the case of Asia, the primary form of domestic tourism occurs by way of pilgrimages and VFR visitations, both of which adhere to local norms of social conduct and are culturally distinct. More often than not, this creates a divide between these native categories of travellers/holiday-makers and the modern tourists (Michaud and Turner, 2006). Furthermore, the privileges asserted and claimed as a right by international tourists impart an elitist flavour to these modern-day tourists. In countries where such claims are less in evidence, such elitism has little purchase among the natives for whom access to the commons (e.g. open beaches) is assumed, and can at most be regarded as an informal indicator of hospitality or a gesture of inclusion.

Societies are represented by their perception and value systems that tend to be closely aligned with prevailing political ideology. Ideological (in)compatibilities tend to have a significant bearing on the experiences and perceptions of guests and hosts. Thus, if the two share somewhat similar values, as might be in some cases of the VFR segment, then can the visitor cultures of the locals be termed as tourism in the commercial (or capitalistic) sense of the word? Furthermore, how does the relative familiarity with the host's culture affect the experience of a guest who shares almost similar culture? Would it be that they bond as people of the same land? Alternatively, it is also possible that this familiarity may breed contempt among native hosts and guests. Moreover, what is the relevance of 'commodification', 'authenticity' (staged or otherwise), 'consumerism' and 'exotics', to name a few, in native holiday-making and travel practices? Equally pertinent is the notion and nature of community involvement in domestic tourism. These are a few of the many problems of terminology that scholars must contend with in their encounters with this theme. Perhaps it is these issues that make this dimension of tourism difficult to quantify, and to be legitimated for qualitative empirical investigations.

Asian domestic tourism: A discourse

Although the region claims a distinct oriental flavour (see Richter and Richter, 1985), much of Asian domestic tourism can best be termed as a *bricolage* where traditional and popular modalities of leisure and travel (such as pilgrimages and VFR) and holidaying (such as religious and secular festivals) have retained their endemic genre to appreciable extents in both puritanical and permissive forms.

There is a haphazard mélange of conventional and contemporary within and among the Asian countries. Conventions have been tempered with some novel or extraneous influences that have been permitted largely with the purpose of some form of organized facilitation, as will be discussed further on. This way, the native travel and touring practices continue on, albeit with some measure of modification. In contrast to this, since the region lures international (overseas and regional) tourists in considerable numbers, a high-end formalization of the tourism sector has been brought (actually grafted) into existence in most of the Asian countries. These provisions also attract vacationers from the domestic market for participation. However, there is a relatively smaller proportion of the indigenous population. Another group of tourists, not included in our definition here, are the migrant and diaspora community who return to travel in their home frequently. This segment has been set apart from the domestic tourists as their socio-temporal and economic circumstances are incongruent with the resident population at large. An additional matter of pertinence in the domestic tourism scene of Asia is that certain countries – namely, Nepal, Bhutan, Burma, Tibet, Ladakh and Sikkim – that apparently have very informal (or pre-capitalistic) sacred and secular systems of travelling and holidaying scarcely interpret these travels and leisure holidays as tourism. Hence, although their conventional life and living patterns include generic forms of festive celebrations, along with leisure and movements, 'domestic tourism' is (mis)construed as being non-existent. In actuality, the discourse of tourism studies tends to centre on a kind of 'tourism' that is, by and large, capitalistic.

If, then, a major proportion of Asian tourism is domestic in character, why does it remain an unexplored area of study? In response, aside from the fact that research-based or 'hard evidence' (Aramberri, 2004; Cochrane, 2006) are, by and large, a rarity, perhaps the reason lies more in the inapplicability of the conventional terms of reference of global tourism studies to the study of domestic tourism activity in this region. The misfortune of the 'Tower of Babel' seems to rest on the region. The following section is an effort to discuss the nuances of some of these terms, whose currency is somewhat restricted by the dictates of international tourism and precludes our understanding of domestic tourism, in general, including indigenous holiday and travel practices.

Sacred–secular complicity

Themes of sanctity and sacred journeys often overshadow Asian travel and holiday-making, both regionally and nationally. Owing to the preponderance of religiosity, the culture of its peoples is informed through a sense of piety and reverence. These senses are visibly manifest in secular aspects of people's lives, livelihoods and leisure, and have sustained their heritage of pilgrimages. In Bhutan, Tibet, Bangladesh, Ladakh and Sikkim, enactments of piety displace indigenous 'tourism'. In its stead, leisure displaces contemporary travel, as the former is so entrenched in the people's way of life and livelihood. Extensions or entanglement of the sacred into the secular are commonplace in the region to the point of obscuring pilgrimage and secular modes of tourism, thereby initiating a 'dual' tourism industry (Gladstone, 2005, pp177, 187). In this broader frame of reference, almost everyone is a tourist at some point or another, regardless of his/her economic and social standing. This explains the enormous and continuous volume of domestic leisure migrations in the countries of the Asian region, especially India and China.

Although tourism, in its politico-economic secular sense, is 'different' from the culturally specific performances of the spirit, the two are intimately comparable in the mode of engagement. Pfaffenberger's (1983) study of Sinhalese at pilgrimage sites in Sri Lanka reveals the illusory difference between the indigenous tourists and pilgrims. Indonesians maintain a lingering respect for their wild places, caves and mountain-tops through mystical interpretations (Cochrane, 2006); the 'pray, pay and play' philosophy (Graburn, 1983) edifies Japan's travel industry, especially the native population; Tibetan nationalism is certainly an offshoot of its traditional pilgrimages that are performed by its nomads, traders, farmers and urbanites (Klieger, 1992); and we can point to the constraining impacts of Confucian philosophy on travel patterns of senior Korean citizens (Lee and Tideswell, 2005): the strong family ties and family-oriented leisure among Muslim populations owing to the moral dictates of Islam (Stodolska and Livengood, 2006); the Vedic philosophy of human life stages that extols the virtues of *Vanaprasthan ashrama* (incessant travelling for the benefit of others as a way to one's spiritual uplifting in later life) (see Singh, 2004) are a few examples. Even in current (modern) times, the secular continues to be informed by and/or dependent on the sacred for its meaning and values: the latter tends to foreground the pleasure, visits, sightseeing, purpose and outcomes of travelling and vacationing. For example, when contemporary Japanese visit Buddhist temples or poetry sites without any sectarian orientation, the sense of reverence in their performances is unmistakable (Foard, 1982).

In addition, the religiosity of Asians is ever present in their economic, social, geographical and political life, and is made evident through the ritualizing of their routines. Their way of life and thinking draws from, and converges at, the religious-cultural 'core', with the sacred determining the constraints of human thought and action. In this regard, the paradigm of *dharma* (Hindu philosophy of humanitarian obligation) is binding for hosts and guests alike (see Srivastava, 2005; Dayal, 2007). Herein rests yet another uniqueness of Asian domestic tourism that sets it apart from its global/Western counterpart. Hence, while 'tourism' is perceived as a politico-economic force that is rooted in Western secularity, the eastern traditional performances of travelling, visiting and *kama* (pleasure) derive their character from the religious and mystic wisdom of the lands. Even though both ideologies provide the foundation for asserting and organizing the social conduct of people, they tend to contradict each other in that the subtlety (e.g. pleasure-seeking) of one is made prominent in the other, inasmuch as the foreground of one (e.g. piety) fades into the other's background.

Tradition and modernity

Tourism is very often referred to as a modern phenomenon despite its distant origins. The interpretations of tourism by international visitors to the Asian destinations are thus not often informed ('skewed') by the perceptions of their own cultural moorings. In this regard, the two terms – tradition and modern – are, indeed, typically inclusive, and any discussion of either invariably brings in the other. Frequently, both seem to be in conflict with each other. Traditional patterns in the way of life and thinking of the Asian people are the visible manifestations of centuries of adaptations for social evolution. Since national culture is familiar, besides an evolving phenomenon, local people are aware of the continuity of their tradition through generations. As a result, they view their traditions as 'sensible' and even appropriately 'updated'. New infusions of 'modernity' may either be rejected entirely or transformed into a cultural tradition or practice as it undergoes cultural rationalization. Bovair's (2008, p339) documentation of the emerging ('parody' of) neo-orientalism in Tibet is a useful illustration of blending tradition (and nationalism) with modernity, as the locals gather in *nangmas* (dance and karaoke clubs) to dance, sing and enjoy native songs. Why, then, should the majority of native holiday-makers and travellers ignore and abandon this perceptive sensibility of vernacular practices in order to adopt a relatively unfamiliar style and pattern of 'touristic culture' in their own social, geographical and economic conditions? On the contrary, the introduction of the new culture presents a dilemma to comprehend. The conversion of 'the health-restoring fountains, meant as a refuge for disease, into the resorts of vanity for those who have no disease but idleness?' (Hannah More, cited in Sodeman, 2005, p787) or the transformation of the open-access common pool into a privatized, exclusive and perhaps gated enclave (see Singh and Singh, 1999) are examples of such cultural fractures and discontinuities. If the purpose of touristic travel and holidaying is to observe, encounter and experience episodes in order to be able to cultivate sense and sensibility (Adler, 1989), would not the traditional and the modern be able to coexist in their own rights? While the practice of leisure travel and holidaying is only as traditional as tourism (in the contemporary context), the difference lies in the context of the two, which brings back into focus the conditions that have given rise to native travel/holiday traditions, on the one hand, and domestic tourism, on the other. Without a context, modernity is just as false (see Oakes, 1998) as the fake authenticity of invented tradition.

In view of the dichotomy between tradition and modernity, scholars of tourism may benefit from diverting this polarization to the singular theme of continuity or change in order to grasp the realities of changes and practices in indigenous tourism in the Asian context. This recommendation emerges from the fact that although 'tourism' *per se* is posited as a modern/Western phenomenon, it is not an entirely 'new' idea, owing to the fact that almost all Asian nations have been subjected to colonization, during which travel and holidaying were introduced to the natives through the establishment of hill resorts, wildlife sanctuaries and health sanatoriums. The emulation of recreational modes of the colonizers by the indigenous populations in post-colonial times can perhaps be regarded as the beginning of tourism in these countries. Since then, Asian domestic tourism on a Western model has slowly, and surely, evolved on the domestic and international fronts. In the case of the former, the introduction of 'leave travel allowances' or 'paid holidays' for government employees (e.g. India and Vietnam) and the regulation of the 'five-day week' (e.g. China), besides official holiday periods that coincide with significant events (such as annual school closures), serve as visible examples of the blending of tradition and modernity or, preferably, the theme of continuity. The inscription of World Heritage sites and living heritages for the purpose of conserving localized patrimonies for posterity is yet another process that formalizes the juxtaposed presentation of tradition with modernity, aiming to reconcile the past with the future. Another area of interest for scholarly engagement may be in exploring ways in which modernity opens up 'newer' interpretations and avenues for reinforcing, sustaining and living these traditions (see Foard, 1982; Ichaporia, 1983; Aiken, 1987; Creighton, 1995; Rea, 2000; Brunet et al, 2001; Hiwasaki, 2006; Michaud and Turner, 2006). 'Discoveries' and 'narratives' of international visitors to these Asian destinations are not really 'new' but become so as the everyday realities are interpreted and explored ('skewed') by the perceptions of their own culture, thereby infusing modernity into tradition. Ichaporia's (1983, p90) study provides evidence of Indian domestic tourists going 'modern by going traditional' as architectural vestiges are revived and presented anew by way of World Heritage sites. A related interest would be to investigate ways and types of these 'disembeddings' or embeddings through domestic tourism in order to document the histories of society's continuing cultural legacies. In conclusion, 'tradition' can least afford to stagnate; on the contrary, 'cross-cultural feeding is very traditional' (*TDR*, vol 23, no 2, p2, cited in Schechner, 1989, p155). Thus, the challenge for Asian domestic tourism is to find creative ways of working modernity into tradition (or *vice versa*) in order to co-create a mosaic of cultural continuity.

Nostalgia and novelty

For the most part, the socio-cultural moorings of Asia are founded in shared histories of religion and colonialism. Nonetheless, intra-regionally, its countries project a bizarre range of socio-political environments and developmental ideologies. For instance, while the micro-state of Singapore or the Japanese archipelago present an enhanced level of (infrastructural) development, other states (e.g. Laos and Sri Lanka) exhibit a differentiated level and scale of development. Very often, economic evolution remains strongly influenced by the reality of a lived socio-historical mosaic. Economic advancements of these nations alone have not been very successful in transforming their established indicators/notions of quality of life, which can be restated in ways that affirm their traditional values. Bhutan's commitment to gross national happiness (GNH) over gross national product (GNP) or gross domestic product (GDP) is a remarkable assertion of its people's rejection of Western consumerist values. This is also reflected in the vernacular tourism modes of most of the region's countries. An interesting and recurring theme in travel and holiday practices is the native's search for nostalgia in conjunction with novelty. For example, Singaporeans are seemingly disappointed by the replacement of colonial vestiges with the more modern (in their view 'faceless' and 'homogenous') landscapes that have overtaken their cityscape (Teo and Huang, 1995). When compared with their Association of Southeast Asian Nations (ASEAN) neighbours (such as Thailand, China and the Philippines), Singaporeans experience a sense of loss (of character and identity). Likewise, Japanese nostalgia for precapitalistic lifestyles has accentuated the native population's sense of belonging and attachment to aspects of their lived or inherited culture, of which the notion of a rural *furusato* (home) and the emergence of travel-craft vacations are visible indicators (Creighton, 1995, 1997). However, this does not translate into a rejection of novelties existing in their own land or being ushered in by global trends. On the contrary, the innovation is sought and engaged with as an extension of the same mosaic. These examples illustrate the Asian tourist's quest for nostalgia and novelty in combination with, rather than just for, each separately. Perhaps another conclusion is that travel and holidaying are not essentially lodged in modern capitalism and that pre-capitalistic modes of tourism are a pragmatic and conscious option to evade alienation from one's roots. This reconciliation between nostalgia and novelty testifies to the 'strength and adaptability' (Crook 1980) characteristic of most traditional cultures.

Travel and journey

In the context of experience, journeys and travels are synonyms. Yet, travel is somehow perceived as a 'fast-track' (Varma, 2000), 'fashionable' (Sodeman,

2005) performance, where being mobile (on the move) is at the forefront. For many, (air) travel is a statement of a modern (life) style that enables high flyers to hop from one urban hub to another in the shortest possible time with far greater ease. Thus, travel is, by and large, perceived as a means to an end – arriving at the destination. Journeys, on the other hand, are perceived as an act of setting out and bracing oneself for all that the process may bring with it. In this way, a journey becomes a means, an end and an agency for an experience. In many Asian cultures, physical movement is understood in spatial and temporal context, as may be evident in its people's movements during pilgrimages, wanderings or simply roaming. Interestingly, while these journeys implied short stays (rest places), travellers are constantly mindful of the temporality of their act and existence. This awareness not only has implications for the conduct of the sojourners, but is critical to elevating journeying as an art. Thus, the journey becomes a 'performance', while travel is understood as a necessary (even mundane) ritual. In commenting on the Indian treatise, *Ghummakad Shastra* (Sankrityayan, 1948, cited in Srivastava, 2005) analogizes the sojourner's journeying with the 'disappearing ripple' that vanishes without a trace. The author conceptualizes journeying within the philosophy of *dharma* (principle/obligation), thereby implying a conscious awareness of impermanence, while the act of setting up a base (home or stay place) posits an antithesis. Consequently, the stay is usually conceptualized in terms of people rather than locations – staying 'with' rather than 'at'. The recent interpretation of travel, as in 'going to a destination', is currently replacing the previously held notion of journeying. How, then, might scholars of tourism reconcile the two apparently similar, yet dissimilar, notions of travel and journey?

Escape versus pursuit of change

Tourism is usually undertaken with an explicit purpose of escaping from the everyday routine lifestyle. Haldrup (2004, p435) reiterates de Botton in concluding that the phenomenon is charged by a desire to 'flee the horror of home' and to go to any place that 'is out of the world'. Indigenous tourists rarely aspire to a place 'out of the world', and Asian holiday-seekers scarcely conceive of such a thought. The usual reason for travel and holidaying, for most Asians, is 'change', as in taking a 'break' – a change of scene or place. In the case of Japanese *furusato* (see Creighton, 1997), the popular desire is to go 'home' to a familiar past, which is the known and the pastiche, where they can find a brief interlude from the alienating work life and pace of urban living. This is a classic example of the Asian disposition to return to the comforts of the familiar setting. Michaud and Turner's (2006) exposition of the Vietnamese *Bien Che* (employer provision of annual and free statutory trips) also reflects similar inclination for a partial respite, essentially in the circumstances and/or the setting of domestic holiday-making men. They describe these trips as relaxation in the familiar company of co-workers, taking leisurely group strolls and gazing at the relatively unfamiliar scene. The experience of change is in the setting, while the sense of escape is almost non-existent. The camaraderie of co-workers transforms into a *communitas* of *Bien Che* vacationers as they celebrate this time with karaoke singing, drinking, dining, singing, relaxing and prostitution. In China, domestic tourists and day trippers go in huge masses to the beautifully restored or reconstructed gardens, such as the gardens of Suzhou (sightseeing) or to the Westlake of Hangzhou or to the completely (re)constructed Song dynasty town. How different is 'change' from 'escape' in terms of motivating tourists is an unexplored field so far.

'Gaze' and otherness

Encountering the other (people and places) is at the core of all leisure travel and visitations, regardless of specific purpose and market segment. Curiosity to know and engage with other people and settings is an innate desire. This desire, however, is by and large aroused through acquired knowledge, skills and abilities. For many modern tourists, the agency of tourism serves to establish or affirm a self-identity – ethnic, class, cultural or hegemonic. Such intentions and abilities tend to 'taint' the experience and outcomes of people's travels. Often, perceptions and engagements of tourists are limited to 'gazing' (seeing), 'grazing' (consuming) and amusement (diversions). On the other hand, given the familiarity and shared values of native guests and hosts, what would be the nature of perceptions and encounters between people of the same nationality? Would the gaze be a reciprocal one – a 'mutual gaze' (Chan, 2006) between the local hosts and guests whose hegemony will hold sway – or is this aspect of tourism relevant at all? Also, owing to the large populations of many Asian countries – namely, China and India, how would mass tourism or holidaying be conceived or would this be a moot point altogether? What new facets of inclusion–exclusion would be revealed through examining the traditions of Asian domestic travel and holiday-making? These are some of the many questions that open avenues for scholarly engagement in domestic tourism in Asia and elsewhere.

Tourism design and control

Holidaying and touring practices tend to either emerge from existing social, economic and political ideologies, or practices may be adopted to facilitate alignment with existing regimes. Differences between the emerging and adaptation approaches are subtle, yet have significant implications. When tourism is deliberately designed or modelled, then the intention of these efforts (usually economic advantages) defines its consumption and production processes. Varying degrees of controls and opportunities made available through the delivery processes have a bearing on the continuation and the future possibilities for innovation and diversity. Stylized provision of opportunities (a method of control) during holidays and leisure travel is an interesting proposition, but can also be a matter of discomfort and can even generate a sense of alienation or resentment (Taylor and Altenburg, 2006), besides escalating costs (and pricing). Gladstone (2005, p163) illustrates that most Indian tourists spend most of their time in the 'informal space' and that it is this space that accounts for the country's maximum commercial activity. As another example, the age-old practice of relying on word of mouth as advertisement continues to be an effective channel of communication, as opposed to reading the printed word from guide books or surfing the internet. The former tends to be a preference among locals rather than foreign travellers since their participations or performances are generally informal. In essence, the commercialized provisioning of touristic opportunities impedes the pleasure of holiday-makers – both hosts and guests – as much native holiday-making in Asian countries occurs by way of a culturally inconspicuous participation, such as in VFR travel, visitation to shrines and temples (inscribed as heritage sites) and participation in festivities (packaged into events). Varying degrees of control and opportunities are evident in the state provisioning for, and people's enjoyment of, holidays (also travel) in Vietnam, China and India. Chinese tourism authorities have a 'macro-control' and 'deep involvement' in the performance of its domestic tourism sector (Butler and Wall, 1985; Wang and Qu, 2004). State intervention in the travels and holiday activities of Vietnamese citizens provides for 'group' and 'packaged' opportunities that are more or less a 'preformatted' undertaking (Michaud and Turner, 2006). In this case, the government has apparently taken on the 'responsibility' of catering to the inhabitants, and in so doing aims to define a vernacular tourism that is distinctly Vietnamese. By contrast, the leave travel concession (LTC) rules (a well-calibrated financial reimbursement of travel expenses of Indian government employees and their families) and the discounts on the travel fares of the 'senior citizen' and 'freedom fighters' (now virtually non-existent) are major nation-wide interventions of the Government of India that significantly affect the travel and tourism potential of its citizens. Through these provisions, the central government primarily intends to facilitate home visits, holiday and religious travels (see Srivastava, 2005).

The dual aspects of opportunity and control are not only relevant for an understanding of the profiles and nature of Asian domestic holiday travels, but also for exploring the implications of each on the other. Even more important is the documentation of the evolution and processes of informal (including community-scale) enterprises, as well as their stability/weakening and/or disappearance in time.

Reality and surreal perspectives

Tourism scholars have thoroughly investigated the notion of authenticity. However, not many may have projected the concept from an indigenous domestic tourist's perspective. Indeed, if such an attempt were to be made, the term could easily translate as 'reality' (which is what many seem to be 'escaping' from). Tourism – whether indigenous or cross-cultural – is designed to conjure up fantasies as an escape mechanism. Given the genre of religiosity, common in most Asian societies, the locals have their 'fantasy' provided in their traditions of myth and mystique. With such an elaborate and deep system of imaginative conjuring already in place, tourism may not necessarily be sought out by Asian domestic tourists primarily for its fanciful illusions. Instead, their play with reality is utterly unproblematic and amusing. In this context, these holiday-makers could be less concerned with a search for 'authenticity' (as they may be well aware of their 'authentic past') or the spectres of 'fantasy'. Instead, given the relative familiarity with their culture and its people, besides the reality of changing times with its implications for their life and the inclination to sustain their collectivist culture, Asians may find the opportunities and possibilities of modern tourism surreal. Such a surrealist approach permits the locals to remain in touch with the actualities of their lives and their world, which then provides a context to encounter and interpret the bizarre or the uncommon. This further leads to rationalizing the passive casualness with which most Asians participate in domestic tourism. Spectacular modernity may thus not be much 'admired'; in fact, its ostentations are known to have generated resentment (Richter and Richter, 1985; Teo and Huang, 1995). For many domestic tourists, while tourism is certainly a 'foreign' notion, their performance in it or its offerings (products/services) seem to be all too familiar. Nevertheless, this 'familiar' is now afflicted by competition,' quality controls, high costs and conspicuousness – all of which are intended to revolutionize these societies.

In sum, empirical investigations in Asian domestic tourism will benefit from the broad array of sub-themes discussed previously. Moreover, the twin themes of continuity and change, in conjunction with revolutionary and/or evolutionary processes, are generic to the study of domestic tourism and can be interpolated with the above concepts. A recommended approach to these potential areas of investigation is in researching ways in which the local/native considerations take precedence over all other (global) considerations. Subsequently, the following section makes an incipient clustering of Asian domestic tourism in the local, global and 'glocal' contexts.

The future: Endogenous scenarios

As the tourism industry surges ahead towards consolidating nations, cultures and regions into one large playground, what might be the future of domestic traditions of travel and holidaying? Will it be subverted by the levelling dictates of global standardization? How far can the global forces of change penetrate to capitalize on group/social culture? What may possibly be the profile of the domestic traveller/holiday-maker in times to come? These concerns assume pertinence in the Asian context where visible politico-economic and cultural changes are currently under way and where the 'tourists' (*per se*) are essentially the foreigners (nationally and regionally). Sceptics (e.g. Crick, 1989) resent current trends in the standardizing force of the system of tourism. There is a tussle between the opinions of sociologists, anthropologists, economists, business agencies and policy analysts regarding the 'right' step forward.

In the discourses of these agencies of influence, the will and wisdom of the performers may not always be referred (or deferred) to since their role is defined by, and restricted to, 'consumption'. However, this role in itself is a potent tool of participation, rather than a tool of 'democratic engagement'. Thus, while plans and decisions are made by a select ensemble of representatives, the locals go about making cultural choices to fashion their holiday-making and leisure travel. Possibilities do exist in that the resilience of native-style tourism is as much a probability as the gradual assimilation of exogenous styles/models. Of course, room must be made for experiments with either in order to permit selective acculturation and evolution.

Asia's pre-colonial and colonial pasts, along with its post-colonial presence in world affairs today, testify to the region's potential for acculturation. Also, since, 'borrowing is natural' (Schechner, 1989, p157), cross-cultural exchanges are a very traditional phenomenon and domestic tourism provides an opportunity for the locals (hosts and guests) to encounter each other – not merely to assert self-identity, but instead to appropriate current winds of change to enhance their sense of the world and its people. In this regard, 'domestic tourism' in Asian countries promises to continue its journey into the future.

Possible domestic tourism scenarios

Present-day Asian tourism contains both local and global flavours. Presuming that domestic tourism comprises the most popular forms of holiday-making and travel among populations within the confines of their national boundaries, such that the practices reflect the ethos of the people, their land (geopolitical) and the times in which they live, three distinct subcategories emerge in the region's domestic tourism – namely:

1   endemic;
2   embedded;
3   *bricolage.*

Endemic domestic tourism relates to those forms of leisure travel that emerge from a community's patterns of life. The patterns may have been completely informal or perhaps formalized through dependence on institutions, social ordering and localized technologies available to them. In due time, the praxis refined into 'an enduring art of travel' (Adler, 1989, p1366) and emerged to enshrine a definite set of social, cultural, communitarian, geographical, political and economic values that defined the concerned population. Internal pilgrimage systems are an unmistakable example of endemic domestic tourism. Specific secular forms of travel such as seasonal leisure migrations, VFR trips, local celebrations, events and festivities may also be identified under this category.

Embedded domestic tourism can be witnessed when native travel and holidaying occur within the formal structures and systems that have intentionally been established for international visitors (clientele). The domestic tourist then mimics and lives up to the projected chimera of modernity (tourism) and the culturally biased imagery of the consumer (tourist). Luxury resorts that target international visitors (primarily) and domestic urbanized elites who have the leisure and purchasing prowess (usually during off season) are a fair illustration. More often than not, these measures have the explicit support of, or have even been initiated by, the government. Examples of bureaucratic involvement with this agenda can be witnessed in the Philippines, China, India, Hong Kong and Singapore, to name but a few. The products and services accessed by these latter consumers are inflected by 'other world' charms and fantasies. This is made possible by hiring foreign 'consultants' (usually in non-Euramerican countries) or partnering with culture brokers (usually local). In the former case, investment, planning and management are sought from 'tourism experts' from the tourist markets of the West (Jenkins, 2006). Tourism, thus imported, then becomes a 'new' opportunity for the privileged few to set themselves apart from the 'common herd'. New kinds of *communitas* are formed, while the existing communities of domestic hosts and guests are estranged – the 'two worlds' exist side by side. Often, the local bathing places are brought under private ownership and commodified, and a commercial culture emerges to be nourished by the increasing disenfranchisement of local culture. Subsequently, locals become unable to participate since they have little or no conceptualization/endowment to join in contemporary or Western-style tourism.

Domestic tourism bricolage constitutes an array of transmuted varieties of endogenous holiday and travel practices that lie in between the prior two categories. These are characterized by styles that cannot readily be grouped by their origins or exemplify a distinct culture as they are the product of selective assimilation or fusion. The assimilation occurs over a considerable period of time, during which the native and non-native versions of travel and holidaying co-evolve through negotiations between the traditional and the new. At times, during this process, evidences of local sensibilities of holiday-making threaten to disappear, thus giving way to (ir)rational modernity of contemporary times (see Jackson, 1999). But then, later, the tradition may resurface and prevail in an 'improvised' form or the imported style may be 'reinvented' in the new cultural context to suit local tastes and sensibilities. The reinvention, rather than the co-evolution, of 'traditional' holidays and travel is the visible indicator of acculturated local values (or 'enculturated' non-local ideas) that may, by and large, reflect politico-economic shifts.

Researchers, particularly in tourism studies, may find the continuing evolution of Asian domestic tourism fascinating for sustainability discourses. Another question that may be posed is: how, then, would authenticity be defined in the context of 'traditional' domestic tourism? Would the notion of the post-tourist become relevant here? Since many Asian countries exhibit such evolving forms of domestic tourism (see Chan, 2006; Hiwasaki, 2006), it may be possible to gather evidence of these tourism discourses, among many others. In closing, then, the evolution of endogenous alternatives to prevailing forms, patterns and trends of tourism is an enigmatic proposition – one that requires patience, time and persistence. Endogenous alternatives continue to 'emerge' from the twin processes of 'borrowing' and 'transformation', alongside the continuation of critical legacies that identify the collective. As a consequence, locals maintain a sense of belonging with these transformations and extend it to their guests. Without doubt, 'tourism' today is, in its academic sense, a borrowed notion for most countries in Asia; but this borrowing is bound to transform into 'indigenous' material – one that the citizens can assimilate and practice as an aspect of their traditional workmanship. Perhaps this enculturation of tourism within native travels may lend to the furtherance of tourism studies and, more importantly, the enrichment of its language.

In this book

The title of this book, *Domestic Tourism in Asia: Diversity and Divergence*, suggests that domestic tourism embraces both the native and nativized versions of travel and holidaying. More importantly, differences within the styles not only coexist but also persistently interact, both among themselves and with the external environment, to give a shape to various tourism systems that are unique to each country. As a consequence, native tourism dynamics concomitantly reflect and effect transformations through the pluralities of *continuity* and *change* and *revolutionary–evolutionary* continua.

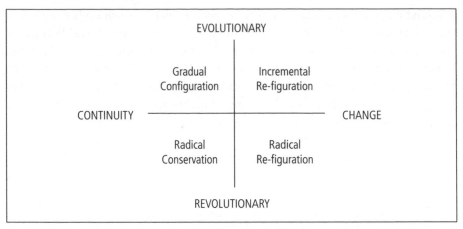

Figure 1.4 *Domestic tourism dynamics: A framework for investigation*

Source: Shalini Singh

While most submissions in this book roughly fall within any of the three scenarios of endemic, embedded and *bricolage* categories, it is pertinent to state that the classification cannot be generalized to an entire country. Also, owing to the dynamic processes that continue to shape the tourism system of a country, native tourism may shift from one category to the other easily. Domestic tourism thus obtains myriad hues arising from the synchronization of the bipolar continua. Consequently, four possible outcomes can be identified:

1   Within the continuity/evolutionary coordinates, *gradual configuration* illustrates a development where new situations (assets, resources, images and cultural contexts) significantly reflect the preceding ones. However, practice and performances in tourism reflect their own distinctive logic and paradigm.

2   *Incremental re-figuration* is also a gradual change, but one that is substantial and brings about situations that differ substantially from the original states (e.g. from traditional to modern) in order to accommodate global trends. Hence, it is appropriately located within the change–evolutionary coordinate.

3   In the revolution–change section, *radical re-figuration* highlights situations and processes where the production and consumption of domestic tourism are connected to radical changes to a new order. This happens in those cases where the political ideology shifts to a new form of ordering, bringing about a paradigm shift in ways of thinking.

4   *Radical conservation* can be represented as a radical turn back to traditions or nostalgia. This usually represents a forward process, but in the same sense as when fundamentalist notions become connected eclectically with

elements from the past in order to use them as icons of identity or 'truth', such as a radical ecosystem approach, or returning to an ideologically and ideally 'primeval' state.

These coordinates will, perhaps, be useful in situating and elaborating upon the critical issues raised in this and subsequent chapters.

Notes

1   The term 'native' implies resident populations who have their roots in the country, and/or identify with it, as their current residence.
2   Asia and the Pacific was the second-best 'performing' region in 2006, with South Asia (+11 per cent) and South-East Asia (+9 per cent) outdoing the region's average (8 per cent).
3   Here, the competition relates to tourism developments that are increasingly undertaken with the singular objective of attracting the wealthy national and international tourist. For example, the idea of the 'authentic replica' is often at the core of Asian scenic/ethnic theme parks (see Notar, 2006; Nyiri, 2006; Oakes and Schein, 2006).

References

Adler, J. (1989) 'Travel as a performed art', *The American Journal of Sociology*, vol 94, no 6, pp1366–1391

Aiken, S. R. (1987) 'Early Penang Hill Station', *Geographical Review*, vol 77, no 4, pp421–439

Alneng, V. (2002) 'The modern does not cater for natives – travel ethnography and the conventions of form', *Tourist Studies*, vol 2, no 2, pp119–142

Aramberri, J. (2004) 'Domestic tourism in Asia: Some ruffle and flourish for a neglected relation', *Tourism Recreation Research*, vol 29, no 2, pp1–11

Beaver, A. (2002) *A Dictionary of Travel and Tourism Terminology*, second edition, CABI Publishing, Wallingford, UK/Cambridge, MA

Bovair, E. A. (2008) 'Journeys to Shangri-La: The neo-orientalism of Tibetan culture', in J. Cochrane (ed) *Asian Tourism: Growth and Change*, Elsevier, Oxford, UK, pp335–343

Brown, R. M. (1935) 'The business of recreation', *Geographical Review*, vol 25, no 3, pp467–475

Brunet, S., Bauer, J., De Lacy, T. and Tshering, K. (2001) 'Tourism development in Bhutan: Tensions between tradition and modernity', *Journal of Sustainable Tourism*, vol 9, no 3, pp243–261

Butler, R. and Wall, G. (1985) 'Introduction: Themes in research on the evolution of tourism', *Annals of Tourism Research*, vol 12, pp287–296

Canadian Tourism Commission (1996) *Domestic Tourism Market Research Study: Main Report*, Canadian Tourism Commission, Ottawa, Canada

Chan, Y. W. (2006) 'Coming of age of the Chinese tourists – The emergence of non-Western tourism and host–guest interactions in Vietnam's border tourism', *Tourist Studies*, vol 6, no 3, pp187–213

Christaller, W. (1963) 'Some considerations of tourism locations in Europe', *Papers and Proceedings of Regional Science Association*, vol 12, pp95–105

Clawson, M. and Knetsch, J. L. (1963) *Economics of Outdoor Recreation*, John Hopkins Press for Resources of the Future, Baltimore, MD

Cochrane, J. (2006) 'Indonesian national parks – Understanding leisure users', *Annals of Tourism Research*, vol 33, no 4, pp979–997

Cochrane, J. (2008) (ed) *Asian Tourism: Growth and Change*, Elsevier, Oxford, UK

Cohen, E. (1995) 'Contemporary tourism – Trends and challenges: Sustainable authenticity or contrived post-modernity?', in R. Butler and D. Pearce (eds) *Change in Tourism: People, Places, Processes*, Routledge, New York, pp12–29

Creighton, M. R. (1995) 'Japanese craft tourism – Liberating the crane wife', *Annals of Tourism Research*, vol 22, no 2, pp463–478

Creighton, M. R. (1997) 'Consuming rural Japan: The marketing of tradition and nostalgia in the Japanese travel industry', *Ethnology*, vol 36, no 3, pp239–254

Crick, M. (1989) 'Representations of international tourism in the social sciences: Sun, sex, sights, savings and servility', *Annual Review of Anthropology*, vol 18, pp307–344

Crook, J. H. (1980) 'Social change in Indian Tibet', *Social Science Information*, vol 19, p139

Dayal, S. (2007) 'Repositioning India: Tagore's passionate politics of love', *Positions*, vol 15, no 1, pp165–208

Dulles, F. R. (1966) 'A historical view of Americans abroad', *Annals of the American Academy of Political and Social Science*, vol 368, pp11–20

Edensor, T. (1998) *Tourists at the Taj*, Routledge, London

Enzensberger, H. M. (1996) 'A theory of tourism', *New German Critique*, Special issue on literature, vol 68, pp117–135

Foard, J. H. (1982) 'The boundaries of compassion: Buddhism and national tradition in Japanese pilgrimage', *The Journal of Asian Studies*, vol 41, no 2, pp231–251

Ghimire, K. B. (2001) *The Native Tourist – Mass Tourism Within Developing Countries*, Earthscan, UK

Gladstone, D. L. (2005) *From Pilgrimage to Package Tour – Travel and Tourism in the Third World*, Routledge, New York, NY

Graburn, N. (1983) *To Pray, Pay and Play: The Cultural Structure of Japanese Domestic Tourism*, C26, Centre des Hautes Etudes Touristiques, Aix-en-Provence, France

Haldrup, M. (2004) 'Laid-back mobilities: Second-home holidays in time and space', *Tourism Geographies*, vol 6, no 4, pp434–454

Harrison, D. (ed) (2001) *Tourism and the Less Developed World: Issues and Case Studies*, CABI Publishing, Wallingford, UK

Helleiner, F. M. (1990) 'Domestic and international tourism in the third world nations', *Tourism Recreation Research*, vol 15, no 1, pp18–25

Hiwasaki, L. (2006) 'Community-based tourism: A pathway to sustainability for Japan's protected areas', *Society and Natural Resources*, vol 19, pp675–692

Hughes, G. (1992) 'Changing approaches to domestic tourism', *Tourism Management*, vol 13, no 1, pp85–90

Ichaporia, N. (1983) 'Tourism at Khajuraho: An Indian enigma?', *Annals of Tourism Research*, vol 10, pp75–92

Jackson, P. (1999) 'Commodity cultures: The traffic in things', *Transactions of the Institute of British Geographers*, vol 24, no 1, pp95–108

Jafari, J. (1979) 'The tourism market basket of goods and services: The components and the nature of tourism', *Tourism Recreation Research*, vol 4, no 2, pp1–8

Jafari, J. (1986) 'On domestic tourism', *Annals of Tourism Research*, vol 13, pp491–496

Jenkins, C. M. (2006) 'An area of darkness? Tourism in the third world revisited', *Tourism Recreation Research*, vol 31, no 3, pp87–91

Kaur, J. (1985) *Himalayan Pilgrimages and the New Tourism*, Himalayan Books, New Delhi, India

Klieger, P. C. (1992) 'Shangri-La and the politicization of tourism in Tibet', *Annals of Tourism Research*, vol 19, pp122–144

Lee, S. H. and Tideswell, C. (2005) 'Understanding attitudes towards leisure travel and the constraints faced by senior Koreans', *Journal of Vacation Marketing*, vol 11, no 3, pp249–263

Lee, Y. S. (2006) 'Myth, spirituality and religion in travel: Pre-industrial Korea', *Tourism*, vol 54, no 2, pp97–106

Li, H. (2006) 'Emergence of the Chinese middle class and its implications', *Asian Affairs*, vol 33, no 2, pp67–84

Martin, S. K. (2004) 'Destruction and revival: The fate of the Tibetan Buddhist Monastery Labrang in the People's Republic of China religion', *State and Society*, vol 32, no 1, pp7–13

Medlik, S. (1996) *Dictionary of Travel, Tourism, and Hospitality*, second edition, Butterworth-Heinemann, Oxford, UK

Michaud, J. (1991) 'A social anthropology of tourism in Ladakh, India', *Annals of Tourism Research*, vol 18, pp605–621

Michaud, J. and Turner, S. (2006) 'Contending visions of a hill-station in Vietnam', *Annals of Tourism Research*, vol 33, no 3, pp785–808

Mitchell, L. S. (1969) 'Toward a theory of public urban recreation', in *Proceedings of AAG*, vol 1, Washington, pp103–108

Moeran, B. (1983) 'The language of Japanese tourism', *Annals of Tourism Research*, vol 10, pp95–106

Mowforth, M. and Munt, I. (1998) *Tourism and Sustainability: New Tourism in the Third World*, Routledge, London

Notar, B. E. (2006) *Displacing Desire*, University of Hawaii, Honolulu, HI

Nyiri, P. (2006) *Scenic Spots*, University of Washington Press, Washington, DC

Oakes, T. (1998) *Tourism and Modernity in China*, Routledge, London

Oakes, T. and Schein, L. (eds) (2006) *Translocal China*, Routledge, London

Ogilvie, F. W. (1933) *The Tourist Movement: An Economic Study*, P. S. King, London

Pearce, D. G. (1996) 'Domestic tourist travel in Sweden: A regional analysis', *Geografiska Annaler*, Series B: Human Geography, vol 78, no 2, pp71–84

Pfaffenberger, B. (1983) 'Serious pilgrims and frivolous tourists – The chimera of tourism in the pilgrimages of Sri Lanka', *Annals of Tourism Research*, vol 10, pp57–74

Pigram, J. (1983) *Outdoor Recreation ad Resource Management*, Beckenham, Kent

Porananond, P. and Robinson, M. (2008) 'Modernity and the evolution of a festive tourism tradition: The Songkran Festival in Ciang Mai, Thailand' in J. Cochrane (ed) *Asian Tourism: Growth and Change*, Elsevier, Oxford, UK, pp311–321

Rea, M. H. (2000) 'A furusato away from home', *Annals of Tourism Research*, vol 27, no 3, pp638–660

Rian, A. (1969) 'The promotion of domestic tourism', *World Travel*, vol 87, pp21–22

Richter, L. K. (1989) *The Politics of Tourism in Asia*, University of Hawaii Press, Honolulu, Hawaii

Richter, L. K. and Richter, W. L. (1985) 'Policy choices in south Asian tourism development', *Annals of Tourism Research*, vol 12, pp201–217

Rose, F. (1997) 'Toward a class-cultural theory of social movements: Reinterpreting new social movements', *Sociological Forum*, vol 12, no 3, pp461–494

Schechner, R. (1989) 'Intercultural themes', *Performing Arts Journal*, vol 11, no 3, pp151–162

Singh, S. (2004) 'India's domestic tourism: Chaos/crisis/challenge?', *Tourism Recreation Research*, vol 29, no 2, pp35–46

Singh, S. and Singh, T. V. (2009) 'Aesthetic pleasures: Contemplating spiritual tourism', in J. Tribe (ed) *Philosophical Issues in Tourism*, Channelview Publications, UK

Singh, T. V. (1989) *The Kulu Valley: Impact of Tourism Development in Mountain Areas*, Himalayan Books, New Delhi, India

Singh, T. V. and Singh, S. (1999) 'Coastal tourism, conservation and the community: Case of Goa', in T. V. Singh and S. Singh (eds) *Tourism in the Critical Environments*, Cognizant Communication Corporation, New York, pp65–76

Sodeman, M. (2005) 'Domestic mobility in persuasion and sanditon', *Studies in English Literature*, vol 45, no 4, pp787–812

Srivastava, S. (2005) 'Ghummakkads, a woman's place, and the LTC-walas: Towards a critical history of home, belonging and attachment', *Contributions to Indian Sociology*, vol 39, no 3, pp375–405

Stodolska, M. and Livengood, J. S. (2006) 'The influence of religion on the leisure behavior of immigrant Muslims in the United States', *Journal of Leisure Research*, vol 38, no 3, pp293–232

Taylor, K. and Altenburg, K. (May 2006) 'Cultural landscapes in Asia-Pacific: Potential for filling World Heritage gaps', *International Journal of Heritage Studies*, vol 12, no 3, pp267–282

Teo, P. and Huang, S. (1995) 'Tourism and heritage conservation in Singapore', *Annals of Tourism Research*, vol 22, no 3, pp589–615

Thompson, K. and Matheson, C. M. (2008) 'Culture, authenticity and sport: A study of event motivations in the Ulaanbaatar Naadam Festival. Mongolia', in J. Cochrane (ed) *Asian Tourism: Growth and Change*, Elsevier, Oxford, UK, pp233–243

UNWTO (2007) 'Tourism highlights 2007 edition', *Facts & Figures*, www.unwto.org, accessed 18 June 2008

Varma, H. (2000) Presentation at the National Seminar on Tourism, Ahmedabad, India, 18 February

Verbeke, J. M. (1988) *Leisure, Recreation and Tourism in Inner Cities*, Institute Katholieke Univeritiet, Nijmegen, The Netherlands

Wang, N. (2000) *Tourism and Modernity: A Sociological Analysis*, Pergamon Press, Oxford

Wang, S. and Qu, H. (2004) 'A comparison study of Chinese domestic tourism: China vs the USA', *International Journal of Contemporary Hospitality Management*, vol 16, no 2, pp108–115

Williams, A. M. and Balaz, V. (2001) 'From collective provision to commodification of tourism?', *Annals of Tourism Research*, vol 28, no 1, pp27–49

Williams, T. A. (1979) 'Impact of domestic tourism on host population: The evolution of a model', *Tourism Recreation Research*, vol 4, no 2, pp15–21

Young, C. A., Corsun, D. L. and Baloglu, S. (2007) 'A taxonomy of hosts – Visiting friends and relatives', *Annals of Tourism Research*, vol 34, no 2, pp497–516

2

Zen and the Art of Tourism Maintenance: A Meditation on So-Called Proto-Tourism in Vietnam

Victor Alneng

The quest for the proto-touristic

Who is a tourist? The question appears as impossible to answer as it is necessary to pose. The almost obsessive preoccupation of this question has given fruit, and a previously grossly ethnocentric tourism studies now stands corrected. The fact that people outside the Western world can be tourists, and not merely immobile hosts, is today an indisputable fact. Because of this, instead of rushing ahead in search of every new tourism type, it is now appropriate to take a moment to reflect on the specifics of this expanding category of tourists. There is, for starters, a crucial distinction to be made between asserting the empirical fact that the indigenous elite in early 20th-century French Indochina was touring the country along with the colonialists, and to search history and pre-modern cultures for primitive tourism or 'proto-touristic' (Nash, 1981) features or elements such as pilgrimage.

It might be said, paraphrasing Hegel, that moderns do not go on pilgrimages because tourism *is* their pilgrimage.[1] This assertion, however, remains empty as long as the passage from pilgrimage to tourism is not scrutinized. In what follows, I will try to do just that and, in the process, put the notion of pilgrimage as proto-tourism to test. I will start with some ethnographic examples from Vietnam in order to set the context for the concluding discussion of the role of the so-called proto-touristic in tourism theory.

Pilgrims in cable cars

If we follow the broad definition of the World Tourism Organization (WTO), religious pilgrims are tourists, and there are also those who suggest that tourism is a kind of modern pilgrimage (MacCannell, 1976; Pfaffenberger, 1983; Graburn, 1989). According to these scholars, it is not (only) pilgrims who are tourists, but tourists who are (metaphorical) pilgrims. Kevin Meethan is not impressed with either assertion. Standing up for the rights of the pious, he determines that 'many of these pilgrims may well be insulted at such a suggestion'. Although recognizing that religious and secular elements may coexist at tourist spots, Meethan (2001, p13) insists: 'there is still a difference between those motivated to travel to sacred places out of a sense of duty and obligation, and those motivated to reside temporarily and seasonally on beaches and in resort areas'.

Meethan is, of course, right, but only to the extent that his argument is circular – he presents two different motivations and then asserts that there is a difference between the two. How does he know pilgrims will be insulted if called tourists and that pilgrimages are always undertaken only with 'a sense of duty and obligation'? Who is to say that one and the same person cannot travel to a sacred place and make some enjoyable stops at touristic spots on the way? Indeed, the fact that a sacred place can even be the same as the enjoyable touristic spot (see Pfaffenberger, 1983) is hard to dispute. Referring to Edensor's study of the Taj Mahal (1998), Meethan knows as much, which, of course, only makes his insistence on the radical difference between pilgrims and tourists all the more confounding. What it comes down to, then, is this: in what kind of symbolic order is duty as a means of self-realization radically opposed to the enjoyment of recreation?

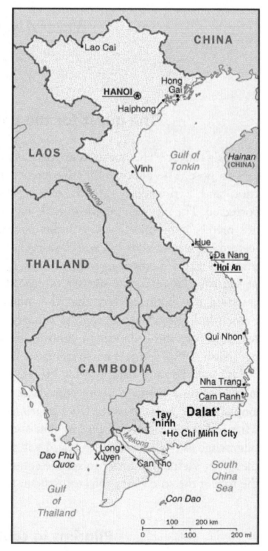

Figure 2.1 *Map of Vietnam*

Source: adapted from www.wordtravels.com

Meethan does not offer any examples, so I will, as opportunistic as it may be. Núi Bà Đen (Black Lady Mountain) in the southern Vietnamese province of Tây Ninh gets well over 1 million visitors per year, of which all but a few are Vietnamese. For them, Núi Bà Đen is both a pilgrimage site and a tourist site, and they seem to have no difficulties shouldering an amalgamation of these presupposed incompatible identities. Western guidebooks represent Núi Bà Đen as a pilgrimage site for pious Vietnamese – 'pilgrims still visit the site' (Footprint, 1999, p271), and 'plenty of old [Vietnamese] women in sandals make the journey to worship at the temple' (Storey and Florence, 2001, p509), while it is promoted as an exotic tourist spot for Westerners. Vietnamese visitors are thus exclusively cast as pilgrims, while Westerners play the role of tourists.

In the Vietnam National Administration of Tourism's (VNAT's) guidebook, however, the pilgrim and tourist identities are rolled into one: 'Many pilgrims go there to pray, but also to go sightseeing and enjoy the entertainment' (VNAT, 2000, p402). While Western guidebooks frame the site as relatively untouched by tourists, the pilgrimage site of Núi Bà Đen is the flagship of the local tourism authority, Tay Ninh Tourism, who, in 1996, invested some US$2 million in building a cable-car ride up the mountain, the first in the country. Ever since, pilgrims can enjoy the scenic view from their cable car on their way up to offer at the temple. The Vietnamese language does include discrete terms for 'pilgrim' (*khách hành hươ'ng*) and 'tourist' (*khách du lịch*); thus, the merger of tourists and pilgrims in the presented example does not derive from problems of translation. Meethan's (2001) claim is obviously relevant only in a context where there exists a sharp distinction between the secular (tourism) and the sacred (pilgrimage), and where the former is vulgarized and the latter is an ordeal. Ironically, Meethan himself criticizes this kind of modernist worldview for having wrongfully informed the study of tourism; but his is a critique of the metaphorical binary opposition championed by MacCannell (1976), Pfaffenberger (1983) and Graburn (1989) that suggests tourism as a kind of secular pilgrimage by which alienated Westerners worship at the temples of modernity. In the end, it seems, this critique is but the mirror image of what it criticizes.

Zen tourists at the bamboo grove

Trúc Lâm monastery and pagoda – *Thiền Viện Trúc Lâm* in Vietnamese – is located in Vietnam's Central Highlands on Phượng Hoàng Hill overlooking Tuyền Lâm Lake some 4km outside the renowned hill station and tourism haunt Đà Lạt. The monks and nuns of the pagoda are devoted to promoting a renaissance of the Zen Buddhist tradition (*sư' Thiền* in Vietnamese) of the ancient Trần Dynasty (1225–1400), during which Emperor Trần Nhân Tông abdicated to become a monk. As a monk, Trần merged the then three dominating Zen sects in the country – Vô Ngôn Thông, Tỳ-ni-đa-lưu-chi and Thảo Đường – into one, which he named Trúc Lâm (literally, Bamboo Grove): hence, the name of the pagoda. Trúc Lâm monastery was inaugurated in 1994 by renowned Zen Master Thích Thanh Từ. Author of titles such as *Vietnamese Zen in the Late Twentieth Century, The Key to Buddhism* and *Buddhism and the Youth*, as well as several Vietnamese titles, Master Thanh Từ is now regarded as an international authority of some rank. In his tireless effort to spread the teachings of the Trúc Lâm sect, he has inaugurated 15 *Thiền* meditation centres in Vietnam, as well as several others in Australia, Canada and the US.

Despite its short history as well as the popular opinion that the pagoda 'hasn't got the traditional beauty of other pagodas' (Trương, 2003, p189), Trúc Lâm has quickly become one of Vietnam's most important pilgrimage sites. It easily competes with traditional pilgrimage sites such as Núi Bà Đen in the south and Chùa Hương (Perfume Pagoda) in the north and it is without a doubt *the* most important Zen Buddhist centre in the country. Its fame has even reached cyberspace and Trúc Lâm can now boast an entry in the internet-based encyclopaedia Wikipedia. The overwhelming majority of visitors are tourists on holiday in the nearby tourism town Đà Lạt. Đà Lạt has around 1 million visitors per year, of which roughly 80 to 90 per cent are domestic tourists. These typically include a visit to Trúc Lâm while on day trips around Đà Lạt and its surroundings. Before arriving at the pagoda, most will have made a stop at Prenn Waterfall, a smallish natural waterfall turned into a kitschy tourism site complete with a mini-zoo, paddle boats and souvenir shops selling plastic trinkets imported from China. Many also combine their visit to the pagoda with a boat trip on nearby Tuyền Lâm Lake, which is another official tourism site. To celebrate the 110th anniversary of the City of Đà Lạt, a cable car was built in 2003, connecting the city with Phương Hoàng Hill and the Trúc Lâm meditation centre. This, in combination with the development of the tourism site of Tuyền Lâm Lake, has increased the number of visits to Trúc Lâm.

As its success in attracting visitors has grown, so too has the myth of origin of its popularity. I have on several occasions been told this myth by people in Đà Lạt where I have conducted fieldwork on and off since 1999. A Taiwanese monk, a legendary Feng Shui expert, so the story goes, came to Vietnam to find a site for the building of the Zen Buddhist meditation centre. After careful considerations and all necessary geomantic tests, he found two spots on the opposite side of Tuyền Lâm Lake. Whatever was built at these two spots, the monk declared, would attract visitors from both far and near. That the name of the lake is a combination of the Vietnamese words for water stream (*tuyền*) and forest (*lâm*) helps to ground this myth in Eastern philosophical tradition, in which the five elements are connected so that water leads to wood, wood to fire, fire to earth and earth to metal – Tuyền Lâm Lake 'is the source of all living beings because here "water leads to wood"' (Trương Phúc Ân, 2003, p187). To further secure the spell, a ritual was conducted, burying some sacred relics at the two spots. The pagoda was then swiftly built on one of these spots. The rest is, as they say, history.

According to superior bonze Thích Trúc Thông Tánh, this is 'pure nonsense'.[2] Before Trúc Lâm was built, there were ten *Thiền* pagodas in Vietnam. All of them were in tropical areas. Thông Tánh explains the success of Trúc Lâm with reference to how the temperate climate of the Central Highlands is very suitable for the practice of meditation. While this seems a reasonable, and most likely at least a partial, explanation, it is interesting to note how this echoes the reasons why the French colonialists chose the Langbian Plateau to build their hill station Đà Lạt. Alexandre Yersin 'discovered' the Langbian Plateau during the late 1800s and in 1900 the colonialists decided to establish Đà Lạt as a recreational region. With its favourable temperate climate and big-game hunting opportunities, it proved a successful venture. Once the local minority peoples had been violently deported and forced into reservations, native coolies were brought in to build the city. Although built from scratch in unexplored hostile territories, Đà Lạt was soon established as a military outpost, a sanatorium and a seat of government rolled into one, thus combining all dominant themes of the colonial rule. There thus seems to be some correlation between the success of Đà Lạt as a tourist town and the success of nearby Trúc Lâm as a pilgrimage site. The history of this sacred place is here linked to the violent history of colonialism.

On a more general level, this correlation is also evident in superior bonze Thông Tánh's denouncing of this myth of origin:

> *This information, people just spread as a rumour for fun. It is not true. We [the monks and nuns of the Trúc Lâm sect] do not care about geomancy. We tried to build this place in such a way that it blends in with the natural view in these surroundings, but that has nothing to do with geomancy. After the pagoda was built, some geomancy practitioners from Taiwan did come here. They praised our pagoda a lot. They asked who choose the spot and the design of the meditation centre. We absolutely did not consider anything about Feng Shui when we built this place. For Thiền Buddhists, these things are not important. That rumour is not true! The reason why so many tourists come here is because we do not charge any fees. We have all services, from parking to toilet, and all of it is free of charge. We don't even have a donation box to encourage people to donate money. That is why people feel free and at ease here. They feel like no one is trying to pick their pockets. In other places, each*

car or bus has to pay many thousand đồng for parking. One motor-
bike has to pay 1000 to 2000 đồng. A visit to the toilet costs 500 to
1000 đồng.³ Everything is money, but here, everything is free.

This stress on the absence of commercialism in explaining the success of the
pagoda at attracting visitors was a topic the bonze kept coming back to
throughout the interview. Paradoxically, as we shall see, this strong emphasis
on the absence of commercialism revealed what the bonze searched to deny –
the importance of the role of money and tourism as commercialized hospitality. Thông Tánh went on to talk about the motivation of the visitors themselves:

The view here is quite beautiful, so it attracts tourists. The reason
why people come here also depends on psychology; but most tourists
who visit Đà Lạt also come here. Not everybody who come here are
Buddhists. Some Buddhists come to visit the pagoda, but most are
tourists. They come here for sightseeing – not everybody comes here
only to pray [to] Buddha! Some Buddhist monks, nuns and lay
people come to pray [to] Buddha. And other people come here for
the beautiful view because they are tourists. Some people come here
with food and drinking and have picnics here all day.

To accommodate these picnicking pilgrims, the monks and nuns have built walking paths dotted with pavilions overlooking Tuyền Lâm Lake. In the pavilions
there are park benches and tables for the picnickers. On the backs of these
benches one can read the names and country of residence of visitors who have
made large donations to the Trúc Lâm sect. The walking paths are lined with flowers, next to which Vietnamese visitors enjoy posing: pictures are taken for a fee by
local photographers catering to tourists.⁴ Rather than the traditional landscape
commonly associated with Zen Buddhism, this gives the area an atmosphere similar to the many parks inside the City of Flowers, as Đà Lạt is often called.

It seems, then, that Trúc Lâm as a religious site has very little to do with its
success at attracting visitors – the touristic rather than the sacred has taken the
front seat. While the international guidebook *Lonely Planet for Vietnam* lists
only Tuyền Lâm Lake but not Trúc Lâm as a tourist attraction, national guidebooks and tourism literature more often than not write about Trúc Lâm as an
integral part of the tourism site of Tuyền Lâm Lake:

Coming to Tuyền Lâm Lake, visitors can't miss Monastery Trúc
Lâm, a destination that all the people in Đà Lạt bear in mind ...
although built only in 1994, it has attracted a lot of visitors from the
city as well as from other places, especially in tourists seasons.
(Trương Phúc Ân, 2000, p232)

Figure 2.2 *Enterprising local photographers catering to pilgrim/tourists –*
as much an integral part of the business-as-usual of the pagoda
as the monks and the nuns

Source: Victor Alneng, 7 August, 2003

The same author also notes:

> *Recognizing the romantic and mysterious sight of Tuyền Lâm Lake*
> *and Trúc LâmPagoda, in 1998, specialists of the Viet Nam Research*
> *and Development of Tourism Institute coordinated with the local*
> *offices to establish a functional project of Tuyền Lâm Lake tourist*

> *site, [which is] determined as a tourist site of ecology and cultural*
> *resort including: lake, forest, natural landscape and pagoda.*
> (Trường Phúc Ân, 2003, p193)

I want to suggest that all of this points to how the pagoda has been subsumed under tourism. Indeed, this is even evident in the interview with the superior bonze. What is most interesting here is in what ways and to what extent the bonze is able to repress the fact of his sacred site being subsumed under tourism. To gain some understanding of the dynamics at work here, it is useful to introduce the distinction between formal and real, or material, 'subsumption'.

The formal and real 'subsumption' of tourism

From the philosophical tradition of German Idealism, Marx borrowed the term 'subsumption'. Before Marx, philosophers Kant, Schelling and Hegel used the term to designate the general tendency of a universal form to incorporate particulars that did not seem to belong to it conceptually. Marx developed the concept of 'subsumption' to analyse the process by which capital, as a social relation of production, penetrates and finally subordinates the productive forces and the labour process. In certain versions of Marxism, the process of subsumption is discussed more generally as the subordination of labour. My references here are, however, to the section entitled 'Results of the immediate process of production', published as an appendix of the second edition of *Capital* (Marx, 1867/1976, vol 1, translated by Ben Fowkes), in which Marx elaborates on the concept of subsumption as the process by which the particularities of the process of labour is subsumed under the abstract universality of capital as a social relation and process of valorization. It is here that he develops the crucial distinction between formal and real subsumption.

Formal subsumption refers to the process by which capital takes hold of a local labour process previously untouched by capital. At this initial stage, which can exist as a particular form side by side 'the specifically capitalist mode of production' (Marx, 1867/1976, p1019), the labour process pretty much continues as before, only now capital has monopolized the means of production. The labour process of previously independent workers, merchants, peasants and artisans is transformed into wage labour, while the existing local market is exploited for the extraction of surplus value. As the term suggests, then, while remaining the same in content, the labour process as such is *formally* transformed in that the valorization of it is brought under the wage form (which makes possible the extraction of surplus value).

This purely formal subsumption, insignificant as it may seem, paves the way for the real, or material, subsumption, by which capitalism as an encompassing mode of production comes of its own. The capitalist can now intervene directly in the local market, and all social relations between people are now transformed into relations between things (commodities). This transformation of social reality, concomitant of capitalism as a mode of production, is what Marx famously has dubbed commodity fetishism. Thus, the real subsumption is 'real' precisely in the sense of it changing not only the economic, but also the social, reality. The real subsumption – that is, the establishing of a new synchronic order – thus transforms how we relate to and experience our social surroundings. What should not be missed here is that in doing so, *the real subsumption transforms in a highly subversive way the very framework with which we can (retrospectively) account for this said transformation.*

My claim here is that the process by which the labour process is first formally than materially subsumed under capital is a process that forms the underlying structural support for the organization of domestic tourism as *endemic, embedded* and *bricolage*, as Singh discusses in Chapter 1. Endemic tourism is, Singh writes, more or less pre-capitalist tourism where local cultural traditions and local commercial interests form the dominant guiding principle. Where this form of tourism exists, national or international commercial interests often come in and formally subsume it. This is done in such a way that the local labour process (artisans) and local ways of travel (e.g. pilgrimage) remain the same in form, but the flow of capital is impeded and directed in favour of dominant, often outside, actors, leaving locals barred from direct access to the fruits of social and material production.

Where this tendency grows stronger, one is likely to see more of, what Singh calls, embedded domestic tourism, where local tourists travel in a tourism infrastructure organized for international tourists. Local cultural forms of travel are now being monopolized by a formal tourism industry driven by national, even international, rather than local interests. This change in the labour process brings with it changes in social production and valorization in such a way that the 'domestic tourist then mimics and lives up to the projected chimera of modernity (tourism) and the culturally biased imagery of the consumer (tourist)' (see Chapter 1). Just as (as Marx notes) 'the specifically capitalist mode of production' can exist, at least temporarily, side by side with a formally subsumed labour process, so, too, can (as Singh notes) fully embedded domestic tourism exist in combination with endemic tourism. This is what Singh calls domestic tourism *bricolage*. This framework can be used to understand the dynamics of places such as Trúc Lâm, where religion and tourism intermingle and, more importantly, where it is evident that capitalism as a mode of social production is transforming the practices of both visitors and hosts.

Zen and the art of tourism maintenance

As mentioned, the superior bonze of Trúc Lâm dismissed the myth of the pagoda being charmed by Feng Shui experts as laughable:

> [Laughing] If this place was charmed, but we did not take care of the garden and the flowers, if we would not keep the buildings in good repair, and if we would charge 10,000 đồng for a small tour bus, and 20,000 đồng for a big, and if each guest who comes through the gate has to pay 5000 đồng for an entrance ticket – if we would do all that, then nobody [would] come here.

For him, it is thus hard work in combination with good services and, above all, a lack of commercialism that is behind the success of his pagoda. What is so interesting here is how the emphasis on the lack of commercialism here explicitly reveals the monk's understanding of himself and his pupils as tourism workers. In tourism, as is well known, it is common to hide charges so as to enforce the experience of hospitality. Examples abound here, ranging from hidden charges in air ticket sales to more down-to-earth examples of socially compulsory (yet formally free) charges such as tipping and the social play of bargaining for souvenirs, which seldom result in an actual lowering of the purchasing prices.[5] As the bonze himself explains, even the spatial organization of the monastery was, from the very beginning, explicitly organized with tourists in mind:

> This is a place for Thiền and there are four departments. The area outside here [where the pagoda is situated] is for tourists and pilgrims, another part is for monks of high position, one part is for those training to become monks, and one part is for nuns. So, the area for tourists is far from the areas for monks and nuns; thus the noise of the tourist does not disturb. But anyway there is a cultural limit to this – it is up to the tourist guides. Some tourists do not have consciousness. They scream very loud. But it's ok. It does not disturb the study area; it's far away from here.

In the passage above, the bonze seems to suggest that it was precisely by taking tourism into account from the start that the monks and nuns of Trúc Lâm can now manage to continue undisturbed with their practice of *Thiền* and leave the managing of tourism up to the tourist guides. It might then be said that Trúc Lâm has escaped being subsumed by tourism by this pre-emptive managing of tourism. It is precisely here, however, that Marx's insights into the ability of the synchronic system to retrospectively write the history of its genesis are crucial.

What the bonze is doing in the passage above is, of course, to retroactively presuppose the existence of tourism in order to explain away how his sacred place has been transformed into a tourism site. There are more than a few indications that the subsumption of this religious site under tourism is real enough (in Marx's sense) to have transformed the practices and the attitudes of the people of Trúc Lâm. For instance, by the stairs leading from the parking area up to the area of the pagoda there is a big sign instructing pilgrims and domestic tourists to dress according to cultural norms. The sign provides a painted illustration of people walking across the open area in front of the pagoda. The main focus of the painting is a family of four, with the husband in white shirt and tie and the woman in *áo dài*, the traditional Vietnamese dress. This perfectly neat family is contrasted with a couple standing nearby, the man wearing shorts and a sleeveless t-shirt and the girl wearing a miniskirt and a revealing top. This couple are crossed over so that no one misses the message. When asked about this billboard, and the fact that many visitors ignore these dress codes, Thông Tánh had this to say:

> *Compared with other religions, Buddhism has a more open attitude towards dress codes. The most important thing is the soul. Even if they are naked but they know how to kneel down in the front of Buddha to pray, then it is no problem. For Buddhists, to meet with Buddha is always an unplanned sudden event. So we cannot stop people to meet Buddha because of how they dress. Before we were more intolerant – this used to make us very angry. We put a signboard both in English and Vietnamese; but later we had to accept people not following these rules. We cannot stand by the signboard by the gate and check each tourist and only let those in who dress appropriately. So the signboard is just to remind tourists. Then it is up to the conscience of each person. If they are aware that they dress wrong, then they stand outside the pagoda. If they see they dress appropriately, then they come in the pagoda.*
>
> *We have to have a sympathetic attitude towards this, and cater for tourists also. Because they are tourists, they want to dress beautiful and modern when they go on a sightseeing tour, which happens to include the pagoda. For them it is normal to do that, so we have to think it is normal too. If tourists think it is normal, but we do not think it is normal, then we become un-normal [laughs]. And if we don't accept it, then we destroy the beauty of the culture that is not touristic.*

This might be interpreted as being perfectly in line with the Trúc Lâm version of Buddhism, which emphasizes the everyday presence of Buddha. From this

Figure 2.3 *The gates of Trúc Lâm meditation centre and pagoda, which features a large sign board instructing visitors on the proper dress code*

Note: To accommodate visiting pilgrims and tourists, the monks have built small pavilions along the walking paths around the pagoda. Here pilgrims and tourists can enjoy a picnic and rest on benches that display the names of visitors who have made considerable donations to the Trúc Lâm sect.

Source: Victor Alneng, 2 April, 2004

perspective, it might be argued that inappropriately dressed visitors provide the monks and the nuns with an opportunity to practice tolerance. But in the end, here it is evident that tourism sets the standard of what is normal.

How, then, does the superior bonze himself make a distinction between tourists and pilgrims?

> *Tourists and pilgrims are the same because both visit the same places like pagodas and other tourist spots as well as the market. They do the same things when they are on tour. The difference is that pilgrims as a group are devoted to Buddhism, and they care more about praying. When they come in to [the] pagoda they are more serious about praying. They wear the traditional long dress for praying. They visit more pagodas. Tourist groups are mostly organized by companies. If tourists see a pagoda when they are on tour,*

*they will stop to make a visit. If pilgrims see a tourist site when they
are on tour, they will stop to make a visit. So, generally speaking,
both have the same tour route.*

It seems, then, that the superior bonze does not share Meethan's (2001) view
that insists on a sharp distinction between pleasure-seeking tourists and duti-
ful pilgrims. Indeed, his view on the matter is strikingly similar to that of
anthropologists Edith and Victor Turner: 'A tourist is half a pilgrim, if a
pilgrim is half a tourist' (Turner and Turner, 1978, p20). Here it is crucial to
insist that it is tourists that form the imperative for pilgrims. *Paradoxically, it is
the tourist who (retrospectively) preconditions that which went before – the
proto-touristic.*

The secret of so-called proto-tourism

In his seminal outline of tourism as an anthropological subject, Dennison Nash
(1981) asserts that 'in less differentiated societies it is obviously more difficult
to distinguish leisure from non-leisure and consequently to identify tourism …
if we are going to get at the bases of tourism we must look into societies in
which leisure and, consequently, tourism are not easy to distinguish'. He goes
on to recount various pre-modern activities that had 'elements of tourism in
them' and concludes by stating:

> *It is probably fair to say that in industrial society more people are
> able to travel greater distances than ever before, but we must
> eschew any simple general evolutionary notions of touristic
> progress... In any case, forces which tend to generate tourism or
> proto-tourism would seem to be present in most, if not all, societies.*
> (Nash, 1981, pp463–464)

I could not agree more, and I would start here by claiming that it is precisely
such a quest for the proto-touristic that Nash engages in that constitutes what
(he rightfully argues) we must eschew. The ethnocentric affirmation of the
tourist as Westerner can be said to betray a vista from what Timothy Mitchell
(2000a, 2000b) calls 'the stage of modernity', characterized by a 'European-
centred cartography', 'a singular history' and a modernity with an 'autocentric
picture of itself as the expression of a universal certainty'. Like two sides of the
same coin, while this tourism destroys its object with its presence, this is a
modernity that creates the world by its very presence. On this same stage,
Western exoticists become self-styled 'explorers' with the ability to 'discover'
picturesque non-Western peoples and places. Ironically, while what Nash is

doing appears as the direct opposite of this, I argue that he is actually engaged in a similar expedition. When critically scrutinizing a particular content of a universal form, one must be mindful that one is always doing this in a way and from a position within the terrain opened up by the form of that content itself. Thus, when Nash sets out on a historical and cultural pilgrimage of sorts, in search of the proto-touristic, the very fact of him doing this, of him *being able* to do this, silently insists on, and thus secures, the abstract universal form of tourism itself. Instead of viewing tourism as a historically determined phenomenon, Nash defines it as natural and eternal when claiming: 'In any case, forces which tend to generate tourism or proto-tourism would seem to be present in most, if not all, societies' (Nash, 1981, pp463–464). Nash's quest for the proto-touristic thus bears witness to how tourism, as a synchronic system, retrospectively appropriates the pre-touristic as the building blocks of a myth of the proto-touristic origin of tourism. What this myth serves to cover up is nothing but that constitutive 'something' that is able to turn the pre-touristic into the proto-touristic.

The problem is that Nash treats the differentiation (or lack thereof) of society as a given, thus erasing the immediate link between capitalism, as a differentiating force, and tourism. The differentiation he refers to is, of course, that of the division of labour and the socio-cultural differentiation that it entails. The emergence of tourism, its subsumption of cultural expressions, signals a societal transubstantiation by way of which we no longer simply *live*, but are required to *earn a living* so that we then can take a holiday from our lives. What the quest for proto-tourism forecloses from the analysis is nothing short of the crucial insight of tourism as a predominant mode of travel in global capitalism. Nash forecloses how capitalism is the violent force that serves as the precondition for tourism to subsume other forms of travel.

The desire to search history or cultural space for proto-touristic practices that are then used to explain, and naturalize, the existence of what one might call really existing tourism constitutes a failure to address the properly dialectical paradox of change. Change somehow presupposes the continuity of a subject who can formulate the change in retrospect, a subject who endures the change unchanged. The problem is that if the change is radical enough, as in the case of a revolution, it will have changed the very coordinates with which to measure and comprehend the occurred change. A proper change is, thus, by necessity always self-relating. Setting its own standard, it can only be measured by measures that it has itself sanctioned. When a system becomes, what in Hegelese is called *for itself*, it sets itself apart and becomes indifferent to its own origin. In the process of doing this, it also recreates its history of origin in such a way that history, now a myth, becomes a story designed to explain the natural existence of that system itself.

Here one should insist on the distinction between the diachronic (the factual historical development of a system) and the synchronic (that system as it has come into its own and established itself as such). Marx's *Capital* is the pre-eminent example of this. First, he spent closer to 900 pages on dissecting the *logos* of capital – that is, capitalism as a synchronic system. Not until Part 8, Chapter 26, entitled 'So-called primitive accumulation', does he address the history of the self-referential chronically self-revolutionizing system that is capitalism. As it turns out, the keyword in the title of this chapter is not, as one would have expected, 'primitive accumulation', but 'so-called'.

As discussed above, the distinction between formal and real subsumption is crucial, and it is entirely misleading to think that the transition between the two is somehow a smooth and natural one. Marx has something entirely different in mind. From the outset, Marx's object of study in *Capital* is *fully developed* capitalism. It is only once examining every detail of capitalism as a logical system in its own right that Marx turns to its genesis. As Žižek (1991/2002, p210) notes: 'Marx's reasoning [here] is far more interesting than may appear at first sight. The gist of his argument is that once capitalism establishes itself as a fully articulated system, it is indifferent towards the [empirical] conditions of its emergence' (see also Balibar, 1968/1970). Marx's claim is that so-called primitive accumulation, or, what one might call, proto-capitalism, which bourgeois political economists such as Adam Smith point to as the dawn of capitalist accumulation, is nothing but the myth of origin that *Capital* tells about itself. As such:

> ... *primitive accumulation plays approximately the same role in political economy as original sin does in theology. Adam bit the apple, and thereupon sin fell on the human race. Its origin is supposed to be explained when told as an anecdote about the past. Long, long ago there were two sorts of people: one, the diligent, intelligent and above all frugal elite; the other, lazy rascals, spending their substance and more in riotous living... Thus it came to pass that the former sort accumulated wealth, and the latter sort finally had nothing to sell except their own skins. And from this original sin dates the poverty of the great majority who, despite all their labour, have up to now nothing to sell but themselves, and the wealth of the few that increases constantly, although they have long ceased to work. Such insipid childishness is every day preached to us in the defence of property.* (Marx, 1867/1976, pp873–874)

In other words, in explaining its own origin, capitalism presupposes a subject who acts like a capitalist. Thus, the myth of so-called primitive accumulation, like all myths of origin, is circular, as it presupposes that which it pretends to explain. Suffice here to recall that the formula Marx introduces to illustrate the speculative incessantly self-revolutionizing virtuality of capital reads as follows:

money–commodity–money (MCM) 'i.e. *value valorizing itself*, value that gives birth to value' (Marx, 1867/1976, p1060, emphasis in original). What is crucial for Marx is, of course, that the result of this circular myth is the foreclosure of the diachronic – the violence with which capitalism subsumes new areas of extraction in order to establish itself as a synchronic system:

> *In actual history, it is a notorious fact that conquest, enslavement, robbery, murder, in short, force, play the greatest part [in the defence of the reign of law of property rights]… As a matter of fact, the methods of primitive accumulation are anything but idyllic.* (Marx, 1867/1976, p874)

After this theoretical excursion, it is high time to get back to the subject at hand. Drawing on these insights, I argue that, when analysing the emergence of non-Western domestic tourism, or tourism in more or less pre-modern settings, it is crucial to avoid this kind of mythologizing that presupposes a subject who acts like a tourist. This would be to ignore tourism as the predominant mode of travel in global capitalism, thus ignoring the history of plunder and death that is the history of capitalism. As is implicitly clear in the case of the success of Trúc Lâm to attract visitors, tourism presupposes capitalism, not a subject (such as a pilgrim) acting as, and then somehow naturally transforming into, a tourist. Capitalism should here, of course, be understood in its dialectical totality as a mode of *social* production by which 'all that is solid melts into air, all that is sacred is profaned' as Marx and Engels (1848/1977, p224) famously celebrated its revolutionary de-territorializing force.

What Marx shows is that so-called primitive accumulation has nothing to do with some sort of proto-capitalist accumulation that naturally develops into fully fledged capitalism. This is, rather, the retrospective fantasy – the myth of origin – that capitalism entertains about itself and its origin. It serves to naturalize the very existence of capitalism as something that has had a natural and smooth development. *Mutatis mutandis*, the search for the proto-touristic in pre-capitalist times and cultures, serves the same purposes of naturalizing the existence of current international tourism and foreclosing from the analysis of the crucial insight of *tourism as a predominant form that travel takes in global capitalism*. In such a way, the violence – both the symbolic violence of cultural uprooting and the material violence of merciless expropriation – that necessarily precedes the emergence of tourism is conveniently erased.

If 'so-called primitive accumulation … is nothing else than the historical process of divorcing the producer from the means of production' (Marx, 1867/1976, pp874–875) then proto-tourism is nothing else than the historical process of divorcing a cultural producer from the means of cultural production – in other words, of transubstantiating a cultural life world into a touristic event. What we are confronted with here, then, is the properly dialectical paradox of an included exclusion – an excluded thing whose very exclusion secures that which is included and which is always already *formally* included as a constitutive lack (akin to a door as a productive lack of a wall, to put it in somewhat more Zen Buddhist terms). The covering up of the traumatic rupture of the symbolic field that this exclusion creates constitutes what in psychoanalysis is called a *phantasmatic object*. By providing support for the existing ideology, the function of the phantasmatic is to make the present state of affairs, the present symbolic reality, appear natural (e.g. see Žižek, 1989).

Thus, the historical link between the proto-touristic pilgrim and the domestic tourist is far from immediate; the transition from the former to the latter is far from natural or straightforward. The missing link, or the vanishing mediator, to use a further technical term, between the two is capitalism. The precondition of tourism is not proto-tourism, but capitalism as the force that transforms previous forms of travel into tourism.

So-called proto-tourism, then, is to tourism studies what so-called primitive accumulation is to bourgeois political economy. It functions to cover up the constitutive excluded thing, the truth of which is uncanny (*unheimlich*) in the Freudian sense and, as such, unspeakable. As we have seen, the success of Trúc Lâm at attracting visitors was, in part, attributed by the superior bonze to the absence of formal charges for services such as entrance, parking and toilette. This theme, which, of course, served to create an aura of honest hospitality untouched by the commercial forces is obviously a widely applied strategy of the tourism industry. At Trúc Lâm, this was even taken into the pagoda, a space officially not designated for tourism. In most places, it is common for pagodas to have a donation box where visitors can, after praying, donate some money for future luck. At Trúc Lâm, this donation box has been replaced with a big bronze bell to put money in. While there are no instructions about this, few visitors will miss it. As the superior bonze explains:

> In that bell, people can offer money. If we put a donation box in clear display, then it means we force people to donate money. Instead, we use this bell. If people know then they put money there, and if they don't know then they don't. Some people don't see it; but if they look for it, we will show it to them. So this is done voluntarily. They really want to offer money, and we don't force them at all. All pagodas have a box where people offer money after they pray to Buddha; but here we don't have any box like that and it surprises people.

As we have seen, the superior bonze does not really deny being a tourism worker; but, just like Nash on his quest for the proto-touristic, *precisely as a tourism worker, as a subject of tourism, a subject speaking from within the terrain opened up by tourism as a fully articulated system, the bonze is forced to deny the relation between tourism and capitalism* (tourism as *a priori* and *imperatively commercialized* hospitality). There is, thus, a very precise limit to what the superior bonze can admit to – in Lacaninan terms, the barrier between the symbolic and the unspeakable excluded real cannot be transcended simply because the symbolic itself *constitutes* this very barrier between the symbolic and the real. In the interview with the superior bonze, this barrier appeared precisely as such – that is, as unspeakable:

> *To say we do not get an income from tourists would not be true. We use the money that tourists donate also but … [hesitate] but we don't know how much. A different department takes care of that money … we don't know … but about money [laughing nervously] … nobody asks about that!*

At this point, my assistant who conducted the interview, herself a Buddhist, felt obliged to apologize to the monk for having forced him to talk about the unspeakable.

Notes

1   Hegel famously noted that moderns do not pray in the morning because reading the morning paper *is* their prayer.
2   The taped interview with Thích Trúc Thông Tánh was conducted on 9 May 2005 at Trúc Lâm Zen meditation centres. It was conducted in Vietnamese by my assistant.
3   At the time of the interview, US$1 was approximately 15,500 Vietnamese đồng.
4   Since Vietnamese tourists usually do not have cameras, it is a common practice to hire a photographer who follows you around and takes pictures while visiting a tourist site. The photographers develop the film and deliver the pictures to the hotel later the same day. As digital cameras and mobile phones equipped with cameras have become more common, these photographers have seen a decline in the demand for their services.
5   See, for example, Alneng (2007) for an example of the latter.

References

Alneng, V. (2007) 'The right price: Local bargains for global players', in *e-Paper presented at ASA07: Thinking Through Tourism*, 10–13 April 2007, London Metropolitan University, UK, Panel on The Cultural Politics of Touristic Fantasies: Addressing the 'Behind-the-Scene' Scene

Balibar, É. (1968/1970) 'Elements for a theory of transition', in L. Althusser and È.

Balibar (eds) *Reading Capital*, New Left Review Edition, London, pp273–308

Footprint (1999) *Vietnam Handbook*, Footprint Handbooks, Bath, UK

Graburn, N. (1989) 'Tourism: The sacred journey', in V. Smith (ed) *Hosts and Guests: The Anthropology of Tourism*, second edition, University of Pennsylvania Press, Philadelphia, PA, pp21–36

MacCannell, D. (1976) *The Tourist: A New Theory of the Leisure Class*, Schocken Books, New York, NY

Marx, K. (1867/1976) *Capital, Volume 1: The Process of Production of Capital*, Penguin Books/New Left Review, London

Marx, K. and Engels, F. (1848/1977) 'The communist manifesto', in D. McLellan (ed) *Karl Marx: Selected Writings*, Oxford University Press, Oxford, pp221–246

Meethan, K. (2001) *Tourism in Global Society: Place, Culture, Consumption*, Palgrave, New York, NY

Mitchell, T. (2000a) 'Introduction', in T. Mitchell (ed) *Questions of Modernity*, University of Minnesota Press, Minneapolis, MN, ppxi–xxvii

Mitchell, T. (2000b) 'The stage of modernity', in T. Mitchell (ed) *Questions of Modernity*, University of Minnesota Press, Minneapolis, MN, pp1–34

Nash, D. (1981) 'Tourism as an anthropological subject', *Current Anthropology*, vol 22, no 5, pp461–481

Pfaffenberger, B. (1983) 'Serious pilgrims and frivolous tourists: The chimera of tourism in the pilgrimages of Sri Lanka', *Annals of Tourism Research*, vol 10, no 1, pp57–74

Storey, R. and Florence, M. (2001) *Vietnam*, Lonely Planet Publications, Hawthorn

Tru'o'ng Phúc Ân (2000) *Bí Mật Thành Phố Hoa Đà Lạt* [*The Secrets of the Flower City of Đà Lạt*], The Ethnic Culture Publisher, Lam Dong Printing and Publishing Company, Đà Lạt

Tru'o'ng Phúc Ân (2003) *Đà Lạt: Một Trăm Mười Mùa Xuân* [*Đà Lạt in Her One Hundred and Ten Springs*], The Ethnic Culture Publisher, Lam Dong Printing and Publishing Company, Đà Lạt

Turner, V. and Turner, E. (1978) *Image and Pilgrimage in Christian Culture: Anthropological Perspectives*, Colombia University Press, New York, NY

VNAT (Vietnam National Administration of Tourism) (2000) *Vietnam Tourist Guidebook*, VNAT, Hanoi, Vietnam

Žižek, S. (1989) *The Sublime Object of Ideology*, Verso, London/New York

Žižek, S. (1991/2002) *For They Know Not What They Do: Enjoyment as a Political Factor*, Verso, London/New York

3

Cultural Solutions to Ecological Problems in Contemporary Japan: Heritage Tourism in Asuke

Christopher S. Thompson

The annual meeting of the Asuke Tsukimi-kai (Moon Viewing Society) began promptly at 6:30pm on a late September evening in 2007, out of doors in a court-yard adjacent to the gatehouse at Asuke Yashiki, an authentically recreated rural mountain homestead once typical throughout Aichi and neighbouring prefectures in central Japan until after World War II. Well known as a first-rate cultural heritage tourism site in the region, during the last decade, Asuke Yashiki has often been touted as the model to follow for economic development and commu-nity revitalization in Japan's increasing number of depopulated peripheral communities (Iguchi, 2002; Thompson, 2004).

Chairman Ozawa smiled as paying guests sat facing each other along two parallel rows of wooden Western-style picnic tables, looking up at a cloudless dusk sky in anticipation of darkness to glimpse the namesake of his event. At the eastern end of the dining area was a display booth stocking a huge variety of Asuke's commercially available native foods, beverages and other renowned hometown products, donated by local producers. As the founder of Asuke Yashiki and the brainchild of reviving this traditional seasonal celebration locally – dormant during the majority of the post-war period – Chairman Ozawa could not be happier with the weather or the turnout. The glimmer of globed Asuke-made candles provided the only table lighting as the sun began to fade. Placed carefully at each table setting was a beautiful configuration of Japanese-style dinnerware – a rice and soup bowl, a small plate, a split-cylinder receiving dish, chopsticks, a tea cup and other service items – all handcrafted from bamboo, harvested from the surrounding forest by the artisans, administrators and staff of Asuke Yashiki who had also prepared a celebratory meal. The bamboo artefacts were as striking as the message represented by their use: even for entertainment purposes, renew-able natural resources, available locally, can be used elegantly to reduce waste.

As the celebrants waited for darkness, they were served their choice of delicious locally brewed sake *(rice wine) or Asuke-made fruit juice – in bamboo cups poured from bamboo urns – by members of the Asuke Yashiki board of directors. As each guest sipped their chosen beverage, relaxed and talked, it quickly became apparent that most people did not know each other. In fact, a majority of those present were not even from Asuke at all. Their only commonality was some level of voluntary involvement with Asuke Yashiki, a sincere respect for its founder and a genuine appreciation for the role that this living historical museum is playing in the region and in their lives.*

Suddenly, a large silver disc appeared just above the gatehouse in the eastern sky. The crowd cheered. On cue, the collective of Asuke Yashiki hosts responded in choreographed precision to serve each guest course after course of expertly prepared local fare (see Figure 3.1). The menu consisted of Asuke-procured specialties such as tofu, assorted sansai *(mountain vegetables) and* ayu *(sweetfish), caught in the Tomoe River nearby. Three kinds of salt seasoned the food.*

As the evening progressed, the guests, having thoroughly enjoyed their sumptuous feast, stood up and moved about to continue meeting and talking with one

Figure 3.1 *Guests waiting for the next course at the annual Asuke Tsukimi-kai (Moon Viewing Society) dinner held at Sanshu Asuke Yashiki in late September 2007: An Asuke Yashiki board member (standing, upper right) is pouring a drink*

Source: Christopher S. Thompson, 2007

another. The mood was jubilant. There were about an equal number of men and women in attendance, several young families, a few college students, but mostly middle-aged professional types with their spouses – many of whom worked at Toyota Motors, the largest employer in the area. Topics of conversation revolved around their Asuke Yashiki-related experiences and how much they were looking forward to the remaining cultural events scheduled for the calendar year. Many new friendships were formed.

At about 9:30pm, the final stage of the celebration began. The MC's turn of a lottery wheel united each guest with a take-home gift: a local product from the display booth. The boxes of tsukimi-mochi *(pounded rice cakes shaped like the moon) went first, followed by the bottles of* shôyu *(soy sauce), plastic tubs of* umeboshi *(pickled plums) and packaged* soba *(buckwheat noodles). Bottles of* sake, *bags of* sumi *(wood charcoal),* waraji *(old-fashioned straw sandals) and a bolt of naturally dyed hand loom-woven cloth were also dispersed. Finally, guests were invited to take with them any leftover food as well as bamboo dishes made for the dinner – their own and any other serving dishes and service items – for use at home. All food and everything bamboo was fair game. To aid in the removal process, several sizes of* furoshiki *(reusable carrying cloths once utilized extensively in Japan before the introduction of paper sacks and plastic bags) were quickly provided (the candles and globes, collected discretely by Asuke Yashiki staff, were returned to storage boxes for reuse). As the crowd cleared, only the picnic tables were left behind.*

From the start, the purpose of the Tsukimi-kai was clear. Hosting this old-fashioned cultural festivity annually at Asuke Yashiki was one of Ozawa's many consciousness-raising strategies designed to bring like-minded people together for the purpose of affirming his message that solutions to many of Japan's contemporary ecological problems can be found locally in the traditional lifestyle and natural resources that have always existed there. Asuke Yashiki is Ozawa's vision for how to put forth this philosophy locally in a politically relevant, economically viable and ecologically sustainable way. To accomplish this goal, Ozawa and his supporters use cultural heritage tourism as their strategic medium. The Tsukimi-kai represented a microcosm of his approach.

Introduction

This chapter examines the aims, functions, conditions, and provisioning for cultural heritage tourism (often called cultural tourism in Japan) at Sanshû Asuke Yashiki, a working reproduction of a mid-19th-century mountain farmstead that attracts domestic and international tourists to Asuke, a rural inland township at the cross-section of Gifu, Nagano and Aichi prefectures in Japan's Chubu (central) region (see Figure 3.2). As its name implies, Sanshû (meaning

'three regions') Asuke Yashiki (which renders as 'Asuke homestead') is modelled after the Edo-era (1603 to 1857) agricultural compounds that were once
prevalent in the area until well into the mid-20th century. Founded in 1980,
this functioning vintage mid-1800s farm is known nationally as Asuke Yashiki,
a modern, cutting-edge cultural tourism venue designed to facilitate direct interaction on-site between tourists from out-of-town and Asuke-based artisans.
Asuke Yashiki's traditional crafts professionals practice time-honoured domestic skills and construct a variety of daily-use items from Japan's pre-modern
past, using proven, age-old, ecologically sensitive techniques. Yet, this tourism
venue disperses Asuke's historical technologies and local wisdom not just to
preserve nostalgic techniques from the community's by-gone days, but for posterity – as effective, practical solutions to the world's contemporary
conservation issues, demographic changes and environmental concerns that
are fully viable and highly relevant to the present. At Asuke Yashiki, visitors are

Figure 3.2 *Map of Aichi Prefecture showing the location of Asuke in relation to
Nagoya and Gifu and Nagano prefectures, as well as Mikawa Bay: A miniature
map of Japan highlighting the location of Aichi Prefecture is inlaid*

Source: Christopher S. Thompson, 2008

urged to relearn long-forgotten domestic skills and to purchase products made there not just for their amusement or to support Asuke Yashiki's cause, but for immediate incorporation within their modern-day lives. The purpose of this chapter is to explain why and how Asuke Yashiki came into existence, and to describe how its founder, Chairman Ozawa Shôichi – a lifelong local resident – has been able to help fulfil a unique vision for Asuke Township and its neighbouring communities through this facility in 21st-century Japan.

Geographically, Asuke Yashiki is located in the north-eastern quadrant of Aichi prefecture, nestled snugly within the natural confines of a flat embankment on the north-eastern side of Korankei Gorge between Mount Iimori and the Tomoe River (see Figure 3.3). For tourists, entrance into Asuke Yashiki occurs through the Kaedemon, a large, rustic, period-authentic farmstead gatehouse at the western edge of the property (see Figure 3.4), which opens onto a modest-sized barnyard designed to complement an authentic 200-year-old thatch-roofed farmhouse from the late Edo period built on the compound's mountain-side boundary (see Figure 3.5). A small stable, several work buildings and multiple display and sales areas, under roof, surround the barnyard on its southern and eastern sides. Also within this space, homestead staff maintain a small collection of livestock (a beef cow and egg-laying hens), a *koi* pond – home to approximately 25 large multicoloured carp – a cat, a vegetable garden and fruit trees. The entire assembly is spread out across roughly

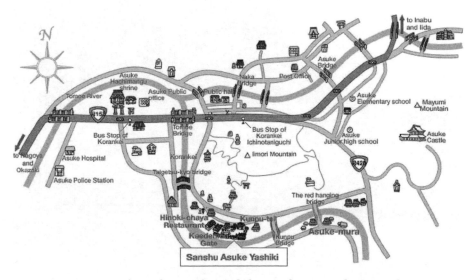

Figure 3.3 *Map of Sanshu Asuke Yashiki in relation to the Korankei Gorge (south of the Tomoe Bridge), Mount Iimori (centre) and the Tomoe River (which runs south to north into its upper estuary)*

Source: Sanshu Asuke Yashiki, 2008

Figure 3.4 *The Kaedemon Gate at Sanshu Asuke Yashiki*

Source: Christopher S. Thompson, 2007

Figure 3.5 *The 200-year-old farmhouse inside the Sanshu Asuke
Yashiki compound*

Source: Christopher S. Thompson, 2007

3000m², or about half the area of a modern-day regulation soccer field (Suzuki, 2005, p4). Even with its contemporary touristic adaptations, Asuke Yashiki looks, feels and smells remarkably like the written descriptions (contained in the town archives) of local working farms from 150 years back (see www.asuke.aitai.ne.jp/~yashiki).

Inside the stable, work buildings and display areas, visitors can observe, interact with and take lessons from craft experts who practice ten different Edo-era farmstead fundamentals. These skills include hand loom-weaving, *aizome* (Japanese indigo dyeing), bamboo crafts, blacksmithing, paper-making, straw crafts, umbrella-making, wood charcoal-making and wooden tub construction. The sales areas include two restaurants that serve homestead-made ingredients utilized in healthy, historically verified Asuke-style dishes, a souvenir shop full of old-school gifts crafted from natural materials still available in the local mountains and streams, and a café serving teas made from herbs well known in the region since the 1600s (see Figure 3.6). Roughly 100,000 tourists visit Asuke Yashiki each year, with foreigners (mainly Asians, but also Europeans and North and South Americans) accounting for approximately 10 per cent of this total (Suzuki, 2005, p4).

Figure 3.6 *Domestic tourists shopping for traditional seasonal foods made at Sanshu Asuke Yashiki from barnyard booths positioned under the fall foliage*

Source: Christopher S. Thompson, 2007

The chapter begins by offering a description of Asuke Township and Japan's post-war rural–urban dynamic that brought about the need for economic development through cultural heritage tourism in this rural mountain setting. Next, the means by which Asuke residents under the leadership of Chairman Ozawa – a former Asuke bureaucrat – refined their purpose for heritage preservation and tied this vision to a workable economic model that brought Asuke Yashiki to fruition is described. Finally, the structural and philosophical characteristics that have enabled Asuke Yashiki to emerge as a cultural heritage site quite different from anything in Japan's historical past are identified and explained.

Situating Asuke

Asuke is a community of approximately 10,000 residents located in the northeastern sector of Toyota-shi (Toyota City, home of world-famous Toyota Motors Corporation), population 400,000, which shares a boundary with a portion of Nagoya (population 2 million), Japan's fourth largest metropolis (Asahi Shimbun, 2006, p86). Fully 86 per cent of Asuke's land area consists of uneven, difficult-to-utilize terrain. Traditionally, independent and cooperative forestry and agriculture have been the main occupations here and in the surrounding Mikawa region (considered to be the central third of Aichi prefecture, north to south). Famous in domestic tourism circles since the 1970s for the beautiful autumn foliage at Korankei Gorge (which boasts 4000 Japanese maple trees), Asuke Township is also known for its dedication to the preservation of its unique 19th- and 20th-century mountain river-front commerce-town architecture, promotion of a mountain village lifestyle sensitive to global ecological concerns, and as a famous outpost during the Edo period on the salt route from the Pacific Ocean to the nation's high-plateau region called the Japan Alps (Asuke Tourism Association, 1996, pp35–51).

Topographically, Asuke ranges in altitude from about 170m to nearly 2000m (Asuke Tourism Association, 1996, pp35–51), which makes the municipality seem (especially from 800m and higher) quite remote from the city. But surprisingly, on a clear day, from the town's many high-altitude roadside lookouts and scenic mountain passes, it is easy to glimpse the skyscrapers of Nagoya and the smokestacks that mark this city's industrial region that lies just beyond. By car, the global headquarters of Toyota and its mother plant (in existence in this location since 1947) are less than 100km away. The modern high-tech urban sprawl of Nagoya, visible in the distance from Asuke, contrasts sharply with the rugged beauty of Aichi's north-eastern mountains. For residents of Asuke, this relative isolation from, but closeness to, metropolitan Nagoya has been both a blessing and a curse. Asuke Yashiki as a tourist destination in the 21st century is, in large part, a local outcome resulting from Asuke's proximity to Nagoya, the history of domestic tourism in Japan, the nation's pattern of post-war rural decline, and the legacy of state policies designed to stimulate the economies of small rural townships in this country's peripheral areas since World War II.

The origin of Japanese domestic tourism

Historically, the origin of modern domestic tourism in Japan can be tied closely to the religious pilgrimages that became popular among the masses during the Edo period. Pilgrimages by commoners during this time featured travel by members of *kô* (mutual aid associations) who took turns taking trips to the nation's most scenic spots and prestigious Shinto shrines and Buddhist temples, typically located in remote rural settings. Miyajima, for example, often cited by Japanese as one of their nation's *sankei* (three most beautiful locations),[1] world famous for its 1200-year-old Itsukushima Shrine and gigantic vermillion-coloured torii-gate,[2] is situated on an isolated mountainous island off the coast of Hiroshima in the county's south-west. Ise Shrine[3] in Mie Prefecture, famous domestically in association with Japan's Imperial family, and Kumano Hongû in Wakayama Prefecture (the most important of Japan's hierarchy of 3000 Kumano shrines) are both located in the mountains of central Japan near the outskirts of Nagoya, but far from other major cities. The most well-known temples and shrines in Nara (Japan's capital from 710 to 784) and the ruins of Heijô Palace (then the Imperial residence) are adjacent to Kasugayama Primeval Forest two prefectures west of Aichi, also a remote rural location. Similarly, many of the most esteemed religious landmarks in Kyoto, the nation's capital from 798 to 1868 north of Nara, exist in rugged out-of-the-way mountain settings. During the Edo period, domestic tourists are reported to have felt spiritually rejuvenated and mentally refreshed by visiting these and other popular difficult-to-access sites. Souvenir purchases from remote locations such as these by travellers for their *kô* associates waiting at home are said to have jump-started the nation's travel gift industry during the 18th century (Formasek, 1997, p165).

As a result of Edo-period religious pilgrimages focusing on travel to isolated rural locations, Japan experienced its single biggest increase in domestic travel unconnected to politics or commerce to date (Ishimori, 1989, p170; Formasek, 1997, p167). Historians of Japanese tourism have posited that many unquestioned beliefs about the origins of Japanese culture that natives continue to perpetuate, such as a reverence for Shintoism (a form of animism) as Japan's indigenous religion, the supposition that Japanese society evolved out of rice agriculture, and the emphasis on rural Japan as a repository of all that is considered truly Japanese, became fossilized through reinforcement in part due to domestic travel to visually stunning, difficult-to-access, religiously and culturally significant locations on a mass scale at this time (Knight, 1993; Formasek, 1997, p170). Touristic travel to rustic domestic locations to learn about and experience local cultural variations has been fashionable among Japanese ever since.

During Japan's post-war period, domestic travellers have continued to envisage rural, regional Japan as a sanctuary of the nation's recuperative traditional cultural values. However, during the late 20th and early 21st centuries, this is largely an urban construction that flippantly ignores the hardships endured by people such as the residents of Asuke, who have lived their lives in the Japanese countryside following World War II. In contradiction to what urban Japanese often perceive as the pride and prestige associated with rural agricultural Japan as the foundation of the nation's modern origins, during a majority of the post-war period, the country's political authority, economic might, cultural leadership and a large percentage of the population have been situated in Tokyo or within the Tokyo–Osaka industrial corridor (Nagoya is located near Osaka) that stretches from the national capital 800km south-west (OECD, 1993, p11). This structural disparity between Japan's urban and rural areas during the post-war years has produced an array of social, economic and political problems in the nation's periphery that for local tourism in many rural communities has had a deterministic effect (Asahi Shimbun, 2006, p255).

Rural decline and local tourism in post-war Japan

Rural decline in Japan since 1945 is widely regarded as having been caused by three major factors: high levels of local depopulation resulting from domestic and international labour demands in the nation's urban areas from the 1950s to the 1970s; constantly changing national tax policies throughout the entire post-war period that made full-time single-family farming financially unfeasible (Juassaume, 1991); and economic decline caused by the drain of human and natural resources from rural areas for use in the nation's cities (Kelly, 1990). These deficiencies, in turn, caused a myriad of problems related to family income and lifestyle maintenance. Realistically speaking, the economic uncertainties of rural life in post-war Japan have made provisioning for local tourism an impossible proposition for most communities (even those with great potential) except for those located near noteworthy natural phenomena, famous temples and shrines, or for local residents with the most creative entrepreneurial minds. However, in the absence of any other income-boosting public- or private-sector opportunities locally, many townships have continued to pursue (often unsuccessfully) tourism-related economic development options.

While Japan's periphery still tends to be regarded by urbanites as the nation's cultural utopia, the best resources, most lucrative companies and a huge portion of the national government's tax income have been centralized in the country's largest cities. As a result, during most of the post-war years, a majority of Japan's rural communities have had to rely on large amounts of economic aid from the state, generated mostly in the nation's urban centres, just to balance their municipal budgets. To the detriment of rural townships across Japan, state tax subsidies to regional areas during this period have also been based primarily on local population figures and lobbying power in Tokyo instead of being driven by local needs (Thompson, 2003, p95). Asuke is a prime example.

Immediately following World War II, as the nation's post-war economy began a rapid growth phase, Asuke residents, attracted by the allure of high-paying cash-yielding factory jobs at Toyota Motors and other automobile industry-related companies in Nagoya, began moving out of their community permanently in huge numbers. During the five years between 1949 and 1954, Asuke lost nearly half of its residents, seriously depleting the town treasury. Unable to recover from the lack of population based funding that it once received, by 1955, Asuke was forced by state mandate to consolidate with three bordering townships just to preserve basic municipal services (Thompson and Traphagan, 2006). Agricultural restrictions during the 1960s and ever-changing tax laws and regional development policies in the 1970s were equally disheartening for town halls and their local constituents seeking funding just to make ends meet (Sanshû Asuke Yashiki, 1990).

During the 1980s, the state, in an attempt to rectify this situation, tried to re-popularize historical rural tourism in Japan (Creighton, 1997, p240). Prefectural governments in out-lying areas were required to initiate mass commercial tourism plans. Hefty block grants of 100 million Japanese yen (roughly US$750,000 in 1989) were provided with no strings attached as seed money for local 'hometown cultivation' projects (Thompson, 2003, p94). Many rural communities highlighted their local traditions or built ski resorts and golf courses with these monies and the help of corporate financiers with the intent of drawing large numbers of urban tourists back, at least seasonally. But a national economic downturn in the mid-1990s terminated these funds and reduced the amount of population-based tax aid earmarked for the periphery, ending this dream (Thompson 2001, 70).

In 2000, following another round of national-level agriculture and rural development policy changes, state tax subsidies to rural cities and towns were cut again. Asuke and its neighbouring communities were forced to consolidate for a second time during the post-war period in 2005, this time into the much larger city of Toyota. Most recently, the aging of Japanese society (almost one in four residents are over the age of 65) and lowest ever national birth rates have exacerbated depopulation, the lack of farm income, the shortage of welfare funding for the elderly, and other endemic social problems. A revamping of the national health insurance and pensions plans in 2006 has resulted in further mandatory reductions of automatic tax subsidies to rural municipalities, only making things worse. In 2008, the social, economic and cultural well-being of rural communities in Japan is once again at a critical point. While municipal independence is no longer possible, formerly autonomous townships such as Asuke have been struggling to find ways to bolster the incomes of the residents who remain and to ensure that their local heritage is not completely lost (Thompson, 2008).

Asuke's distinctive heritage asset

As post-war socio-economic circumstances have threatened the survival of Japan's regional municipalities, heritage preservation has become a major priority. Because of Japan's domestic tourism history (which values rural locations), the growing number of resident senior citizens, knowledgeable about local history and customs with time to spare, desperate to supplement municipal coffers however possible, many rural township beaurocrats consider heritage preservation and local economic development to be inextricably linked. Since the mid-1990s, the most successful examples of such linkages have occurred in the communities where local leaders have activated the economic value of local traditions by connecting them to a distinct local heritage asset (human, material or conceptual) that distinguishes that locale in some special way (Suzuki, 2006, p5). In Asuke, the township's historic crafts heritage and traditional folk practices are undergirded by an ecological philosophy that hinges on the idea that the most desirable way to exist in the world is to cultivate a sustainable way of life that uses local, historical and cultural resources that already exist there. Through Asuke Yashiki, Chairman Ozawa and his Asuke proponents have utilized this heritage asset concept to full socio-economic advantage.

From a Western viewpoint, the philosophy behind Asuke's heritage asset sounds suspiciously familiar. The influence of John Ruskin, 19th-century British social thinker, artist, naturalist and landscape conservationist, upon this way of thinking – and, by extension, upon the concept for Asuke Yashiki – seems almost certain (Kikuchi, 2004, p24).[4] But while Ruskin's ideas have had a significant impact on Japanese environmental thinking from the 1890s to the present, as Chairman Ozawa and his Asuke supporters have considered ways to preserve their mountain heritage through tourism during the post-war years, practical socio-economic considerations and Japanese cultural precedents have had much more sway. From the beginning of recorded history, the Japanese have regularly looked religiously and culturally to the natural environment for solutions to the problems of daily living. An indigenous belief in a national origin based on a rural lifestyle close to nature, a community organization and problem-solving ethos hundreds of years old that continues to value the use of local resources advantageously, and the habit of perpetually re-examining age-old ideas as virtuous ways of improving the present are (at least officially) the ideals that motivate their efforts. The implied connection between heritage preservation and community survival is no coincidence. However, a failure to recognize the syncretistic way in which foreign contributions have been incorporated within Japan's domestic post-Edo society and the political economy of post-World War II rural life results in a misunderstanding of the indigenous socio-cultural significance of how and why the formula for Asuke Yashiki was derived.

'Heritage politics' in Asuke

Strategically speaking, during a majority of the post-war period, the residents of depopulated rural towns such as Asuke that have lacked private-sector industries to support local jobs or supplement the local tax base have had to rely heavily on the human and informational resources available through their local town hall for help when addressing community problems. Since almost all town hall bureaucrats, elected officials and town council representatives in such towns are themselves part-time farmers and/or foresters, or local small business owners (which is not the case in large cities where bureaucrats are transferred regularly to posts outside of their residential districts), they have a vested interest in volunteering their time and public-sector experience for the good of their hometown (Bramwell and Lane, 2000, p98; Thompson, 2008).

In Asuke, it was these 'hometown bureaucrats' who organized themselves and their community during non-work-hours under Ozawa's leadership who eventually discovered a workable strategy to contest their local socio-economic problems and heritage preservation concerns. As a grassroots organization independent of local government that could spearhead Asuke's community revival from the private sector, during the late 1950s, the Asuke Tourism Association (ATA), originally a private volunteer citizens' group disbanded in 1955 (before Asuke's first post-war amalgamation in April of the same year), was re-established with the help of the second-generation Asuke Town Hall in 1961. The mandate of the ATA was to be a conduit for 'heritage politics': the utilization of the personal hometown social and professional networks of association members to coordinate the information, resources and personnel available through the Asuke Town Hall and other local public-sector resources to systematically identify methods for local economic development, depopulation reversal and heritage preservation in Asuke. 'Heritage politics' also meant that the ATA would utilize similar means to implement any plan that might be derived as a result (Sanshû Asuke Yashiki, 1990, p8).

Initially, local structural and financial obstacles seemed insurmountable. During the early 1960s, the ATA board of directors (consisting of Ozawa, town hall bureaucrats, local business owners, and representatives from several of the town's remaining farming households) was so alarmed by the lack of prospects for Asuke that through town hall connections, the membership began instigating city council and neighbourhood association meetings in the hopes of generating local advancement ideas from public study sessions, lectures by knowledgeable guests and open discussion meetings. The ATA board knew from the start that in order to couple any kind of economic development with the preservation of what they felt was a unique local history, the solution would have to be considerably different from the cookie-cutter (one-pattern-fits-all) measures being implemented by the state in some of the other similarly depopulated rural towns in the prefecture and across the country at that time (Sanshû Asuke Yashiki, 1990, p9; Creighton, 1997, p249).

Reflecting inward, not outward, for local socio-cultural solutions

Owing mainly to the absence of any immediately viable models to emulate, in 1965 the ATA encouraged Asuke residents, town bureaucrats and civic leaders to do what, in retrospect seems so obvious and so historically Japanese. Instead of looking outside the community for local solutions, they looked inward, turning to their township's distinctive local history for inspiration. Drawing on the legend of Sanei, a local Zen priest who in 1634 began planting hundreds of maple and cedar trees on the hillside near Kojakuji (his temple) as a meditative exercise, funding from the state through Asuke Town Hall was procured to build a seasonal resort area where visitors could enjoy Asuke's beautiful fall foliage. Synchronized with cultural events at Kojakuji and other local temples and shrines each season, the project was a hit with domestic tourists, as Korankei Gorge began attracting thousands of visitors a year. However, local income and tax revenue increases resulting from this project alone were not sufficient to turn the tide on Asuke's socio-economic condition (Sanshû Asuke Yashiki, 1990, p9).

Capitalizing on the success of the Korankei Gorge Project, which was subsequently made permanent, in 1969, the ATA board decided to tap even deeper into the local history of their town, the product of four consolidated *yamazato* (mountain communities) along the salt route from Mikawa Bay (located off the south-central Pacific coast of Aichi Prefecture) to the mountains of Shinshû (the 19th-century name for the territory that is now Nagano

Prefecture) on the Chûmakaidô (Chûma Road, literally, the 'inside horse passageway') for economic development ideas. Until the beginning of the 20th century, it was along this Chûmakaidô at Asuke that the Tome River became so shallow that the flat-bottomed riverboats carrying hundreds of straw bales full of salt upriver from the Pacific Ocean could not travel any further. At Asuke, the salt bails had to be transferred onto oxcarts and pulled to a main stable for reloading onto horseback for mountain transport. The ATA-led community process of systematically reflecting back historically on Asuke's heritage is what first resulted in the idea of establishing a facility that could recapture the essence of this unique mountain river town while generating even a small amount of local income to supplement Korankei profits (Sanshû Asuke Yashiki, 1990, p9).

Origin of the Asuke Yashiki concept

By all accounts, the original idea for Asuke Yashiki can be traced to discussions that took place at an ATA-sponsored heritage seminar held during the mid-1970s under the leadership of Ozawa Shôichi, born and raised locally, then chief of the Tourism Division in Asuke Town Hall. Ozawa, who had studied rural development practices in many parts of Japan as part of his job, was well known for a variety of successful local, high-profile economic stimulus initiatives implemented through his town hall position. Among his accomplishments was the 'Moo Moo Ox-Cart' event, a re-enactment of the ox procession that once pulled salt bails from the Tomoe River through local streets to the Asuke horse stables for reloading onto horseback mountain transport. Ozawa was also the instigator of Asuke's efforts to preserve the unique Edo period architecture of its rustic riverfront using state funding. But while receiving plenty of media attention, neither of these projects had successfully attracted domestic tourists to Asuke on a permanent year-around basis. 'At a time when our local cultural values were in danger of being re-configured in diverse directions', Ozawa now says, 'It was vitally important for Asuke to revisit its local heritage, not so much for the tourists, but for ourselves' (Sanshû Asuke Yashiki, 1990, p11).

Informed by years of studying the history and heritage of their hometown, Ozawa and his advocates felt confident that the Asuke lifestyle contained in its ecological emphasis a worldview that could contribute significantly towards addressing many contemporary local, national and global lifestyle issues. As a consequence, Ozawa's community development approach was grounded in the idea that Asuke should not mirror the influence of the city (Nagoya) which had taken so much from the town already, but should proudly project outward Asuke's best values, wisdom and cultural practices, cultivated throughout its history, in a way that would elevate the quality of life in modern society – not just locally, but much more broadly in the prevailing world. The idea for how this way of thinking might be applied to a tourism project in Asuke was inspired in part by the economic development work of Urabe Shigetarô, a restoration specialist, who had once been a guest speaker at an ATA-sponsored 'heritage preservation' brainstorming event. During the early 1970s, Urabe had taken a dilapidated pre-war cotton-spinning factory in a working class neighbourhood in Osaka and nurtured it into a highly successful interactive urban tourist destination using similar heritage preservation principals. At the time, Urabe's work was well-known among local development aficionados in Japan as the Ivory Square Project (Sanshû Asuke Yashiki, 1990, p11).

Motivated by the success of Urabe's work, it was Ozawa and his supporters who first contemplated the possibility of trying to attract heritage tourists by exhibiting, at interactive displays, forestry equipment, relics from the packhorse era, and paper-producing equipment from the Sanshû region (Gifu, Nagano and Aichi prefectures) in an open storefront available in Asuke's riverfront shopping district for tourists coming to visit the Korankei Gorge. Through this experience and the ongoing process of ATA-led historical reflection, Asuke townspeople came to realize that along with their ecological philosophy, the community's folk craft expertise in the context of mountain agriculture was probably its most distinguishing characteristic. Following many rounds of revisions, it was Ozawa and his Asuke supporters working as volunteers within the structure of the ATA who finally refined the idea that led to the Asuke Town Hall's formal adoption of an ingenious proposal to establish an old farmhouse and annexed work areas on an available lot located between the Tome River and Mount Iimori in the heart of Korankei Gorge to demonstrate indigenous traditional crafts for heritage tourists.

What made Ozawa's Asuke Yashiki concept extraordinary, however, was not merely that the facility sought to preserve the traditional lifestyle and inherited historical technologies of the Asuke and Mikawa regions through person-to-person contact with outside visitors. The proposal was outstanding because it identified the historical and cultural value of the folk craft skills and indigenous knowledge possessed by local senior citizens as a financially viable cultural treasure, and advocated the use of this resource as the underpinning of the facility in a way that would make it financially self-sufficient. The attraction of heritage tourists of all ages to an interactive venue to learn cultural skills, the preservation of local lifeways in danger of disappearing in a commercial enterprise designed to produce young successors who could make money while sharing this knowledge with successive generations of tourists as facility employees, and the utilization of skilled senior citizens from the local community to carry out the process constituted the proposed vision. The Asuke Yashiki concept not only addressed local economic and heritage preservation

issues, but, by including senior citizens, added a social welfare dimension to local development that in Japan at this time was truly unique (Arai, 1998;
Yoshida and Higuchi, 1998).

At the height of Japan's post-war Rural Nostalgia Boom during the mid-
1970s, there were plenty of rural hometown venues where potters sat at potting
wheels demonstrating old-fashioned throwing techniques in public locations, or
where craftspeople in glass-enclosed booths moulded cast-iron teapots using
traditional materials and old-fashioned methods, never having any meaningful
contact with tourists (Creighton, 1995, p270). Conversely, Asuke residents felt
that they had more to offer. By utilizing the knowledge, expertise and historical
experience of their local senior citizens, Ozawa and his supporters wanted to
display the entire lifestyle of Asuke craftspeople by defining their function at
Asuke Yashiki and in the Asuke community more broadly. With Ozawa's help,
what Asuke residents decided that they wanted to create was a facility that
would be a catalyst for reactivating the use of authentic lifestyle practices from
the region's past applicable to the problems of the present that could be easily
accessed by anybody who took time to visit (Sanshû Asuke Yashiki, 1990, p12).

Asuke Yashiki: Finalizing the blueprint

An authentic recreation of the *yamazato* (mountain village) lifestyle required
that everything be prepared the old-fashioned way. Wood charcoal would be
made in a real kiln, wooden dishes carved on foot-powered lathes, and traditional cloth woven on authentic hand-operated looms. The purpose of Asuke
Yashiki would be to question the methods and philosophies of the modern
world by restoring the region's mountain community ethics and values through
Asuke's folk craft heritage and creating an alternative to what was available in
the city. But as the conceptualization and planning for Asuke Yashiki continued, the project had its critics.

In 1977, the Asuke Town Council challenged the Asuke Yashiki concept as
being too ambitious. Who was going to pay the estimated US$1.1 million that
it would cost to build the facility? And how was such a concept going to be
economically sustainable? Would the Asuke Town Hall eventually have to be
bailed out like so many other heritage preservation projects around the country, or was there something different about the Asuke Yashiki plan?

The initial question was answered shortly when, with the help of the Asuke
Town Hall, Ozawa and the ATA applied for and received a Remote Area
Promotion Grant (a precursor to the mass tourism grants that the state began
offering during the 1980s), fully funded jointly by the national government
(Ministry of Land, Infrastructure, Transport and Tourism), the Aichi prefec-
tural government, and the Asuke municipal government. In essence, this meant

that the construction cost of Asuke Yashiki was fully covered (Suzuki, 2006, p3). But Asuke Yashiki would not be able to operate on public funds alone, and would have to generate an income, even if modest, to be financially solvent. The challenge for Ozawa and his Asuke Yashiki proponents would be to devise a creative business model that could enable the facility to simultaneously take full advantage of a diverse range of income-generating resources and possibilities (Sanshû Asuke Yashiki, 1990, p13).

After a long and thorough consideration process, Ozawa and the ATA decided on a third-sector model – a financial paradigm that could combine funding from public-sector sources with private investment. Because the ATA board was becoming increasingly busy with Korankei Gorge tourism and other projects, it was decided that a separate management organization dedicated exclusively to Asuke Yashiki and other possible future projects of this type would be formed. The board of directors of the new management organization was composed of local residents who either worked in the prefectural government or the Asuke Town Hall, owned businesses locally or in the prefecture, or were involved in professions sensitive to Asuke Yashiki-related interests. Established in 1979, this organization was named the Asuke-Midori-no-Mura (Asuke Green Village) Association, and began managing four major financial components of the Asuke Yashiki project sanctioned by its board. These included:

1   income expected from the daily operation of Asuke Yashiki, such as admissions and membership income, craft skill classes fees and purchases of traditional foods;
2   funds generated by an Asuke Yashiki investment group made up of local and prefectural businesses, including Toyota Motors and public-sector partners such as the Asuke Town Hall;
3   revenue to be earned through a percentage of the commercial sale of craft products made on site; and
4   funding from grants and subsidies applied for and received from both the public and private sectors.

Management of these facets of the Asuke Yashiki financial structure were to create the capital necessary to cover all facilities expenses, including six full-time administrative salaries. The Asuke Green Village Association, which eventually embarked on two other third-sector industry economic development projects in Asuke, established an Asuke Yashiki board of directors to oversee and advise the facility's daily operation as well.

As Asuke Yashiki was preparing for its first year of operation, in early 1980, once again with the help of a town hall grant application, Asuke Yashiki (now an incorporated third-sector enterprise) became the recipient of more state money. This time, the financial aid came as long-term renewable subsidy funding from the Ministry of Agriculture Forestry and Fisheries (MAFF) as a Mountain Village District Special Measures Project for the purpose of promoting *ningen-sei sôzô no tame no bunka kei kankô* (meaningful cultural tourism for the purpose of [preserving] the human imagination). Asuke Yashiki was now officially sanctioned as a facility to 'preserve the rich heritage of local mountain culture in the Sanshû region through the revival and uninterrupted practice of the historic arts by transmitting the values and philosophies contained therein to visitors via interactive experiences on site' (Sanshû Asuke Yashiki, 1990, p13).

This designated mission matched perfectly the original vision for Asuke Yashiki proposed by Ozawa and the ATA. Asuke Yashiki supporters were delighted. However, the MAFF label also required that the 'historic arts' at Asuke Yashiki be 'cultivated as an income-generating regional industry to improve the standard of living and cultural awareness of local residents while heightening their love of, and appreciation for, their hometown and lifeways that are a part of their distinct regional heritage' (Sanshû Asuke Yashiki, 1990, p13). Unfortunately, concrete plans for how to achieve this goal through craft products had yet to be finalized. Therefore, in late 1979, the Asuke Yashiki board began holding marathon meetings to come up with a way of actualizing this requisite.

Within weeks, the Asuke Yashiki board, in consultation with the ATA, the Asuke Green Village Association, its many public- and private-sector contacts, and the Asuke Town Hall devised a plan. Operationally, the Asuke Yashiki artisans (consisting of retired local senior citizens as long as they were available) would be placed on retainer and, as tenants of Asuke, be assigned to a work area where tourists could watch them work, ask questions and have access to them in close proximity. In addition, Asuke Yashiki would help each artisan to find and support an appropriate apprentice, as well as attempt to secure long-term contracts with domestic wholesalers to whom they could sell their products at regular monthly intervals, as well as making them available directly to tourists onsite. In exchange for workspace and the support of a potential successor, artisans would share a percentage of their profits with Asuke Yashiki and as crafts experts would be considered staff members of the facility. Farmstead programming would be planned and implemented by Asuke Yashiki administrators jointly with the artisans on staff and their apprentices. In retrospect, these tenets – crafts skills preservation and programme management – became key to Asuke Yashiki's initial and long-term success. With the renewable source of MAFF support secured and operational details outlined, the basic fiscal, philosophical and structural foundations necessary to begin the operation of Asuke Yashiki were finally firmly in place as the facility opened its doors to the public early in April 1980.

Asuke Yashiki's state funding successes at this time were not so much the result of good grant writing at the ATA, but came about because of the changes that began to occur in Japanese regional development policy during the last quarter of the 20th century to accommodate the economic decline that began to be particularly noticeable in rural townships such as Asuke across Japan. During the early 1970s, the national government initially advocated the rural adoption of high-tech communication and transportation networks (such as enhanced radio, telephone and television connectivity, as well as high-speed rail service and connectors to the nation's evolving super-highway system) to promote regional development through tourism as part of the emerging information society (Rimmer, 1992, p1610; Thompson, 2001, p70). But due to the extensive infrastructural investment that was necessary, progress was slow. To bring about faster and more visible economic results, this strategy was subsequently supplemented in the late 1970s by an expansion of the policy that also advocated the construction of leisure and resort facilities which emphasized the cultivation of local culture and heritage resources through rural tourism in economically disadvantaged rural areas (Creighton, 1995, p270; Thompson, 2004, p583). Asuke Yashiki is one example of many hometown tourist venues that benefitted financially from this policy shift.

As is often the pattern in public-sector fundraising, secured grants attract new grants. During the next few years, the ATA, working through the Asuke Town Hall, was also able to help Asuke Yashiki secure a 'hometown cultivation' block grant (referred to earlier) during the 1980s. Many rural townships in Japan also received these funds. However, the difference between Asuke Yashiki and most other hometown tourism venues around the country was that from its planning stages, the facility was supported structurally and financially by a diversified array of income-generating divisions connected to people and institutions in the public and private sectors locally, and at the prefectural and national levels. Furthermore, the various individuals and institution connected to Asuke Yashiki had a vested interest in its success.

Asuke Yashiki's financial viability

In its first year of operation from 1980 to 1981, Asuke Yashiki was able to attract slightly more than 100,000 paid visitors, nearly twice the number of initial estimates. Despite changing government policies and state pressure to initiate mass commercial tourism, over the next two decades, Ozawa (at this time in his 50s), who was appointed first-generation director of Asuke Yashiki as part of his town hall tourism division job, stuck with the original vision for the facility and financial management plan. During the first decade and a half, paying visitors steadily increased, peaking at 189,000 in 1995. But due to the slowing of the Japanese economy during the late 1990s, attendance figures declined slightly thereafter, levelling off at between 100,000 to 120,000 visitors per year after that. These numbers could have been much lower, but Asuke's proximity to Nagoya is thought to have helped to minimize the slide.

During the first few years of operation, Ozawa tried to generate as much income as possible through admission fees, craft classes, commissions on the sale of folk craft items, a menu of seasonal foods and special cultural festivities (such as the Tsukimi-kai). But, not surprisingly, in subsequent years, he had to harness his entrepreneurial creativity to broaden Asuke Yashiki's earning potential. Using lessons learned from Urabe's Ivory Square Project, one way in which Ozawa accomplished this was by slowly adding small specialized attractions within Asuke Yashiki, such as restaurants and display areas using building grants from the state designated for cultural preservation (Suzuki, 2005, p5).

Since 1980, the greatest amount of revenue at Asuke Yashiki has been generated through cultural skills classes taught by expert artisans (27 per cent), followed by income from the restaurants (the Kunpootei and the Katakago) and Hinokichaya, the onsite teahouse (24 per cent). The tenant areas (featuring Asuke artisans who engage in both contract work and direct marketing) produces 23 per cent of the budget. The admissions and membership fees now typically garner 15 per cent of Asuke Yashiki income. Surprisingly, traditional foods and pickles and the Asuke Lodge (a nostalgia museum with special exhibits that remind visitors of life during Japan's 1950s to 1960s) yield only approximately 6 and 5 per cent of profits, respectively (Suzuki, 2005, p5). The highest monthly income total ever recorded was in 1998 during the month of November, which resulted in revenue of US$2.79 million (US$1 = 110 Japanese yen). This figure has not ever again been matched. Yet, to date, according to Suzuki Megumi, a knowledgeable female 40-something Asuke Yashiki insider, with the help of public-sector funds, the facility has broken even financially each year. During the 2000s, however, Suzuki reports that overall income at Asuke Yashiki has been affected by what some economists have called Japan's millennial economic downturn – currently in its eighth year (email correspondence, 21 February 2008).

As expected, a considerable seasonal variation in the number of visitors is noticeable. January and February are typically the slowest months. The highest number of tourists have always been recorded when the foliage is most beautiful each autumn – usually during the period from late October to late November. Unexpectedly, however, statistics also show that Asuke Yashiki has had a very positive economic impact on extra income generated in Asuke Township, as a whole, in local businesses beyond Asuke Yashiki by attracting repeat visitors to the municipality over the course of an annual cycle. Interestingly, Asuke Yashiki is also given credit by locals for slowing (some statistics would suggest stopping) population outflow by helping to make Asuke a desirable residential location close to Nagoya for individuals and groups interested in community participation, local heritage preservation as well as ecological and environmental issues. Asuke is also thought of by Nagoya residents as a good retirement location for seniors (some of them originally local natives) interested in actively pursuing such interests without being too far away from their children and grandchildren working Toyota-related jobs in the suburbs of Japan's fourth largest city (Suzuki, 2005, p5).

Analysing Asuke Yashiki's success

Scholars of Japanese tourism maintain that the reason why Asuke Yashiki has been so successful over the years simultaneously as a 'cultural tourism venue' and a viable business is fourfold. First, Asuke Yashiki was conceived according to a heritage politics model. This is significant because Asuke Yashiki is a combined result of the funding know-how and business expertise available locally and through the Asuke Town Hall, but structurally and financially completely independent of it. Therefore, the success or failure of Asuke Yashiki does not depend directly on the local tax base, population figures or the local business climate. This distinguishes Asuke Yashiki from other municipal and private cultural tourism venues of its kind in Japan.

Second, Ozawa's concept for Asuke Yashiki as a cultural heritage facility extends far beyond the idea of merely preserving local lifeways in a contained setting. His vision also includes the practical application of this legacy interactively to contemporary problems even outside the walls of the facility. This emphasis connects the past with the present in a practical way within Asuke Yashiki and the extended community through elaborate seasonal, holiday and special events, the frequency and scale of which are still unusual in Japanese domestic heritage tourism circles. A third potent component has been Asuke Yashiki's third-sector status. The MAFF grant and other public-sector funding provide a fundamental foundation of financial support and a purpose for Asuke Yashiki to exist that can remain consistent no matter how much business fluctuates from year to year within the income-producing dimensions of the farmstead.

A fourth reason for the success of cultural tourism at Asuke Yashiki is that Ozawa (now retired from the Asuke Town Hall and, thus, no longer director of Asuke Yashiki, and who has taken on the chairmanship of the ATA full time) has not been afraid to adjust his existing approach to changing social, economic and political trends domestically and internationally. Working with his hand-picked successor chosen for many qualities, including his international community development expertise, Ozawa continues to create new ways of harnessing the appeal of Asuke Yashiki that might never have been imagined at its genesis. For example, since 1998, Asuke Yashiki has been consulting with public and private counterparts in Vietnam and China about how to implement tourism venues in these countries using Asuke-devised cultural tourism paradigms adapted to local circumstances. As a result, the success that Asuke Yashiki has achieved in revitalizing the Asuke community through cultural tourism has been recognized nationally and internationally during the early 21st century as one of the best examples of this practice in Japan (Suzuki, 2005, p5).

Asuke Yashiki in the New Millennium

In Asuke Yashiki in 2009, for a nominal entrance fee (about US$5 for adults and half this amount for students and seniors), not only can tourists watch artisans engage in a variety of crafts once practised in every farm household locally, they can also enjoy a wide variety of displays and live demonstrations designed to educate them about topics ranging from proper social etiquette in a mountain village setting to safe, traditional, eco-friendly ways to fish in a mountain stream. By engaging in Asuke Yashiki activities, visitors of all ages – from the elderly questioning the relevance of their life experiences and Baby Boomers nostalgic for farm tools they remember from the 1950s, to youngsters who think the small pieces of wood charcoal on display are mini-nuggets of chocolate – develop an admiration for, and understanding of, the practical wisdom possessed by Asuke's forebears.

Thanks to the MAFF grant, since Asuke Yashiki's first year of operation in 1980, a major educational emphasis at the facility has been on the various ways to utilize the wisdom of the past to address the problems of the present. Since Asuke's consolidation into Toyota City in 2005, access to supplementary municipal development funds and special grants from Toyota Motors (a major corporate taxpayer in Toyota City since 1947) have also become available to support this priority. While educational visits from schools only account for about one third of the children who visit the facility each year, annually about twice as many youngsters attend craft skills classes and participate in seasonal activities with their parents and grandparents. Thus, despite being the least lucrative of Asuke Yashiki's heritage offerings, educating youngsters (and adults) about more efficient ways of living in contemporary society remains a central focus of the farmstead's institutional mission that continues to be expressed at the facility through a profusion of constantly updated topical exhibits.

For example, at the 'traditional fuels' display, clean-burning wood charcoal is touted as a possible replacement for contemporary home cooking and heating fuels and a possible alternative to the world's overdependence on fossil fuels. As a placard in the display reads:

In recent years, citizens the world over have become aware that the mass consumption of fossil fuels has ushered in a host of ills, ranging from the emission of endocrine-disrupting substances such as dioxins to global warming. In this context, wood charcoal has become a focus of renewed attention at Asuke Yashiki. Unlike fossil fuels, wood charcoal is a clean energy source, infinitely renewable as long as forests exist. Furthermore, charcoal has other uses as well. It can purify polluted streams, cleanse drinking water and condition soil. Its moisture-absorbing properties make it a valuable insulation material in building mould-free homes. It is time once again to reincorporate these materials into our everyday lives as residents of the Mikawa region once did. (Aichi Voice, 2007)

The importance of using renewable natural resources in daily life (such as those made at the facility) is reinforced in this text from another display on the importance of using biodegradable materials:

One would never guess, just by looking, how many uses there are for the plant fibres in wood, bamboo and straw. Unlike nylon or plastic, these fibres naturally degrade over time and return to the soil. While this biodegradability may seem like a drawback, the process by which nature creates durable materials, breaks them down and creates them once again in a self-completing cycle is actually a superior feature. The wide range of applications the people of Mikawa devised for the natural materials that grew in the forests around them shows us that these people knew how to live comfortably with minimal waste. (Aichi Voice, 2007)

Similarly, Asuke Yashiki promotes the virtues of the mountain lifestyle as an ideal example of a balanced existence that modern global citizens should learn from and emulate, as described in this posting:

The early settlers in the Mikawa region depended on the mountains for everything, from food to tools and implements. Life revolved around working the tiny mountain vegetable fields and rice paddies in the spring, raising silkworms in the summer and making charcoal in the winter. Some communities extracted lacquer from trees in the summer and made paper in the winter. During the agricultural off-season, blacksmiths were kept busy repairing metal farm implements, such as scythes and hoes. At one time, Asuke had four or five blacksmith shops; now only one remains. To power essential operations, such as threshing and lathing, mountain villages relied on the water wheel – a distinguishing feature in the landscape of Japan's old farming communities. (*Aichi Voice*, 2007)

Perhaps the most interesting thing about Asuke Yashiki is not the artefacts or the exhibits, but the resident artisans (all but one of the men and women are senior citizens from Asuke) who practice more than just their craftwork. In the spirit of community building, they and all Asuke Yashiki employees cook meals, collect eggs in the hen house and cut wood for the *irori* (pit hearth) in the thatched-roofed farmhouse where all Asuke Yashiki staff eat their noon meal together. Artisans also have various Asuke Yashiki-related administrative responsibilities and participate as facility representatives in Asuke-hosted community meetings and events. Many of them make periodic trips to demonstrate their crafts at tourism promotion fairs outside of Asuke to which they might be invited or assigned, but also visit local elementary, junior high and high schools on a regular basis. They create their craft product, but also try to add to the quality of life at Asuke Yashiki and in the Asuke's broader township community as they live the ideals that their crafts represent. Artisans are seen frequently talking to tourists in the barnyard, taking photographs with them, and sometimes even joining visitors for tea and snacks in one of the restaurants or the teahouse in the farmstead compound. Artisans, along with their full-time administrator colleagues, also train volunteers as docents, activity assistants, and prepare them to perform other specialized jobs. This is important work as over half of Asuke Yashiki's daily operational tasks are dependent on volunteers for completion.

According to Asuke Township residents, this interaction between Asuke Yashiki personnel, townspeople and volunteers has the effect of revitalizing the town and attracting not only tourists, but urban refugees and seasonal residents who crave this kind of contact. In the opinion of Obuchi Takahiro, a male middle-aged local bookstore owner: 'Asuke Yashiki tipped the Asuke tourism scale in a positive direction. Having a facility like this locally has brought an increasing number of weekend visitors to the community all year around' (interview, 20 February 2008).[5] The increased number of visitors to Asuke since 1980 has helped the local tax base and has enriched the community, producing a general feeling of optimism that local residents have about their hometown in the mountains that did not always exist.

As of late, the interactive role of Asuke Yashiki artisans has even begun to mirror Japan's society-wide tendency in recent years to engage in a record number of international projects. In 2005, Asuke Yashiki added a new facility, the Asia Studio, where guest artisans from China, Nepal, Vietnam and other Asian countries are invited to live and work for a contractual period to demonstrate their traditional crafts. Asuke Yashiki has been attracting increasing numbers of traditional Japanese culture enthusiasts from Euro-America as well. In 2007, students from Ohio University in the US

Figure 3.7 *An Asuke Yashiki bamboo artisan teaching visiting Ohio University students a traditional cutting technique*

Source: Christopher S. Thompson, 2007

participated in a one-week cultural immersion programme designed and implemented solely by Asuke Yashiki artisans, administrators, and staff (see Figure 3.7). Ohio University is scheduled for a similar session in 2009.

Cultural tourism and Japan's urban–rural dynamic

Until the 1990s, domestic cultural tourism in rural locations within Japan had been regarded primarily as a 'ritual of reversal' that brought relief in the form of exposure to traditional Japanese culture to urbanites who battled the ills of the modern world in the nation's metropolitan areas. But in an about-face from this historically urban-centred model of heritage tourism in Japan, the example of Asuke Yashiki shows that from the perspective of Asuke locals, this retro-farmstead is not only a rural-centric concept, but also an important (almost crucial) way for local residents to validate the importance of their mountain heritage in 21st-century Japan. Asuke Yashiki is simultaneously a local response to the geopolitics of post-war Japan and an expression of Asuke's contemporary culture. Asuke Yashiki empowers local residents and the artisans who represent their traditional way of life to actively reproduce not only the highly valued craft skills native to the area, but also the social and cultural patterns that have engendered this heritage. Cultural tourism at Asuke Yashiki is different from tourism in Japan's historical past for at least five interrelated reasons.

First, Asuke Yashiki is a concept initiated by locals at a time when the national government's answer to the socio-economic problems of the periphery was to consolidate each prefecture's shrinking municipalities and to impose mass commercial tourism using state funds to develop local economies – a top-down proposition. However, unlike many of the post-war tourism venues for which funding ran out, Asuke Yashiki originated locally, and although it utilized, in part, the same state funds, is an original economic development concept that was planned and implemented independently by the people and institutions of the Aichi countryside – a bottom-up response. Second, the Asuke Yashiki Project is a joint venture between state, private, local and regional funding sources. Until Asuke Yashiki, third-sector enterprises of this type in the tourism industry in Japan were virtually unknown (Arai, 1998). Third, Asuke Yashiki-style cultural tourism advocates utilizing traditional ideas to solve modern problems. The use of tourism to facilitate economic development is a post-war phenomenon; but the idea of using traditional products to solve contemporary problems such as how to reduce waste, the overdependence on fossil fuels, and how to provide the nation's increasing number of senior citizens with meaningful activity is distinctive.

A fourth reason why Asuke Yashiki tourism differs from the past is that this facility is an example of a commercially, socio-culturally and ecologically successful venture not dependent on the heritage politics model from which it was derived. Even after Asuke was consolidated into Toyota City in 2005, Asuke Yashiki continued to remain a financially independent and theoretically relevant third sector-enterprise. This is rather unusual given that many post-war municipal heritage preservation venues in rural Japan have generally failed financially or have needed to be subsidized significantly by the public or private sector, or both. Asuke Yashiki has been successful because of the facility's diverse human and institutional ties, a business model suitable to its circumstances, the love for and commitment to Asuke's heritage preservation demonstrated consistently by those associated with the enterprise, and the leadership of a gifted leader named Ozawa Shôichi, who figured out how to combine the human and institutional resources at his disposal effectively.

Finally, Asuke Yashiki has an ecological focus that encourages volunteering, personal growth and the reintroduction of old ways to live on the planet involving interaction with flora, fauna and cultural heritage as its primary attraction. The facility promotes programmes that minimize the negative aspects of conventional tourism on the environment, and enhances the cultural integrity of Asuke locals, who are the focus of this touristic enterprise. An integral part of cultural tourism at Asuke Yashiki is the promotion of recycling, energy efficiency, water conservation and the creation of economic opportunities for the local community and those related to it. The incorporation of all of these characteristics into a single, independent, heritage tourism venue that can theoretically be duplicated in other rural settings domestically and internationally is what makes Asuke Yashi a world class model to emulate in bringing about community revitalization through heritage tourism in regional Japan (Arai, 1998; Iguchi, 2002, p123).

Notes

1   The other two locations are Matsushima, a series of pine-covered islands off the Pacific coast of Miyagi Prefecture in Japan's north-east, and Amanohashidate, a beautiful pine-covered sandbar in northern Kyoto Prefecture on the Japan Sea.
2   A *torii* is a traditional Japanese gate commonly found at the entrance to a Shinto shrine, although it can be found at Buddhist temples as well. It typically has two upright supports and two crossbars on the top, although the *torii* at Miyajima is much more elaborate.
3   The Grand Shrine at Ise is considered to be Japan's most sacred Shinto Shrine because it enshrines the Sun Goddess Amaterasu Omikami, believed to be the ancestor of the Japanese Imperial family.
4   Ruskin's ideas and those of his protégé, William Morris, introduced to Japan as early as the 1890s, have had a strong and positive influence on Japanese academic and popular discourse associated with conservation, ecology and local development. Both men are permanently memorialized in a museum in rural Osaka that continues to promote the modern application of their ideas and those of other foreign and Japanese environmentalists who arrived afterwards and who were influenced by their work (www.ruskin-morris-center.ecnet.jp/en/index.html, 2008).
5   The name and occupation of this informant and all others who are quoted directly in this chapter have been disguised to protect their privacy.

References

Aichi Voice (2007) 'The Ruskin and Morris Center of Osaka Today', *Aichi Voice*, www2.aia.pref.aichi.jp/voice/no9/9_time_travelar.html, accessed 24 December 2007

Arai, Y. (1998) *Rural Tourism in Japan: The Regeneration of Rural Communities*, Rural Life Research Institute, Zenkoku Nôgyô Kyôsai Kaikan, www.agnet.org/library/article/eb457.html, accessed 21 August 2008

Asahi Shimbun (2006) *The Asahi Shimbun Japan Almanac*, Toppan Printing Co., Tokyo, Japan

Asuke Tourism Association (ed) (1996) *Shin Sanshû Asuke* [*The New Asuke*], Taikô Corporation, Nagoya

Bramwell, B. and Lane, B. (eds) (2000) *Tourism, Collaboration, and Partnership: Politics, Practice, and Sustainability*, Channel View Publications, Buffalo, US

Creighton, M. (1995) 'Japanese craft tourism: Liberating the crane wife', *Annals of Tourism Research*, vol 22, no 2, pp463–478

Creighton, M. (1997) 'Consuming Rural Japan: The Marketing of Tradition and Nostalgia in the Japanese Travel Industry', *Ethnology*, vol 36, no 3, Summer, pp239–254

Formasek, S. (1997) *Consuming Rural Japan: The Marketing of Tradition and Nostalgia in the Japanese Travel Industry*, SUNY Press, Albany, NY

Iguchi, M. (2002) *Kankôbunka no Shinkô to Chiiki Shakai [Regional Society and the Promotion of Cultural Tourism]*, Minerva Shobô, Tokyo, Japan

Ishimori, S. (1989) 'Popularization and commercialization of tourism in early modern Japan', in T. Umesao, M. Fruin and N. Hata (eds) *Senri Ethnological Studies*, 26, Japan National Museum of Ethnology, Osaka, Japan, pp179–194

Juassaume, R. (1991) *Japanese Part-Time Farming: Evolution and Impacts*, Iowa State University Press, Ames, IO

Kelly, W. W. (1990) 'Regional Japan: The price of prosperity and the benefits of dependency', *Daedalus*, vol 119, pp209–227

Knight, J. (1993) 'Competing hospitalities in Japanese rural tourism', *Annals of Tourism Research*, vol 23, pp165–180

OECD (Organisation for Economic Co-operation and Development) (1993) *Territorial Development: Regional Problems and Policies in Japan*, OECD, Paris, France

Rimmer, P. J, (1992) 'Japan's "resort archipelago": Creating regions of fun, pleasure, relaxation, and recreation', *Environment and Planning*, vol A 24, no 11, pp1599–1625

Sanshû Asuke Yashiki (1990) *Asuke Yashiki no Jû-nen [Asuke Yashiki: The First Ten Years]*, Asuke Town Hall, 27 April, pp8–11

Suzuki, N. (2005) 'Establishing a traditional craft promotion facility: The effective promotion for regional development in developing countries: Part III', *Bulletin of Japanese Society for the Science of Design*, vol 171, pp11–20

Suzuki, N. (2006) 'Effective Tourism development through traditional craft promotion: Japanese experiences', paper presented at The First International Congress on Tourism and Traditional Crafts and Associated Activities, Riyadh, Saudi Arabia, 7–14 November, http://ci.nii.ac.jp/naid/110004047344/, accessed 28August 2008

Thompson, C. (2001) 'Cyber-chômin@Tôwa-chô: Re-territorializing rurality in regional Japan', *Pan Japan: The International Journal of the Japanese Diaspora*, vol 2, no 1/2, pp64–99

Thompson, C. (2003) 'Depopulation in regional Japan: Population politics in Towa-chô', in J. Knight and J. Traphagan (eds) *Demographic Change and the Family in Japan's Aging Society*, State University of New York Press, New York, NY, pp89–106

Thompson, C. (2004) 'Host produced rural tourism: Towa's Tokyo Antenna Shop', *Annals of Tourism Research*, vol 31, no 3, pp580–600

Thompson, C. (2008) 'The politics of folk performance in northeast Japan: Preserving Ishihatooka Kagura', in *The Demographic Challenge: A Handbook about Japan*, German Institute for Japanese Studies, Tokyo, Japan, pp361–385

Thompson, C. and Traphagan, J. (eds) (2006) *Wearing Cultural Styles in Japan: Concepts of Tradition and Modernity in Practice*, SUNY Press, Albany, NY

Yoshida, K. and Higuchi, M. (1998) 'Econometric analysis of green tourism in Japan using data from the nationwide farmstead operator survey', *Nôgyô Sôgô Kenkyû*, vol 53, no 3, pp45–97

4

Pilgrim Culture of Tīrthā in India: Enculturation of New Age Movements within Age-Old Rituals

Shalini Singh

Introduction

India's landscape is a cultural mosaic of temples, shrines and consecrated monuments that lends the country a distinct identity. But it is the ubiquitous worshipper who reinforces the religious genus of the country's masses. Going to the temple (or any other place of worship) is a daily affair, though setting out on a pilgrimage for a ritual to participate in a faraway festive celebration or to a holy river for a purifying dip are the highlights of many people's lives. This religiosity is a phenomenon of the Indian masses and has attracted the attention of tourists and scholars alike, who have at times remarked on the spectacle with some measure of awe at the fervidity of faith that stirs mammoth crowds for ceremonious undertakings throughout and around India. Some scholars have, however, questioned the pageantry that Hinduism upholds (see Griswold, 1912; Tomalin, 2002, 2004).

Clearly, then, this chapter delves into Hindu pilgrimages (*tīrthā yātrā*) as a dominant form of domestic travel and tourism in India. A pertinent aspect of the *tīrthā yātrā* is that it is not merely a centuries-old practice; its traditions have continued with undiminished fervour in contemporary times of increasing modernity and secularity. This chapter, therefore, begins with an introduction to some colloquial terms that constitute the common parlance for travel, tourism and pilgrimages of the Hindi-speaking Indians. Unique features of domestic tourism in the country are then elaborated upon. Given this contextual backdrop of domestic tourism, the pilgrimage tradition of Hindu *tīrthā yātrā* is discussed. Considerable attention is focused on the background, practices and the systems that characterize these pilgrimages. In doing so, an attempt is made to assert the explicit relationship of *tīrthā* (pilgrimage) *yātrā* (journey) with nature, in terms of both the veneration and the use of nature. This relationship has, in current times, given cause for concern. Hence, in order to present the big picture of vernacular forms of religious and quasi-religious tourism of Indian resident population, particularly the Hindus (as they constitute the largest faith group in the country), the chapter commences with an overview of the practices and uniqueness of Indian domestic tourism. Having presented this backdrop, the chapter zooms in on Hindu religious travels and visitations, accomplishing two purposes. First, it explores the system and practices of *tírthā* (Hindu pilgrimage) in order to understand its underlying principles. Concomitantly, this explanation also intends to provide insights into the secular extensions and implications of the *tírthā* tradition, as well. A critique of contemporary *tírthā yātrā*(s) in practices of pilgrimages and the religious tenets is then briefly presented. Considering Hinduism's claim to be nature-based, the critique intends to question the sagacity of the Hindu pilgrimages (*tírthā yātrā*) in terms of environment and human action. While acknowledging the dichotomy between bio-divinity and bio-consciousness, the chapter concludes with a note on some pragmatic pathways that have been employed by religious institutions as a possible strategy for reconciling environmental friendliness and bio-divinity.

Sojourns of the Indian masses: An overview

Information on the travel and tourism practices of Indians is diffused and amalgamated. One of the reasons for this lies in the fact that the modern tourism system conceptually contrasts the legacy of travel practices of native Indians whose leisure migrations have for long been constructed differently owing to their distinct socio-cultural foundations. As a consequence, the terminological references also vary considerably (see Figure 4.1).

Before the arrival of modern tourism, during colonial and post-colonial times, vernacular forms of travelling (*yātrā*) and touring (*ghumna*) have maintained a vivid and vigorous presence in the country. *Yātrā* and *ghumna* continue to be generic terms, associated with the *ghumakkar* (native traveller), whether in the form of religious travel – namely, *tírthā* (pilgrimage) – or secular travels such as *deshatan* (literally, travel within the national boundary) that included *milna* (visiting people) and *dekhna* (sightseeing). Interestingly, the activity of recreation is implicit in these terms. Hence, while a *tírthā yātrí* (journeying pilgrim) naturally engages in 'purposeful' re-creative activities such as paying homage, praying, singing hymns, and observing religious sanctions and doctrines, a person who travels to friends and relatives or even strangers is expected to partake of and observe the host's familial and communitarian traditions. Documentary evidence of such endogenic tourism practices and

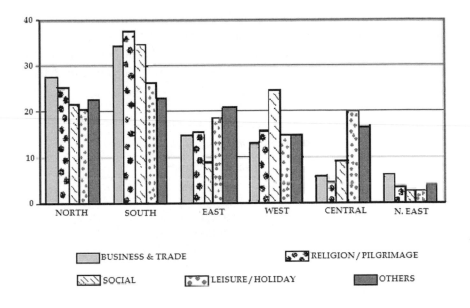

Figure 4.1 *Regional distribution of domestic trips with the purpose of travel (2002–2003): Percentage of trips accounted for by each region for any given purpose of travel*

Source: NCAER (undated, p16)

patterns can be obtained from ancient texts, such as the *Shastra, Upnishada, Paurana* and *Veda.* Notwithstanding these colloquial terms, the phrase *domestic tourism* is interpreted as the internal movement and activities of Indian residents for leisure and recreation pursuits, including religious journeys. This clarification delineates inbound tourist traffic that usually comprises non-resident Indians (NRIs).[1]

In contemporary times, traditional and modern travel and touring practices are collectively referred to as *ghumna*[2] – an accepted term with its all-embracing scope. As simple as the term may be, this conflation, nonetheless, confounds our understanding of current practices and patterns in Indian domestic tourism, with tradition and modernity becoming inextricably coexistent (Joseph and Kavoori, 2001). Such fusion of tourism performance poses a major challenge to researchers of Indian tourism in their effort to take part in discourses or to contribute to the existing tourism literature. Subsequently, studies on tourism in India are few and far between, and are predominantly impact studies. In comparison, literature on India's domestic tourism is almost non-existent. Likewise, reliable statistical data are, by and large, estimates that are generated to serve the specific purpose of interest groups. Recently, the

Government of India has made available some of its official and sponsored reports on domestic and international tourism (NCAER, undated, 2004; MARCH, 2006; Ministry of Tourism, 2006, 2008). According to these official sources, nearly 549 million Indians undertook domestic travel in 2007 (see Table 4.1).

Table 4.1 *India: Domestic visitor volume*

Year	Domestic visitors
1997	159,877,008
1998	168,196,000
1999	190,671,014
2000	220,106,941
2001	234,781,257
2002	271,328,180
2003	309,040,000*
2004	366,230,000*
2005	390,470,000*
2006	461,160,000*
2007	549,000,000*

Note: * = rounded figures.

Source: India Stats 2003a; India Stats 2003b; MARCH (2006); GOI 2007; NCAER (undated)

A foremost feature of domestic tourism in India has always been its 'mass' character. With a population of over 1 billion people, this fact is self-explanatory. More interesting is the revelation that as many as 157 million travellers (two-fifths of the entire volume) originate from urban centres, while approximately 392 million (nearly three-fifths of the traffic) comprise rural inhabitants who are engaged in the country's agrarian economy (NCAER, undated, pi). This feature reflects that a larger segment of the native travellers continue to maintain traditional patterns of living and lifestyles, and, hence, travel practices. These aspects also provide an explanation for the informal nature of India's domestic tourism (see Gladstone, 2005).

The *seasonality* factor is of overarching significance in Indian domestic travels and tours. This feature is found to dominate both traditional travel patterns and modern tourism practices. Indian summers have comprehensibly been associated with 'a time' to undertake journeys and trips. As a result, almost all Hindu festivals are in conformity with the astrological calendar. Hence, while festivals mark seasonal transitions, the summer months open doorways to pilgrims. In addition, the Indian summers (May to July) have assumed significance in the contemporary practice, too, when people seek out cooler locations to escape the sweltering tropical weather. Vacationing during summers is further reinforced by the closure of schools for the season, giving families an opportunity to get together for a reunion in their home communities or to travel together for holiday-making. This 'summer rush' escalates demands for transport, accommodation and other tourist-related amenities in destination areas beyond carrying capacities. Special provisions are made by the government to meet with increased demands for surface transportation – particularly rail. Nearly 90 per cent of resident Indians travel by surface, with as many as six-sevenths of the tourists using buses and the remaining opting for train journeys. Trains, being the most preferred mode of long-distance travel, are especially scheduled to meet with tourist overflows in the summer season and also during festive occasions.[3] Although this effort solves transportation problems, to some extent, it exacerbates those of the destination areas that are consequently deluged by tourist hordes and are, thence, challenged with allocating and provisioning scarce resources. For example Manali, a popular hill resort in Himachal Pradesh, records a host–guest ratio of 1:650 during the tourist season (Singh, 2008). Concomitant issues of limited accommodation, excess waste, traffic bottlenecks and congestion, overcrowding and scarce amenities impact negatively upon product and quality requisites. Under these circumstances, concerns for carrying capacities are rendered meaningless and futile.

Another pertinent factor for mass domestic tourism in India is that travelling and touring among native Indians is largely in the *context of the family*. Since the family continues to be the foundation of Indian society, it occupies a central position in the living and lifestyles of Indians (Mullatti, 1995). Interdependency, nurturing and social support gained through and within family systems is, indeed, a uniquely valued cultural factor (Simhadri, 1989; Madan, 1990) that informs the decisions, motivation, attitude and lifestyles of the majority of Indians. This influence extends itself to the holiday-making process and behaviour of the natives, in this way providing a context. Tripping to peripheral locations during weekends or brief (one- to two-day) work breaks (see Figure 4.2) is interspersed with inter- and intra-state travels to the urban cores and peripheries. Much of the time, the place or visitation becomes secondary to the primary intention of travelling for family togetherness or unification. For example, the visiting friends and relatives (VFR) category of native tourists accounts for nearly 30 per cent of domestic touring. This segment is independent of the VFR category that travels with a definite purpose of attending family events (approximately 31 per cent), such as marriage and religious celebrations. Conventional and contemporary Indian secular travel, such as *milna* (visiting relatives and friends), was born out of familial needs for solidarity, particularly in times of crisis and/or solemnity. These occasions 'warrant' people to travel, either independently or with family members, to nearby or faraway locations of the extended family. Travelling and touring for intergenerational purposes, in terms of destination choice as well as journeying along with, is not uncommon. Therefore, it is appropriate to estimate that 'socializing' occupies over 60 per cent of travel purpose. This further corroborates the culture of 'collectivism' (Triandis, 1995)[4] that sustains the Indian ethos.

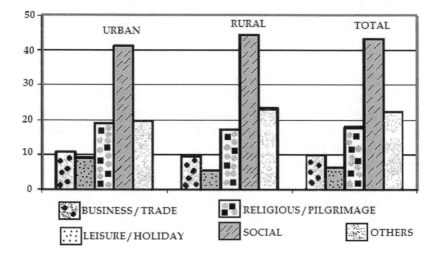

Figure 4.2 *Rural and urban distribution of day trips with the purpose of travel (percentage of all day trips)*

Source: NCAER (2004, p33)

Most travels by Indians exhibit a distinct *preponderance of the sacred*. Secular travel, in India, is known to be decreed by the Hindu gods themselves even before *tírthā yātrā* came into practice.[5] Secular[6] travellers do not observe the strict regimen of the *tírthā yātrā*. However, they are not completely devoid of some religious component. Here, the society serves as the monitoring agent to ensure civic propriety. Religion is seen as complementing the socio-cultural order of lifestyle, where jollity, festivities and celebrations were legitimized with some measure of sanctity. Apart from events of birth and death, other occasions such as marriages, festivals and socio-cultural obligations follow the Hindu astrological calendar, which has been very close to the farming cycle of the Indian agrarian society/population. Festive events such as *Holi*, *Diwali* and *Dusshera* are no less significant quasi-religious celebrations that warrant nation-wide travelling, touring and holiday-making. Numerous local, regional and national fairs and festivals influence the life and mobility of Indians since these occasions are recognized as national/restricted (regional) holidays. It is noteworthy that though traditional domestic tourism conformed to seasonal cycles, the larger ecological and sociological foundations informed the design and organization of the practices (as exemplified later in this chapter). Nature and its principles had so far provided the context for human action and endeavour. To this end, it informed, guided and mobilized individuals to bind all together into a 'cultural syndrome' (Triandis, 1995) by incorporating evaluative and behavioural dimensions. This is particularly true for most forms of secular tourism in the country.

Vernacular travels by Indians also seem to be *needs based* in terms of consumption and provision of facilities. Nonetheless, they are wholesome in relation to the hierarchy of meeting the varied needs of the masses. Clearly, domestic Indian tourism, by and large, is a typical example of 'social tourism' that has been made accessible by the masses – notwithstanding the near absence of promotional marketing. Notions of class, age, gender, income and occupation have had negligible impact on the travel behaviour and patterns of the vast majority.[7] Although these variables influence the decision-making process, they do not segregate the natives from holiday and leisure experiences. This is certainly a noteworthy feature of India's domestic tourism, which is aptly phrased as 'low-value, high-volume market' (Euromonitor, 2004).

Perhaps the most prominent cause of high tourist movements and activities is that the Indian mindset is visibly *religious and ritualistic* (Griswold, 1912; Singh, 1992). Traditionally, Indians have been a religious society and practising faith is an eminent aspect of living and lifestyle of almost all individuals and of all religious beliefs (see Table 4.2). Pilgrimages (*tírthā yātrā*) account for the second largest purpose of domestic travel and tour (see Table 4.3). Two-thirds of this traffic is concentrated in the states of Tamil Nadu, Andhra Pradesh, Uttar Pradesh, Maharashtra and Karnataka (see Table 4.4), owing to the concentration of some of the most prominent sacred sites of Hinduism. Likewise, Buddhists, Muslims and Christians (alongside Hindus), therefore, undertake journeys to shrines of their respective faiths at designated and undesignated times of the year. Buddhist shrines at Sarnath, Varanasi, Dharamshala and Bodhgaya; the *Dargah* of Muslim saints at Aligarh, Ajmer and Ahmedabad; the churches of Goa and Tamil Nadu; and the innumerable Hindu places of worship throughout India, particularly in the Himalaya[8] and along the coasts all exert an influence on the rural and urban masses for homage as well as a touristic 'gaze'. Bathing festivals, such as the *Kumbh Mela* (Allahabad), *Snan Yātrā* (Puri) and *Kartik Purnima* (Pushkar), draw mammoth gatherings to consecrated locales at designated occasions. The large turnout to these 'un-gated' religious and semi-religious events makes it almost impossible to gather statistical data. The *Kumbh Mela*, for example, is estimated to attract no less than 68 million devotees for a dip in the *sangam* (holy confluence point) of the River Ganges at Allahabad (in Uttar Pradesh).[9] This inflow, comprised largely of rural folks, makes this six-week event the largest in the world. In contrast to these informal pilgrimage centres is the highly organized pilgrim destination of Tirupati, whose pilgrim volume/flows and arrangements, besides wealth and assets, seem to surpass the orderly system of Disney World (Gladstone, 2005, p207).

Table 4.2 *Population distribution on the basis of religions*

Religions*	Population	Percentage
Hindus	827,578,868	80.5
Muslims	138,188,240	13.4
Christians	24,080,016	2.3
Sikhs	19,215,730	1.9
Buddhists	7,955,207	0.8
Jains	4,225,053	0.4
Other religions and persuasions	6,639,626	0.6
Religion not stated	727,588	0.1
Total	1,028,610,328	100.0

Note: * = excluding Jammu and Kashmir.

Source: GOI (2008)

Table 4.3 *Rural and urban distribution of Indian domestic tourists by origin and purpose (2002) (percentage)*

Purpose	Urban	Rural	All India
Business and trade	10.7	6.6	7.7
Leisure and holiday	8.7	5.0	6.0
Religious and pilgrimage	16.2	12.9	13.8
Social	52.9	61.0	58.9
Others	11.6	14.4	13.7
Total	100.0	100.0	100.0

Source: NCAER (undated)

To summarize, geographical and cultural features have, for centuries, informed the mind of the majority of Indian domestic travellers in making choices for destination and determining tourist behaviour patterns. Today, despite all the extraordinary shortcomings, accruing from the arrival of the influxes of visitors at various sacred and secular sites throughout India at designated times of the year, domestic tourism continues to record annual growth in tourist numbers. These tourists quite willingly make concessions on 'international' standards for the sake of an affordable visit. This aspect of demand by native tourists may be interpreted thus: *first*, the native tourist does not assign a high value to quality;

Table 4.4 *Relative ranking of states by purpose of visitation of Indian domestic tourists (2002–2003)*

Purpose	Rank				
	1	2	3	4	5
Business and trade	Karnataka (15.0)	Andhra Pradesh (12.7)	Uttar Pradesh (10.8)	Maharashtra (7.9)	Punjab (7.5)
Leisure and holiday	Karnataka (17.8)	Tamil Nadu (9.6)	Uttar Pradesh (9.2)	West Bengal (9.0)	Gujarat (8.6)
Religion and pilgrimage	Maharashtra (17.6)	Karnataka (13.6)	Uttar Pradesh (11.5)	Andhra Pradesh (9.7)	Tamil Nadu (9.3)
Social	Uttar Pradesh (13.1)	Maharashtra (11.0)	Madhya Pradesh (9.3)	Andhra Pradesh (9.3)	Rajasthan (8.4)
Others	Uttar Pradesh (12.1)	Maharashtra (10.7)	Karnataka (10.4)	Bihar (9.2)	Madhya Pradesh (7.1)
All trips	Uttar Pradesh (12.3)	Maharashtra (11.4)	Karnataka (10.0)	Andhra Pradesh (9.1)	Madhya Pradesh (7.3)

Source: NCAER (undated)

second, these tourists place 'purpose' of travel above all other facets of the travel experience – with the 'purpose' commonly being visiting/staying with kith and kin, a short respite from exasperating summer temperatures, family outing, pilgrimage, travelling and short trips outside their everyday environment in varying combinations; and, *third*, the majority of native tourists are more or less inconspicuous consumers during vacations as they are fairly moderate in their expectations of facilities and amenities. These socio-economic factors work discreetly to sustain the local economies, social fabric, cultural norms and natural landscapes of even the heavily visited locations.

The tradition of *tírthā yātrā*

Back of the beyond

Tírthā is essentially the oldest strand of Hindu tradition that represents a people's piety for nature and natural locations. The word *tírthā* entails multiple layers of meanings – all of which are indicative of sanctity and veneration. Hence, *tírthā* invariably translates into a place of pilgrimage.[10] The locations of *tírthā* have traditionally been at riverbanks and fords, notwithstanding their topographical lie. The River Ganga (commonly referred to as the Ganges River), for example, is a spatially diffused sacred landscape (Ramakrishnan, 2003) that constitutes high mountains, holy cities and fertile plains – all of which are made sacred by the ecological system that combines the different subsystems through which the river flows. Scholars, particularly geographers, refer to the physical and cultural landscape of India in terms of 'sacred geography' (Eck, 1981; Kaur, 1985), owing to the existence of innumerable *tírthā sthana* (pilgrim centres) of local, regional and national importance, which dot the entire country (see Figure 4.3). But while the entire continent may be perceived as a spatially diffused sacred landscape, certain sites hold utmost significance for the Hindu pilgrim (see Singh, 2006a, for a taxonomy of *tírthā*). To this end, seven locations are identified as most important (Kashi, Prayag, Mathura, Haridwar, Ayodhya, Dwarka and Kanchipuram), with as many as six of these being located in the north of India. Furthermore, sacred sites are not limited to riverbanks and fords alone – the repertoire of sacred spaces extends to mountain peaks, caves, forests, groves and swamps, besides river sources and confluences. Most such locations are beset in spectacularly scenic and ecologically fragile landscapes (Gangotri, Yamunotri and Nanda Devi, to name a few) that have been consecrated in order to conserve place attributes. Such pristine locations are sanctified to such an extent that no temples were originally localized. This process, identified as *sanskritization*, is understood to be a conscious act on the part of the proponents of the Hindu faith to convert scenic areas and natural resources into loci of devotion and to create a nature-based cultural identity for the nation. Non-aquatic *tírthā sthānā*, usually sanctified by mythological ascriptions and presided over by deities, are referred to as *dhāmā(s)* (abodes). There are four primary *dhāmā(s)* located at the four extremities of India – Badrinath (north), Jagannath Puri (east), Rameshvaram (south) and Dwarka (west). A subset of these four *dhāmā(s)*, alongside a hierarchy of other shrines (see Singh, 1977), has been identified in a smaller geographical space within the Indian Himalaya. These are referred to as the *Chhottā Chāār Dhāmā Tírthā* (smaller four abodes Himalayan pilgrimage), comprising the summits (of Gangotri, Yamunotri, Badrinath and Kedarnath) dedicated to four prominent deities. The *Chhottā Chāār Dhāmā Tírthā* is most popular among the Hindu pilgrims. Besides these primaries, many secondary *dhāmā(s)* are located throughout India. Likewise, several such sub-pilgrim routes establish spatially defined sacred landscapes and are duly recognized in a complex system of sacred regional hierarchy (see Sopher, 1968; Kaur, 1985; Ramakrishnan, 2003). Interestingly, for the north Indian Hindu pilgrims, the southernmost *tírthā* of Rameshvaram is the ideal distant target,

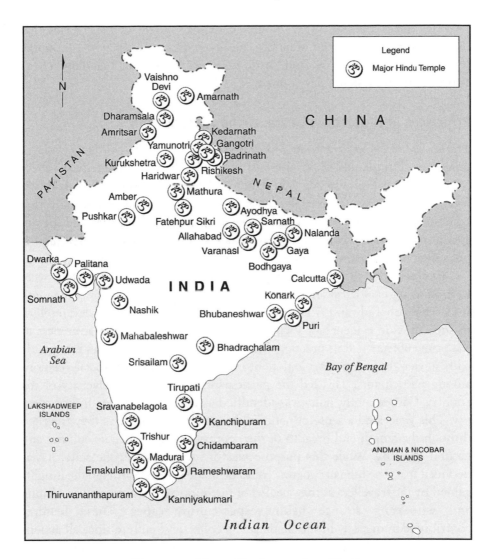

Figure 4.3 *Major Hindu temples of India*

Source: Shalini Singh

while the pilgrims from south India concede to the Himalayan shrines in the north as ideal pilgrimages (Bharathi, 1963).

To reiterate, financial status is, indeed, an indispensable and valuable ingredient of Hindu lifestyle doctrine. However, economics persists in a subservient place to both society and the physical environment. Such an approach leads to the endorsement of man–environment interdependency for the sustenance of life and, hence, sustainability. In asserting the social and contextual rootedness of Hindu theology, Tarakeshwar et al (2003) indicate the existence of a comprehensive, though complex, system of pilgrimages that deftly weaves the principles of nature, society and individuals – the continuing tradition of its structures and institutions testify to the ingenuity of an approach to the system's development.

Principles and practices of the *tírthā yātrā* system

The system of *tírthā yātrā* (sacred journeys) is understood to be highly evolved, unique and unparalleled in the history of civilization (Bharadwaj, 1973; Morinis, 1984; Kaur, 1985). Adi Shankaracharya (788 AD to 820 AD), the founder of this system is duly credited for his ingenious philosophy that combined socio-cultural, geographical and environmental values and ideologies into a unified whole. A brief overview of the tradition of *tírthā yātrā* is presented here to afford a glimpse of the complexities of its system.

Typically, the principles that guided the evolution of the system were formed along ecological and social parameters. In the context of *tírthā yātrā*, researches (Bharadwaj, 1973; Morinis, 1984; Kaur, 1985) on Himalayan pilgrimology provide evidence of social cohesion and environmental awareness as the prime objective of its practices. All provisions and programmes were made with a view to integrating and reinforcing or reproducing social relations among participants. This led the participants to realize the diversity of the country. Consequently, unity was identified as being integral for India's identity. This generated a sense of nationalism in the population as they travelled through the length and breadth of the country to experience its cultural and natural diversity. While this purpose was of importance to the state, it was deduced that true human progress could be made possible through the insights gained by the travellers as they availed of the opportunities of meeting, visiting and witnessing strange nature-scapes/culture-scapes. These features contributed immensely to the shaping of a collectivist culture since all actions were undertaken in the context of the collective good of mankind and nature.

On the identification of these enduring goals, the next dimension was to define the principles according to which the desired outcomes could be achieved. This required efficacious planning for harmonious man–environment integrity. Having traversed and studied the Himalayan resource base, religious philosophers, of the time prepared a detailed inventory of every geographic aspect of these bioregions. The inventory was then used for definite purposes – namely, to:

- determine the levels of sensitivity of these regions to withstanding human numbers and activities;
- identify and monitor the nature and type of visitor activities; and
- select and design appropriate channels for informing the visitor.

To these ends, religion was used as a medium to guide interactions among people and the environment. Deb et al (1997), Pandey (1996, 1998) and Tiwari et al (1998) consider that a religious attitude to nature and others makes it relatively easy to curb misuse or overuse of a resource base. On the contrary, the system was useful in cultivating a sense of reverence towards others and their environments. An obvious outcome of these measures was the moral/ethical behaviour of all participants, a spirit of altruism, enhancement of learning and wisdom, and the evolution of spirituality, which later contributed to the character of the nation as a whole, as well as the formation of national identity.

In order to actualize the above objectives, several subsystems were designed and put in place for the benefit of all participants of the system. First and foremost, the Hindu way of life was determined to follow four definite phases of living, within which the seniors (in the third and fourth phases) were obliged to undertake these journeys by way of a religious obligation. This entailed devoting oneself to performing 'prescribed' (alongside proscriptions) duties and rites for the benefit of all, such as giving alms to the poor, planting trees, contributing donations (cash/kind) to institutions established for social causes, making offerings at designated sites, paying fees for services received, engaging in religious discourses, and interacting with fellow pilgrims as well as local residents. Since this was an obligation that needed to be fulfilled by the citizens, the state patronized these practices by ensuring the security of the travellers and even subsidizing their sojourns. The state joined the religious institutions to set up an elaborate network of agents and agencies that would provide, monitor and facilitate the *tīrthā yātrā*. An indigenous banking system was made operational in order to grant loans and funds to people with limited resources. At the interactional dimension, norms and standards were set for appropriate behaviours and attitudes of the *yātrís* with respect to their interaction with compatriots and their use of environmental resources. By way of resource sustainability, definite formats were determined for the route to be followed, such as the localizing and periodizing places for commencing and concluding the journey, locations for rest and stay, duration of journey, and permissible activities such as singing, interacting, bathing, saying prayer and worshipping. All of these were determined after careful consideration of the geography and ecology of the locations. These norms were delivered to the *tīrthā yātrī* by way of mystical anecdotes and codes of conduct. The local community and the facilitators of services and provisions were equally bound by social norms, metaphorically expressed as *atithi devo bhava* (the guest as a god). These and many other dos and don'ts necessarily translated into 'best practices', given the local conditions of the times.

These subsystems laid the foundations for appropriate action expected of all participants of the *tīrthā yātrā*. Rules and regulations were also formulated to atone for violations, if and when they occurred. Speculating on the volume of these movements and amassing people at stipulated times and locations, flows were monitored and kept regulated between and within locations to avoid spatio-temporal overflows.

The most important aspect of these systems is monitoring and auditing, for which a subsystem was put in place. This subsystem comprised the *pandas* (priests), who were typically the custodians of the larger system as they were given charge to monitor flows and impacts at different levels of the system. The primary function of the *pandas* was to provide information and counsel to individuals on:

- when and how they should plan and undertake the journey;
- the numerous obligations while on the journey;
- the details of the destinations to be visited, alongside a defined purpose for each;
- codes of conduct; and
- the merits or demerits of adhering to or violating the norms and stipulations, respectively.

This was vital information that would prepare the *yātrī* – mentally, spiritually and physically – in this way conditioning the individual's attitude, perceptions and behaviour in order to ensure compliance. This counselling was rendered and reinforced at different times, pre-*yātrā*, through the *yātrā* and post-*yātrā* phase. *Pundits* and *pandas* were delegated the task of monitoring the individuals and their sojourns and were even authorized to pronounce penalties and rewards on a case-by-case basis.

Another critical function of the *panda* system was of documenting and reporting. Every *yātrī* was obliged to report his/her arrival, stay and departure besides furnishing details about family history. This information was used to keep a record of the traveller's background and also to ensure that every eligible member of the society undertakes the journey in fulfilment of his/her rights and duties. The reports also included all cases of benign and erroneous acts, as well as the borrowing and lending of money. This system was used to maintain law and order in society, in general, and during special events such as bathing festivals. Delivering discourses and engaging in prayers and meditation, which have also been part of the priests' duties, served the purpose of information exchange and knowledge enhancement.

Conclusively, *tīrthā yātrā* systems had been successful in yielding the envisaged benefits – namely, formation of national identity; social integration; societal and individual well-being and progress; strengthening of human values through ethics; affirmation of and respect for man–environment synergy; and principles of living and lifestyle. Religion was gainfully utilized as an indispensable ingredient to restrain the negatives of mass movements to sensitive environments, encourage native travel and encase a grand system that was designed to generate the common good for generations. The tradition has thus continued and contributed to the ethos of Hindus in India. Changing times and ways of thinking have, nonetheless, reduced the practices to symbolic rituals. In contemporary times, therefore, the age-old system of Hindu pilgrimages can be considered to be quite divorced from its original purpose and approach.

Analysing current practices: Critical observations

The tradition of *tīrthā yātrās* continues to remain an integral aspect of the dogma-driven (religion-driven) masses. Nevertheless, the current approaches to its practice by the pilgrims and its agencies, in conjunction with prevailing ideological shifts, have begun to interfere and disrupt the wholesomeness of the system's foundations. Apparently, the very tenets that have nourished the system, through the centuries, seem to be instrumental in defiling it. The three primary and interrelated concerns associated with the desecration include accessibility and growth, an increasing thrust towards tourism (secularization) and ritualism.

Enhanced accessibility and growth

India's large population is a fair explanation for *en mass* exoduses and the concentration of pilgrims and visitors at its sacred sites. Not only has there been an increase in its population size; but the twin factors of increased accessibility and economic increments have enhanced the mobility of increasing proportions of the population. This has subsequently been reflected in the demands being placed on resources and amenities. In a recent study on the sacred complex of Tirumala-Tirupati, a popular pilgrimage centre in south India, Shinde (2007) documents the significance of changing scale, frequency and character of pilgrim visitation to the sacred temple and its environs.

In addition, government patronage of, rather than direct involvement in, the organization and facilitation of pilgrim movements in various parts of the country is an unmistakable factor that has spurred a growth in pilgrim activity.[11] Large-scale investments, human and capital, have to be deployed to provide for clean-up and to restore the bathing site at Prayaga (Allahabad), where crowds of millions arrive at a particular time of the year.

Doron's study (2005), on pilgrims and pilgrimage in Varanasi corroborates the 'marked' expansion of pilgrim movements since the advent of railroads and improvements in communication networks across the continent. More pertinently, these modern transportation networks have not changed, modified or 'rearranged' the pilgrimage map of India; instead, all places of significance have been provided with linkages to population concentrations (Sopher, 1968). Even if one were to argue that most Hindu pilgrimages are seasonal migrations, the growth in numbers of both pilgrims and tourist visitations can scarcely mitigate the effects of the use of finite natural and improvised resources in a defined time period. Such advancements are, perhaps, responsible for relegating the traditional pilgrimage phenomenon into a package-tour mode of operation and performance (see Doron, 2005; Gladstone, 2005).

Increasing secularization

Recent past trends in the attitude and interactions of pilgrims with the pilgrimage settings are indicative of sacrilege. Pilgrims are known to increasingly adopt the 'package-tour' model of travelling and sightseeing that combines secular visitations with an obligatory obeisance or two (Gladstone, 2005; Shinde, 2008). In doing so, the pilgrims resemble tourists in their modes of participation. India's socially mobile upper-middle class arrive at these sites more for a visit than for pilgrimage. Although the vernacular term for 'seeing' (*darshana*) as a pilgrim or as a visitors would apply equally to both, some differences are visible. Secular-minded visitors will invariably pay their obeisance to the sacred, but may not necessarily participate as a pilgrim in terms of their interactions with service providers, length of stay, need for comfort and ease, onsite performance of rites and activities, use of services and facilities, or other related prescriptions. They may choose to maintain a studied distance from the more enthused engagements. Changes in the conduct of the visitors/pilgrims have also effected alterations in the approach and conduct of the service providers, as well as the religious institutions that are responsible for the sites and the experience of the sacred (Doron, 2005; Shinde, 2007). Owing to the enmeshing of sacred and secular modes of engagement, as previously discussed, the pilgrim economy and the tourism economy are quite blended (Gladstone, 2005). Hence, in recognition of the economic value of visitors, the public sector and the autonomous religious institutions are explicitly eager to woo the domestic tourist and the pilgrim. To match this, the religious institutions offer special privileges to votaries with paying prowess (see Narayanan, 1997, 2001).

At the secular front, having subscribed to a capitalistic mode of 'development' during the 1990s, the Indian government has begun to consciously engage in marketing efforts (MARCH, 2006). In this regard, the urban middle/upper class (some 300 million people) are a potential market for the promotion of a consumer culture due to the increasing levels of incomes at this segment of the urban population. Rising income levels and overt publicity and promotion schemes have legitimized (tourism) consumerism significantly. Tourism practices of the relatively higher income groups, such as the urbane upper-middle and the upper classes of the society, are distinct from the tourism practices of the masses. The 'class consciousness' of the upper-middle and upper classes compels them to seek out lesser-known pleasure peripheries and to avail of elitist amenities pertaining to high-risk adventure sports, shopping, fine dinning, self-drive travels and the like. Since most pilgrim sites are located in scenic landscapes – often fragile ecosystems – the tourist-pilgrim avails of the twin benefit of homage and holiday in the one trip (see Figure 4.4). To facilitate movement (pilgrim and tourist), throughout India, turnkey projects, such as the construction of a grand national highway connecting the entire country, airport construction and upgrades are making much headway in the country. Accompanying projects such as privatization of public enterprises – namely, Air India – and port facilities; liberalization in the accommodation (especially resort development), retail travel and fast-food sectors; alongside encouraging foreign direct investments in tourism development and management undertakings (see Singh, 2008) are noticeable endeavours towards the commercialization of *yātrā* and *ghumna* or *deshatan*. Apparently, traditional ideologies of purposeful conservatism and wholesome progress are being systematically replaced by modernist (un-progressive) views of 'development' and growth. It is contended that current trends appear to be a 'thrust' for material benefits on the indigeneity of India's ethos over community values, thereby driving a wedge of income-based identity among the natives. Ironically, native leisure travel and holidaying in India is (d)evolving from the 'right of all' to the 'privilege of the few' as the country gradually aligns itself with global trends.

Ritualistic reductionism

As previously stated, many pilgrims to India's sacred sites have a modified (touristic) mode of engagement with the sacred. The relative proportion of these religious tourists is definitely smaller than those whose modes of engagement adhere closely with the prescriptions of the *tírthā yātrā* system of yore. Hence, most pilgrims believe in achieving merit through the performance of rites, while few may seek an awakening through conscientious performance of the same (see Singh and Singh, 2009). Scholars, Indian in particular, have often extolled the virtues of rituals of pilgrims and pilgrimages (Narayanan, 1997, 2001; Gupta, 1999; Ramakrishnan, 2003; Singh, 2004, 2006a, to name but a few), while others (usually Western) have commented on the ritualized religiosity of Hindu pilgrims (Sopher, 1968; Eck, 1981, 1985; Tomalin, 2004; Doron, 2005).

In commenting on the characteristics of Hinduism, Griswold (1912, p164) noted that Hindu religiosity is given to deifying 'whatever is' with an uncritical ('syncretic') religious point of view in all affairs of life. These features point to a tendency for blind-sighted practice of faith, which is quite the practice among

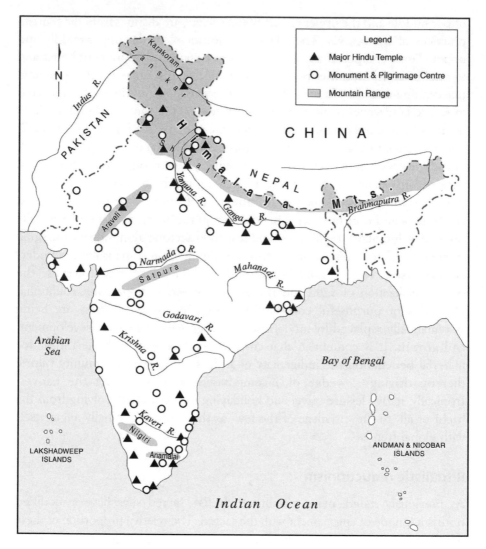

Figure 4.4 *India: Hindu pilgrim and tourist places*

Source: Shalini Singh

the masses. Over the centuries of *tírthā yātrā* practices, ritualization has, indeed, emerged as a strong causal factor, displacing spirituality, which had guided and guarded resource use and the Indian value system for centuries (Dumont, cited in van der Veer, 2001). This is recognized as an issue because of the fact that an increasing number of pilgrims perform the prescriptions with an acute syncreti- cism. Such an uncritical approach to observances obscures the essence of the purpose of the performance or the true religion itself.[12] Nonetheless, those who feel the benefits of their observances consider them to be supererogatory and rebuff such instructions. Thus, it is not so much the religious prescription for spiritual merit that drives religious movements in the country, but the culture-specific custom of going to and/or performing prescribed rites at sanctified places to affirm their own perception of religiosity.

Having studied the relationship between religion and environmental conservation in India, Tomalin (2002, 2004) claims that those religions that recognize bio-divinity or base their religious beliefs on nature and its phenomena are distinct from religions (typically new-age belief systems) that are founded on religious environmentalism as a deliberate practice. The major points of contradiction between the two encompass the dichotomy of old–new, east–west and *archaic religiosity–pragmatic modernity*. In doing so, Tomalin has not only separated the secular from sacred, but also deconsecrated nation-wide grassroots movements in India (see Karan, 1994). Tomalin's observation may be well founded in view of a comprehensive reflection on concerns regarding the growth of religiosity alongside the deterioration of conscientiousness essential to the practice of the rituals of *tírthā yātrā*. Apparently, most Hindu pilgrims, having deified nature and its endowments, have absolved themselves of their responsibility towards their 'centre' of belief altogether (Narayanan, 2001). For instance, the millions of pilgrims who gain 'purification' through their ritual of journeying to and bathing in the holy waters of River Ganga, at the holy cities of Prayaga (currently Allahabad) and Varanasi (traditionally *Kashi*), blatantly refuse to accept that the river could ever be polluted by their ritual or that the river needs to be cleansed of the impurities (substance) cast away by its devotees. In the minds of the pilgrims, the river cleanses them of their 'sins' and it is with this belief that they perform the ritual of taking a bath in its ('divine') water and that the hallowed river is beyond human contamination or sacrilege. Bathing is primarily perceived as the agency or physical medium through which the embodied sin is purged and is a pious act in and of itself. This perception is extraordinarily heightened such that it transcends the physicality of the body, the waters and the act. Hence, the notion of sullied or polluted water/space is denounced as petty worldliness (informal communications with several local boatmen and pilgrims at the *ghats* (riverbank) of Banaras/Varanasi during the author's visits to the location in July 2006).

Few recent studies (Chopra et al, 1997; Manoharan et al, 1998; Maharana et al, 2000), at various sacred locations in India, have documented evidence illustrating that pilgrims, including domestic tourists, tend to be scarcely forthcoming (in terms of willingness-to-pay initiative as a way of returning to nature) for the maintenance and conservation of environmental sanctity. In the pilgrim's perception, the environment does not need managing – it is divinely endowed (actually 'the divine' personified) to restore itself (informal communications with several local boatmen and pilgrims, July 2006). Here is a serious and genuine conflict between moral and religious interests, as well as spiritual merit and sanctimonious obligation. The contradiction raises a major question: 'Can the tenets of nature-(based) religions be juxtaposed with those of religious environmentalism in order to engender environmental sensibility among the masses?' If yes, then, how may the two be juxtaposed such that the *purposive piety* (conscious goodness) of the scientific and the sacred is realized through the agency of pilgrimage?

Evolving tírthā rituals

... it is only spiritual faith that can make men work and enable them to find pleasure in working for the common weal.
(Rajagopalachari, 1953)

Present-day secular tourism pursuits in India, on the other hand, are an assemblage of 'vernacular' culture (Jackson, cited in De Bres, 1996) and 'popular' culture (Glassie, cited in De Bres, 1996).[13] The opposing natures of the vernacular system of *tírthā, yātrā, milna* and *ghumna* and a Western conceptualization of commerce-driven tourism (*paryatan*) are disturbing. Kaur's study on *Himalayan Pilgrimages and the New Tourism* (1985) alludes to the antithesis of the two inasmuch as the latter is typified by Western ideologies of economic growth and the former is representative of collectivist values of the east (Hofstede, 1983). Contemporary tourism (*paryatan*), founded on the principles of modernist views of capitalism, has crept into and mingled with these vernacular practices. As a result of this, technically, tourism (*paryatan*) has come to be interpreted in the plural contexts of the economic culture of the West and the cultural economy of the East (see, for example, Joseph and Kavoori, 2001).

There is no doubt that the age-old rituals of Hindu *tírthā yātrā* have added to the environmental woes of India. Equally pertinent is the fact that rendering *sanskritized* spaces sacred is a cause for concern for scientists, environmentalists, pilgrims and religious institutions – all of whom are potential stakeholders in the scheme of Hindu *tírthā yātrā* and religious tourism. Elsewhere in the world, secular tourism has given rise to new social and environmental movements to respond to the global issues of environmental and cultural deterioration. Similar initiatives have also been introduced in India by international tourists via volunteering holidays. Although domestic tourists in India have yet to warm to the notion of serious/responsible leisure, it is doubtful if the idea of environmental pilgrimages (Singh, 2006b) will resonate with the masses, who perceive the environment rather differently. In this regard, Tomalin's (2004) assertion about religious environmentalism being separate from environmental religiosity holds sway. Nonetheless, Tomalin's analysis also throws light on the pragmatic inclinations of Hindu religious philosophy. It is this pragmatic dynamism of the Hindu mindset that may afford opportunities for the enmeshing of age-old rituals with new-age movements. Mazumdar and Mazumdar (2004) confirm that rituals of place can play a significant role in the 'internalization' process, as rituals serve as 'reminders', as well as sharpen the sense of the sacred while being involved.

Some illustrations of such pragmatism are being reflected in the rituals of the pilgrims at select locations. Many temples (see Narayanan, 1997, 2001; Shinde, 2007) associated with the *tírthā yātrā* tradition have formed religious organizations whose primary agenda is to undertake definitive action to ameliorate location-specific environmental issues. In pursuance of these agendas, several of them have elected to partner with municipal services and/or state forest departments to support and facilitate their functioning, while others have mobilized pilgrims and visitors to perform *seva* (selfless service) as an act of faith/worship. The term *seva* implies humanitarian service by way of active devotion and can be undertaken in various ways – clean-up drives, monitoring activities, assisting with raising plant nurseries, afforestation programmes, awareness activities through the development of 'sacred plants resort', alongside public relations initiatives for ecology consciousness. Thus, the pilgrims devoutly plant saplings, assist in cleaning up, raise plant nurseries for afforestation programmes, aid in awareness campaigns, and volunteer in various conservation schemes of the temples as a way to earn merit and appease their deity. In this way, religious authorities of specific temples have been innovative in converting stale rituals into acts of meaningful devotion.

In conclusion, then, sacred landscapes are human-designated spaces for rituals of geo-piety, where consciousness is afforded an opportunity to exalt people–planet symbiosis. Therefore, as long as the sense of reverence can be maintained, and their capacity for sacrifice and a love for rituals abides in the Hindu way of thinking, it could be a matter of time and patience before the hordes ritualize environment-friendly *tírthā*.

Acknowledgements

The author gratefully acknowledges permission to excerpt material from a previously published article (in *Tourism Recreation Research*, 2004, vol 29, no 2, pp35–46), granted by Professor. T. V. Singh, editor-in-chief, for inclusion in this work.

Notes

1   It is presumed that NRIs constitute a significant part of the VFR market; however, since this chapter focuses on the tourism system of the country, it is important to consider the larger masses of resident population for our analysis of the tourism system.

2   '*Ghumna*' literally means roaming or wandering. The term implies some measure of purposelessness. The 'real' purpose of travel and tourism, in the conventional (Indian) context, would translate into serious pursuits such as pilgrimages and visiting friends and relatives for socially legitimate reasons. In the absence of such serious pursuits, *ghumna* is loosely (and colloquially) synonymous with tourism.

3   *Puja* specials during *Dusshera* and summer specials during May to July.

4   Collectivism is defined as 'a social pattern consisting of closely linked individuals who see themselves as parts of one or more collectives (family, co-workers, tribe, nation); are primarily motivated by the norms of, and duties imposed by, those collectives; are willing to give priority to the goals of these collectives over their own personal goals; and emphasize their connectedness to the members of these collectives' (Triandis, 1995, p2).

5   God Indra's advice to King Harishchandra is recorded; thus, 'there is no happiness for the person who does not travel; living amongst men, even the best man becomes a sinner; for Indra is the traveller's friend. Hence travel!' (*Aitareya Brahmana*, 1920, vol VII, p15).

6   The term *social* usually implies 'secular' in common parlance. The word *secular* (in the context of India) does not imply the same meaning as it has in the West, where the word is restricted to rationalism and the sole motive of the modern state. In truth, in the Indian context, it is understood to be compatible with faith (see Madan, 2001, p141).

7   While poverty may be regarded as an exclusionary factor, there is evidence of indebtedness, especially among the most deprived who will find the financial means to fulfil a pilgrimage or even a visitation to friends and relatives.

8   The Indian Himalayas are studded by the most prominent Hindu shrines that are high in the hierarchy of sanctity and, thence, relevance. Singh (1977, p49) has mapped out the layout of the five Prayagas (Devprayaga, Rudraprayaga, Karnaprayaga, Nandaprayaga and Vishnuprayaga), the five Kedars (Kedarnath, Madhmaheshwar, Tungnath, Rudranath and Kalpeshwar) and the five Badris (Badrinath, Dhyan Badri, Yog Badri, Bhavishya Badri and Narasingh Badri).

9   Although the *Kumbh Mela* occurs on a very grand scale every 12 years, the bathing ritual is observed every 6 years as the *Ardh Kumbh Mela*, and also annually at the same time in the Hindu calendar year on a lesser magnitude.

10 See Eck (1981) for the multiple meanings of Hindu *tírthā*; the tantric term for the same is *pithā*, which literally means 'seat' or centre of learning.

11 The annual *yātrā* to Amarnath Cave (4270m above sea level) is organized by the state government during the month of July and August. With a view to work out and finalize different arrangements, a series of core meetings are held between the state and central governments. Among other issues connected with this *yātrā*, a decision has been taken to regulate the *yātrā* traffic within a prescribed daily ceiling, on specific routes. Detailed information with regard to *yātrā*, including other related issues such as dos and don'ts, and installation of free *langers* (free kitchen) by non-governmental organizations (NGOs) is publicized by the Tourism Department in leading national dailies as well as local newspapers, as well as from all the tourism offices located within and outside the state (Amar Nath Ji yātrā,

http://kashmirdivision.nic.in/about/services/amrYātrā.htm, accessed 22 July 2008).

12 Hindu schools of thought have often minimized the importance of pilgrimages in the face of 'true devotion' and instructed people to avoid outward religious observances as redundant and superfluous (*Bombay Gazetteer*, vol XXII, p105).

13 Vernacular culture is described as traditional or homemade practices that define a society/community. It portrays the endogenous ingenuity of a social group and is steeped in tradition. Whereas popular culture is relatively more amicable to frequent temporal changes, it is considerably more widespread than vernacular culture.

References

Aitareya Brahmana (1920) *Rigveda Brahmanas* (translated from original Sanskrit by A. B. Keith), vol VII, Harvard University Press, Cambridge, MA

Bharadwaj, S. M. (1973) *Hindu Places of Pilgrimages in India*, Thompson Press Ltd, New Delhi, India

Bharathi, A. (1963) 'Pilgrimage in Indian tradition', *History of Religions*, vol 3, no 1, pp135–167

Chopra, K., Chauhan, M., Sharma, S. and Sangeeta, N. (1997) *Economic Valuation of Biodiversity: A Case Study of Keoladeo National Park, Bharatpur*, Report, Part II, Institute of Economic Growth, New Delhi, India

De Bres, K. (1996) 'Defining vernacular tourism', *Annals of Tourism Research*, vol 23, no 4, pp945–948

Deb, D., Deuti, K. and Malhotra, K. C. (1997) 'Sacred grove relics as bird refugia', *Current Science*, vol 73, pp815–817

Doron, A. (2005) 'Encountering the "other": Pilgrims, tourists and boatmen in the City of Varanasi', *The Australian Journal of Anthropology*, vol 16, no 2, pp157–178

Eck, D. L. (1981) 'India's "tirthas": "Crossings" in sacred geography', *History of Religions*, vol 20, no 4, pp323–344

Eck, D. L. (1985) 'Banaras: Cosmos and paradise in the Hindu imagination', *Contributions to Indian Sociology*, vol 19, no 1, pp41–55

Euromonitor (2004) *Euromonitor Travel and Tourism in India – Executive Summary*, www.euromonitor.com, accessed 15 January 2004

Gladstone, D. L. (2005) *From Pilgrimage to Package Tour – Travel and Tourism in the Third World*, Routledge, New York, NY

GOI (2007) *Incredible India 2007: Top 10 States/UTS of India in Domestic Tourist Visits in 2006*, Market Research Division, Ministry of Tourism, Government of India, North Delhi

GOI (2008) 'Census data 2001: India at a glance and religious composition', www.censusindia.net, accessed June 2008

Griswold, H. D. (1912) 'Some characteristics of Hinduism as a religion', *The Biblical World*, vol 40, no 3, pp163–172

Gupta, V. (1999) 'Sustainable tourism: Learning from Indian religious traditions', *International Journal of Contemporary Hospitality Management*, vol 11, no 2/3, pp91–95

Hofstede, G. (1983) 'Dimensions of national cultures in fifty countries and three regions', in J. B. Deregowski, S. Dziurawiec and R. C. Annis (eds) *Explications in Cross-Cultural Psychology*, Swets Zeitlinger, Lisse, The Netherlands, pp335–355

India Stats (2003a) 'Tourist statistics 2001', Ministry of Tourism and Culture, Government of India, statistics dated 15 December 2003, www.indiastat.com, accessed 2 February 2004

India Stats (2003b) 'State-wise Domestic Tourist Visits in India (1997 to 2003)', www.indiastat.com, accessed 2 February 2004

Joseph, C. A. and Kavoori, A. P. (2001) 'Mediated resistance – Tourism and the host community', *Annals of Tourism Research*, vol 28, no 4, pp998–1009

Karan, P. P. (1994) 'Environmental movements in India', *Geographical Review*, vol 84, no1, pp32–41

Kaur, J. (1985) *Himalayan Pilgrimages and the New Tourism*, Himalayan Books, New Delhi, India

Madan, G. R. (1990) *Social Welfare and Security*, Vivek Prakashan, New Delhi, India

Madan, T. N. (2001) 'Religion in India', *Daedalus*, vol 130, no 4, p141

Maharana, I., Rai, S. C. and Sharma, E. (2000) 'Valuing ecotourism in a sacred lake of the Sikkim Himalaya, India', *Environmental Conservation*, vol 27, no 3, pp269–277

Manoharan, T. R., Muraleedharan, P. K. and Anitha, V. (1998) 'Economic valuation of non-market benefits', in P. K. Muraleedharan, K. K. Subramanianan and P. P. Pillai (eds) *Basic Readings in Forest Economics*, Kerala Forest Research Institute, Peechi, India, pp77–95

MARCH (2006) *Study on Evaluation of the Scheme Domestic Promotion and Publicity including Hospitality (DPPH)*, Submitted to Ministry of Tourism, Government of India, New Delhi, MARCH Marketing Consultancy and Research, Hyderabad, India

Mazumdar, S. and Mazumdar, S. (2004) 'Religion and place attachment: A study of sacred places', *Journal of Environmental Psychology*, vol 24, pp385–397

Ministry of Tourism (2006) *India Tourism Statistics 2005*, Market Research Division, Ministry of Tourism, Government of India, New Delhi, India

Ministry of Tourism (2008) *Annual Report 2007–08*, Ministry of Tourism, Government of India, New Delhi, India

Morinis, E. A. (1984) *Pilgrimages in the Hindu Tradition: A Case Study of West Bengal*, Oxford University Press, New Delhi, India

Mullatti, L. (1995) 'Families in India: Beliefs and realities', *Journal of Comparative Family Studies*, vol 26, no 1, pp11–25

Narayanan, V. (1997) '"One tree is equal to ten sons": Hindu responses to the problems of ecology, population and consumption', *Journal of American Academy of Religion*, vol 65, no 2, pp291–332

Narayanan, V. (2001) 'Water, wood and wisdom: Ecological perspectives from Hindu traditions', *In Daedalus*, vol 130, no 4, pp179–206

NCAER (undated) 'Domestic tourism survey 2002–03', National Council of Applied Economic Research, New Delhi, www.tourism.gov.in/survey/dtsurvey.pdf, accessed 18 August 2008

NCAER (2004) *Domestic Tourism – A Feasibility Study 2002–03*, Sponsored by Ministry of Tourism and Culture, NCAER, New Delhi, India

Pandey, D. N. (1996) *Beyond Vanishing Woods: Participatory Survival Options for Wildlife, Forests and People*, CSD and Himanshu, Mussoorie/New Delhi/Udaipur, India

Pandey, D. N. (1998) *Ethnoforestry: Local Knowledge for Sustainable Forestry and Livelihood Security*, Himanshu/AFN, New Delhi, India

Rajagopalachari, C. (1953) quoted in *Indian Express*, 1 June

Ramakrishnan, P. S. (2003) 'The sacred Ganga river-based cultural landscape', *Museum International*, vol 55, no 2, pp7–17

Shinde, K. (2007) 'Pilgrimage and the environment: Challenges in a pilgrimage centre', *Current Issues in Tourism*, vol 10, no 4, pp343–365

Shinde, K. (2008) 'Religious tourism: Exploring a new form of sacred journey in north India', in J. Cochrane (ed) *Asian Tourism Growth and Change*, Elsevier, Oxford, UK, pp245–257

Simhadri, Y. C. (1989) *Youth in the Contemporary World*, Mittal Publications, New Delhi, India

Singh, R. P. B. (2006a) 'Pilgrimage in Hinduism: Historical context and modern perspectives', in D. J. Timothy and D. H. Olsen (eds) *Tourism, Religion and Spiritual Journeys*, CABI, Oxon, UK, pp220–236

Singh, S. (2006b) 'Secular pilgrimages and sacred tourism in the Indian Himalayas', *GeoJournal*, vol 64, pp215–223

Singh, S. (2004) 'India's domestic tourism: Chaos/crisis/challenge', *Tourism Recreation Research*, vol 29, no 2, pp35–46

Singh, S. (2008) 'Destination development dilemma: Case of Manali in Himachal Himalaya', *International Journal of Tourism Management*, vol 29, pp1152–1156

Singh, S. and Singh, T. V. (2009) 'Aesthetic pleasures: Contemplating spiritual tourism', in J. Tribe (ed) *Philosophical Issues in Tourism*, Channelview Publications, UK

Singh, T. V. (1977) 'Opening Garhawal for tourism: Towards research-based planned development', *The Himalaya*, vol 1, no 1, pp44–52

Singh, T. V. (1992) 'Development of tourism in the Himalayan environment: The problem of sustainability', *IE/PAC, UNEP*, vol 15, no 3/4, pp22–27

Sopher, D. E. (1968) 'Pilgrim circulation in Gujarat', *Geographical Review*, vol 58, no 3, pp392–425

Tarakeshwar, N., Pargament, K. I. and Mahoney, A. (2003) 'Measures of Hindu pathways: Development and preliminary evidence of reliability and validity', *Cultural Diversity and Ethnic Minority Psychology*, vol 9, no 4, pp316–332

Tiwari, B. K., Barik, S. K. and Tripathi, R. S. (1998) 'Biodiversity value, status, and strategies for conservation of sacred groves of Meghalaya, India', *Ecosystem Health*, vol 4, pp20–32

Tomalin, E. (2002) 'The limitations of religious environmentalism for India', *Worldviews*, vol 6, pp12–30

Tomalin, E. (2004) 'Bio-divinity and biodiversity: Perspectives on religion and environmental conservation in India', *Numen*, vol 51, pp265–295

Triandis, H. C. (1995) *Individualism and Collectivism*, Westview Press, Boulder, CO

van der Veer, P. (2001) *Imperial Encounters: Religion and Modernity in India and Britain*, Princeton University Press, NJ

5

From Community to Holiday Camps: The Emergence of a Tourist Economy in Mongolia

Amartuvshin Dorjsuren

Introduction

Domestic tourism in Mongolia is less researched and largely overshadowed by research on international tourism (JICA, 1998; TASIS, 1998; MRTT, 2005). By way of reliable data, only one domestic tourism survey, conducted by the Ministry of Road, Transport and Tourism (MRTT) in 2004, is available. Nonetheless, the absence of studies on the country's domestic travellers and holiday-makers does not mean that Mongolians are oblivious to holiday travels and visitations in their own country. On the contrary, domestic tourism in Mongolia is an increasingly popular activity that most certainly affects the country's economy, environment and society.

This chapter presents the growth of domestic tourism in Mongolia during the communist or socialist period (1921 to 1990). Contemporary trends in native tourism are then examined with reference to political, economic, cultural and geographical factors. The second half of the chapter empirically explores the positive and negative consequences of increasing domestic tourism in Mongolia. To this end, it is useful to delve into the tourism potential of the country for its natives.

Leisure/holiday/travel potential of Mongolia

Country's background

Sandwiched between Russia and China, Mongolia occupies 1,566,000km² and is almost three times the size of France (see Figure 5.1). However, it is inhabited by slightly more than 2.7 million people, of whom 38 per cent live in the

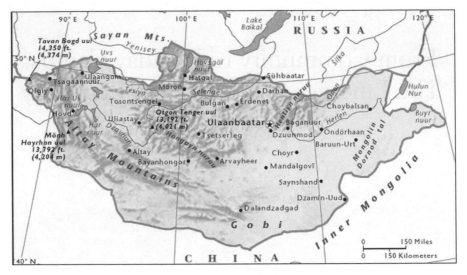

Figure 5.1 *Map of Mongolia*

Source: adapted from map supplied by Department of Socioeconomic Geography and Tourism at the National University of Mongolia

capital city of Ulaanbaatar (Mongolian National Statistical Office, 2008a). Geographically, Mongolia stretches over the Gobi Desert in the south and the Siberian taiga with lush forests, lakes and rivers in the north, while towering Altai (4374m) and Khangai (4021m) mountain ranges dominate in western and central Mongolia, respectively. Eastern Mongolia is predominantly flat steppes, with the lowest altitude of 560m in the country. The climate of the country is continental: winters (November to February) are cold with average temperatures range between –20°C and –25°C. In January, temperatures sometimes drop below –45°C with abolsute minimum drops below –57°C; but stable clear days dominate. Springs and autumns are windy, and strong dust storms occur that can commonly reach 28 metres per second. Summers (May to August) are warm, with light breezes and patchy showers. July is the warmest month, with the average air temperature around +20°C to +25°C and its maximum reaches +48°C. The precipitation distribution in the area depends greatly on the relief and landscape; it is 650mm in the mountainous areas and 55mm in the desert regions a year. There are long rivers in the northern, western and eastern parts of the country, but many small springs, oases and wells are a major water supply for people and animals in the Gobi region (Mongolian Academy of Science, 1990).

Mongolia experienced extensive political, economic and socio-cultural changes during socialism, which covers the period from 1921 to 1990. Following the revolution in 1921, Mongolia gained independence and became the first Asian nation to adopt communism with the socialist ideology. The communist government of Mongolia introduced an extensive modernization plan, including a free healthcare and a free educational system, as well as a five-yearly industrialization plan. The national alphabet was also replaced by Cyrillic in 1941. Schools and hospitals were established in almost every village since the 1920s. At the beginning of the 1940s, Mongolia had the first modern university.

Development of modern industries resulted in rapid urbanization in Mongolia during socialism. Although Mongolia had only three major towns – Orgoo, Uliastai and Hovd before the revolution in the 1920s (Badarch et al, 2002) – a number of new cities were established, including Erdenet and Darkhan, which eventually emerged as the two largest cities after Ulaanbaatar. Urbanization and modernization took place at the same time, and a large proportion of traditional society settled in newly formed towns followed by changes in rural traditional life. A complete nationalization of private livestock was undertaken in 1958/1959 and collectives were established (Bold, 1996). As the communist government did not favour private property, nomadic families were made to collectivize their private property, which consisted largely of live-stock. This took place in order to fulfil the social norm of equality and to provide raw materials to the state-owned new industries. The state was in charge of all aspects of society to the extent that even the nomads were instructed on which animals to herd, and when and where to migrate.

Socialism and domestic tourism

Travelling habits during the socialist period were also distinctive because of extensive interventions by the government. Holidays and recreational activity were an integral part of the extensive state healthcare system in Mongolia. As a consequence, recreation and excursion became popular among the urban population and youth organizations – namely, the Association of Mongolian Revolutionary Youth (AMRY). Recreation is widely understood as free fun time in holiday camps and outdoors. Major recreational activities among most Mongolians consisted of group of colleagues, friends and relatives driving to natural scenic spots where they could enjoy themselves, play different sports and card games, set up traditional barbecues, sing along and sip vodka. Excursions, mostly short and organized outdoor tours, are largely amongst student groups and schoolchildren as a means of gaining knowledge about wildlife and to practise physical education.

Thus, holiday camps were established in order to provide recreational and holiday facilities for the expanding urban population under a centrally planned economy. Those who worked for state-run organizations, including the nomadic herders, would travel as a group to holiday and recreational camps.

The types of holiday centres in Mongolia comprise spas and sanatoria, holiday camps and children's camps. Geographically, children's camps and holiday camps are located near major population centres. In contrast, spas and sanatoria are usually located at curative hot and cold mineral springs and natural resources that are relatively distant from the populous centres. Before the 1990s, there were 113 spas and sanatoria, holiday camps and children's camps (Mongolian Academy of Science, 1990, p131). The number of holiday-makers who visited these spas and sanatoria and holiday camps increased 2.8-fold and 8.3-fold, respectively, during the period of 1960 to 1984. There were a number of year-round spas and sanatoria, with a capacity of more than 500 beds – namely, Khujirt, Otgontenger, Orgil, Janchivlan, Gurvannuur and Ar Janchivlan, where visitors could receive various mineral and physical treatments in scenic landscapes (see Table 5.1). The central part of Mongolia, including the surrounding areas of Ulaanbaatar, had the maximum number of these facilities (totalling 79), while western and eastern Mongolia had 19 and 14 leisure facilities, respectively.

Almost half of all holiday camps were exclusively for children. These camps were for schoolchildren during their summer holiday – mainly between June and August. School groups usually spend 14 days at the camp, where they participate in various themed, cultural (e.g. talent competitions, including singing, dancing and creative writing), sporting and educational activities. It is clear that children's camps served as holiday centres for children to make friends and learn something new or to uncover their talents, as they continue to do today (see Table 5.1).

The location of holiday camps in scenic landscapes with fresh air and wildlife mainly attracts domestic holiday-makers with busy working hours who live in congested urban areas. When winter approaches (November to February), urban residents travel as day visitors to skiing centres near Ulaanbaatar, Erdenet and Darkhan. Skiing and sledging were particularly popular among urban residents and Khandgait was one of the most-visited skiing centres outside Ulaanbaatar (as it still is today).

Naadam, a nationwide festival in July that takes place in every district level, involving the three sports of horse racing, archery and wrestling, is one of the major holiday seasons when most Mongolians (including nomads, school friends and relatives) involve themselves in extensive travel activities. Nomads train racehorses and travel for long distances to spend several days taking part in this festival, while other people aim to participate in archery and wrestling matches. After the *Naadam* festival, school friends of all ages (including nomadic herders in the countryside) spend at least one to three days together travelling to scenic or famous places for a holiday or school reunion.

Table 5.1 *Domestic tourism centres during the socialist period in Mongolia*

Region	Province	Spa and sanatoria	Holiday camps	Children's camps	Total
Western Mongolia	Bayan-Olgi	Chigertei	Aksu and Uujim	Zost and Uujim	5
	Uvs	Khar Termis	Tsunkheg and Kharkhiraa	Kharkhiraa	4
	Khovd	Bayanbulag	Nevt	Bayanbulag	3
	Gobi-Altai		Khunkher and Guulin	Nokhorlol	3
	Zavkhan	Bayanzurkh, Zart, Otgontenger	Zart	Tsetserleg	5
	Total	**6**	**8**	**6**	**20**
Eastern Mongolia	Khentii	Berkh, Avargatoson, Bor-Ondor and Khajuu-Ulaan	Gurvannuur	Onon and Kherlen	7
	Dornogovi		Dalanturuu	Jargalan	2
	Sukhbaatar		Dariganga	Dariganga	2
	Dornod		Tsagaankhondii	Ulz, Enkh	3
	Total	**4**	**4**	**6**	**14**
Central Mongolia	Khovsgol	Bulnai and Salbart	Tunel	Urandosh	4
	Arkhangai	Shivert		Tamir	2
	Bayankhongor	Shargaljuut	Shargaljuut	Ovgonjargalant	3
	Ovorkhangai	Khujirt, Khuremt		Tsagaanzalaa	3
	Bulgan	Erdenet	Khyalganat, Saikhanhulj	Bugat, Nairamdal and Jargalant	6
	Selenge	Khadat, Darkhan and Shariin gol	Khond, Shaazgait, Shariin gol and Kharaa	Gunnuur, Zulzaga and Artsag	10
	Tov	Ar Janchivlan, Ovor Janchivlan and Baganuur	Dugankhad, Elkhad, Bayanbuural, Suuj and Khairthaan	Dugankhad, Elkhad, Och, Shonkhor, Baigal and Olziit	14
	Omnogovi		Khavtsgait and Gurvansaikhan	Gurvansaikhan	3
	Dundgovi		Burdiin-Uyanga	Sumkhokhburd	2
	Total	**13**	**16**	**18**	**47**
Surrounding areas of the capital city of Ulaanbaatar		Orgil and Uurkhaichin	Sognogor, Bayangol, Tsagaanguna, Sanzai, Oin bulag, Narst, Selbe, Songino, Nukht, Terelj and Kharzai	Soel, Bayangol, Tsagaannuga, Khaiguulchin, Gachuurt, Khandgalt, Yanzaga, Tamirchin, Solongo, Dol, Bayan-uul, Nairamdal, Narst, Sansar, Javkhlant, Gorkhi, Kharzai, Jargalan and Osvoriin oichid	32
	Total	**2**	**11**	**19**	**32**
Overall total		**25**	**39**	**49**	**113**

Source: Mongolian Academy of Science (1990)

Aspects of domestic tourism in contemporary democratic Mongolia

Nowadays, domestic tourism is defined by people's income, seasonality and festivity, as well as frequent holiday breaks. After the 1990s, major political and economic changes took place in Mongolia and the country opened its doors to international travellers. There was a shift from the centrally planned economy to the market economy. As a consequence, the state-run organizations and collectives, including livestock collectives, began to be privatized during the 1990s. Private businesses emerged and large numbers of people became self-employed. After the transition began, Mongolia experienced economic crisis. As with other industries, Mongolia's domestic leisure industry also slowed down. Holiday camps had less visitors compared to the past and, consequently, many of these holiday camps were shut. Mongolians were less willing to travel due to the fact that they were trying to adjust themselves to a new political and economic system. However, Mongolia's economy has been recovering since the New Millennium and there is increasing affluence in this society. In the context of current employment patterns in Mongolia, 44.3 per cent are in various private businesses, including banking, construction, real estate, hotel and restaurant, mining, wholesale and retail trade; 37.65 per cent in agriculture, hunting and forestry; and 18.05 per cent in public service and other sectors (National Statistical Office of Mongolia, 2008b). These statistics show that a strong private sector emerged and grew after the 1990s. The private sector also tends to offer competitive salaries and people now have more disposable income for travelling within the country. The major population centres of Ulaanbaatar, Erdenet and Darkhan and their surrounding areas are becoming popular weekend holiday centres while upholding the tradition of holiday camping.

In recent years, Mongols share the travel lodges (*ger*) of the international tourists. *Ger* is a traditional Mongolian dwelling, a mobile domed structure with circular walls, used both in urban and rural areas. The main frame of a *ger* is assembled wooden parts with a circular domed crown, poles as a roof, a door and walls that are held together by ropes. The layers of square-shaped tick felts and water-proof canvases are applied against the outside of the wooden structure of a *ger* as insulation. Over the winter, more of these layers are needed to keep a *ger* warm inside. Camps use a large *ger* as a restaurant and the small ones for accommodation for up to four people. Some of the camps use two attached *gers* an en-suite accommodation with private bathroom facilities. The number of *ger* camps in rural areas is growing in order to meet the increasing demand from domestic and international tourists. Although the *ger* camps began to be established after the 1950s, it is during the last five years, in particular, that the majority of the *ger* camps developed in Mongolia. According to the MRTT, the number of *ger* camps in Mongolia had already reached more than 220 in 2008.

Figure 5.2 *Bayan Uul holiday camp, near Ulaanbaatar (1998)*

Source: Elma Bayan-Uul Co Ltd, 2008

Figure: 5.3 *Bayan Uul holiday camp, near Ulaanbaatar (2008)*

Source: Elma Bayan-Uul Co Ltd, 2008

In contrast, holiday camps established during the communist period comprised European-style buildings and were located further into the natural areas beyond the urban hinterland (see Figures 5.2 and 5.3). These holiday camps were state-owned; however, a large majority of them were privatized after the 1990s. The main function is to accommodate domestic holiday-makers during their holidays. Most holiday camps are open year round in contrast to the majority of *ger* camps, which only operate during the summer. *Ger* camps also offer two different price packages for domestic and foreign travellers, while holiday camps have only one standard service charge. Affluent domestic travellers often use these facilities during their holidays. Many of these camps are located alongside hot and cold curative springs, lakes and other scenic landscapes. However, camping is still popular, not only because it offers close attachment to nature, but because it provides cheap accommodation. Recent growth in the urban population followed by the expansion of *ger* districts that rely primarily on coal for fuel and growing traffic have resulted in increased air pollution in Ulaanbaatar. Thus, urban populations seek fresh air during weekends, and more particularly during the winter months when urban air pollution often exceeds permissible levels.

In general, domestic tourism takes place within limited distances, social groups and at varying frequencies. Domestic travellers also tend to arrange their holidays independently instead of travelling through travel agents or tour operators. Families and relatives, friends and colleagues travel together as a group and spend at least one day away from urban settlements in the wilderness or in a holiday camp, a sanatorium or children's camp. Today, notable changes are also emerging in the domestic tourism market. The number of domestic tourism-oriented tour operators is growing, along with an increasing frequency of domestic travel adverts on television and radio during the summer.

Visiting friends and relatives and events

One of the most popular reasons for travelling in Mongolia is to visit friends and relatives (VFR). In most cases, it is the city dwellers who visit their friends or relatives over the summer season. A large percentage of Mongolians still have family members or relatives out in the countryside maintaining their nomadic way of living, or relatives in their home areas. These groups tend to be nostalgic about their traditional culture and ways of living and spend time close to nature in tranquility away from busy city life.

In particular, the nationwide *Naadam* festival is still one of the main periods when most Mongolians get together. Horse racing is one of the three main sports of *Naadam*. There are six different categories in the traditional horse race based on the age of the horse and different racing distances. The youngest age category is two-year-old horses that race for 12km to 15km, while mature horses (older than eight years) race for 28km. Training and taking part in these races is part of almost every nomad's leisure activity. It takes at least a day or overnight horse ride for many nomads to get to the *Naadam* ground. Some people travel for more than 1000km to take part in big-scale *Naadams*. The main change since the socialist period is the increased frequency of small-scale *Naadams* besides the nationwide *Naadam* in July. For instance, 'ovoo' worshipping is a ritual where local people pay tribute to sacred mountains and pray for sufficient rain and good luck. The ritual is almost a small version of the *Naadam* festival and involves not only religious ritual but also horse racing and wrestling matches.

Along with horse racing, wrestling is one of the main features of *Naadam*. Many Mongolians travel long distances in order to take part in the wrestling matches, which are open to all men who enjoy the sport. This is also the same for archery, which is not so popular at local and small-scale *Naadams*. It is apparent that *Naadam* attracts not only manly sport participants, but also large audiences. *Naadam* is an occasion for people to enjoy the sporting matches while meeting their friends and relatives. These people join together for a family feast, famously known as *horhog* and *boodog*. These are traditional Mongolian barbecues that people enjoy having together. At the same time, singing along while drinking *airag* (fermented mare's milk) and milk vodka is part of almost every adult's holiday activity in scenic landscapes.

In contrast to the urban-to-countryside flow of holiday travelling, a reverse travelling trend also occurs in Mongolia. Around the advent of autumn and the beginning of winter (from the end of August to the end of November), students travel to urban areas for their new academic year and are usually accompanied by their parents. The beginning of winter is also a period when Mongolians prepare their winter food, which involves butchering animals. Given the culture of courtesy, Mongolians have a tradition of sharing this winter food among their relatives. So these Mongolian nomads travel for long distances to deliver winter food to their relatives living in urban areas. This is an opportunity for rural nomads to meet or 'see' their relatives and experience the modern way of living in a city and to visit and pray in the large monasteries, particularly those in Ulaanbaatar.

Religious tours are one of the main types of travel activities for domestic travellers. The return to freedom of worship and Buddhism since the 1990s has a visible influence on the daily life of many superstitious Mongolians. The monasteries of Gandantegchilen, Erdenezuu and Amarbaysgalant, alongside famous historic and architectural sites, are also the most popular worshipping places among Mongolians. Gandangechilen Monastery is located in the capital city and is the most popular pilgrimage site that was the only functioning monastery since the communist period. Erdenezuu Monastery, established in 1586 – the oldest Buddhist monastery in the country – is a popular destination for Buddhists and is easily accessible from Ulaanbaatar by road. Thus, visiting monasteries and the birth places of famous saints is considered a spiritually renewing and positively energizing activity for worshippers. The main season for domestic travellers is May to October (personal communications with a director of a domestic tour operator in the area, 2008). Besides the mainstream summer holidays, religious tours usually occur during the low tourist season. In this regard, certain periods, such as weekends, new year and after Lunar New Year festivals, are particularly busy. For instance, the traditional Lunar New Year festival is followed by the annual Buddhist ritual of offering and mantra practising in monasteries during the spring season. Recently, the Buddhist monastery of Khamariin Khiid, in Dornogovi Province, has emerged as one of the most famous religious destinations among domestic visitors. This monastery, located 40km to the south of Sainshand, is believed to be the world energy centre that infuses nature's positive energy within people.[1] The Trans-Mongolian Railway that passes through the area makes the monastery more accessible to the public. Visitors from a wide age group travel from all parts of the country to Khamariin Khiid throughout the year. Most of the travellers visit the area independently either by private transport or by train. This tour has been gaining in popularity since 2003. Trains to Sainshand, the provincial centre town of Dornogovi, runs twice daily, with each trip carrying 1120 and 1280 passengers totalling approximately 2400 passengers a day. The Mongolian Railway Tourism Bureau organizes a two-night, all-inclusive package tour for domestic travellers, selling as many as 30 package tours a week. The overall number of travellers reached more than 2000 between 2006 and 2007. Currently, three *ger* camps operate in Khamariin Khiid. As a result of increasing domestic tourism, residents in Sainshand have established guiding and transport associations that assist the domestic travellers, who visit the monastery and surrounding areas.

Student group travel

Students seem to be the ones who have disposable income and time to travel in a group, regardless of the culture of dependence on their family. There are 170 universities and colleges with more than 120,000 students in Mongolia, with a large majority of these (as many as 132) located in Ulaanbaatar (Ministry of Education, Culture and Science, 2008). The academic year in the country runs from September to June, which includes at least three weeks' breaks throughout a year: one in September when they start the new academic year, the second one around December as a winter break to go skiing or simply enjoy the fresh air out in the mountains, and the third occasion is a celebration of the arrival of summer before the end of the academic year. One exceptional occasion is the graduation ceremony when students spend at least two to three days in holiday camps or *ger* camps. Currently, there are no official statistics about the patterns of student holidays and weekend breaks. However, the overall number of students taking part in regular recreational activities in Mongolia could almost equal the number of international tourists a year in the country. In economic terms, student group travels to holiday camps and *ger* camps near Ulaanbaatar is notable. Despite the fact that student spending on a single visit may be less than that by international travellers, the relatively higher frequency of visitations compensates for the low returns.

Health tourism

Health tourism has a relatively long history of development and extensive support by the government in Mongolia. Major destinations for health travellers are established sanatoria from the socialist period – namely, Orgil, Khujirt, Shargaljuut, Avargatoson, Otgontenger, Ar Janchivlan, Ovor Janchivlan and Biger sand sanatorium. These sanatoria offer a wide range of drug-free treatments. Avargatoson, for example, offers hydrotherapy for various forms of allergies; neurological diseases; rheumatism or arthritis; stomach, kidney and liver diseases; and gynaecological problems. Shargaljuut also offers hydrotherapy for epilepsy; cardiovascular disorders; respiratory and digestion problems; heart and kidney problems; various forms of allergies; and neurological diseases, using a hot mineral spring, therapeutic mud combined with massage, and acupuncture. In addition to these mineral springs and therapeutic mud services, mare's milk treatment is also offered. Biger is the only sand sanatorium where people are treated for kidney affliction. The treatment is essentially a natural therapy that combines camel milk drinking and sitting in a sand bath that is enriched with wind-blown minerals from the saline lake next to the sand dunes.

There is an ever-growing demand for health tourism amongst the urban population. According to a general manager of Shargaljuut sanatorium, the summer season is always fully booked, even though the facility is not promoted publicly. As a consequence of the increasing demand, the sanatorium is planning to undergo expansion. Due to treatment restriction (visitors are required to stay in well-insulated houses and to keep themselves warm), some sanatoria open only during the summer season between May and August. Those who take part in health tourism in Mongolia travel regardless of the distance of the sanatoria. For instance, both Shargaljuut and Biger are not readily accessible to Ulaanbaatar residents and require driving on dirt roads for long distances. Nonetheless, the demand is still very high. The travelling expenses are reasonable and it is all inclusive. However, the disadvantaged groups in society (orphans and low income people) and those who have medical insurance can travel free of charge or at cheaper fares, respectively.

One of the negative impacts observed around such natural resources is the increase in tourism infrastructural development, particularly of those sanatoria

Figures 5.4 *Avargatoson Sanatorium offers hydrotherapy, for which* ger *camps are set up all around the lake*

Source: Amartuvshin Dorjsuren, July 2008

that are near large urban areas. In Avargatoson, for instance, the original sana-torium is surrounded by *gers* and land-leasing local residents, *ger* camp developers and short-stay campers. It seems that there is a lack of regulation on the arrangement of land use (see Figure 5.4). Since the area is not serviced by a proper sewage system, unpleasant sewage smells are very common. Although such natural resources are becoming a good revenue generator for local residents, the future of this therapeutic lake is at severe risk.

Domestic tourism destinations

Both VFR and student groups often travel for long distances throughout the summer, particularly between July and August when most people have their summer holidays. The trips often occur as jeep tours, as groups of friends and families travel through popular scenic landscapes of the country. According to a domestic tourism survey conducted by the MRTT (2005, p83), 53 per cent of respondents stated that the Arkhangai region is the most popular long-distance destination, followed by the Ovorkhangai-Kharkhorin region (50 per cent) and the Khovsgol region (46 per cent).

The Arkhangai region is famous for its lake Terkh and the dormant volcano of Khorgo and Taikhar Chuluu, along with the monolith in the Tamir River basin, Mount Bulgan and a Buddhist monastery of Zayiin Gegeen. Domestic travellers visit the region for the panoramic views of its wooded mountain regions and the lakes, and for the opportunity to sample local dairy products. The Ovorkhangai-Kharkhorin region is home to the World Heritage Site of the Orkhon Valley. The area is renowned for Mongolia's oldest Buddhist monastery – Erdenezuu – and the remains of the Kharkhorum, the 13th-century capital of the Mongol Empire. Tovkhon Monastery in the Khangai Mountains is also a popular pilgrimage site for Mongolians. The monastery was erected on the mountaintop surrounded by lush coniferous forest under the supervision of the head of Mongolia's Buddhists, the first Bogd, Zanabazar, which is a teaching centre for meditation practices and Buddhist art. The region is also popular for its ancient ruins and burial sites from the Uigur and Turkic periods, including Uigur's Khar Balgas (ninth to tenth century AD) and Khusuu Tsaidam (sixth to eighth century AD) – a Turkic-inscribed monument. This Orkhon-Enisei inscription, written by a grandson of Kultegin and devoted to Bilge Khan of Turkic origin and his brother Kultegin in 732 AD, is the first alphabet of the Central Asian nomadic tribes (UNESCO, 2004). Another popular area within Ovorkhangai region is Khujirt hot spring spa, established during the socialist period. Since the curative water of the spa contains bicarbonate, carbonate, sodium and hydrogen sulphide, it is very popular among domestic visitors for the treatment of nerves, backaches, extremities and cardiovascular diseases (Shagdar, 1997).

The Khovsgol region has a well-developed tourism image that centres on the pristine Lake Khovsgol. The lake is the deepest inland water body in Central Asia (with a depth of 262m and a length of 136km). This area has been protected since 1992. Besides these three regions, a fourth region – the Khentii region, associated with the birth place of Chenghis Khaan – is also frequented. This area constitutes the southern ridge of the Siberian taiga. Within the region, Mount Burkhan Khalduun, which was historically worshipped by Chenghis Khaan, is still one of the state-recognized holy mountains in the country, where regular state worshipping rituals take place. Such rituals were prohibited during the communist period and returned after the 1990s. Today, there are five such holy mountains throughout Mongolia. These mountains are officially recognized as 'state worshipped mountains' by the president of Mongolia and the ritual takes place once every four years.[2]

The impact of domestic tourism on the nomadic lifestyle of Mongols: An exploration

The existence of a nomadic way of life is one of the advantages of Mongolian tourism that has become extinct in many cultures and countries. Thus, conservation of such a unique culture may be vital in the future. In contrast, there have been changes in external tourism demand. Some tourists seek emerging destinations that offer authentic cultural experiences and wildlife explorations. This helps to explain why the nomadic way of life in Mongolia is becoming one of the major attractions for international tourists.

In order to meet the basic requirements of tourism policy and planning, tourism should be developed only within the limits of the carrying capacity of society. Despite extensive research on carrying capacity in tourism international-ally, there has been no previous attempt to define carrying capacity in any area of Mongolia to tourism. In particular, social carrying capacity (SCC) is always controversial to determine and is highly dependent on people's views and perceptions. The SCC of nomadic peoples in Mongolia has not yet been part of academic research and is new to the field of tourism studies.

The process of conserving locals' authenticity should not be regulated in a tokenistic manner or left to a third party's views. Rather, it should be the choice of the host community. Thus, Crick (1989, p336) complains that there is a lack of local voices in the literature (based on Pearce et al, 1996, p98). In addition, the study of the SCC of nomadic people further led to investigating the role and impacts of domestic travellers in destination areas, particularly those described in the previous section. It can be seen that the higher number and frequency of travellers correspond to higher impact. Therefore, popular desti-nation areas may need to be more concerned about the impact of domestic tourism.

In studying the impact of tourism, the perceptions and behaviours of insti-tutions (e.g. tour operators and governing bodies), as well as those of individuals (nomads and nomadic families), can be a useful approach. Furthermore, Robson (2002, p276) states that open-ended questionnaires are particularly useful in gaining the confidence of participants without the test of any prior knowledge as the questions are quite elastic and can be stated in ways that can minimize the hidden meaning of the responses and interviewees. Hence, respondents are known to speak confidently to explain and respond to the probes of the researchers, affording unexpected insights. At the same time, a researcher can verify the validity of the answers via accompanied observations. Thus, open-ended questions were utilized in order to obtain rich explorative data.

The primary data on the impacts of domestic tourism in Mongolia were extracted from research conducted in 2005 by the author of this chapter in order to fulfil an MSc dissertation. The focus of the study was on the social carrying capacity of nomadic peoples in relation to international tourism in the Omnogovi area in Mongolia between 17 August and 26 September 2005, covering 27 nomadic herders, aged between 19 and 77 years, and one *ger* camp and two tour operator managers.[3] The questions related to tourism impact, the tourism carrying capacity and the social carrying capacity, and other issues were investigated by questions 1 to 25. Questions 1 to 11 aimed to identify the environmental, economic and socio-cultural impacts and the level of these impacts on local communities. The original questions were intended to explore the changes caused by tourism and the attitudes of tourists towards the places and people visited. The aim was to understand how these impacts affected relations between the community and international travellers. Many questions were prefaced by 'why' in order to uncover the reasons and the values of local herders and tourism enterprises.

A purposive sampling approach was utilized as opposed to random sampling, following the snowball technique, with each interview influencing the choice of the subsequent interviewee in 2005. Due to the nomadic culture of the case study area, interviewees were more or less homogeneous in terms of way of life and basic industry, which is animal husbandry. However, indefinable divisions exist amongst the population. Therefore, basic criteria for the selection of the respondents were age group, gender, the level of involvement in tourism, and the geographical and tourist area. Thus, the interviewees were selected from the surrounding areas of the major tourist camping destinations of Yoliin Am, Khongoriin Els and Bulagtai. However, the personal communications conducted during 2007 to 2008 were selected on the basis of random sampling purely in order to explore the unidentified themes and issues in domestic tourism development in Mongolia.

In order to obtain a richer and deeper understanding of the subject, individual and focus group semi-structured interviews, informal conversations and participant observations were also employed in empirical data collection. A number of informal personal communications were conducted between 7 to 13 July and 15 to 18 August 2008 in Avargatoson sanatorium and in Khamariin Khiid, respectively, involving four travellers, a local resident and a sanatorium manager, a manager of a domestic tour operator and a holiday camp director, in total. The research in 2005 was not purely on the impact of domestic tourism in the destination area. In order to reveal a full picture of domestic tourism development in Mongolia, it was necessary to include conversations with people who have a certain level of experience in the domestic tourism industry and interactions with domestic travellers, as well as the actual domestic travellers themselves. Personal communications (semi-formal and informal) with tourism industry workers and local communities during the period of 2006 to 2008 have been incorporated in the following discussion by way of appropriate representation of facts. Alongside these, observations made during the interviews and casual conversations between the interviewees as well as from everyday life were also recorded.

Owing to limited financial resources and restricted logistics in terms of accessing people and places, despite sufficient time availability, the selection of the research methods was deemed relatively appropriate, at best.

Contributions and conflicts of domestic tourism in Mongolia

Despite burgeoning domestic tourism, little attention has been paid to its impact in Mongolia. Based on the qualitative data collected, this section presents the economic, environmental and social implications of domestic tourism in some major destination areas in Mongolia.

Ironically, despite the paying capacity of international tourists visiting Mongolia, rural nomads near Lake Khovsgol in northern Mongolia revealed that income from the horse-riding activities of domestic travellers frequently outweighs that from their foreign counterparts. Part of the reason for this is the fact that rural nomads find it difficult to communicate with foreign travellers who are not accompanied by a guide. Herders who hire horses on a commission basis to *ger* camps seem to earn less compared to the earnings from domestic travellers; therefore, it is more beneficial for nomads to serve Mongolian travellers and to earn commission-free income. There are also some additional opportunities – for example, selling dairy products and meat onsite without extra travel costs. The shopkeeper and retail business runners at Avargatoson sanatorium also revealed significant economic benefit from domestic travellers. There is visible growth in local retail businesses as a result of the influx of visitors at the sanatorium, with more shops carrying a variety of goods than the village nearby. According to a shopkeeper, the villagers make their living by running domestic traveller-oriented shops, land leasing, and selling meat and dairy products at the sanatorium. Despite significant economic benefit for locals, domestic tourism tends to trigger inflation as well. In 2005, the local people of the Kharkhorin region were paying inflated prices due to the higher number of domestic and international travellers. Thus, while the economic impact of domestic tourism is generally positive for local herders, a minority of the interviewees thought that the benefits were insufficient. However, the economic benefits of domestic tourism are accompanied by negative environmental implications.

The common environmental problems are litter, desertification and reduction in groundwater levels, as well as damage to pastures from the numerous new vehicle tracks. In some national parks, many nomads find the litter and pollution levels alarming. Herders complain that 'increasing tourist camps result in many roads and deteriorate the pasture … and generate dust'. According to tourism impact research in the Gobi Desert region in southern Mongolia in 2005, the majority of nomads interviewed believed that domestic travellers are the main waste generators in Yoliin Am. Observations in Terelj National Park near the capital city of Ulaanbaatar further support that the excessive amount of litter is largely caused by domestic travellers who either have limited travelling experience or have lost their respect for nature. Observations and interviews in Lake Khovsgol National Park also show notable environmental damage along the shore of the pristine lake. Although the national park has a designated camping area for campers, there are no control measures on the behaviour of the domestic travellers who tend to do their washing in the lake and generate litter. *Ger* camp runners are concerned about the image of the area and potential damage brought to their long-term travel business.

The environmental impact of domestic tourism in major tourism destinations in Mongolia thus includes soil erosion, water pollution and litter. All of these issues are on the increase and could potentially lead to severe environmental damage in the future if no adequate measures are taken. In particular, the damage to pastures by new dirt roads was seen as the main impact in the area because herders make their living by herding animals and they are dependent on pastures and environment. These impacts seem to concentrate in certain areas that are classed as national parks or are under state protection.

The socio-cultural impacts, on the other hand, are intertwined with the environmental and economic impacts, and are thus complex. The perception of these impacts as positive, neutral or negative varies with people's own outlook, including how their values and beliefs are affected; what is acceptable in society; and how they themselves perceive these effects. Observation in Avargatoson sanatorium indicates that local entertainment, concert and regular weekend ballroom dance are organized only for the domestic travellers. At the same time, nearby villagers and nomads join in and enjoy these activities. Thus, a positive aspect of domestic tourism is that rural communities gain modern social skills through such entertainments. The interviews in the Gobi region documents that tourism transforms the monotonous and ordinary life of the herders into a livelier one as people learn how to communicate and encourage tourists to ride horses. Some of them have gained the knowledge and art of delivering better services and they 'have organized a rangers' association with certain regulations to support' themselves. The study shows that jobs in the tourism sector are perceived by nomads as interesting since they afford opportunities to meet different people, gain communication skills and become involved in various types of activities, including handicraft and horse hiring. The reasons for these perceived opinions may be attributed to the lack of socializing activities amongst the scarcely populated nomadic communities across large territories of Mongolia. When combined with the monotonous cycles of animal husbandry involving animal herding for most of the year, the lifestyle of these nomads is far from enviable. Therefore, tourism-related activities and festivals could be the major socializing events causing locals to appreciate tourism.

But the socio-cultural impacts are not altogether positive. There are, indeed, some negative impacts that need mentioning. Prominent concerns include disruption to nomadic daily life, the antisocial behaviour of domestic travellers, discriminatory practices of tourism stakeholders, inadequate policy and unfair trade. According to a study in the Gobi Desert, nomadic herders noticed some significant destruction due to travellers' behaviour and tourism development in the area. The majority of domestic travellers are perceived as 'bad' tourists and could most likely generate 'some conflict between domestic travellers and the herders'. As a result, national park rangers are required to carry an identity card that legitimizes their authority to ask misbehaving visitors to comply with national park regulations. In the absence of any identification, travellers tend to disobey rangers and even violate the rules. Additionally, the herders feel that their values and beliefs are frequently disrespected by the tourists. In this regard they revealed that domestic tourists consciously violated Mongolian customs, especially those of maintaining propriety while defecating or urinating in the direction of the holy mountains and springs. The locals find such misdemeanour of the visiting Mongolians as inexcusable: visitors are expected to be aware of these local customs.

Tourism is also apparently blamed for fewer family interactions. According to one interview, 'it seems difficult to work as a horse guide for the camp' since his wife and child cannot look after the animals. Seasonal tourism has a larger impact on the small households. As mentioned earlier, pastures and water wells are the most important aspects of the nomads' lives. Increasing camping activities, infused by tourism development, have adversely affected locals' lives significantly. According to the respondents, 'the water is sucked for the camp

Figure 5.5 Ger *camp development in Terelj National Park*

Figure 5.6 Ger *camps in Terel National Park are particularly busy over the weekend due to the influx of visitors from Ulaanbaatar*

consumption, so it is not enough for us in a hot summer'. In this regard, again, the nomads expect domestic travellers to have an understanding of traditional Mongolian lifestyles and value system. However, since the visitors ignore these values, their activities are perceived as negative.

Indeed, these impacts have so far not been acknowledged or addressed in any government policy. The permission to use land for *ger* camp developments also does not seem to follow legal procedures. According to the country's regulations, the distance between *ger* camps must be at least 10km; however, these rules have already been broken (see Figures 5.5 and 5.6). Although there are currently 29 *ger* camps operating with official permission in Terelj National Park, there are at least triple the number of *ger* camps operating without official permission. Some of these camps are located very close to each other. There are as many as 61 *ger* camps and 31 holiday camps currently operating around Ulaanbaatar (personal communication, Tourism Information Centre in Ulaanbaatar, 2008). In Lake Khovsgol National Park, such irregular *ger* camp development is taking place as well. Furthermore, the nomadic people in Terelj National Park, and in the Govi Gurvan Saikhan National Park, are being pushed aside as *ger* camp developers overtake the pastoral lands. Hence, while demand for domestic (also foreign) tourism continues to increase, the adverse effects of these increases are also becoming increasingly apparent.

Conclusions

Domestic tourism in Mongolia is distinctive in its own right. The socialist period (1921 to 1990) resulted in enormous socio-economic and political changes, as did the democratic changes since the 1990s. Recreation and holiday activities were made an integral part of the extensive healthcare system in Mongolia, with 113 spas and sanatoria, holiday camps and children's camps throughout the country serving domestic holiday-makers and schoolchildren (Mongolian Academy of Science, 1990). However, the democratic revolution has effected a reconfiguration of the centrally planned economy into a market economy, leading to a dramatic increase in the Mongolian private sector. This is reflected in Mongolia's leisure industry. Nearly 220 *ger* camps have been newly established during the past 17 years, alongside the traditionally existing holiday centres.

The contemporary domestic tourism trend is also distinctive and reflects the changes in Mongolia's society and economy after the 1990s. Mongolia's culture itself resulted in a unique form of domestic tourism. Along with major VFR-type domestic travellers, event-motivated domestic tourism emerged in relation to the *Naadam* festival. Student groups also seem to be an important segment in the domestic tourism market, particularly the short weekend breaks at regular frequencies near main population centres. Central and northern Mongolia, including Arkhangai, Ovorkhangai and Khovsgol regions, represent the main long-distance domestic tourism destinations, while Terelj National Park attracts mainly day and weekend travellers according to the survey conducted by the MRTT (2005).

Domestic tourism is becoming more important for contemporary Mongolians. Some travelling activities are not seen as holidays by locals. For example, pilgrimages, annual *Naadam* festival events and the new academic year for students are considered as everyday activities rather than holidays. Due to increasing disposable income and private car ownership, burgeoning numbers of people are involved in frequent weekend breaks in areas surrounding the main population centres – namely, Ulaanbaatar, Darkhan and Erdenet. Today, tour operators specializing in domestic travel have emerged in Mongolia. In contrast to a few years ago, the number of domestic travel companies and the frequency of television and radio adverts on domestic tours have increased in Ulaanbaatar. However, these new trends are followed by growing environmental impacts on destination areas. Terelj National Park is a clear example of the boom in *ger* camps, some of which were established without official permission. Despite domestic tourism's significant potential (with its associated problems), the government has turned a blind eye towards development and planning policy in Mongolia.

Domestic tourism has also resulted in various economic, environmental and socio-cultural impacts. Economic impacts were perceived as positive by a large majority of the interviewees. In particular, nomadic herders, local shopkeepers and retailers seem to be the ones who have benefited most. The main reason for such perceptions is that tourism generates additional revenue for rural villagers and nomads besides animal husbandry. Tourism is the only main income source for a few families, while it is the second most important source of revenue for the majority of herders, according to the interviews in the Gobi region. In some areas domestic tourism is the major livelihood for many people, namely in Avargatoson. However, there are potential threats to the economic benefits of tourism. Residents in major destination areas seem to pay inflated prices as a result of the influx of tourists. The case in Kharkhorin region documents increased living expenses due to the inflated prices of general commodities.

Environmental damage in major domestic holiday destinations is also growing in relation to tourism development. Although national parks were established in order to conserve wildlife and to preserve it for future generations, the positive and negative consequences of tourism seem to be disproportionate. The study in Omnogovi province in southern Mongolia shows that the majority of interviewees recognized the negative environmental impacts, such as degradation of animal pastures by travellers' cars and damage to the major tourist attractions, including the glacier in Yoliin Am and the oasis in the Khongoriin Els area. Similar environmental impacts are observed at the Avargtoson sanatorium.

Socio-cultural impacts are complex and predominantly positive. Education, various festivities and the improvement of living standards are noted as the major positive effects of tourism by many interviewees. Holiday centres in rural areas seem to organize frequent cultural and educational activities which rural communities are also able to enjoy in the case of the Avargatoson sanatorium. Negative socio-cultural impacts can be summarized as one of the major drawbacks of tourism in some areas. Some nomads believe that domestic travellers' antisocial behaviour tends to destroy their daily life. Herders also complain that they have been subjected to various discriminations, such as access to water resources and pastures, employment opportunities at tourist camps and their tourism-related initiatives.

Finally, domestic tourism in Mongolia has a bright future in terms of natural resources and market demand, and both consumers and travel business are increasing. Domestic tourism development is currently taking place on its own without any intervention from the government. Although domestic tourism is being increasingly overshadowed by growth in international tourism in government policy, it continues to expand its infrastructural base. As a consequence, there are growing positive and negative impacts on the economy, the environment and society in Mongolia. In particular, the use of natural resources (land, pasture and water) for establishing new holiday centres seems to be controversial and may cause wider consequences among domestic travellers, rural communities, travel business and the government in the future. Therefore, developing well-planned domestic tourism seems to underpin the long-term sustainability of the domestic leisure industry in the country.

Notes

1   People believe that this is where the monastery was erected by the 19th-century noble Danzanravjaa (1803–1856).
2   The ritual of Mount Sutai (4090m) in Govi-Altai Province in western Mongolia took place for the first time in the summer of 2008 and attracted 10,000 visitors to the area.
3   The interviews in 2005 are tape-recorded and last approximately 45 minutes. However, some interviews were longer than others because of focus group interviews.

References

Badarch, D., Zilinskas, R. A. and Balint, P. J. (2002) *Mongolia: Science, Culture, Environment and Development*, Routledge London

Bold, B. (1996) 'Socio-economic segmentation-Khot-ail in nomadic livestock keeping in Mongolia', *Nomadic Peoples*, vol 39, pp69–86

JICA (1998) *The Master Plan on National Tourism Development in Mongolia-Interim Report*, JICA, Ulaanbaatar

Lattimore, O. (1962) *Nomads and Commissars*, Oxford University Press, UK

MECS (Ministry of Education, Culture and Science) (2008) *Statistics of Universities and Colleges in 2007–2008*, www.mecs.pmis.gov.mn/index.php?option=com_content&task=view&id=621&Itemid=168, accessed 3 March 2008

MRTT (Ministry of Road, Transport and Tourism) (2005) *Report of Survey Conducted on International and Domestic Tourism in 2005*, Ulaanbaatar, Mongolia

MRTT (2008) *Tourism Sector Profile*, www.mongoliatourism.gov.mn/index.php?action=menudata&id=7, accessed 2 March 2008

Mongolian Academy of Science (1990) *National Atlas*, National Geodesy and Cartographic Office, Ulaanbaatar, Mongolia

Mongolian National Statistical Office (2008a) *Review of Mongolian Socioeconomic Situation*, Report from Mongolian National Statistical Office, Ulaanbaatar, Mongolia, www.nso.mn/eng/e-tanilts.php, accessed 1 March 2008

Mongolian National Statistical Office (2008b) *Mongolian Statistical Yearbook 2008*, National Statistical Office of Mongolia, Ulaanbaatar, Mongolia

Pearce, L. P., Moscardo, G. and Ross, F. G. (1996). *Tourism Community Relationship*, Elsevier Science Ltd, Oxford

Robson, C. (2002) *Real World Research*, second edition, Blackwell Publishing, Oxford

Shagdar, S. (1997) *Fifty Routes Through Mongolia: A Guide for Tourists*, Ulaanbaatar, Mongolia

TACIS (1998) *TACIS Project Development of Tourism for Mongolia-Visitor Survey*, TACIS, Ulaanbaatar

UNESCO (2004) *Nomination of Orkhon Valley Cultural Landscapes for Inclusion in the World Heritage List*, http://whc.unesco.org/en/list/1081/documents/, accessed 1 December 2007

6

'Domestic' Tourism and Its Discontents: Han Tourists in China's 'Little Tibet'

Christopher Vasantkumar

The visit is always easier for the traveller. (Minca and Oakes, 2006)

Introduction

In recent years, cultural anthropologists and critical human geographers have mapped the ideational and material contours of Chinese domestic tourism with increasing specificity. Scholars such as Timothy Oakes (1998), Eileen Walsh and Peggy Swain (2004) and Pal Nyiri (2006) have sought to understand Chinese tourism on its own terms rather than assume *a priori* that tourist practices in the People's Republic of China (PRC) proceed according to familiar Western models. Nyiri especially has devoted considerable attention to analysing mainstream Chinese tourism's emphasis on the act of authenticating and on confirmation over authenticity and discovery as the ultimate goals of the journey. While these interventions have been largely salutary, I suggest that in contrast to visions of tourist itineraries that brook no semiotic dissent via a thoroughly over-determined presentation of sites worthy of visitation, tourism in contemporary China is productive of at least two sets of discontents.

Specifically, I refer, first, to the increasing number of Chinese tourists who model their journeys on Western modes of backpacking and, second, in a rather different vein to the local Tibetans who are confronted with a rising tide of urban Han tourists. In this chapter I illustrate the degree to which the intersecting practices and interests of both of these groups are insufficiently captured by recent work on domestic tourism. In place of a seamlessness of tourist meanings, I attempt to reinsert the plurality of Chinese tourist practices into ongoing debates in the field of tourism studies. I do so by focusing ethnographically on Han tourism to Tibetan areas of the PRC. Such an approach highlights the degree to which accounts of current Chinese tourism as (in important respects) fundamentally different from Western-derived forms underplays the increasing significance of independent, 'backpack' forms of sojourning. In addition, through an extended ethnographic example – focusing on a day spent on the grasslands with a local Tibetan informant and two tourists from Guangzhou – I foreground the ambivalences of the 'domesticity' that is commonly thought to be manifest in domestic tourism.

Ultimately, I suggest that rather than being somehow more local, more naive or more organic than more familiar globalized forms of tourism, Han travels to Tibetan areas are fraught with encounters that highlight the ethnic, regional and nostalgic contradictions of contemporary China. Tourism here is emblematic of access to money and power and serves as a mechanism not necessarily of tying the nation more closely together, but of throwing its internal disparities into bolder relief. I now turn to an ethnographic example that I present at some length.

The incidents detailed below are drawn from ethnographic field research into quotidian interethnic interaction that I conducted in Gannan Tibetan Autonomous Prefecture in south-east Gansu Province, north-west China, between 2003 and 2007. Gannan lies outside the Tibetan Autonomous Region (TAR), in what historically was the region of Amdo at the north-east edge of the Tibetan cultural area (now divided between China's Gansu, Qinghai and Sichuan provinces). It lies along a transition zone between Han, Tibetan and Hui Muslim populations. Until the riots of March 2008, which resulted in the placing of much of the region off limits to foreign tourists, life in Gannan for locals and tourists alike was generally more relaxed and less subject to government restriction than in Lhasa and other places inside the TAR. Thus, while I aim, in this chapter, to make general points about tourism in Tibetan areas of China, I must note that my account proceeds from a specific place that may not be representative of all interactions between Tibetan hosts and Han guests.

The events I relate took place in and around the small multi-ethnic (roughly, 50 per cent Tibetan, 35 per cent Han and 15 per cent Hui Muslim) town of Xiahe. Also known by its Tibetan name Labrang, it has long been a centre of religious pilgrimage and instruction and, in recent years, has increasingly become a key locus for domestic and international tourist itineraries. Home to a large and important Tibetan Buddhist monastery (as well as a mosque and a Daoist temple) and open to foreign tourists since the early 1980s, Xiahe, despite its diverse population, has been widely promoted as 'China's Little Tibet' (*Zhongguo de Xiao Xizang*). For many decades, an important centre of political power in the region, it has in the communist era been usurped by nearby Hezuo as prefectural capital, but remains an important market town for Tibetan nomads living in the surrounding grasslands.

Although it sits almost exactly in the centre of the map of contemporary China, in actuality, it is located at the meeting point of multiple frontiers – the transition from Han lowlands to Tibetan uplands, the threshold between settled agricultural and nomadic pastoralist modes of life, and the intersection of tourist itineraries and economic backwardness. As such, it is a particularly compelling prism through which to view the problematic 'domesticity' of contemporary Chinese tourist practices.

A day on the grasslands

On 30 January 2004, around 1.00pm, I went down to Rinchen's[1] quarters by the backside of the prayer wheel ranks that line the southern edge of the monastery, only to find him out and his older brother, also a monk, in the process of welcoming his father and mother to town for Monlam (the Tibetan Great Prayer Festival). About ten minutes later Rinchen called to say: 'Meet me at the Henan restaurant: I have a few errands to finish running and then we can get going.' Ironically, I had eaten there just prior to going to look for him and was stuffed, but I went anyway. When I got there I found that he had not yet arrived; but, sitting dispersed around a large round table, fiddling with the lazy Susan, were his friends: Zhuoma (Drolma) and Tsering, 22-year-old Cantonese-speaking Han women from Guangzhou City (Canton), one of whom had given herself the striking English name of 'Purple'. Rinchen had originally met them two years before when he was a Chinese-language tour guide at the monastery and wanted them to have a nice day on the grasslands in Sangke, a few kilometres up the valley from Xiahe. Laterally, he had extended an invitation to me to do the same, though I am still unsure as to whether he intended for me to have an experience of touristic pleasure or, as I like to think, he thought the Cantonese tourists would be as interesting to observe as the nomads.

Purple and her friend brought along expensive looking SLRs and a tripod and were dressed in standard semi-sporty urban Chinese fashion: impractical windcheaters, jeans of varying wash and hiking boots. They had been to Xiahe three times and when asked what the most interesting thing here was, they said: 'The temple [si: the monastery], of course' and looked at me as if I was slightly daft to have asked such an obvious question. I asked them if they were Buddhists and they said, somewhat obscurely: 'No, we're teachers' – they teach special needs students ('They're very slow') – and one of them works part time for Prudential Insurance. In English, she said she liked that job because she 'learns lots of games there'. The conversation shifted quickly enough that I forgot to ask what kind of games one learned working for a multinational firm. Sometime over the course of their previous two visits, Purple and her friend (whom Rinchen addressed ostentatiously by their Tibetan names,[2] or in the case of 'Zhuoma/Drolma', the Mandarin version) had met and made friends with another monk named Rinchen. Only later did I find out from my friend Rinchen that this was the first time he had ever met Rinchen II, too. This second Rinchen, older and more solidly built than the first, was from the prefectural capital of Hezuo and seemed to have been invited to accompany us solely to operate the video camera.

Once we got going, the Cantonese women stopped in the market to buy fruit to give to the nomad family we were to visit. The errands were finally done and having met up with Rinchen at the side of the main road through the monastery we hailed a *miandi* (microbus) and set off for the grasslands. The Cantonese women called Rinchen *laoshi* (teacher) and asked fairly knowledgeable questions about the chief reincarnate lama of the monastery, who would soon be moving back to Labrang from his current posting in Lanzhou. They knew that he hadn't lived in Xiahe since he was eight and speculated that he wasn't really a monk. They asked about the grand residence being built for him in the 'Tibetan part of town'. Yet, even as they asked Rinchen topical questions and called him *laoshi* to indicate respect in a religious/'cultural' realm, Purple and her friend still subtly reaffirmed their own sense of ethno-regional superiority.

Despite speaking primarily Cantonese, a southern regional dialect within the vast linguistic rubric of 'Chinese',[3] they still found time to jokingly criticize Rinchen's tones (which sounded fine to my ear). Implicitly, they marked themselves off as the proper or, at least, more proper speakers of Chinese by virtue of geographic or historical proximity. Rinchen was talking about renting the whole minibus rather than travelling more cheaply by sharing a taxi with a number of other parties. Purple (Zhuoma) and Tsering teased Rinchen for pronouncing the first syllable of the phrase *baoche* (to hire the entire vehicle) as a third tone (in this position, a low tone) instead of a first tone (high level). 'You pronounced it like *chibaole* [I'm stuffed]! If you had said it in fourth tone [falling tone], that would have meant "explosion", *baozha*, like his hair!': they pointed to my six months' worth of curls and giggle.

The place we were going to took some finding. At first Rinchen had said he had friends out there; but later on when I pressed him as to whether they were friends or kin, he averred that they were family (*keyi suan shi qinqi*). They stayed with him when they came to town; but this was the first time he had been to their place. We went first to Sangke village, little more than a crossroads in the centre of a broad valley where grassland swept up to white-tipped peaks on the horizon. Impressively paved roads led out of the valley towards Qinghai and Xiahe, and smaller gravel tracks arced off towards the distances. It all reminded me very much of big sky country in Montana. Here, Rinchen asked directions and we turned around and, leaving the pavement behind, headed off down the rough gravel road that, if we would let it, would eventually carry us to the town of Amchog. After Rinchen had slid back into his seat in the *miandi*, the Cantonese women teased him again. This second form of teasing worked less on ethnic or linguistic levels and had more to do with regional and economic differences between Canton and Xiahe, wealthy East and impoverished West in their particular contemporary infra-China versions. When he commented on how good the new (and admittedly smooth and well-graded) road from Xiahe to Sangke was, he called it a *gaosu gonglu* (a highway). Purple and Tsering chastised him as mothers might chastise a well-meaning but deluded child: 'This isn't a highway!', they giggled.

We had to ask directions two more times before we found the proper turnoff, a rutted dirt road that, in parts, looked like a frozen streambed. The *miandi* driver became increasingly frustrated as we failed several times to crest an icy slope, spinning the minivan's little wheels and cursing under his breath. Finally we arrived at a settlement of a few houses set beneath hills that gradually rose to angular, erosion-marked mountains, dun coloured on the horizon. In the other directions, grasslands, yellow in their winter coats, stretched away. Near the settlement, they were fenced off into pastures where sheep were grazing. Giant Tibetan mastiffs guarded the tiny brick houses. We pulled up at one of these, the home of a large nomad family. Four generations lived here under one roof. They were obviously poorer than many of the Tibetan townspeople from Xiahe itself; their elbows were cloaked in grime and the food they offered to us when we sat down in the place of honour on their *kang* reserved for guests was noticeably stale and scanty. But they welcomed us warmly. Milk tea was served in mugs cleaned laboriously with dirty rags. They obviously did not have much. It was possible that in the eyes of the visitors this made them seem more authentic.

Soon after we arrived, Purple and Tsering commenced the process of being made to look like Tibetan nomads. The first order of business was to have their hair braided in the 'traditional' Tibetan fashion. The white-haired Tibetan grandmother, her daughter and her granddaughter, already a mother in what must be her late teens or early twenties, bent over the Cantonese women one by one, braiding their hair with deft movements. They did all this by moistening the hair, braiding it and securing with small scrunchies that the Cantonese women had bought especially before we left Xiahe. As Purple had her hair braided, Tsering giggled and commented on the process, with the other Rinchen recording it all on video. When her hair was finished, the roles were reversed; the nomad women swarmed around Tsering, while Purple clucked and giggled. Hair braiding was followed by dressing the Cantonese women in the festival clothes of the nomads – from the brightly patterned collared shirts to the giant fur-lined robes held in place by long red sashes. After an hour or so Purple and her friend had been transformed into a state where they might pass for Zhouma and Tsering if only you didn't look too closely. Yet, no matter how complete the transformation in dress, no matter how 'authentic' the nomad drag, no one could remain in any doubt as to the ultimate difference between the Cantonese women and the Tibetans who surrounded them. Indeed, one was reminded of opportunities to dress up like Manchu emperors at sites such as the Forbidden City in Beijing.

In the midst of this process, a Tibetan boy in his late teens wearing a dirty Western-style mountaineering jacket poked his head in the door and said in Chinese: 'The horse is up on the hill, I will have to go get it' (*qu zhua ta*). He returned a little later with the horse in tow. Tsering rode first; she was the slimmer of the two with a pretty smile and Dhonjub, the teenage horse wrangler, took a shine to her. Instead of leading the horse he got on behind her after joking to the monks in Tibetan (they translated for me once she was out of earshot): 'I'd like to take her to a remote place and not come back for a while.' As it turned out, Dhonjub was a joker who excelled at winding people up. Rinchen said that he used to be a monk, but no longer was. I responded that his temperament seemed particularly ill suited to that vocation. At various points in the afternoon, he brought out a basketball and queried my ability to play, played (feathered) hacky-sack with the Guangzhou women dressed in their Tibetan finest, and wrestled with me in the usual nomad fashion – grabbing me low and trying to lift my feet off the ground. At one point he said in Chinese:

> 'I'm coming to America next year and I want to contact you'.
> 'Contact me when you get there', I reply.
> 'Now how will I do that? America is a big country like China.
> If I live in Shanghai and you live in Lhasa, how will I find you?'
> 'I'll give you my email address.'
> 'Email? On a computer? I can't do that!'[4]
> 'Okay, I'll give you my phone number' (but in the chaotic end
> to the day, I don't).

Later, in his continuing wooing of Tsering, he 'practised' his English on the Cantonese woman. This time leading the horse she was riding, he wondered: 'You're beautiful; what does that mean?' 'You're beautiful: *you shenme yisi?*' '*Ni hen piaoliang*', she replied, translating the phrase into Mandarin. I said to him on the sly: 'I think you already knew what that meant', and he grinned: 'Yeah, I understand a little!' Much later, when it was getting dark, he was still angling to seduce her. Sitting over the remains of a modest noodle dinner, consumed to loud proclamations of deliciousness by the two Cantonese women, he unveiled his last gambit: 'It's getting dark, there's no transportation and there is no hotel [*zhaodaisuo*] so I guess you will have to sleep here!' But by then Rinchen had his own reasons for wanting to leave.

I had remained aloof from all offers of being made up as a Tibetan nomad and when hoisted onto the horse, the poor beast soon made it clear that he had no interest in being ridden by a 275lb ethnographer. But as horse-riding led gradually to photo-taking, I became more involved, if only in order to record the strange ordinariness of the touristic encounters I was witnessing. It had turned into a gloriously sunny day – crisp and not too cold in the light, though a little too windy to be really comfortable. In addition to having the other Rinchen record their adventures on their video camera, Purple and her friend took massive amounts of pictures of various poses on horseback, with the monks and with the freakishly large and ill-coifed (in their opinion) anthropologist. Everything had been proceeding reasonably smoothly when, at dinnertime, they insisted on going out riding again to take some pictures at the magic hour when the light was turning the prairies into an extraordinary lake of gold. Rinchen tried hard to talk them out of this final excursion – the light was failing and if they tarried too long, not only would dinner be delayed, but we stood a very real chance of being unable to find any transport back (the original *miandi* driver having packed up long ago). Despite his protests, they rode out again, heading to the pasturages with Dhonjub in tow.

After a moment of indecision, we decided to follow along just to make sure things were okay. They had gone quite a ways ahead, and when we caught up with them, it looked as if there had been an accident – the horse and its rider were down in a ditch. But they were only playing a joke on Rinchen for being a wet blanket. It was in poor taste, if you ask me. Rinchen again asked them to come back to the settlement for dinner, but they insisted on going even further and he began to worry more intensely, on the one hand, about making our hosts feel put out (*weiqu*) and, on the other, more proximately about the risks the Cantonese women were taking with the horse. Forsaking the wide dirt road on which Dhonjub had previously taken them on slow loops, they had headed off-road to a large expanse of grassland separated from the road by a wire fence.

Here they were galloping at high speed and from a distance the rider appeared to be losing control. From our angle on top of a low rise, it looked as if Tsering was heading directly for the fence. She tried to slow the horse, without much success, and it appeared as if she would be thrown and the horse injured. Rinchen set off at a run to try and save them. He needn't have: the horse was making for a gate in the fence that we couldn't see from our vantage and eventually Tsering was able to slow to a stop with no physical harm done. But Rinchen was flustered: 'If anything happens to them, it's my responsibility [*wode zeren*]', he sighed, and I found myself annoyed by how lightly the Cantonese women took this charge. Once we got to the pasture, he relaxed a little, even taking a spin on the horse himself: he grew up on the grasslands and had been riding since he was young. When he rode fast, his robes trailed out behind him, vermillion on the wind, a lone rider at speed and dust rising to the failing light in the horse's wake.

After 40 minutes or so, Dhonjub's 11-year-old sister arrived and led the horse home. Rinchen and I turned back too, but the Cantonese lingered for *another* half hour taking pictures. Before we turned back, he told them several times: 'We have to leave before sundown, because we are walking!' They ignored him blithely. On the way back, as the Cantonese frolicked oblivious on the prairies, Rinchen said: 'I've known them for two years, but I won't bring them back. I didn't know they would act like this.' He was afraid of bothering our hosts.

Finally, they came back, bringing dusk with them, and they began to change out of their Tibetan finery; but having changed half way, they relented and, insisting on a group photo before dinner, they cajoled the nomad family into helping them put the nomad clothes back on. Before the group shot (of the monks, the family, themselves and me), they took a picture of the two Rinchens. To ensure proper authenticity, they asked my friend to remove his maroon fleece even though it was cold and it matched the colour of his robes perfectly. Apparently, proper monks do not wear synthetic fleeces. After this everyone came together and posed, Dhonjub making wild eye-rolling faces until he was told to stop. I took some pictures that I would later give to Rinchen to pass along to the family. Purple and Tsering took one set of photos and began preparation for another. They attempted to order various family members into more aesthetic alignments – 'Okay, you, little child [*xiaohaizi*], over there!'; but after the first picture the group dispersed and Rinchen said with a measure of annoyance: 'That's enough!'

At dinner, having changed out of their nomad finery, Zhuoma and Tsering tore into the gristly meat with gusto. Tsering shrugged off Dhonjub's final attempt at wooing and with a modicum of ceremony, we were off downhill in the last grey light of evening. Purple and her friend were bouncing down the hill with delight. Rinchen asked them if they had enjoyed themselves ('*Kaixin ma?*': 'Did you have a good time?). They responded giddily: '*Kaixin! Kaixin!*' ('Yes! Yes!'). For a while, though, it looked like my friend's fears about having to walk the 13km or so home were well founded. The wide rutted road ran empty to the horizon. A couple of vehicles passed us and left us up to our noses in their dust. In response, when we heard the noise of an approaching jeep, the five of us blocked the road from shoulder to shoulder. Briefly, I feared that the other Rinchen was going to be flattened, but the jeep shuddered to a stop in the nick of time and luckily for us was heading directly back to Xiahe without stopping in Sangke village. Wedged in the warm jeep, Rinchen looked visibly more relaxed: it had been a weird day – his Cantonese friends found what they wanted and tried to be polite, but even these good intentions resulted in sometimes very awkward situations. I still wonder about his original motivations in inviting them – and me, for that matter.

A fortnight or so later, Rinchen cooked dinner for me in his monks' quarters. As he cooked I sat on the *kang*, while the *Harry Potter* video I had brought along to pass the time played in the background. I asked him about our day on the grasslands:

> '*Did the Guangzhou girls leave happy?*'
> '*I'm sure they must have. The other Rinchen saw them all the way to Lanzhou.*'
> '*Did you know him?*'
> '*No, not at all.*'
> '*Is he a classmate of yours at the Buddhist Studies Institute [Foxueyuan]?*'
> '*No he's just an ordinary Labrang monk [Labulengsi yiban de sengren]. I didn't know who he was; but the girls knew him before so he ended up coming along.*'
> '*So are Zhuoma and Tsering Buddhist?*'
> '*One was and one wasn't.*'
> '*Which one was Buddhist, the skinnier one or the pudgier one [Purple]?*'
> '*Well, the thin one is Buddhist, but the other one doesn't believe in anything [Shenme dou buxin].*'
> '*Why are they so interested in this place if they are not Buddhist?*'
> '*I'm sure I don't know [Wo kending bu zhidao]!*'

Analysis

I present this example at length because it illustrates the sorts of misunderstandings that can result from the supposed intimacies of domestic tourism. I spent most of the day in question talking to Rinchen and observing the Cantonese women from a distance; thus, in my recounting of the story, I necessarily erred on the side of emphasizing Rinchen's worries over the Cantonese tourists' pleasures. While this bias was accidental, I think in retrospect that it provided an unusual perspective into the tangled domesticity of Chinese tourist encounters.

The intentions on both sides were good. Rinchen had positive experiences with the Cantonese women in the past and wanted to provide them with a special window into Tibetan life. Zhuoma and Tsering, for their part, were legitimately interested in, and reasonably informed about, Tibetan culture, especially its religious aspects. They attempted to conform with the expectations that accompany visiting a Tibetan household by purchasing fruit from the market to give to the family. Yet, in the end, it was hard to get away from the impression that they used this attempt at conforming with cultural expectations as a licence to then act as if they were in something like a Tibetan theme park, where hair-braiding, horse-riding and playing dress-up stood in for any sort of extended dialogue with the pastoralist family who served as our hosts for the day. The Cantonese women left having thoroughly enjoyed themselves. Yet, they remained oblivious to the stress and concern that their larking about had caused Rinchen, who, weeks after their visit, remained ambivalent about its motivations and ramifications. As it was, things turned out okay; but at the time, the possibilities of injury from horse-riding accidents or of having to walk back to town in darkness seemed very real and kept him from having any fun at all.

The narrative I have just presented provides a concrete illustration of two of the main themes of this chapter: the emergence of discovery-based tourism paradigms among urban Chinese and the foreignness of domestic travel in the PRC. In addition, unlike many accounts of tourism in China that focus on its codified state-sponsored aspects, this account provides a window into the sorts of unruly tourist practices that are emerging in today's China and also into the stress that such encounters place on their local mediators (compare with Minca and Oakes, 2006, on their shared visit to Venice). At this point, having set the stage with the story of the day on the grasslands, I turn to a more detailed meditation on the ambivalences of domestic tourism in contemporary China.

Tourist supernovae

As the introduction to one of the best-selling English language travel guides to China notes: 'domestic tourism is in a state of supernova, showering sights around the land with much needed investment (and less-needed noise pollution and litter)' (Harper et al, 2005, p3). According to the website of the Chinese National Tourism Authority, in 2007, the number of domestic tourist trips exceeded 1.6 billion, up from 719 million in 1999 and 240 million in 1985 (www.cnta.gov.cn/, accessed 18 February 2008; data on 1999 and 1985 from Meszaros, 2003, cited in Nyiri, 2006). Even allowing for the somewhat idiosyncratic manner of measuring these movements statistically,[5] it is clear that human mobility and its ensuing profits have increased exponentially over the last decade and a half.

In his recent work on 'scenic spots', Pal Nyiri attributes the startling growth in domestic tourism to a combination of factors, which together have reshaped the human landscape of the PRC. Nyiri notes that only since the late 1990s has tourism become a mass phenomenon in the PRC. Key elements in this process have included rising personal income; the introduction of the five-day work week in 1995; the introduction of three week-long holidays in 1999;

and government promotion of tourism as a remedy to economic woes beginning in earnest in 1998 (Nyiri, 2006, pp5–6). Despite its relative recentness, however, domestic tourism in China, according to Nyiri, draws on longstanding traditions of sojourning – key here are practices of literati travel that date back at least to the 16th century (Nyiri, 2006, p7). Central to these modes of travel and their contemporary analogues is a focus on a (now state-) codified set of scenic spots (as Nyiri translates *lüyou jingdian*) that serve as the key nodes, *par excellence*, in the constellation of tourist itineraries.

In place of more familiar Euro-American models of travel premised on notions of discovery and of leaving the beaten track behind in order to gain access to a realm of more immediate and authentic encounters, Nyiri argues compellingly that in contemporary China, domestic tourism is essentially about beating a path to state-sanctioned points of predefined interest. Journeys of discovery here are replaced with journeys of 'confirmation' (Nyiri, 2006, p93).[6] In a context where culture and economic development are viewed not as antonyms but as 'synergistic' (Nyiri, 2006, p78),[7] Nyiri argues that the vast majority of PRC domestic tourists are not pursuing authenticity through a romanticizing tourist gaze, but are instead approaching their itineraries from a rather less familiar angle. This otherness of Chinese modes of tourist consumption is manifest in ways that relate to the local:

> For the Western traveller, the local interlocutor – particularly in the role of the 'native guide' – is valuable because he authenticates the experience of place. For the Chinese tourist, there is no need for a 'native guide'. For him, as for the Westerner, the local is an object of contemplation and consumption; however, the local is not an interlocutor, since authentification of the experience comes from the professional tour guide, the travel agency or the site management as they are supposed to be more familiar with the cultural cannon. Indeed, as interlocutor, the local is suspicious and potentially threatening. (Nyiri, 2006, p68)

Tourism, here, is again less about leaving paths than beating them, less a supposedly liberatory[8] geography of encounter than the 'consumption of bounded and controlled zones' (Nyiri, 2006, p7), less concerned with authenticity[9] than with authentification.[10]

While Nyiri's interventions are useful in tracing the contours of the human and symbolic territory of mainstream domestic tourism, I think he overplays the uniformity of domestic tourism in contemporary China.[11] In part, I think his emphasis on authentification over authenticity as the driving force behind tourist itineraries stems from the particular moment in which he did his research during the late 1990s and early 2000s. In retrospect, these years appear to be on the cusp of a transition from a 'theme park fever' (Oakes, 1998, p50) to a more guidebook-centric set of practices. Building on Timothy Oakes's pioneering work on tourism in China, Nyiri highlights the significance of theme parks (of ethnic or historical theme) in the initial stages of the growth of domestic tourism. The 2000 to 2500 theme parks that opened in the 1990s 'reproduc[ed] *en masse* a canon of sites and attach[ed] new cultural references, such as ethnicity, to some of them' (Nyiri, 2006, p16). In the process, they also became models for tourist interaction, shaping the expectations of planners, visitors and visited, alike. On mention of theme parks, one's first instinct might be to think of entities along the lines of Disney World; but what Nyiri is describing differs from such received models in subtle but crucial ways. Specifically, in the discussion that follows, pay special attention to themes as an active process of forming people's modes of interaction with tourist sites.

Nyiri relates Xu Xinjian's conversation with village officials in a Qiang village in Ngawa (Aba) autonomous prefecture in Sichuan:

> *For these officials, 'developing' a tourist village meant undertaking what the leisure business terms 'theming': creating a 'tourist product' with a clear narrative of meaning, supported by a multitude of performative and interactive features – displays, shows and visitor activities. '* (Nyiri, 2006, p50)

Nyiri posits that this emphasis on 'theming' – on message control – stems from the formative role of theme parks on Chinese tourist practices, building on what he calls rather nebulously 'the historical memory of Chinese travel'. The key here, however, is the formal similarity that Nyiri constructs between theme park and scenic spot'[12] each is marked by a standardization of meaning and narrative. In such contexts, the point of tourism is not to make one's own meaning through novel or fortuitous encounters, but to participate in a specific, state-sponsored structure of feeling (Nyiri, 2006, p78).

Yet, especially within the last five years, alongside these themed modes of mostly group tourism, something like a backpacker culture has started to blossom at least among urban youth from China's wealthy Eastern Seaboard. One manifestation of this trend is the explosion in guidebooks[13] devoted to independent or self-guided tourism (*zidong you* or *zizhu you*), which now make up a sizeable chunk of the travel sections of bookstores in urban centres. Nyiri notes this trend, devoting several pages to a discussion of 2002's *Zangdi Niupi Shu: Beishangbao Jiu Zou de Ganjue* (Yi Zhi, 2002), which he translates as *A Cowhide Book of Tibetan Lands: The Feeling of Pick up Your Backpack and Go!*, a visually stunning guide for independent travellers. Ultimately, however, he is dismissive of the genre, noting that 'Western backpackers' guidebooks and websites can make new destinations fashionable; Chinese guidebooks lack the intention and the power to do so' (Nyiri, 2006, p89). This assertion is belied by the impact that Chinese guidebooks (particularly the *Guzhenyou*, or *Ancient Village Travel* manuals; e.g. Zhou, 2006) have had on Western guidebooks to China. Attractions such as the leaning towers of Kaiping in Guangdong Province and Fenghuang in Hunan appeared prominently in such books before making their way first into *Frommer's*(!) and only recently into *Lonely Planet*, which, until the 2007 edition, appeared to have been written entirely in ignorance of Chinese-language guidebooks.

I highlight this not to suggest the passing of the theme park modes of tourist practice, but to foreground the degree to which idioms (or, dare we say, themes) of discovery are beginning to function alongside those of confirmation in the organization of independent travel at the present (compare with Nyiri, 2006, p95). In the context of the recent spate of *zidong lüxing*, or independent travel guides, new forms of tourist desire modelled on transnational backpacking practices are posed as alternatives to official theming practices.[14] The authors of a recent guide to Tibet (*Xizang*) explicitly construct independent travel (*zidong*[15] *lüxing*) as a way of creating one's own meanings independently of official discourse. They exhort the independent traveller to *yong ziji de yanjing faxian, yong ziji de yanjing xunzhao* (Zhang and Zhao, 2001): 'Use your own eyes to discover, use your own eyes to seek.'[16] Thus, the contemporary domestic travel landscape is perhaps more multifarious than that which Nyiri traces in his book. While it is difficult to obtain statistics on the growth of independent domestic travel, my field research in Xiahe, a heavily touristed[17] Tibetan monastery town in north-west China's Gansu Province, suggests that the number of Chinese backpackers is roughly equal to that of foreign backpackers; the trend is, in other words, not insignificant. These are tourists who, in Nyiri's words, may be in pursuit of 'the internal exotic', in doing so, 'self-consciously embracing the Western model of the tourist as solitary adventurer' and (even if they travel in packs) often equating such a model with cosmopolitan modernity.

While these more adventurous forms of tourist discourse re-envision the proper criteria for understanding the value of particular places, actual touristic flows in the PRC re-inscribe existing topographies of wealth and exclusion. During ten months of fieldwork among tourists and other travellers in Xiahe, I encountered many domestic tourists: most were young, all were urbanites, the vast majority hailed from Beijing, Shanghai or Guangzhou. Tellingly, all were Han (rather than members of one of China's 55 minority ethnicities). Tourist practices and discourses in contemporary China are productive of a particular constituency delimited by being unmarked in class, ethnic and place-based terms. Independent tourism in China, at present, is predicated on the detour of a particular kind of self through another conceived of in historical or spatio-cultural terms. This touristic self is most often urban, middle-to-upper middle class, Hanzu and Eastern. It is not that country folk, the poor or ethnic minorities do not travel for business or even undertake journeys of personal significance; it is that these sorts of itineraries are not 'touristic', as officially or popularly defined.

In his provocative, though flawed, essay on the 'illegibility of the "non-white" adventure traveller' in contemporary risk culture, Bruce Braun describes the ways in which the assumption of the whiteness of the adventurer is linked to the naturalization of a particular racial and economic order. For Braun, this particular racio-economic order 'assumes a world divided in two: a European modernity alienated from nature, and a non-European pre-modernity peopled by natural cultures' (Braun, 2003, pp195, 201). Braun errs in overemphasizing the racial components of exclusion at the expense of accompanying class factors; but his argument is useful to think about in approaching 'the Chinese case' in that it pushes us to address the illegibility of the rural tourist (usually glossed 'migrant') or the *shaoshu minzu* (or minority nationality) tourist (for Tibetans, usually glossed 'pilgrim'). In doing so, one runs up against certain assumptions about the nature of particular types of people in Chinese society. By focusing solely on the non-white adventurer in racial terms, Braun misses an opportunity to look critically at the ways in which race and class (let alone gender) intersect. In the Chinese case, class and urban–rural divides are tightly bound up with ethno-*minzu*[18] identities. It is not just about the illegibility of the non-Han tourist *per se* in that rural Han are just as likely to be marginalized as Tibetans, it is about the invisibility of the non-privileged tourist where privilege is conceived of as a complex intersection of various axes of difference that include ethnicity, *hukou* (place of household registration), region and class. Key here is the difference between the local and the cosmopolitan: only the latter is capable of tourism.

These class, *minzu* and/or regional cleavages between the tourists and the toured highlight the problematic status of the domesticity posited by the formulation of 'domestic tourism'.[19] In English, the word 'domestic' has unavoidable resonances of intimacy, deriving from the Latin *domesticus*, or 'belonging to the household'. In the phrase 'domestic tourism', the nation-state is constructed as analogous to a household. Where foreign tourists might follow itineraries that detour a self through an unknown other, the supposed proximity and familiarity of the domestic would seem to indicate a greater intimacy, a self-touring self,[20] an itinerary that is, as it were, all in the family. While the Chinese government has put considerable effort into the successful production of visions of the PRC as a 'family nation' (see Pan et al, 2005), in practice, the 'domestic' encounters that occur in the context of Han tourism to Tibetan areas of the PRC are considerably more fraught affairs.

A 2001 article in *Time Asia* entitled 'China falls for Tibet chic' foregrounds both the increasingly seductive appeal of sojourns in Tibetan regions for urban

Han and the ambivalences of such peregrinations (Forney, 2001). Highlighting a trend that has intensified only in recent years (and resulted in a whole raft of guidebooks), the author of the piece notes that 'Chinese have fallen for Tibet. Growing numbers of Chinese now practice Tibet's form of Buddhism, fill their glasses with Tibetan booze and consider a jaunt on the high plateau a badge of cool.' The consequences of this flirtation with Tibetan culture have not been entirely pretty: 'Many of the Tibetan practices [Han Chinese now] ape can be as tacky as white men in redface doing a rain dance. Yet', the author continues, 'given that official propaganda has for decades blamed Tibetan culture itself for keeping Tibetans poor, ignorant and not above suspicion of cannibalism, this sudden interest shows the government's decreasing ability to mould public opinion, and the growing independence of Chinese trend-makers' (Forney, 2001). In place of older official dicta that Tibetan Buddhism was a feudal superstition deserving eradication, 'mysterious' (*shenmi*) and 'spiritual'[21] Tibetan culture now draws Eastern urbanites to China's Western fringes, seeking the same sort of spiritual charge that draws Anglo-Americans to the reservations and mesas of the south-west.

Forney (2001) acutely notes the central paradox in the increasing tourist fascination with Tibet:

> *Given what [the] Chinese have learned of Tibet for the past half century, it's hard to believe they would venture near the place. Eighth-grade textbooks omit mention of Buddhism, emphasizing instead that before China's army 'peacefully liberated' the province, 'it practised the darkest, most barbaric system of slavery in human history'. Films like the 1963 Serfs, seen in childhood by nearly all Chinese, show venal monks digging out people's eyeballs to settle debts and stretching the skin of dead serfs over drum heads... Such images die hard. Yang Bo, a 30-year-old Chinese tourist who absorbed many propaganda films on Tibet, recoiled while visiting one of Tibetan Buddhism's holiest places, the Labrang Monastery in Gansu Province: 'It was dark, and the spinning prayer wheels sounded savage.'*
>
> *Official propaganda hasn't changed – Tibetan song-and-dance troupes still pirouette on television to folksy ditties such as 'The Communist Party turned bitter to sweet'. The change comes instead from people such as artist Li Bing, whose father once oversaw Chairman Mao's travel plans. Backpacking through China, she grew enamoured of Tibet. After studying its language for a year, she spent six months on the plateau in 1998 and later produced an exhibition of her work featuring Polaroids of Chinese and Tibetans next to their overlapping handprints. Since then, travel to the Roof of the*

> *World has become as common for artists as a paint-spattered studio,*
> *and many galleries peddle their renderings of noble Tibetan rustics.*
> *'Chinese who go to Tibet can't help but see it as foreign', Li says.*
> (Forney, 2001)

We can see from this passage that part of the allure of independent travel to Tibetan areas for Han Chinese lies in these areas' very *foreignness*. The consequences for understandings of 'domestic' tourism of conceiving Tibet as an internal 'other' are manifold. As previously noted, the encounter between privileged Han Chinese backpackers and their Tibetan 'compatriots' is often fraught with misunderstanding and anxiety. Furthermore, it is worth noting the degree to which mappings such as those described by Forney (2001) obscure the degree to which places such as Xiahe/Labrang are not in any simple mono-ethnic-way 'Tibetan places', but are complexly multi-ethnic locales that count local Han among their inhabitants.

Even if Chinese backpackers are simultaneously drawn to and repelled by the foreignness or 'savagery' of Tibet, their journeys are also informed by a sense of consonance between the wild places on China's fringes and the potentially 'transgressive' quality of discovery-based tourist paradigms. Backpacking among urban Han Chinese is, as Nyiri reminds us, often explicitly linked to discourses of Western-influenced cosmopolitanism. This consonance between Tibetans and youthful cosmopolitans is beginning to seep into mainstream media. In the summer of 2006, a commercial for bottled water was played frequently on Chinese television (and is only slightly embellished in my retelling of it). The commercial begins with a scene of a young, well-dressed man (wearing, if I remember correctly, rather stylish glasses) sitting in a café (precisely the same sort of individual who, in my experience, might entertain notions of backpacking or driving off the beaten track). He is, as it turns out, a drummer and is unable to resist drumming on the table, practising his chops much to the annoyance of the other patrons. They make their disapproval clear and we cut to a scene where our hero has retired to his house; here, seemingly, he can drum to his heart's content, this time on a full kit. Unfortunately, after a few moments of blissful pounding, a purposeful brick shatters his window and his spirits.

Then we cut to the drummer at his kit amidst the emptiness of big sky country – stereotypical Tibetan nomad country where the vast, empty green pastures stretch away to the mountainous horizon. Surely here the drummer can find a place for his craft. He takes to his skins with renewed vigour; but is shortly startled by the arrival on the scene of a group of fearsomely tall Tibetan nomads dressed in their characteristic giant cloaks bedecked with coral and turquoise, the very picture of the intimidating 'other'. As they draw closer to him, looking menacing, he, recalling previous instances of societal disapproval, or perhaps simply terrified, stops playing. At this, the Tibetans look even more annoyed and they gesture towards his kit. After a moment, the drummer realizes that they are not threatening him with bodily harm as a result of his racket intruding on their rangeland, but are, in fact, beckoning him to resume playing. He does so with great gusto and the commercial ends with a scene of the nomads bopping along happily to his exertions, a perfect encapsulation of the perceived simpatico between stylish urban youth and the rugged peoples on China's fringes. A happy picture, but one that, as one might imagine, does not always play out as smoothly in real life.

Where Forney discusses the foreignness of Tibetan culture for urban Han, conversations I had with local Tibetans in and around Xiahe highlighted their ambivalence about the growing influx of Chinese tourists and made explicit their distaste at perceived notions of entitlement among urban Han. The day after getting back from the excursion described above, I discussed tourism with Ngawang, a monk from Xiahe who had spent a year in India and Nepal from 1996 to 1997 and still bears the marks of that experience. In response to my comment: 'It's very quiet here right now', he replied, speaking almost entirely in English:

> 'In a few days, many people will come for New Year celebrations: to see the monks dance.'
>
> 'Both Chinese and foreigners?'
>
> 'So many Chinese. Ba-da-da-da!' He makes the noise of feet tromping over monuments.
>
> 'Is this a good thing or a bad thing?'
>
> 'Foreigners coming is okay, we welcome them; but the Chinese tourists are not good. The foreigners, when they come, many of them want to learn about Tibetan history and religion. Or they already know about it and they want to study this temple [Labrang Monastery]. They know what to ask: "What things can I do? What things I cannot do?" The Chinese, on the other hand, don't take the time to do this. They're like monkeys [makes hooting noises] hopping around the place [and causing problems]. Where Westerners are very sensitive, the Chinese [feel entitled to] say: "I paid money for this ticket, I should be able to do X; you should show me X." I have many Chinese friends; but the difference in thinking between Chinese and Tibetans is a barrier to mutual understanding. With the Hui [Muslim Chinese], it's the same thing. I have Muslim friends, but their thinking is different. Muslims are focused on business. This is the one thing: this is how you have a good life, best life, perfect! Tibetans maybe care about religion or about people, but Muslims are very narrowly focused on

making money. As for Chinese [Han] people, they go to school and
they hear from a very young age how wonderful their country is. In
school, Chinese people hear that they are number 1 and that
number 2 is the others, Tibetans, maybe. Same thing on television,
the news is always positive, constantly proclaiming how good China
is. "Today a company made this much money, building a new city,
a nice car; today the president visited this foreign country. China is
great and powerful." The Hanzu are made to feel that they are the
ones responsible for the greatness of their country. But all these
great things: do you see them here? You know the Xibu Dakaifa
[Great Develop the West Strategy]? Well, has the West caught up
with the East yet? Where are all the nice cars [and other markers
of development]?'
     'Somewhere else?'
     'Exactly. But if you watch television, all you see is this
[triumphalist] picture of China.'

Ngawang's take on Chinese tourism attests to the degree to which tourism can re-inscribe rather than break down boundaries of class, ethnicity and region. If young Han are drawn to Tibetan places by their perceived foreignness, then the inhabitants of these places are also forced to confront an influx of strangers in their own territory, but not necessarily on their own terms. For us as scholars of tourism and of contemporary China, the ethnographic examples presented in this chapter push us to bring the messiness of actual tourist practices back into scholarly accounts. Young urban backpackers are reshaping the landscape of Chinese tourism and are participating in moral revaluations of the ethno-scape of the nation, recasting an aversion to brutal Tibetan superstition into a romantic, if naive, enthusiasm for mysterious sacred culture. Yet, even as backpacking reshapes the tourist and human landscapes of the nation, it simultaneously re-inscribes existing class and ethnic and region-based cleavages within the population.

As analysts we must be able to apprehend what is qualitatively new about journeys such as the Cantonese tourists' sojourn on the grasslands, and be cognizant of the way in which tourist innovation and overtures towards intercultural dialogue rest on a foundation of societal inequality and unthinking ethno-regional and class bias. By doing so, we can formulate an analysis of domestic tourism that follows the logic of scholars such as Doreen Massey who have argued that 'home places' are not the ordered secure worlds that many (men) take them to be, but are rather fraught with the ambiguities, tensions and contradictions of modernity' (Massey, cited in Minca and Oakes, 2006, p17).

Notes

1   A Tibetan Buddhist monk in his early 20s, then studying at the Provincial Institute of Buddhist Studies (*foxueyuan*).
2   One might suggest that this 'Tibetanizing' of their names was an effort at constructing temporary bonds of a sort of fictive kinship. Alternately, one could see it as part of the process by which the Cantonese sought to temporarily adopt the external trappings of being Tibetan (e.g. by having their hair braided and dressing up in Tibetan festival clothing: a sort of ethnic karaoke?).
3   See Ramsay (1989), Dwyer (1998) and Gladney (2004) for more on the hierarchy of languages within China and the complexity of the Chinese-language family.
4   Two years later, meeting him again on the grasslands with Rinchen (although in a very different context, a pasture by the Sangchu River where locals go to hang out, shoot some hoops or go swimming), he still wasn't using email but did pass along his QQ (internet chat) address.
5   Nyiri (2006, p109) notes that these very high numbers, currently higher than China's total population, 'are based on surveys of rail and road traffic' and 'therefore, although they are used by most tourism research publications ... reflect mobility, in general, rather than tourism specifically'.
6   Nyiri (2006) cites Ivy's description of tourism in Japan prior to the 1970s: 'Travel to these landscapes [Mount Fuji, Lake Towada, etc.] was an exercise in confirmation: the sightseer ... expected no unusual encounters, no solitary experience. The purpose of travel was to see what one was supposed to see, to view an already culturally valued scene, and to acquiesce to general opinion' (Ivy, 1995, pp44–45, cited in Nyiri, 2006, p93). Such orientations began to change only after the Discover Japan campaign in the 1970s fostered an increasing focus on individualized discovery. Lest we think that this sort of orientation is some sort of 'Eastern' proclivity, compared with the following passage from Andrew McGregor's work on Torajaland, cited in Mike Crang's (2006) essay on 'Circulation and emplacement':

> *The travellers' expectations had been so well shaped by their guide-books that they were no longer surprised or astonished when they finally arrived at the 'exotic sites'. Viewing the unknown, while an integral part of their trips, was not considered a fantastic part of their experiences because, in a sense, they had already done it... Predestination images made gazing on upon the tau-tau a fulfilling experience, not because of the tau-tau themselves, but because they were at the very spot that had been made famous in their minds by countless previous exposures.* (McGregor, 2000, p40, cited in Crang, 2006, p52).

Or consider the oft-repeated travellers' mantra: 'We can't go there, it's not in the book.'
7   As a result, commercialization is not necessarily seen as destructive of a site's attractiveness.
8   Minca and Oakes (2006, p18) suggest that a focus on travel as transgressive or as innately freeing obscures the degree to which 'while we may travel in order to transgress, if only for a day, the boundaries and routines that order our lives, we find that travel becomes more of a routinized homage to shoring up those binaries; it merely reifies boundaries by reinforcing a subject-object binary'.

9   In my fieldwork I did encounter Chinese independent travellers interested in the consumption of authenticity. The comments of a Han film-maker – a practising Buddhist – visiting the region for the first time, were in this regard instructive. Queried as to his impressions, he replied: 'It's not like I imagined it would be' (*gen wo xiangxiang bu yiyang*). 'The culture of today's Buddhist', he continued, 'is not like it was in the past – it's changed' (*Xianzai Fojiao wenhua gen guoqu bu yiyang; you bianhua*). Specifically, 'lamas' behaviour doesn't match their teaching; they eat meat, drink alcohol and patronize prostitutes' [*chi rou, he jiu, piao ji*] and they are, above all, commercialized [*shengyihua* or *maimaihua*].' 'They depend on average Tibetans; but the gap between them has grown and grown.' Of course, such opprobrium for the practice is not universal even among tourists. In response to the film-maker's comments, a Han TV producer from Beijing visiting Xiahe at the same time suggested that the former's disappointment had to do in part with his being Buddhist and a corresponding gap between the expectations of the believer and the tourist. '*Youshihou women de yaoqiu bu gongping*': 'Sometimes our expectations aren't fair – we expect them to preserve their original culture; but aren't their lives entitled to progress as well?' (*Tamen de shenghuo ye yao jinbu*).

10   Hence, Nyiri's (2006) focus on what he terms 'cultural authority': the role of the state in identifying sites worthy of being toured. See, for instance, his discussion of the publication of tour guide manuals (*daoyou ci*).

11   See, for example, his assertion that 'one encounters no dissent at scenic spots' (Nyiri, 2006, p81).

12   See, for example, the comment in Wei et al (1999, p231, cited in Nyiri, 2006, p83) that 'ancient relics, "in a sense could also be understood as theme parks built by people in antiquity"'. On this line of thinking, see also James Hevia's essay (2001) on the cultural and historical stakes of including Chengde on the list of UNESCO World Heritage sites.

13   This is not to say that guidebooks themselves do not do 'thematizing' work. Some ways of 'theming' tourist space (through the employment of possible itineraries) include cost (*10 Trips for 1000 Yuan*), historical routes (*The Silk Road*; *The Tea Horse Route*), mysterious or religious places (*Xizang Niupi Shu*, Buddhist monuments of China), activities (trekking, 4WD routes, photography), traditional architecture (the *Guzhenyou*, or *Ancient Village Travel* series, which deserves a full treatment for the novel relationship that they construct between some very out of the way places and the metropolitan gaze).

14   In their preface, Zhang and Zhao (2001) note that 'in the West, independent travel is almost a required course [*bixiuke*] for every young person. It is not only a way to appreciate the significance of life [*tiwei shengming yiyi de fangshi*], even more so it is essential to growing up [*gengshi chengchang de bixu*]'. The authors go on to contrast the situation abroad where guidebooks and independent travel information are widely available with that in China where their guidebook series is an attempt to get things off the ground.

15   *Zidong* has connotations of voluntariness, spontaneity and, less directly, related connotations of automation – and, hence (although this may be stretching things), technological modernity.

16   Compare this with Nyiri's treatment of the *Discover Japan* campaign of the 1970s (Nyiri, 2006, pp93–94).

17   According to the webpage of the South Gan Tibetan Autonomous Prefecture People's Government (*Gannan zhou renmin zhengfu*), Labrang Monastery is one of the three great tourist sites of the province (*sanda lüyou jingdian zhiyi*). It was designated in 1982 as a national-level target (*zhongdian*) of cultural preservation and was

opened to foreign travellers in 1984. The tourist resources (*lüyou ziyuan*) in Labrang and its surroundings are especially rich (*shifen fengfu*). According to the government website, in 2002, Xiahe welcomed (*jiedai*) 4.1 *wan*, or 41,000 foreign tourists, and 23.84 *wan*, or 238,400 domestic visitors. From this custom, tourism-related businesses raked in 1345 *wan* or 13.45 million yuan (approximately US$2 million). Since the implementation of the *Xibu Da Kaifa*, or Great Western Development Strategy, in 2000, tourism has explicitly been cast as one of the most important means of 'developing locally specific economic resources' (*fazhan tese jingji*). Thus, both backpacker and organized tourism in Xiahe take place in a context where tourism is explicitly conceived as a means of developing the local economy (www.gnzwdt.gov.cn/CenterIntro/ViewData.asp?CenterIntroId=27, accessed June 13, 2008).

18 See Lipman (1997) and Harrell (2001) on the translation of *minzu*.
19 In this respect, the Chinese term *guonei* (or internal to the nation) is less suggestive of troubling resonances.
20 The map of the Beijing Minority Cultures Park, for example, says in English: 'Let us know ourselves, let the world know China.'
21 From the back blurb of a 2006 guidebook to Gannan Tibetan Autonomous Prefecture (Woniu Zhizao, 2006), 'Tibetan areas signify the mysterious, the miraculous, the sacred' (*zangqu yiweizhe shenmi, shenqi, shensheng*).

References

Braun, B. (2003) '"On the raggedy edge of risk": Articulations of race and nature after biology', in D. Moore, J. Kosek and A. Pandian (eds) *Race, Nature, and the Politics of Difference*, Duke University Press, Durham, pp175-203

Crang, M. (2006) 'Circulation and emplacement: the hollowed-out performance of tourism', in T. Oakes and C. Minca (eds) *Travels in Paradox: Remapping Tourism*, Rowman and Littlefield, New York, NY

Dwyer, A. (1998) 'The texture of tongues: Language and power in China', in W. Safran (ed) *Nationalism and Ethnoregional Identities in China*, Routledge, New York, NY, pp68–85

Forney, M. (2001) 'China falls for Tibet chic', *Time Asia*, www.time.com/time/asia/magazine/2001/0129/china.tibet.html, accessed 18 February 2008

Gladney, D. (2004) *Dislocating China: Muslims, Minorities and Other Subaltern Subjects*, University of Chicago Press, Chicago, IL

Harper, D., Fallon, S., Gaskell, K., Grundvig, J., Heller, C., Huhti, T., Mayhew, B. and Pitts, C. (2005) *Lonely Planet China*, Lonely Planet Publications, Oakland, CA

Harrell, S. (2001) *Ways of Being Ethnic in Southwest China*, University of Washington Press, Seattle, WA

Hevia, J. (2001) 'World heritage, national culture and the restoration of Chengde', *Positions*, vol 9, no 1, pp219–243

Ivy, M. (1995) *Discourses of the Vanishing: Modernity, Phantasm, Japan*, University of Chicago Press, Chicago, IL

Lipman, J. (1997) *Familiar Strangers: A History of Muslims in Northwest China*, University of Washington Press, Seattle, WA

McGregor, A. (2000)   'Dynamic texts and the tourist gaze: Death, bones and buffalo', *Annals of Tourism Research*, vol 27, no 1, pp27–50

Meszaros, K. (2003) 'Tourism – the Chinese are coming', *Newsletter of the Institute for*

World Economics, Hungarian Academy of Social Sciences, vo. 20, no 51, February

Minca, C. and Oakes, T. (2006) 'Introduction: travelling paradoxes', in T. Oakes and C. Minca (eds) *Travels in Paradox: Remapping Tourism*, Rowman and Littlefield, New York, NY, pp1–21

Nyiri, P. (2006) *Scenic Spots: Chinese Tourism, the State and Cultural Authority*, University of Washington Press, Seattle, WA

Oakes, T. (1998) *Tourism and Modernity in China*, Routledge, New York, NY

Pan, Z., Lee, C., Chan, J. and So, C. (2005) 'To cheer for the family-nation: The construction of Chinese nationalism during the Hong Kong handover', in D. Tao and Y. Jin (eds) *Cultural Studies in China*, Marshall Cavendish Academic, Singapore

Ramsay, S. R. (1989) *The Languages of China*, Princeton University Press, Princeton, NJ

Walsh, E. and Swain, M. (2004) 'Creating modernity by touring paradise: Domestic ethnic tourism in Yunnan, China', *Tourism Recreation Research*, vol 29, no 2, pp59–68

Wei, X., Liu, Z. and Zhang, S. (1999) *Zhongguo lüyouye xin shiji fazhan de qushi* [*Trends in China's Tourism Development in the New Century*], Guangdong Travel Press, Guangzhou

Woniu Zhizao (2006) *Gannan xingzhi shu* [*Gannan Travel Information Book*], Shaanxi People's Press, Xi'an, China

Yi Zhi (2001) *Zangdi Niupi Shu: Beishangbao Jiu Zou de Ganjue* [*Cowhide Book of Tibetan Places*], China Youth Press, Beijing, China

Zhang, T. and Zhao, J. (2001) *Xizang (Tibet)* (*Zanglingyang Zidong Lüyou Shouce*), Guangdong Travel Press, Guangdong, China

Zhou, H. (ed) (2006) *Zhongguo guzhenyou* [*China Ancient Village Travel*], Shaanxi Normal University Press, Xi'an, China

7

Year Zero! From Annihilation to Renaissance: Domestic Tourism in Cambodia

Trevor H. B. Sofield

Introduction

On 17 April 1975, Cambodia began Year Zero. Pol Pot, the commander of the Communist Khmer Rouge revolutionary movement, took control of the capital, Phnom Penh, on that date and so began 3.5 years of one of the most brutal regimes of the 20th century. An extreme Marxist who believed that many communist revolutions had been unsuccessful because of their failure to totally destroy all vestiges of capitalism, Pol Pot embarked on a reign of terror and destruction that the world has rarely seen (Becker, 1986). In less than 4 years, some 1.7 million Cambodians out of a total population of 11 million had perished under his paranoia. Cambodia's cities and towns were depopulated, most of the infrastructure of the towns and cities was destroyed, and its entire society was reduced to just two categories: soldiers and peasant slaves. The objective was to create a pre-industrial rural utopia. Every person older than the age of six years was drafted into a work gang and relocated to the country-side where he or she toiled from dawn until dusk without wages on a semi-starvation diet (which itself was a control mechanism applied universally to all but the soldiers on grounds that underfed people would lack the strength and will to offer any resistance). All schools were closed; education ceased. Hundreds of thousands of Cambodians identified as 'educated' (above primary school level 7) were exterminated on the simplistic basis that if they could read and write, they must have participated in the corruption of the military regime of General Lon Nol that Pol Pot overthrew. Their extended families were also killed on the rationale that they were parasitical beneficiaries of the corruption and could not be allowed to survive to exact revenge. Together with monks who were also singled out for death, they were 'the enemies of the state'. In Pol Pot's terminology, uneducated people were 'blank slates' who could be manipulated into performing even mass killings without remorse (Chandler, 1999). For 'intellectuals', as defined by the Khmer Rouge, 'to keep you is no gain; to kill you is no loss' (Dutton, 2007, p32). The scale of the killing has been described as 'systematic political slaughter' (Dutton, 2007) or 'democide' (Rummel, 1997), rather than genocide, because it was carried out by the Khmer government against its own ethnic Khmer citizens (with the exception of some minorities such as Chinese Cambodians and Cham–Muslim–Cambodians, who were also targeted as enemies of the state). The distinction is that while both genocide and democide are mass killings that are government driven, a democide can include annihilation of a group because of its symbolic political meaning (Rummel, 1997). Because the violence in Cambodia was directed at Cambodians who were racially identical to the perpetrators, it was not a true genocide, which would logically imply auto-extermination (Dutton, 2007, p31). Ideology was the basis for differentiating between 'them' and 'us'. The introduction of Year Zero was symbolic of the dawn of a new era: history and the past were eliminated and reference to them was punishable by instant death.

Pre-Pol Pot, there was limited domestic tourism in Cambodia as we know it today. It was a poor country where the Cambodian elite, including the Royal Court of Prince Norodom Sihanouk, often copied French notions of leisure and recreation – indeed, many of them took their holidays in France (Osborne, 1973). There were some relatively luxurious beach homes and hill station residences, most of them built by the French colonialists, in several towns along the south coast that were used as occasional 'retreats' after the French exit in 1953. The early years of Prince Norodom Sihanouk's rule after Cambodia gained independence from France in 1953 to the mid-1960s, are sometimes referred to as 'the Golden Age' by elderly Cambodians (*Phnom Penh Post*, 2008) where many forms of recreation and entertainment flourished. Under Sihanouk's personal direction, the public education system expanded from just 12 high schools and 2 universities in 1955 to 180 high schools and 48 universities by 1968. During the same period, the number of children enrolled in primary school jumped from 311,000 to more than 1,025,000; high school enrolments increased from 5300 to 117,000 (Osborne, 1973). It was also a decade of thriving cultural advances, with the king promoting a Cambodian film industry (producing several films himself) and music, and the Royal Court sponsoring a number of singers and actors and actresses of the day (Nette, 2008). The king and the royal family participated in many festivals and Buddhist ceremonies, the majority in the capital, Phnom Penh, and the environs of the Royal Palace (now a national monument open to the public). Angor was not a destination for Cambodians (although French colonialists used to make safaris to visit the ruins) and it had not been developed for tourism.

There was a burgeoning professional class and middle class for whom recreation and touring were common. The general population was active in pilgrimage and religious and cultural festivals at the local level, a popular feature at the village level was entertainment by touring musical bands, and sport and recreation at the local level were also popular (Nette, 2008). The Khmer New Year was widely celebrated over a four-day period each April.

Some of these activities were significantly reduced in the five years before the overthrow of Sihanouk in 1970 by General Lon Nol, however, because the Vietnamese War stretched over the border into Cambodia, with American bombing of infrastructure, and then because of the civil war with the Khmer Rouge until Pol Pot assumed total control in 1975. The recreational ferries that used to ply the Mekong disappeared, and internal travel was difficult and dangerous.

All tourism, sport, religions and, therefore, ceremonies, festivals and pilgrimage, as well as leisure and recreation activities, ceased the day Pol Pot entered Phnom Penh: all holidays were banned (Etcheson, 2006). Theatres, musical studios, film studios and all other elements of the arts and culture were destroyed. Singers, actors, actresses, dancers, cultural performers, entertainers of all kinds, poets, novelists and all others with similar cultural and artistic associations were systematically exterminated. One of the crimes punishable by death was 'reminiscing' about the past: the public expression of memories of past times was banned publicly. To say: 'It was better before the revolution' brought instant death. Libraries were burned. Other prohibited activities included praying, flirting, expressing joy, contacting the outside world and owning private property of any kind. As with all other towns in Cambodia, the coastal towns and hill stations were emptied of their populations and virtually all of the 'capitalist' beach homes and resorts were destroyed by the Khmer Rouge. The ruins of the Bokhor Hill Station behind the beaches of Kampot, where there was a casino, a church and numerous residential buildings, are a good example, with not a single habitable structure remaining to this day.

'Year Zero' was exactly that: the beginning of a thankfully short-lived regime that decimated its own population. Not only was Cambodia pre-tourism in the Western sense, but under Pol Pot there was no tourism.

Following Pol Pot's constant provocation of Vietnam, the Vietnamese army invaded Cambodia in 1979 and for the next 12 years ruled the state under a military government. Pol Pot and his soldiers retreated to a series of rural and jungle strongholds from where they continued guerrilla attacks and mass killings, and again leisure and recreation were suppressed, not as a matter of ideology, but as a matter of the prevailing lack of security and continuing warfare. Finally, peace of a kind was negotiated in October 1991 (the Paris Peace Accords); Vietnam withdrew and a United Nations peacekeeping force; the United Nations Transitional Authority of Cambodia (UNTAC) was established; and elections for a new civilian government were held. Slowly, tourism began to emerge from the shadows, although many places remained off-limits because elements of Pol Pot's Khmer Rouge soldiers continued to cause bloodshed (including the kidnapping and killing of several foreign tourists) and visitation numbers were miniscule – less than 50,000 per year between 1993 and 1997. Cambodians themselves were so preoccupied with trying to reconstruct their shattered lives, in many cases with only remnants of their extended families, that the pursuit of leisure and recreation had little priority.

The uncertain internal security situation was again disturbed in 1997 when fighting broke out between the elected coalition parties then ruling Cambodia, the FUNCINPEC (Front Uni National pour un Cambodge Independant, Neutre, Pacifique et Coopératif) Party under then first prime minister, Prince Rannaridh, eldest son of the former King Sihanouk who had been overthrown by General Lon Nol in 1971 and Hun Sen, second prime minister and leader of the Cambodian People's Party. The Cambodian People's Party triumphed and Hun Sen became prime minister, a position he continues to hold today even after three successive elections since then. Following Pol Pot's death in an isolated rural village in 1998, stability has prevailed for the last decade.

Figure 7.1 *Map of Cambodia*

Source: Cambodian Ministry of Tourism

However, it is a stability that has brought no accountability for the crimes against humanity committed by the Khmer Rouge. Only in 2006 was an agreement finally reached between the United Nations and the Cambodian government to set up an international tribunal to bring the leaders of the Khmer Rouge to trial, though as of January 2009, only four leaders had been brought before the court, with the now aged remaining Khmer Rouge leaders denying any responsibility for the mass killings. It is also a society in which many surviving adults have refused to talk about or share with their children the years of Pol Pot. His attempted revolution has been expunged from schools and history curricula, so the younger generation have little knowledge about it. It does not feature in the National Museum in Phnom Penh. Nor does the government support the Genocide Museum established in the school that Pol Pot turned into the most notorious of his many torture prisons, Tuol Sleng, in the capital city, where out of more than 14,500 prisoners (all meticulously photographed and recorded) (Short, 2004) only 7 survived: this museum is run by non-governmental organizations (NGOs) with international funding. In addition, the Cambodian government does not support the Documentation Centre of Cambodia (DC-CAM), which was established as part of Yale University's Cambodian Genocide Project in 1995 to document the Khmer Rouge regime and the crimes committed during that era with the objectives of promoting the rule of law, accountability and reconciliation. Cambodia thus has a government and much of its population who deny or are ignorant of its recent past and take few lessons from it. Kiernan (2004, p16) argues that only tribunals bringing Khmer Rouge leaders to justice can recapture their history and dignity: 'Although a legal accounting of the crimes of the Khmer Rouge era cannot restore to Cambodians their lost loved ones, [it] could give them back their history.' Etcheson (2004) also argues that true reconciliation between victims and oppressors of the Khmer Rouge regime can only occur with the accountability that a tribunal would bring.

Psychologists such as Matthias Witzel (2007) claim that relative political stability has come at a significant psychological cost to individuals. Given the magnitude of the Khmer Rouge crimes and the deaths of so many people, the failure to articulate notions of individual responsibility, conscience and human dignity leaves the victims suspended in powerlessness and confronting unresolved personal trauma (e.g. Odenwald, 2002; Vinjamuri and Snyder, 2004; Baum, 2008). Carlson and Rosser-Hogan (1991) reported that a high proportion of Cambodian refugees in the US demonstrated a strong correlation between the amount of trauma they experienced during the Pol Pot years and the severity of symptoms, such as post-trauma stress disorder, dissociation, avoidance, depression and anxiety, and hypothesized that the Cambodian population at home would demonstrate a similar relationship. The Transcultural Psychosocial Organization (TPO), a UN World Health

Organization collaborative centre associated with the Free University of Amsterdam in The Netherlands, started work with democide survivors in Cambodia in 1995 in an attempt to deal with this community-wide problem (the TPO also operates in other countries which have experienced genocide, such as Burundi, Ethiopia and Uganda). The TPO recognized that post-trauma stress disorder was evident throughout the community, with collective responses discernible through coping mechanisms such as dissociation, avoidance and numbing. Because of its widespread manifestation throughout the 'adult over 40s' community, psychologists from the TPO have described this as 'societal trauma' (Sotheara Chhim, 2007). Boyden and Gibbs (1998) found similar symptoms, and these findings were echoed by a group of 70 American psychologists and psychiatrists who received special funding from the US government to visit Vietnam and Cambodia in early 2007 in order to gain a better understanding of post-trauma stress related to their Cambodian and Vietnamese refugee patients in the US (Meyers, 2007). They considered that they could not fully comprehend the level of trauma inflicted on the Cambodian people by the Khmer Rouge until they had visited the country and talked to survivors (Meyers, 2007). In personal discussions with the author at the time, several members of the group commented that in Vietnam there was more of an individual response to the stresses faced during the Vietnamese War; but in Cambodia, where every person they interviewed had lost at least six or seven family members because of the democidal policy of Pol Pot, they also described the prevailing situation as one of 'societal trauma inflicted by the Khmer Rouge' (Meyers, 2007, p40). Their conclusions included the identification of the same symptoms as those documented by the TPO: continuing high levels of post-trauma stress, dissociation, avoidance and numbing as coping mechanism that required community-wide and collective treatment. They also noted that because all Cambodian psychologists and psychiatrists had been killed by the Khmer Rouge and training in these fields had recommenced only through international aid agencies after 1995, there was very limited clinical capacity to deal with the problem. They could discover no adults who had availed themselves of such services and treatment in Phnom Penh. As Meyers (2007, p40) noted: 'In Cambodia, mind cannot be separated from spirit or body, and the individual cannot be separated from the collective. Treating trauma literally involves the whole community.' Clinical psychologists such as Baum (2008), Dutton (2007) and Witzel (2007) support the conclusions of the TPO and the American group that for many Cambodians who lived through the Khmer Rouge years, the lack of counselling and opportunities to heal have left them in a state of dissociation characterized by detachment and suppression of feelings.

National esteem and Cambodia's international image have also suffered from the reluctance of Cambodian authorities to re-establish the generally accepted social norm that crimes and atrocities should not go unpunished (Crocker, 2004), despite the United Nations Commission on Human Rights (UNHCR) pushing for more than 15 years to establish a special tribunal. As noted above, only in 2006 did the Cambodian government bow to international pressure to establish such a tribunal, although many Cambodians are quick to argue that it would be better not to confront people with the horrors of the atrocities after more than 30 years of suppressing them (another manifestation of dissociation). Some mental health experts also believe that the upcoming tribunal process will revive stressful memories for a certain percentage of the population (Sotheara, 2007). In one sense, the reluctance of the Cambodian government to work with the UNHCR mirrors the trauma-based avoidance mechanisms of the population whom it governs, although there are also significant political considerations at work since some members of the current political and military leadership of Cambodia were closely associated with the Khmer Rouge itself.

This chapter holds that leisure, recreation and domestic tourism for Cambodians have taken a particular path in the last decade that is consistent with this pervasive psycho-social environment. The recent past is avoided and the focus is on the glories of the ancient Khmer civilization of six centuries ago in an attempt to demonstrate to the world the worth and merit of Cambodians and Cambodia, and to establish a national image of a peaceful and harmonious society: there is a collective response to the trauma that 'buries' the immediate past but resurrects the glorious ancient past as a coping mechanism.

Tourism as a sector for post-conflict development

Where international and domestic tourism had again been reduced to zero following the outbreak of civil war in 1997 and its political resolution in 1998, the intervening years have continued to witness a steady development in tourism as the Hun Sen government made it a priority sector for national reconstruction. From less than 10,000 international tourists in 1998, numbers, in 2007 increased to almost 2 million and the industry was estimated to have brought US$1.95 billion in revenue to the country (Ministry of Tourism, 2008). At the same time, as the country slowly stabilized politically, and security and economic conditions improved, domestic tourism began to grow. With such a devastating recent history, people who were decimated and suffering post-democide trauma (Dutton, 2007) and a country whose physical infrastructure had been almost completely destroyed, it is perhaps not surprising that Cambodians turned away from recent events to seek respite and relief in ancient glories, the peace of the past and Buddhist pacifism. In this psychosocial environment, drawing on their history and heritage, traditional and religious festivals, especially those that demonstrated the worth of Cambodians, began to re-emerge. Monasteries and temples were rebuilt or reopened, providing both spiritual renewal and centres for community and leisure (non-work) activities. Perhaps most significant of all in this context, given the need to rise above the horrors of Pol Pot and to reaffirm their dignity and self-esteem, Cambodians began flocking to their ancient capital Angkor, which 500 years ago ruled over the largest land empire that South-East Asia has even seen.

By 2007, about 1 million Cambodians were visiting their world-famous heritage site, the temples of Angkor (APSARA, 2008), and more than 1 million Cambodians from around the country were descending every year to join the 1.5 million residents of Phnom Penh for the reinstituted annual festival called *Bon Om Tuk*, or boat races to celebrate the reverse flow of the Tonle Sap River and to seek blessings for a prosperous harvest. This phenomenon of the re-emergence of domestic tourism, leisure and recreation in Cambodia, founded on traditional festivals and ancient heritage as part of a search that transcends the individual sense of self, has an underlying focus on demonstrating national worth and national unity. Celebrating the 'glorious past' of the ancient Khmer Empire and the impressive spectacle of colourful festivals and pageants provides both an escape and a healing process for traumatized people.

Heritage and history: The Khmer Empire and Angkor

In contextualizing contemporary 21st-century recreation and tourism by local residents in Cambodia, it is necessary to examine the historical record of socio-cultural power and the role of traditional socio-religious events in the ancient Khmer kingdom centred around Angkor. There are two key 'texts' that provide insights into recreation as enjoyed during the five centuries of the Khmer Empire that ruled much of Indochina – Cambodia, eastern Thailand, southern Laos and large swathes of Vietnam – from the ninth to the 14th centuries. First, there are the several kilometres of *bas relief* panels, friezes, decorated lintels and pediments, inscriptions and thousands of other carvings that adorn the 250 temples and other structures of Angkor. Second, there is the remarkable chronicle of Zhou Daguan, a young Chinese diplomat who lived at Angkor for a year in 1296 AD and who on his return to China wrote *A Record of Cambodia: The Land and Its People* (Daguan, 1296 AD, translated by Harris, 2007). While the *bas relief* panels and other carvings at Angkor mainly depict religious themes (Hindu and Buddhist ceremonies, festivals, events in the lives of the gods and their acolytes, and the myths and legends of Rama, Shiva, Vishnu and Brahma), the kings and their royal courts, and many famous battles, they also provide tantalizing glimpses of everyday life and the pursuit of leisure and recreation 800 years or more ago. Zhou's travelogue-cum-diary follows a standard format of old Chinese travel literature with a strong focus on describing the royal court as the apex of power and governance and trade opportunities (much the same objectives of current diplomats around the world); but he also wrote in some detail about 'curious local customs' and thus also touched on leisure and recreation. The collective evidence from the *bas reliefs* and Zhou's account is that while the record of daily life at Angkor is limited, there is enough material to determine that 'many of the mundane aspects of Khmer life have remained similar almost to the present day, particularly in the countryside where houses, markets, ox-carts and so on are almost identical to those carved in sandstone eight centuries ago' (Freeman and Jaques, 2002, p37).

All of the visible buildings at Angkor, now a protected World Heritage site (since 1993) that stretches out over more than 250km², are religious monuments because they were constructed of brick and stone; the royal palaces and other residences and buildings were wooden edifices and have long since disappeared. However, the base of the royal reception hall of Angkor Thom overlooking the royal square is evidenced by its stone foundations, a raised 3m high platform more than 300m long and 50m wide, known today as the Elephant Terrace because of the carvings of elephants along its walls. Zhou provides descriptions of this hall (which consisted of a number of pavilions) and some of the ceremonies that were conducted there (Murray, 1994). The centre of power revolved around the Khmer kings as religious figureheads with major religious responsibilities, and events of the royal courts attracted participant observers from many sections of society. Although all of the major roles in such festivals and events were the exclusive prerogative of royalty, the governing elite and senior religious leaders, they were ceremonies that drew pilgrims from all socio-economic levels down to the poorest peasants. Zhou describes one of these royal processions and, despite a general tone of disparagement of his Cambodian hosts, he acknowledges that the 'southern Barbarians' could honour their princes in majestic style. Preceded by a large band of female bodyguards and accompanied by musicians, dancers, jugglers and acrobats, the king went forth, with the princesses and ladies of the court carried beside him in palanquins: 'The ministers and princes are all on elephant back, from afar their innumerable red parasols can be seen... Behind them at last comes the king, standing upright on the back of the largest elephant and holding in his hand a sacred sword' (Zhou, cited in Daguan, 1296, translated by Harris, 2007). This procession is also captured in a 94m long series of *bas relief* panels in Angkor Wat. A major feature of these ceremonies was a series of traditional dances performed by *apsaras*, celestial maidens, and they are depicted in friezes and *bas relief* carvings all over Angkor – more than 2200 of them in total. The forms and styles of this rich dance heritage have been passed down over the centuries, and in contemporary Cambodia *apsaras* remain a favourite component of cultural performances and will be a feature of most major Cambodian festivals and celebrations, such as wedding ceremonies. The contemporary tourism industry was quick to co-opt the *apsaras* tradition, and *apsaras* performances are standard components of all two- or three-day tours to Angkor by international tourists, and more than 50 hotels and restaurants have their own nightly *apsaras* cultural dances with the evening meal.

Other friezes and *bas relief* carvings at Angkor Wat and Bayon temples depict a variety of leisure and recreational vignettes (Murray, 1994). There are several scenes of a barbecue with skewered meat being grilled over a fire; forest scenes with archers hunting deer; mothers playing with their children; high-caste ladies with elaborate coiffures being attended by female servants; the Bayon depicting a cockfight about to start, the two owners presenting the cocks to each other with onlookers placing their bets (Figure 7.2); a ruler reclining on his couch surrounded by women and attendants while being entertained by musicians, singers and dancers; a chess game; wrestlers, gladiators and a boar fight for sport; cooks preparing a banquet; feasts; an acrobat supporting three children; a tightrope walker; musicians and jugglers performing; boats carrying ladies of the court across a lake where a group of three *apsaras* dance on lotus flowers; other women walking in a garden, another being rowed in a small boat by a servant to gather lotus flowers; and other forms of entertainment. Among

Figure 7.2 *Placing bets on a cockfight, Bayon temple frieze*

Source: Trevor Sofield

the many panels depicting battles and wars, there are also carvings of animals – deer coming down to a river to drink; cranes in a mating dance; a cormorant catching a fish; a line of forest animals such as elephants, bears, rhinoceros, deer and tigers, and parrots, hornbills and other birds. In various ways many of these forms of leisure and recreation are reflected in contemporary form today. Barbecue picnics in the countryside are popular weekend pastimes, often beside lakes and rivers; and the animal sanctuary south of Phnom Penh, Phnom Tamao, is thronged with Cambodian visitors every holiday and weekend, outnumbering foreign tourists by ten to one.

Originally, the kingdoms and societies of the Khmer Empire were of Hindu origin, and its ceremonies and festivals were therefore based on the Hindu calendar. King Jayavarman VII (1181 to 120 AD), however, was 'a fervent Buddhist' who introduced Mahayana Buddhism and 'crammed into his 30-year rule the largest building programme ever undertaken at Angkor' (Freeman and Jaques, 2002, p13); subsequently, the great Hindu temple of Angkor Wat became a major pilgrimage site for centuries as a Theravada Buddhist centre of worship for Cambodians, a role that it continues to play today. Until the Khmer Rouge moved into the area and systematically destroyed many images in the 1970s, one of the galleries of Angkor Wat was known as the 'Hall of the Thousand Buddhas' (Roveda, 2002, p22). Following peace in Cambodia after the internecine struggles of 1997 when all tourism ceased, Angkor has become the premier attraction and destination for international tourists, with almost 2 million international visitors recorded in 2007 (Ministry of Tourism, 2008) and more than 1 million Cambodian visitors, as noted above.

Angkor as pilgrimage tourism

On the basis of three years of residence in Cambodia (2005 to 2008) as a senior adviser within the Ministry of Tourism, more than 20 visits to Angkor, supervision of major tourism developments for Siem Reap and Angkor (as team leader of the Mekong Tourism Development Project), chairing and participating in many meetings and conferences on Angkor, and numerous discussions with a wide range of Cambodians (including ministers, senior officials and 'ordinary' citizens), my overriding conviction is that Angkor represents the apogee of Khmer identity for contemporary Cambodians, which is above and beyond its religious significance. Their visits to Angkor in many thousands each year constitute a pilgrimage in a social sense as much as, if not more than, in a religious sense: not only do they visit Angkor for Buddhist propitiation, but they visit to reaffirm their identity and heritage and to idolize the glories of the past. Drawing pride from the fact that Angkor was the capital of 'the great-

Figure 7.3 *Cambodians worshipping at Buddhist shrines established inside the main temple of Angkor Wat (June 2007)*

Source: Trevor Sofield

est land empire that South East Asia has ever known' (Osborne, 2000, p35), is the overwhelming emotion of Cambodian visitors to the site. Winter (2007) has an excellent description of the way in which many Cambodians visit Angkor at the time of the Khmer New Year as a deliberate act of Khmer identity reconstruction.

Angkor is not just a 'visited place' for Khmers, however. There are now more than 120,000 Cambodians living and residing in 112 villages close to the ruins (APSARA, 2005), thousands of them inside the core-protected reserve where they farm the land using water from the many *barays* (reservoirs) constructed by their ancestors centuries ago (the largest, East Baray, is 7km long and 2km wide, built circa 896 AD). In 1992 at the time of the Vietnamese withdrawal from Cambodia 12 years after ousting Pol Pot, the UNTAC census revealed only 22,000 residents in and around Angkor. Now, in addition to daily rural/farming activities, they have re-established Buddhist shrines all over Angkor, taking advantage of the archaeological restoration work, and they worship at these sites regularly, often several times a week, and in some cases with daily offerings of fruit and flowers. In November 2007, I counted more than 40 such active worship sites with 'resident' monks and nuns acting as stewards for them (in March 2005, by contrast, I counted less than 10). Many of the shrines are now attracting thousands of worshippers daily, hundreds of whom are international visitors as well as Khmers. One of the sites, a 4m high statue of Buddha restored by a German conservation team, was repositioned in an alcove adjacent to the main entrance archway to Angkor Wat in early 2007, and a majority of visitors, Khmer and foreign tourists, alike, now detour to the right from the causeway arch to enter the complex through this side alcove. No Khmer proceeds any further without stopping for a moment of prayer and offerings of incense, flowers or fruit. Angkor is thus reverting in a number of ways to a dynamic living culture rather than just a UNESCO museum-style site, an archaeologists' playground or a commercialized spectacle for tourists to 'Oooh!' and 'Aaaah!' over. Khmer ownership of Angkor has thus been reinforced. This multiple use of Angkor, of course, brings tensions with it, some of which are discussed below.

The social significance of heritage lies in its association with identity: it is fundamental in helping individuals, communities and nations to define who they are, both to themselves and to outsiders. It provides a sense of 'belonging' in a cultural sense and in terms of place. For the Khmers, their custodianship of famous heritage sites such as Angkor and Preah Vihear constitutes a key element in defining their socio-cultural identity. In this context, 'place' – territoriality – has always been important for the Cambodians (Osborne, 2000).

Alterity and identity are produced simultaneously in the formation of 'locality' and 'community' in the sense that community 'is never simply the recognition of cultural similarity or social contiguity, but a categorical identity that is premised on various forms of exclusion and construction of otherness' (Gupta and Ferguson, 1997, p13). The Khmer of Cambodia engage in processes of exclusion and 'othering' that assist in forming their collective identity as holistic and markedly different from their neighbours in Thailand, Laos and Vietnam. When they visit Angkor, they may share religious sentiments with these 'other' visitors and pilgrims from the Buddhist ecumene –

global connectivity; but they remain ethnically and culturally disconnected from them and constantly/consciously take steps to differentiate themselves. They are particularly rigorous in highlighting Angkor's heritage as theirs, dismissing out of hand each and every claim, especially by the Thais, to the contrary. In 2004, in response to an alleged remark by a Thai actress engaged in making a film at Angkor that Angkor was, in fact, Thai (a claim that dates back at least to the 15th century when Thai armies ransacked the capital and removed many of its treasures to Bangkok), mobs[1] went on a rampage in Phnom Penh and burned the Thai Embassy to the ground in protest.

Cambodian visitors to Angkor also mindfully map themselves (Moscardo, 1999) very firmly as different from *tourists*: they are owners and custodians who 'belong', paying homage to their ancestral heritage, not wandering travellers motivated by curiosity. The same concept of alterity may be applied not only to Thais and tourists, but to locality: the issue is not simply that one is located in a certain place, but that the particular place is set apart from and opposed to other places. The issue of identity for the Khmer at Angkor demonstrates with special clarity the intertwining of place and power in the conceptualization of 'culture' (Gupta and Ferguson, 1997).

For French visitors to Angkor, there are some parallels with Cambodian secular visitation. There is connectivity with the historical heritage of colonial French Indochina that is an important part of their identity in the larger world. It is frequently said that Europeans 'discovered' Angkor in the 19th century and the French naturalist Henri Mouhot is widely acknowledged as the individual whose notes, published in Paris in 1863, first drew international attention to Angkor. This is, however, a Eurocentric perspective that grew out of the European fascination with 'the age of exploration' to uncover 'darkest Africa', the 'Far East' and other isolated places (isolated from the capitals of Europe, that is!), since in reality the Khmer had never 'lost' Angkor even if many of the monuments became neglected after the fall of the last great Khmer Empire in the 14th century. 'Angkor Wat always remained occupied and a place of worship' (Freeman and Jaques, 2002, p40).

The Ecole Francaise d'Extreme Orient (French School of the Far East), founded in 1899, assumed responsibility for the conservation of the monuments under colonial French Indochina in 1907. Since that time, with only a 20-year break due to wars, the Pol Pot regime, the Vietnam invasion and subsequent political unrest, a succession of distinguished French archaeologists have excavated the ruins and restored many buildings. France now co-manages the International Conservation Coordinating Committee (established in 1993) with Japan, under the honorary chairmanship of the King of Cambodia. The United Nations Educational, Scientific and Cultural Organization (UNESCO) provides the secretariat in Phnom Penh and the committee works closely with the Cambodian national authority, the Authority for the Protection of the Sites and Administration of Angkor (APSARA), to coordinate conservation and archaeological research assistance from nine or ten countries. There is a wide and varied literature of French explorers and activities in the Mekong sub-region, and with Angkor, in particular (Osborne, 2000); the 'French connection' thus remains very strong. Much French visitation to the site is in the nature of a touristic pilgrimage to recapture the vanished glories of the French colonial empire and to bask in the current level of French archaeological and historical leadership related to Angkor's conservation, a French version of Urry's 'romanticized nostalgia' (2002, p94).

Visits by Cambodians and others to Angkor may be 'read' in other ways as well. MacCannell (1976, p2), for example, describes tourism as 'a ritual' and tourist attractions as 'precisely analogous to the religious symbolism of primitive peoples' (based on Emile Durkheim's 1912 *Elementary Forms of the Religious Life*), drawing a dichotomy between the sacred (the non-ordinary experience) and everyday work and life (the ordinary, or the profane). In MacCannell's construct, attractions are 'sacred sites', objects are 'venerated' and 'sacred', and monuments that are elevated and framed for viewing are 'enshrined', and so there is a blurring of distinction between the secular and the religious. MacCannell maintains that there is normally a process of '*sacralization*', which renders a particular natural site or cultural artefact a sacred object of the tourist ritual. A key difference between the pilgrim and tourism-as-pilgrimage is that whereas the pilgrim pays homage to a single centre, the tourist pays homage to an enormous array of very diverse centres/attractions.

Nelson Graburn (1977) described tourism as 'the sacred journey' and used the long tradition in anthropology of the structural examination of events and institutions as markers of the passage of natural and social time, as 'rites of passage', the sacred/non-ordinary/touristic and the profane/workaday/stay-at-home dichotomy. He distinguished between the excited anticipation of departure from the 'profane' state of everyday life and work and the transition into the liminoid (uplifted spiritual) state of the holiday ('holy day') and its associated *communitas*, where normal social conventional behaviour was suspended in *ludic* activities (playfulness) while on holiday, with the sadness of re-entry at the end of a carefree vacation. Tourism, he suggested, is the modern equivalent for secular societies of the annual and lifelong sequences of festivals for more traditional, religiously oriented societies. This is the case for virtually all sacred sites where non-believers are permitted access even if that access is often restricted for 'outsiders' to the periphery and not 'inside' to the core. The foregoing outline of the analogies between pilgrimage travel and tourism as pilgrimage confront each other when sights/sites that have been sacred to pilgrims for centuries become sights/sites to be consumed by secular visitors. Angkor, receiving both Cambodians and foreigners, both Buddhists and non-Buddhists, exhibits elements of this dichotomy.

In examining further the literature on pilgrimage tourism, the seminal work of Turner (1973) provides a useful starting point from which to analyse current Cambodian visitation to Angkor. Shrines as major places of pilgrimage are visited by all the adherents of a religion, regardless of divisions into sects, ethnicity or some other characteristic, and Angkor receives Buddhists from all over the world. For the last three years, Koreans have replaced Japanese as by far the largest foreign contingent of visitors – more than 350,000 in 2007 – and the majority of them utilize Angkor not only as an exotic attraction of the other, but as a site for worship. Turner's concept was of sacred centres 'out there', peripheral and remote, 'excentric' to the centres of population and the socio-political focus of secular power, often located beyond a stretch of wilderness in the 'chaos' surrounding the ordered, 'cosmicized' socio-political world (Sofield, 2001). While this may be accurate in the context of some Christian shrines, it is less accurate in the context of Hinduism and Buddhism, as Cohen (1992) outlined in relation to Buddhism in Thailand. Cohen suggested that where there is a fusion of religion and politics, the same place will be the centre for both, although the institutions are separate. There is, thus, a 'concentric' rather than an excentric pilgrimage centre. This can be further refined for Cambodia: for as long as Angkor was the capital of the Khmer Empire and its kings were considered as reincarnations of Vishnu or other gods, so that both spiritual and governmental authority resided in the one (as with the former kings of Nepal until very recently when the monarchy was abolished in May 2008), pilgrimage to Angkor could be termed 'a unicentric place of conjoint authority' (Sofield, 2001). Angkor has long lost that combination of politico-spiritual power; but for Cambodians it remains the most important place for asserting their national identity – its current bucolic landscapes are a reaffirmation of the peace and harmony that is central to their Buddhism. It is a triumphant disavowal of the darkest pages of their history and a proud celebration of the most glorious era of their civilization.

Concurrence

If we take the Turner/Cohen theses and apply them to Angkor, we arrive at a concept I have elsewhere termed 'concurrence', concerning visitation to sacred sites (Sofield, 2001). This is the simultaneous presence of a range of different motivational activities and behaviour carried out by different visitors to Angkor. Concurrence will be manifest in a variety of ways: visitations will *concurrently* include both the sacred (the pilgrim) and the profane (the tourist). The site, its temples, *stupas* and history will simultaneously be both sacred and familiar (to the believer) and a place of religious and historical significance, but exotic (to the tourist). It will be a place of immense significance and mindful mapping for the pilgrim, but placeless for the tourist in need of a map. In this context, a pilgrim may be clearly differentiated from a secular (profane) tourist by virtue of the motivation for travelling, which is intrinsically religious, often accompanied by collective asceticism, sacrifice and symbolic behaviour: without the religious element, the journey would not be undertaken (Vukonic, 1996).

For Buddhists from Cambodia, a pilgrimage to Angkor will be a journey to the traditional socio-cultural and political centre of their society, but motivation based on the religion cannot be divorced from the current political situation in terms of displaying a peaceful image of a united Cambodia to the world. It is not Cohen's concentric place; but it displays concurrence where the two factors meet and coexist with little or no tension. For Buddhists from Thailand, Korea or Japan, however, whose major motivation is religious, the same journey could validly be regarded in Turnerian interpretation as pilgrimage to an excentric place. For the secular visitor, it can still be regarded as a pilgrimage in the sense of paying homage to one of the great architectural wonders of South-East Asia, and that in itself is also a source of pride for Cambodians. A journey for secular international tourists is also one to the periphery, away from the centre of their own society and its religious and cultural institutions: it is an example of the search for the 'other' (Cohen, 1992, 1998). Even in the 21st century with the superior technology of transport now available for the journey from Europe, the Americas, Africa, Asia and Australasia, travel to Cambodia is still distant, time consuming and 'out there'.

Angkor will witness quite different simultaneous behaviour: that of the pilgrim determined by religious protocol or liminal experience, and that of the tourist motivated by curiosity, a desire for an educational/cultural experience, *ludic* (playful) recreation or some other secular rationale. Tension may be apparent over the different approaches to the site, especially when religious sensitivities are ignored. Angkor will simultaneously accommodate participation and observation, the former by pilgrims in individual or collective acts of worship and religious ceremonies, and the latter by tourists. Tourists as non-believers may occasionally also be participants, depending on the nature of the worship or ceremony, and may be able to participate at the margins. It is common to see non-Buddhist tourists at various worship sites around Angkor buying several sticks of incense and burning them before a statue of Buddha. In a *ludic* sense, they will also join in stroking or caressing a piece of statuary for good luck, whereas believers will be motivated by their faith in undertaking such behaviour.

Non-Cambodian tourists, especially group tours, will invariably operate to a fixed itinerary, seeing the major sites in prearranged sequence in a morning tour under the supervision of a guide before returning to their hotel for lunch, and then an afternoon tour to tick off more sites before returning to Siem Reap

Figure 7.4 *Cambodian families picnicking on the banks of the moat surrounding Angkor Wat, Cambodia (November 2006)*

Source: Trevor Sofield

Figure 7.5 *Cambodians relaxing in their ubiquitous hammocks at a picnic spot, Kulin waterfall, near Angkor*

Source: Trevor Sofield

for their evening meal. Many Cambodians, by contrast, will take mats with them and spend most of the day at a fixed spot (the moat around Angkor Wat is the most favoured place) in picnic style, utilizing the local refreshment and food stalls. For many of the more affluent Cambodian residents of Siem Reap, this is a regular pastime.

Cohen (1992) notes that the farther and more peripheral (excentric) the location of a sacred site from the visitor's own country, the stronger the tourist components of the pilgrimage are; the pilgrim is 'a semi-tourist', depending on the same range of services as the secular visitor (Turner and Turner, 1978). This is particularly so for Korean tourists who, while engaging in acts of worship, frequent three-, four- or five-star hotels in the adjacent service town of Siem Reap. They eat in restaurants all over the town, but rarely eat at the more than 150 food stalls erected in and around the major temples in the core area of Angkor by itinerant Cambodian vendors, in contrast to Cambodian visitors who eat as often at these local stalls as they do in town restaurants and who may stay with friends and relatives as well as in hotels. The differentiation in both accommodation and restaurant behaviour is further example of concurrence.

Festivals and special events

Just as Angkor provides Cambodians with the opportunity to 'bury' the Pol Pot years in celebration of past glories, a range of festivals and special events provide a similar psycho-social environment for them, and Cambodians participate in these occasions in huge numbers. Ceremonies that pay respect to nature's four elements – earth, wind, fire and water – are extremely important in Khmer culture and these festivals are generally free from the inevitable element of suppressed sadness that accompanies the Khmer New Year with the absence of many family members. These festivals and ceremonies can also be traced back to the Khmer Empire, and so the same echo of greatness that exists at Angkor is manifest in them. The five main festivals are the Water Festival, the Fire Festival, the Royal Ploughing Festival, the annual Kite Festival and the Khmer New Year.

The Water Festival, *Bon Om Touk*, and the Fire Festival, *Bandet Pra-tib*, are celebrated during the same three-day period in late October or early November, watched by perhaps 2.5 million Cambodians. Unable to be held for three decades, the festivals now attracts the largest crowds to assemble in Cambodia. A general holiday is declared and hundreds of villages and towns from all over the country bring their traditional long boats to the capital, where they race non-stop in pairs with crews of 20 or 40 from around 10.00am until dusk each day until a final winner is declared. The course is about 2km long down the Tonle Sap River to a point just above its entry into the Mekong River in front of the Royal Palace. The festivities are presided over by the King, and the prime minister and all government ministers share a pavilion with him on the banks of the river in the heart of the city.

The three-day Water Festival marks the changing of the flow of the Tonle Sap River[2] and is also seen as thanksgiving to the Mekong River for providing the country with fertile land and abundant fish. In the Angkorean period, the Water Festival honoured the Khmer navy of King Jayavaraman VII, regarded as perhaps the greatest of the kings partly because of his major naval victories over the Cham and Vietnamese. *Bas relief* carvings and inscriptions in the Bayon Temple complex and in the Banteay Chhmar Temple, which are both at Angkor, describe the naval procession, and some scenes depict the king commanding his navy during battles and vanquishing the Cham. Since that time, the naval festival has synchronized with animist and Buddhist beliefs so that it now also represents the propitiation of the water spirit, *Nata*, to bring prosperity to farmers and fishermen and water for humans and animals, thus providing stability for nature. As the sun sets on the last day of the festival, the hundreds of boats line up on the river for a 'grand sail-past', saluting the King with raised oars, and the most beautifully decorated vessel then sails out alone into the centre of the river where it performs the 'cutting of the string' ceremony. This symbolizes the freeing of the *Nata* to return to the sea. Only when this has been completed can the people be sure that they have dutifully honoured the mighty Mekong and

Figure 7.6 *Cambodian crowds at the annual Boat Festival, Phnom Penh (October 2007)*

Source: Trevor Sofield

ensured that the floods are over for the year. The link with Angkor sets the Cambodian Water Festival apart from other water festivals around Asia that focus on the *Nata* and thus reinforces for Cambodians the celebration of their mighty civilization, of which they are now proud custodians.

Each evening after the boat races for the day have finished, hundreds of thousands of onlookers linger to watch a fireworks display and parade of about ten large boats emblazoned with lights that combined represent the *Bandet Pra-tib*, or Fire Ceremony. According to a Buddhist text, after the Buddha died his four main teeth were each sent to a different place. The first was kept in *Trai-Treng* (heavenly third paradise), the second was kept in dragon's lair (the kingdom under the sea), the third in Kunthearak (an Indian kingdom), and the fourth in Tuant-borak (a kingdom in Nepal). The *Bandet Pra-tib* ceremony is to show respect to the Buddha's tooth that is kept in dragon's lair, although another aspect of *Bandet Pra-tib* is to show respect to the fire spirit they cook with (Meach Ponn, professor, Buddhist Institute of Cambodia, radio interview, 28 October 2006). In the days of King Norodom Sihanouk, ten years before Pol Pot, the second night of the Water Festival saw thousands of miniature floating lanterns being released onto the river as votive offerings to both *Nata*, the water spirit, and the Buddha. Young people would also pray to find true love using the tiny floating lamps. Today, the tiny *Pra-tib roy* lamps have been replaced by ten large *Pra-tib* boats illuminated with traditional Khmer pictures (e.g. *apsara* dancers) and ministry insignia in 'neon-light artworks' that parade up and down the river opposite the Royal Palace for three to four hours after the fireworks display. The linkage with Angkorian history, myths and legends, animistic beliefs and Buddhist philosophy are all testament to a civilization of grandeur and longevity; thus, participation in, and celebration of, these two festivals make a further statement about present-day Cambodia for its citizens.

Another festival with a similar set of outcomes is the Royal Ploughing Festival, which takes place every year in May in a field kept especially for this purpose outside the main wall of the palace in Phnom Penh, in front of what is now the National Museum. Presided over by the King and senior Buddhist monks, two white oxen pull a gold-painted plough, followed by four girls dressed in white who scatter rice seeds over the furrows from gold and silver baskets. After several circumambulations of the field, the oxen are unhitched and six golden bowls of different food are placed before them. Depending on which bowl is chosen first, the Buddhist monks divine what sort of season will follow, whether there will be floods or drought, a bountiful harvest or scarcity. This festival celebrates the Buddha's first moment of enlightenment, which is said to have happened when he was seven years old and had gone with his father to watch the first ploughing of the new season. Thousands of Cambodians line the field outside the Royal Palace to witness the pomp and spectacle, many taking their young children with them (as with the Boat and Fire Festivals), safe

Figure 7.7 *Annual Ploughing Festival, Phnom Penh, with the King's Pavilion in the background and one of the princesses sowing the first rice seeds*

Source: Trevor Sofield

in the knowledge that this ceremony attests to their glorious past without raising the spectre of Pol Pot. It also provides a link to the more recent imperial past (another 'Golden Age'; *Phnom Penh Post*, 2008) when King Norodom Sihanouk used to preside over the same ceremony during the 1950s and 1960s.

Pithy Banghos Kleng – the Kite Festival

The Kite Festival, *Pithy Banghos Kleng*, (also referred to as *Khleng Pnorng or Khleng Ek*) pays respect to the wind and is celebrated in November or December, usually one month after the Water Festival. Millennia ago, the Khmer believed in *Neak-ta* (animistic spirits), leading to the celebration of the *Pithy Sen Neak-ta* (the Spirit Festival) at the beginning of the rainy season. At the beginning of the dry season, the Kite Flying Festival served to express gratitude to *Preah Peay* (wind spirit) for bringing dry weather to ripen crops, as well as praying for rain for the next season (Simim Sarak, 2002). During the centuries of the Khmer Kingdom the kings used to preside over the festival. A stone inscription dated 972 AD records that *Khleng* (harvest kites) were sacred objects during the Angkorean period.

As the annual festival begins, in villages and towns all over Cambodia, including in the streets and parks of Phnom Penh, kites are flown at this time of the year by hundreds of thousands of people, both young and old. During the night, lantern kites, many of them equipped with flutes that 'sing' in the wind, are flown over open fields, watched by whole communities and families who then return to their homes for a harvest feast. 'The kite festival is an enter-tainment enjoyed by everyone regardless of age or social standing', wrote Sim (2002, p6). 'Cambodians come together at this time without divisions, to enjoy the hard won freedoms of peace.'

The re-emergence of this festival is particularly pertinent to the thesis that it is a coping mechanism to overcome the Khmer Rouge atrocities. In 1994, a private citizen, Sim Sarak, whose family had been decimated by the Khmer Rouge and who had managed to survive by disguising his education and work-ing as a labourer on a rice collective, petitioned the Minister of Culture and Fine Arts for permission to organize the Kite Flying Festival for the first time in Phnom Penh in many years (Sim and Cheang, 2004). Sim documented the role of the Kite Festival under the Khmer Kingdom rulers, and noted that while it had ceased after the destruction of Angkor by the Thai invasion in 1431 (banned as deliberate policy by the Thai conquerors), it had been revived by Cambodian King Ang Duoung (1840 to 1859), a devout Buddhist commit-ted to peace. After his death in 1859, however, there were no royal observations of kite-flying ceremonies by his successors, although kite-flying remained popular among the Khmers during harvest season until 1970. In a short booklet on *The History of Kite Flying in Cambodia*, prepared for a new National Kite Museum opened in Phnom Penh in 2004, Sim and Cheang (2004, p1) wrote that:

> *Unfortunately for the Cambodian people, their country was in turmoil from the successive wars and civil strife of the 1970s. This dark period had caused hunger, misery, sufferings and killings to Cambodian people. Khmer culture was on the brink of extinction and the exercise of kite flying must certainly die forever.*

However, the Minister of Culture and Fine Arts approved Sim's request to revive the *Khleng Pnorng*, or *Khleng Ek*, Festival, and it continues annually. The tenth anniversary of the revival of the Kite Festival was opened by Deputy Prime Minister Prince Norodom Sirivudh on 11 December 2004, and the Kite Museum officially inaugurated. As Sim and Cheak wrote (2004, p3):

> Khleng Ek *gives not only a colour back to the Khmer culture, but also conveys its symbolic identity of peace and happiness to young Cambodians and their friends across the world as well. The revival of* Khleng Ek *explains that our motherland of Cambodia is living at peace and tastes a happiness.*

The Khmer New Year, like the celebration of the New Year in many Asian soci-eties, is centred on family reunification, made all the more poignant for

Cambodians who lost so many members of their families under the Khmer Rouge. It is a week-long celebration involving virtually all Cambodians, including several thousand overseas Cambodians who return at this time each year. Domestically, as many as 4 million Cambodians travel to all parts of the country every April to reunite with parents and/or grandparents. It has many facets – formal feasts with a range of traditional dishes, many informal meals with numerous family members present, and group visits to temples where the old year is 'washed away' and the New Year is welcomed in with non-stop ceremonies. Additionally, many fairs are held in temple grounds with food and refreshment stalls and performing artists and entertainers. *Ludic* participation by the younger people involves 'water-throwing' activities (where passersby and vehicles are doused with water 'bombs', usually plastic bags filled with water, but occasionally buckets of water, and are greeted with much hilarity). It is a time for visiting friends in one's home town or village as well, and day-long picnics are a feature. For those who are richer and have vehicles or the capacity to hire a taxi or truck, family groups travel to a nearby river for a day-long picnic, and bathing in the river is one of the most common activities, along with a picnic lunch (as depicted in the friezes of Angkor). Around Cambodia's third largest city, Battambang, for example, 70km to 100km out of town on the banks of the Sanger River, six to seven 'picnic spots' have been developed. Typically, these spots have been cleared, leaving only mature trees and landscaped with gardens and a variety of statuary, while thatched raised platforms of split bamboo have been constructed. Simple toilet facilities are provided and several of the more elaborate sites have a restaurant producing local dishes. Families hire a thatched platform, set up a barbecue lunch and wander down to the river for a swim. Such picnicking is highly seasonal, restricted largely to the dry season (October to May) because during the monsoon season the river rises some 10m to 12m and becomes a raging torrent. The sites tend to be used almost exclusively by Cambodian nationals and there are none on the itineraries of any tour operators catering to foreign tourists. Emphasizing this informal exclusivity is the fact that not one of these picnic spots is mentioned in the Lonely Planet guide (Ray, 2006). For Westerners, an intriguing facet of these picnic sites is their adornment with gigantic statues of a herd of prancing horses, giant birds, deer and tigers, often painted in bright gaudy colours – blue, red, yellow, green, purple, black and white. They appear incongruous to Western eyes, set as they invariably are in sylvan countryside landscapes where the Western emphasis would be on 'naturalness' and 'ecotourism'; but to Cambodians there is historical and traditional continuity with their ancient Khmer heritage and the statuary of Angkor, and, for them, these monumental reinforced concrete figures enhance rather than detract from the sight/site. The emic rather than the etic perspective provides meaning that is embedded in Khmer heritage.

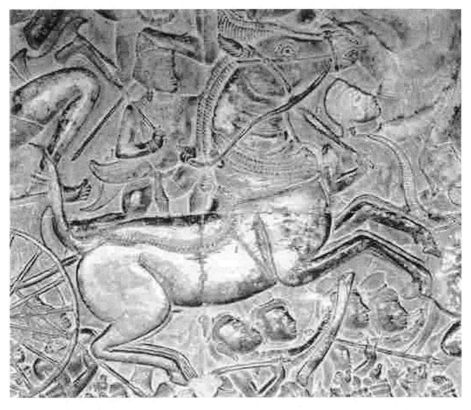

Figure 7.8 *Galloping horse depicted in a wall frieze of Angkor Wat*

Source: Trevor Sofield

Figure 7.9 *'Monumental' statues, Sangker River picnic spot, Battambang*

Source: Trevor Sofield

For some Cambodians, the Khmer New Year is also a time for remembering relatives who were killed during the Pol Pot years, although for many the trauma runs so deep that a form of denial, a 'retreat into the monastery' avoiding all judgement (as Thai author Pira Sudham, 2002, called it³) and a profound desire to forget see them shy away from any public act of remembrance. However, Sampau (Boat) Mountain, 25km from Battambang, is an exception. A holy mountain for centuries with very old Buddhist temples and monasteries that were largely destroyed by the Khmer Rouge (field guns even being deployed on the heights, several of which – now disabled – remain there to this day), the mountain was also the site for a deliberate act of desecration by Pol Pot's soldiers who used one of the sacred caves as a torture prison and two of the cliffs and deep ravines of the mountain as mass-killing sites, hurling several thousand 'enemies of the state' to their deaths. After the withdrawal of the Vietnamese and as order was slowly restored, Sampau Mountain's temples were gradually rebuilt (some rebuilding continues to this day), and a small group of monks and nuns took up residence with the task of praying 24 hours a day in perpetuity to try and rescue the souls of those killed who, in Buddhist theology, are 'lost and hungry ghosts' because they were denied a proper burial with appropriate Buddhist rites. These dark places today experience a Cambodian form of *thana*-tourism at the Khmer New Year when more than 30,000 pilgrims each day of the New Year holiday provide offerings for the monks and nuns to recite continuous prayers for their 'lost' relatives. Many pilgrims detour from the temples to the killing sites and caves to burn incense and recite prayers. Temporally, however, not enough time has elapsed since the horrors of the democide to fade for most Cambodians; and the 'Cambodian *thana*-tourism' to the so-called Killing Fields of Pol Pot that may be found in many parts of Cambodia is not a form of visitation for the vast majority. Such sites are shunned by most Cambodians. In 2007, for example, 140,978 international visitors toured the Choeung Ek Killing Fields, 10km east of Phnom Penh, where some 83 mass graves containing the remains of 27,000 victims have been exhumed; but only 8569 Cambodians (6 per cent) entered the site (MTDP, 2007).

Conclusions

There is no other country that has faced a Year Zero situation and had to contend with the aftermath of democide in the same way as has Cambodia. During the Pol Pot years, virtually all leisure and recreation pursuits were not only banned, but made the object of capital punishment should anyone indulge in them. Tourism ceased to exist, totally, utterly and completely. As Cambodia has struggled to emerge from the dark Khmer Rouge years and sought to embrace tourism as one of the pillars of national reconstruction, its people have had to struggle at the personal level with the 'dystopia' and destruction of their lives and families. One response has been to disassociate from and deny the horror years of Pol Pot, suppressing them and their consequences. This has produced forms of domestic leisure, recreation and tourism that tend to differ from the activities pursued by their neighbours. Cambodia has now enjoyed a decade of peace and stability, although there are those who claim that because of the lack of accountability and the failure, to date, to bring a single Khmer Rouge perpetrator to justice there is an underlying distortion to that stability.

The involvement and participation of millions of Cambodians in tourism and recreational activities is orchestrated to a limited extent by government policy, mainly through its action in restoring national holidays for them. It is argued here that the activities have been taken up by Cambodians in their millions, not because of direct government persuasion (although that is a factor), but perhaps, more importantly, because they not only are non-threatening and 'comfortable', but are perceived by them as positive ways to rebuild their culture and their identity through their children after Pol Pot nullified so much (albeit for a short time). They also project a sought-after image of a peaceful and harmonious country consistent with Buddhist teachings that are elevated in the festivals, ceremonies and events so that they are endorsed and used at the individual level, even if subconsciously, as a coping mechanism.

Obviously, there are other forms of tourism, leisure and recreation undertaken by Cambodians today than those described here, and without the post-trauma stress disorder syndrome that affects so many of their parents, the younger generations are widening the forms and types of activities that they undertake. Nevertheless, there is a unifying theme running through all the largest such tourism, leisure and recreation activities and that is the glorification of ancient and traditional Khmer civilizations, ceremonies and festivals that has its basis in the denial and suppression of recent history. It is perhaps a very specific kind of Cambodian 'nostalgic gaze' where ancient history and heritage are romanticized and form part of a current Cambodian 'collective gaze' (Urry, 2002) that overrides memories of the Khmer Rouge atrocities. In his chapter 'Gazing on history', Urry (2002, pp94–123) acknowledges that different gazes will be determined by cultural factors and that the explosive growth of tourism globally has resulted in 'an epidemic of nostalgia' (Urry, 2002, p94); and in this context, the particular forces that have shaped contemporary Cambodian domestic tourism can be interpreted as not only psycho-socially determined to a significant extent by collective trauma, but also culturally determined through nostalgia for a glorious historical past. The Khmer Empire of Angkor sits unchallenged at the apex of contemporary Cambodian domestic visitation, although numbers are greater for the Water and Fire Festivals, the Khmer New Year and the Kite Festival; with their common genesis dating back to the mighty Khmer Empire, they all share links to Angkor that reinforce the pre-eminent role of Angkor itself.

Notes

1   Cambodian media at the time reported that protests began in universities, and as students spilled out onto the streets they were joined by factory workers and public servants. Crowds swelled all day and in the afternoon more than 20,000, according to press reports, marched on the Thai Embassy. Police and army units were apparently conspicuous by their absence and there was no public statement issued by any government authority requesting the crowds to disperse, nor any overt attempt to control them.

2   The Tonle Sap River drains the Tonle Sap Lake and flows into the Mekong River at Phnom Penh during the dry season. During the wet season, however, the Mekong River is unable to escape through the Vietnam Delta into the sea, and floodwaters back up to such an extent that the Mekong River rises above the level of Tonle Sap Lake, and the Tonle Sap River reverses its flow. The lake expands from about 4500km² to more than 16,000km² to become the largest lake in South-East Asia. It spreads under the so-called inundated forest for thousands of square kilometres, and this protected, highly nutritious habitat creates the most prolific fish nursery in Asia. The lake has been famous for centuries for its prolific fishing industry. Towards the end of October/early November each year, the level of the Mekong begins to subside and the Tonle Sap River once more reverses its flow and drains into the sea. In ancient times, it was believed that the ancient Khmer kings had the power to reverse the river flow – hence, the presence of the king in present-day Cambodia. The Water Festival is timed to coincide with the reversal of the river's flow.

3   Pira Sudham is regarded as one of Thailand's leading authors. His award-winning book, *Monsoon Country*, led to him being nominated for the Nobel Prize in literature in 2004.

References

APSARA (Authority for the Protection and Safeguarding of the Region of Angkor) (2005) *Population Census, Angkor Region, June 2005*, APSARA, Phnom Penh

Baum, S. K. (2008) *The Psychology of Genocide*, Cambridge University Press, Cambridge, UK

Becker, E. (1986) *When the War Was Over: The Voices of Cambodia's Revolution and Its People*, Simon and Schuster, New York, NY

Boyden, J. and Gibbs, S. (1998). *Children of War: Responses to Psycho-Social Distress in Cambodia*, United Nations Research Institute for Social Development, Geneva

Carlson, E. B. and Rosser-Hogan, R. (1991) 'Trauma experiences, posttraumatic stress, dissociation, and depression in Cambodian refugees', *American Journal of Psychiatry,* vol 148, pp1548–1551

Chandler, D. (1999) *Brother Number One: A Political Biography of Pol Pot*, Westview Press, Boulder, CO

Cohen, E. (1988) 'Authenticity and commoditization in tourism,' *Annals of Tourism Research*, vol 15, pp371–386

Cohen, E. (1992) 'Pilgrimage centers: Concentric and excentric', *Annals of Tourism Research*, vol 19, no 1, pp35–50

Cohen, E. (1998) 'Tourism and religion: A comparative perspective', *Pacific Tourism Review*, vol 2, no 1, pp1–10

Crocker, D. (2004) *Reckoning With Past Wrongs: A Normative Framework*, Institute for International Public Policy, University of Maryland, MD, June, pp1–29

Daguan, Z. (1296) *A Record of Cambodia: The Land and Its People*, Silkworm Books, Chiang Mai, translated by Peter Harris, 2007

Durkheim, E. (1912) *Elementary Forms of the Religious Life*, Allen & Unwin, London

Dutton, D. G. (2007) *The Psychology of Genocide, Massacres, and Extreme Violence*, Greenwood Publishing Group, Wesport, CT

Etcheson, C. (2004) 'Faith, traditions and reconciliation in Cambodia', in *Settling Accounts? Truth, Justice, and Redress in Post-Conflict Societies Conference*, Harvard University, MA, 1–3 November, pp1–40

Etcheson, C. (2006) *After the Killing Fields: Lessons from the Cambodian Genocide*, Greenwood Press, Westport, CT

Freeman, M. and Jaques, C. (2002) *Ancient Angkor*, River Books Ltd, Bangkok, Thailand

Graburn, N. H. H. (1977) 'Tourism: The sacred journey', in V. Smith (ed) *Hosts and Guests*, University of Pennsylvania Press, Philadelphia, pp17–31

Gupta, A. and Ferguson, J. (eds) (1997) *Culture Power Place: Explorations in Critical Anthropology*, Duke University Press, London

Kiernan, B. (2004) 'Coming to terms with the past: Cambodia', *History Today*, vol 54, no 9, pp16–18

MacCannell, D. (1976) *The Tourist: A New Theory of the Leisure Class*, Macmillan Press, London

Meyers, L. (2007) 'Remembrance and renewal in Southeast Asia', *Monitor on Psychology*, vol 38, no 4, April 2007, pp40–41

Ministry of Tourism (2008) *Annual Report 2007*, Ministry of Tourism, Royal Government of Cambodia, Phnom Penh

Moscardo, G. (1999) *Making Visitors Mindful: Principles for Creating Sustainable Visitor Experiences through Effective Communication*, Sagamore Publishing, US

MTDP (Mekong Tourism Development Project) (2007) *Quarterly Report, October–December 2007*, Ministry of Tourism, Phnom Penh, Cambodia

Murray, S. O. (October 1994) 'A thirteenth century imperial ethnography', *Anthropology Today*, vol 10, no 5, pp15–18

Nette, A. (2008) 'In Cambodia, a rock 'n roll revival', *Asia Times*, 19 August, p7

Odenwald, M. (2002) 'Ways of coping with trauma lead to further victimization and disempowerment: Combat trauma and substance abuse in members of a former liberation movement, Somalia', in *The International Trauma Research Net Conference Individual and Collective Trauma – Reality, Myth, Metaphor?*, 28–30 June 2002, Wiesbaden, Germany

Osborne, M. (1973) *Politics and Power in Cambodia: The Sihanouk Years*, Atlantic Monthly Press, New York, NY

Osborne, M. (2000) *The Mekong: Turbulent Past, Uncertain Future*, Atlantic Monthly Press, New York, NY

Phnom Penh Post (2008) 'Looking back in fondness on Cambodia's golden era', *Phnom Penh Post*, 12 June, p4

Ray, N. (2006) *Cambodia* (3rd ed), Lonely Planet, Footscray

Roveda, V. (2002) *Sacred Angkor – The Carved Reliefs of Angkor Wat*, River Books, Bangkok, Thailand

Rummel, R. J. (1997) *Statistics of Democide: Genocide and Mass Murder since 1900*, Center for National Security Law, University of Virginia, and Transaction Publishers, Rutgers University, Charlottesville, VA

Sarak, S. (2002) *The Khmer Kite Book*, Ministry of Culture, Phnom Penh, Cambodia

Short, P. (2004) *Pol Pot: Anatomy of a Nightmare*, Henry Holt, New York, NY

Sim, S. (2002) *The Khmer Kite Book*, Ministry of Culture, Phnom Penh, Cambodia

Sim, S. and Cheang, Y. (2004) *The History of Kite Flying in Cambodia*, National Kite Museum, Phnom Penh

Sofield, T. H. B. (2001) 'Sustainability and pilgrimage tourism in the Kathmandu Valley of Nepal', in V. Smith and M. Brent (eds) *Hosts and Guests Re-Visited: Tourism Issues of the 21st Century*, Cognizant Communications Corp, New York, NY, pp257–274

Sottheara Chhim (2007) *Helping the Victims of the Khmer Rouge: A Joint Proposal by the Transcultural Psychosocial Organization Cambodia (TPO) and Documentation Center of Cambodia (DC-CAM)*, DC-CAM, Phnom Penh

Sudham, Pira (2002) *Monsoon Country*, Shire Asia Mahanaga Edition, Bangkok

Turner, V. (1973) 'The center out there: The pilgrim's goal', *History of Religion*, vol 12, no 3, pp191–230

Turner, V. and Turner, E. (1978) *Image and Pilgrimage in Christian Culture: Anthropological Perspectives*, Columbia University Press, New York, NY

Urry, J. (2002) *The Tourist Gaze*, second edition, Sage Publications, London

Vinjamuri, L. and Snyder, J. (2004) 'Advocacy and scholarship in the study of international war crime tribunals and transitional justice', *Annual Review of Political Science*, vol 7, pp345–362

Vukonic, B. (1996) *Tourism and Religion*, Elsevier Press, Oxford

Winter, T. (2007) *Post-Conflict Heritage, Postcolonial Tourism: Tourism, Politics and Development at Angkor*, Routledge, Abingdon, UK and New York

Witzel, M. (2007) 'Trauma in Cambodia,' *Phnom Penh Post*, 24 December, p3

8

Kyrgyz Tourism at Lake Issyk-Kul: Legacies of Pre-Communist and Soviet Regimes

Nicola J. Palmer

Introduction

This chapter considers the influence of historical domestic travel patterns in Kyrgyzstan on modern tourism development, both for the domestic and international markets. In order to accomplish this, the chapter examines the concept of 'domestic travel' in two very distinct epochs of a nation's history. In post-Soviet Kyrgyzstan, it is notable that tourism development has been influenced by both pre-communist and Soviet legacies. One tourism site, in particular, retains national importance and has consistently maintained popularity throughout the country's history – Lake Issyk-Kul. This geographical site is used as the basis for an examination of travel and tourism legacies in this chapter. The location of Lake Issyk-Kul is shown in Figure 8.1, where Kyrgyzstan's geographical position in relation to Kazakhstan, Uzbekistan, Tajikistan and China may also be seen.

First, traditional migration patterns of a Central Asian nomadic population are considered where excursions to summer pastures or '*jailoos*' have given rise to the development of modern ecotourism products offered to Western tourist markets. The importance of natural environmental resources to the lifestyles of this population is noted. Second, Soviet internal travel within the USSR region of Central Asia is examined, highlighting some interesting issues for a broader understanding of the term 'domestic tourism' in communist ideologies. The ways in which heavily institutionalized Soviet travel patterns have affected intra-regional Central Asian tourism are considered. The chapter is centred on a single tourism site, Lake Issyk-Kul in Kyrgyzstan – the second largest high-altitude lake in the world after Lake Titicaca in South America (UNESCO, 2002), a site deemed to be 'the pearl of Central Asia' (Asel, 2007, p1).

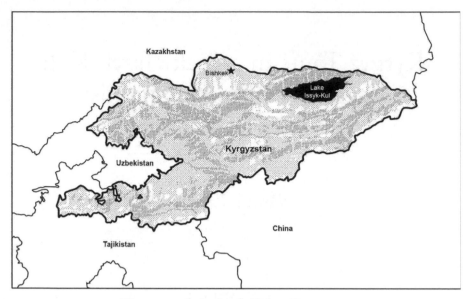

Figure 8.1 *Lake Issyk-Kul in Kyrgyzstan*

Source: www.umsl.edu/services/govdocs

Kyrgyzstan: Past influences

In Central Asia, the culture of each region may be recognized to be a product of thousands of years of spatially constrained historical events (Thompson et al, 2006). The history of the land and the people who now inhabit Kyrgyzstan is complex; but tribal origins may be identified relating to the ethnic Kyrgyz population today. Bashiri (1999) acknowledges a contested view of the history of the Kyrgyzstan, with at least 18 theories in existence relating to the origins of the ethnic Kyrgyz population. He argues that despite the debates, 'what is certain ... is that as a people the Kyrgyz are close to the Kazakhs and that their movement, too, is tied to the march of the Hordes of Chingiz Khan west' (Bashiri, 1999, p1).

The *Manas* 1000-year-old oral epic has often been argued to act as an encyclopaedia of early Kyrgyz history, celebrating the independence of the Kyrgyz people and charting battles to resist rival Arab and Chinese powers. Kakeev and Ploskikh (2002) provide a detailed analysis of Kyrgyz origins and early Kyrgyz lifestyles and traditions, highlighting two important sources in the formation of the concept of a Kyrgyz nation – the 'autochthonous' (local) Tien-Shan roots and the Central Asian Yenisei layer. In support of early inhabitation of these geographical areas, there is Palaeolithic evidence of human activity in the Kyrgyz Tien-Shan area around Lake Issyk-Kul and the Fergana Valley. This is particularly visible around the north-shore area of Lake Issyk-Kul at Cholpon-Ata, where rock drawings (petroglyphs) have been argued to provide evidence of ancient burial sites and the focus of sacred worship dating back to ancient and medieval times (UNESCO, 2008).

The annexing of Kyrgyzstan by Russia in 1864 and Soviet influence from the 1920s (Bashiri, 1999) is significant in Kyrgyz history, resulting in the population being, subsequently, exposed to the processes of Russification and collectivization. Kyrgyzstan gained independence in 1991; as a legacy of Stalin's demographic engineering in the 1930s, the multi-ethnic composition of the population is diverse. While 66 per cent are Kyrgyz, 14 per cent are Uzbeks and 12 per cent are Russians (Sharipov, 2007). In addition, there are estimates that the population of Kyrgyzstan comprises people from more than 80 different ethnic groups (L. Akmatova, pers comm, March 2004; N. Omuralieyv, pers comm, March 2004). Post-independence, Kyrgyzstan, like many other former Soviet states, has undergone immense socio-economic and political change, including considerable shifts in the ethnic composition of the republic (Palmer, 2007).

It has been estimated that 55 per cent of the 4.9 million population of Kyrgyzstan live below the poverty line (Helvetas, 2002). More recent statistics suggest that 40 per cent of the population live below the national poverty line and it is argued that 'with GNI [gross national income] per capita of US$600, the Kyrgyz Republic is among the poorest countries in the world' (World Bank, 2008, p1).

Domestic tourism in the context of Kyrgyzstan

The whole concept of domestic tourism (from definition, to measurement, to management and promotion) has been greatly overshadowed in comparison to international tourism. There are actually surprisingly few definitions of tourism that specifically attempt to explain the term 'domestic tourism', and the blurring of the boundaries of the concept has been recognized in the light of globalization and regional alliances in many parts of the world (Cooper et al, 1998). If we accept Cooper et al's (1998, p12) definition of domestic tourism as 'travel by residents within their country of residence', then we encounter difficulties surrounding modern-day changes in residency and migration patterns. If we examine domestic tourism under the Soviet regime, then we encounter even greater conceptual dissonance, reflecting the ideology and the concept of union states.

Due to the historical past of Kyrgyzstan, however, when exploring domestic or native tourism it is important to recognize the influence of two distinct epochs in the nation's history. This is because a traditionally nomadic population from pre-communist times was 'settled' and boosted by a USSR-wide population under Stalin. In modern times, this has resulted in a diverse multiethnic population group and the existence of nomadic traditions alongside more Russified and Western practices.

Acceptance of the United Nations–World Tourism Organization (UN–WTO, 1999, p3) definition raises questions over the nature of travel purpose:

> *Domestic tourism comprises the activities of residents of a given country travelling to and staying in places inside their residential country, but outside their usual environment for not more than 12 consecutive months for leisure, business or other purposes.*

The extent to which transhumance practices shape modern tourism and may actually be counted as tourism has previously generated academic interest. For example, it has been argued that 'landscapes in Europe valued for tourism are the product of transhumance' (KNAW Onderzoek Informatie, 2007, p1). Furthermore, Hall and Williams (2002), within their examination of tourism and migration, have noted the symbiotic relationships between consumption-led migration systems (including the components of seasonal migration and non-tourism-led migration) and tourism flows. Butler (1999) has further considered second homes as a form of transhumance accommodation.

The way in which traditional nomadic practices of pre-Soviet Kyrgyzstan have given rise to modern tourism products and affected contemporary travel patterns is considered within this chapter, notably with respect to the development of '*jailoo* tourism'. Transhumance is recognized here to constitute a form of travel that has shaped and influenced tourism flows.

In this chapter, a distinction is made between 'pre-communist domestic tourism' and 'Soviet era domestic tourism' in Kyrgyzstan, with the former referring to native tourism (Kyrgyz travel within Kyrgyzstan) and the latter referring to intra-regional USSR travel.

The importance of Lake Issyk-Kul

Lake Issyk-Kul is acknowledged to be the second largest high-altitude lake in the world (after Lake Titicaca in South America) and one of less than 20 ancient lakes on Earth estimated to be more than 25 million years old (Palmer, 2006). The name 'Issyk-Kul' derives from hot lake, reflecting the fact that this drainless lake up to 300m deep never freezes in spite of its high altitude because of the salt content in the water. In the summer months, the water temperature can reach 23°C – the effect of mountain ranges to the north and south of the lake – meaning that it is protected from extreme continental climatic conditions.

In pre-communist times, traditional tribal shamanistic beliefs combined with animism placed a high value on natural environmental resources and resulted in Lake Issyk-Kul being held in high regard by the ethnic Kyrgyz population. For example, there are reports that, at one time, the lake – referred to as 'the pearl of Central Asia' surrounded by 'the heavenly mountains' of the Tien-Shan – was held in such reverence that some ethnic Kyrgyz people refused to swim in the waters (Eckel, 2002). There are even claims that the significance of Lake Issyk-Kul to the ethnic Kyrgyz population may be compared to that of Buckingham Palace to the British (Xhunga, 2006) – an interesting external perception which perhaps overestimates the significance of Buckingham Palace to modern-day Britons. Lake Issyk-Kul is certainly recognized to be a site of national importance even in modern times. In 2004, the Kyrgyz government declared the lake to be 'the property of the nation' (Advantour, 2008, p1).

There are a number of legends surrounding the site of Lake Issyk-Kul, including reports of four drowned cities lying beneath the waters of the lake (Maillart, 2005). In the pre-communist period the south shore of Lake Issyk-Kul formed the northernmost branch of the Great Silk Road, a major trading route between Europe and the Far East, and a stopover was established at Kochkor. There are claims that the discovery of at least one sunken city beneath Lake Issyk-Kul provides evidence of the lake's importance as a commercial and mercantile hub during Silk Road trading times (Sweat, 2007).

A state nature reserve (*zapovednik*) was established at Issyk-Kul during the USSR period, and post-independence, in 1995, a separate, geographically distinct United Nations Educational, Scientific and Cultural Organization (UNESCO) biosphere was established in the Issyk-Kul region. Both environmental designations reflect the value of the site in ecological terms.

Pre-communist era travel patterns in Kyrgyzstan

The ethnic Kyrgyz were formerly Central Asian pastoralists – 'yurt-dwelling, nomadic herdsmen, migrating seasonally with their animals' (Akmoldoeva and Sommer, 2002, pxvii). Although many of their cultural traditions remain in the everyday lifestyles and practices of these members of the Kyrgyz population, some of the longer-term impacts of Stalin's attempts at collectivization in Kyrgyzstan, while not entirely effective, did result in a more settled population.

The travelling of the ethnic Kyrgyz population is now largely limited to the summer months (mainly July and August) when Kyrgyz families, accompanied by their horses and felt tents (*yurts* or *boz-ui*), retreat to summer pastures (*jailoos*) and adopt more primitive lifestyles akin to the permanent existence of their ancestors. In common with many tribal societies and because of the nomadic roots of the ethnic Kyrgyz, there appears to be a strong spiritual relationship between people and nature. For example, the *yurts* are constructed of felt hand spun and dyed from their herds of goats; the fermented milk of their mares – *kymys* – is drunk as a health aid; and the Kyrgyz traditionally hunt on horseback using birds of prey. During their summer migrations, the ethnic Kyrgyz demonstrate some clear examples of nature-based subsistence (Schmidt, 2005). Although this modern domestic travel is based on nomadic transhumance practices, the migrations are now largely limited to 'short stationary periods in the early summer pasture' (Van Veen, 1995), rather than following a transhumance cycle, and the travel that takes place is mainly for recreation rather than livestock grazing.

The early Kyrgyz people are identified as cattle-breeding nomads, and they followed distinct clan and tribe structures that permeated all aspects of their lives. Clans were governed by a leader with the help of elders, and communities were established around a three-wing clan model, with Kyrgyz identity being based on membership of one of three clan groupings – *ong* (right), *sol* (left) and *ichkilik* (neither) (Anon, 1996). Travelling was a constant theme of Kyrgyz life and proximity to natural resources such as water was a key issue in the selection of *jailoo* locations. As Polynsky (V. Polynsky, pers comm, March 2004) notes: 'the more spacious and rich in rivers the plain … the more *yurts* [would] be "built" on it'.

A seasonal aspect of this type of travel can be easily recognized – migration to summer pastures would begin in May or June and would be sited on high-mountain locations, enabling richer livestock-grazing opportunities and also offering the Kyrgyz nomadic population cooler living conditions (Kareem, 2005). Thus, early Kyrgyz travel patterns were heavily based on the conditions of the natural environment, reflecting the strong relationship between the ethnic Kyrgyz culture and the natural environment (Palmer, 2006).

Geographically, '*jailoo* tourism' occurs traditionally around areas of water and at high altitudes. Lake Son-Kul, a mountain lake in the central Tien-Shan Mountains to the south of Lake Issyk-Kul and the second largest lake in Kyrgyzstan, has traditionally attracted the most *jailoo* tourism due to its topography. Son-Kul offers a treeless, high-mountain plateau surrounded by green meadow grazing for livestock. Lake Issyk-Kul is situated at a lower altitude; but there are also records of this area being an important site for Kyrgyz nomads (Beer and Tinner, 2008). Recognizing transhumance as a form of mobility that has shaped and influenced tourism flows, travel to Lake Issyk-Kul might, thus, be recognized to possess pre-tourism roots.

It must be acknowledged that Lake Issyk-Kul was not a specific travel site for ethnic Kyrgyz nomads. However, the ancient legends based on the Issyk-

Kul region do place Lake Issyk-Kul as a sacred site; the site is reported to have been used by a medieval conqueror – Tamerlane – as his summer camp or *jailoo* (Ling, 1998).

Soviet-era tourism in Kyrgyzstan

In addition to narrative accounts of traveller experiences in the USSR, there is a sizeable amount of academic research relating to Soviet era tourism. Koenker (2002, 2003, 2007) has examined the structures, intended outcomes and meanings of tourism in a Soviet context dating from the 1919 Russian Revolution. Her observations highlight the importance of tourism as an integral part of socialist ideology. Soviet era tourism acted as a means of forging a shared national culture and, in particular, domestic tourism was crucial as an expression of patriotism. Examining the way in which heavily structured and prescribed tourist itineraries were employed as a tool to reinforce socialism, Koenker (2007, p82) argues how 'the very act of travelling together helped to create common experiences, common memories and a sense of common belonging to the society'.

Koenker (2003) not only recognizes the significance of mass tourism under the Soviet regime but also acknowledges mass tourism as a deliberate strategy. Gorsuch and Koenker (2006) situate Soviet mass tourism within the context of socialist, collective consciousness-raising activities. They argue that the value of tourism for individual self-improvement was exercised through organized factory worker group tours, Communist Party cadres and other segments of society. Hence, the benefits of tourism for the individual were emphasized – most notably in terms of education and rest or relaxation; but tourism was encouraged to be undertaken as a collective or group activity. The reflexive nature of the Soviet citizen is often under-acknowledged, and within the context of Soviet tourism it must be recognized that tourism (*turizm*) existed alongside and in direct contrast to 'excursionism', with independent travellers aligning themselves with the former activity and regarding excursionists as inferior in that their trips were 'more organized, short-term and [with a] specific goal mainly educational' (Koenker, 2007).

The impact of the Russian Revolution on Kyrgyzstan must be duly acknowledged. Tourism was regarded as an educational- and cultural aware-ness-building activity linked to scientific research. Within this, there was also a focus on youth travel as part of the Soviet educational system and curriculum efforts to enforce identity-building using the concept of 'motherland'. Tourism was an integral part of the socialist ideology. Although Koenker (2007) argues that mass tourism was a deliberate intention of Soviet tourism, policy organizations such as Sovtour and the All-Union Society of Proletarian Tourism and

Excursions aimed to plan individualized itineraries with a view to creating independent tourists. It is evident that highly structured and sophisticated tourism support systems were in place at that time.

Hauser (2004) reports that by 1929 there were already 250,000 Soviet tourists travelling to different areas of the USSR. But it would be a fallacy to suggest that all tourism within the boundaries of the former USSR was internal or domestic. Various travel guide accounts detailing explorations throughout the USSR (e.g. Maillart, 2005) demonstrate that it was possible to travel outside the heavily institutionalized, highly structured systems, and also that inbound tourism to the USSR did occur. The extent of freedom available to the independent traveller should not, however, be over-interpreted, nor should the opportunities for inbound travel to the USSR. Tales of strict visa application processes and highly bureaucratic border control procedures abound. For example, Maillart (2005) recounts her travels through Central Asia during 1932, providing some valuable insights into Western travel patterns under the USSR regime.

Noack (2005) focuses on Soviet tourism in the 1960s and 1970s, recognizing mass tourism to be characteristic of the period of 'devolved socialism'. He identifies a growth in non-organized holiday-makers or 'wild tourists' (independent travellers) during the Krushchev and Brezhnev regimes, and emphasizes the late Soviet Union period to be of vital importance to studies of Soviet tourism. During this pre-independence period, it is apparent that attitudes towards tourism began to shift alongside a weakening of the state ideology shaped by Stalinism. However, he notes how a full understanding of tourist (Soviet) expectations and experiences is hampered by a lack of open discourse under communist conditions.

The Issyk-Kul region of Kyrgyzstan has been identified as a leading USSR recreation area. During the late 1980s, trade union resort houses around the northern shores of Lake Issyk-Kul accommodated up to 350,000 people from across the USSR. Eckford (1997, p3) reports that 'by all accounts, during the pre-democratic period this area [Lake Ysyk-Köl region] was alive with tourism business from within the Soviet Union. Next to the Black Sea it was one of the most coveted vacation destinations in the union.'

Hofer et al (2002) suggest that the unspoiled setting and unpolluted water of Lake Issyk-Kul were instrumental in establishing the site as a popular Soviet tourist attraction. During Soviet times the region was established as a holiday destination for Communist Party cadres. Nathan (2002, p1) reports how 'in Soviet times, despite being the site of secret torpedo tests, Issyk-Kul was a famed rest and restoration spot for party cadres in search of pampering themselves at the area's plush hotels and sanatoria'.

Hofer et al (2002) identify Lake Issyk-Kul as a Soviet era tourist attraction based on two key attractors: the 'unspoiled setting' and the 'unpolluted water' of the lake. Allen (2006, p53) reports that ' on the north shore of Issyk-Kul, scores of lakeside resorts hosted high ranking members of the Soviet government and military. These were among the most "plush" accommodations in the USSR.'

Following the collapse of the USSR, it transpired that many country houses, used for holidaying by Soviet leaders, were beyond Russia's territory. Post-independence, *Altin Kol* on the north shore of Lake Issyk-Kul at Cholpon-Ata became an official summer residence of the Kyrgyz president. The designation of the residence as an official presidential holiday home further increased the profile and status of the Issyk-Kul region as a holiday destination, as did the attraction of dignitaries from other countries. The ex-Russian president Boris Yeltsin has been identified as a repeat holiday-maker in Issyk-Kul. Much can be derived about the level of Kyrgyz tolerance and positive attitudes towards Russia through the fact that during Yeltsin's 2002 holiday to Issyk-Kul, 'a 5000m mountain peak was named in his honour' (Saralaeva, 2003). Furthermore, in 2003, a statue of the former Russian leader was erected at the resort of Cholpon-Ata on the north shore of Lake Issyk-Kul to further commemorate his visits to the area – the only such monument to Yeltsin in any of the former Soviet countries, including Russia. It is important to acknowledge that Issyk-Kul's reputation as a favoured tourist destination of the Communist Party elite (*vlasti*) in Soviet times continued to attract dignitaries from former Soviet states even in post-independence years.

Lake Issyk-Kul: Pre-communist era and Soviet era tourism legacies

The importance or significance of Lake Issyk-Kul for tourism is still recognized today. The type of tourism that takes place is water based (fishing, swimming and water sports), alongside summer beach tourism, and is highly seasonal. It has been claimed that 99 per cent of all tourism money in Kyrgyzstan is located in the Issyk-Kul region (S. Pyshnenko, pers comm, March 2004). There are estimates that 1.2 million tourists visited Issyk-Kul in 2006 and tourist arrivals are forecast to grow further (Madumarov, cited in Asel, 2007). However, there remains difficulty in accessing reliable tourism statistics for Kyrgyzstan, and Nasirdinov (as cited in Mamaraimov, 2007) argues that contrary to official estimates, approximately 500,000 tourists visited Lake Issyk-Kul in 2006, with these being primarily 'foreign' visitors. According to Mamaraimov (2007), approximately 70 per cent of tourists to Issyk-Kul are from Kazakhstan and 20 per cent are from Russia.

It is reported that Lake Issyk-Kul has become increasingly popular with a growing segment of Kazakh middle- and upper-class citizens (Daly, 2008). But in addition to attracting these market segments, there are reports that the destination is popular with some Kyrgyz holiday-makers (Rakin, 2007, as cited in Asel, 2007). Precise domestic tourism figures for Lake Issyk-Kul are lacking; but the Kyrgyz Destination Marketing Association (2006) has reported that Kyrgyz citizens comprised approximately 20 per cent of all tourists in Kyrgyzstan in 2006. On the basis that Lake Issyk-Kul has been identified as one of the most well-established tourist destinations in Kyrgyzstan, it may be asserted that some of the nation's domestic tourism is still taking place at Issyk-Kul. Furthermore, this type of tourism is most likely to occur in the north-shore area of the lake, where the most development has taken place, with facilities including large-scale accommodation establishments, discotheques, cafés and beach-front entertainment. In direct contrast, the south shore is recognized to be a lesser developed and more sparsely populated area, attracting holiday-makers who prefer ecological purity and quiet, simple relaxation. Any true '*jailoo* tourism' practised by Kyrgyz citizens in that region is unlikely to be counted within the official tourism statistics (Kyrgyz tourism estimates are based on border guards' data, information from businesses offering holiday and leisure services, and accommodation establishments).

At first sight, the contrast between the north-shore and the south-shore areas of Lake Issyk-Kul suggests that two very different tourism development paths have been created. Yet, in relation to the issue of domestic holiday-making and legacies from the past, both shore areas illustrate how domestic tourism activities from Kyrgyzstan's pre-communist era and also from the country's period of Soviet rule have shaped modern tourism activities – not solely in terms of domestic tourism, but perhaps more notably in terms of Kyrgyzstan's international tourism.

In relation to the south-shore area of Lake Issyk-Kul, it was acknowledged earlier in this chapter that the area was not primarily a site for traditional Kyrgyz *jailoo* tourism, although the area has been identified as a sacred site for the ethnic Kyrgyz population and is a popular location within ancient Kyrgyz legends. Today, however, there is evidence that the area has gained popularity as a *jailoo* tourism site. Fieldwork conducted by this author in 2004 revealed that local tour operators were deliberately setting up their *yurt* camps, which were aimed at international visitors to Kyrgyzstan alongside local Kyrgyz family holiday-makers, specifically to demonstrate 'natural' cultural activities to the tourists. Thus, ethnic Kyrgyz families – domestic tourists – on holiday have become an attraction and are drawn into the tourism experiences of international tourists (Palmer, 2006). Some of these *yurt* camp developments were reported to exist around the south shore of Lake Issyk-Kul (S. Katanaev and N. Schetinok, pers comm, March 2004).

The south-shore area of the lake is dominated by small- and medium-sized tourist enterprises, catering for adventure, ecotourism and community-based tourism (CBT), with infrastructures and systems having been specifically established to attract international niche tourism markets. In comparison to the north-shore area, the actual scale of tourism activity is much smaller scale (albeit growing if the increasing tour operator itineraries that include a visit to this destination area are interpreted to demonstrate economic viability and, thus, market demand).

With respect to the north shore of Lake Issyk-Kul, Allen (2006, p46) argues that 'history equates to a legacy that has significant impact in how tourism in these cases exists today, in terms of the clientele, the services offered, and the role of the state'.

The resorts and sanatoria were originally constructed from a non-existent tourism infrastructure in Soviet times and were designed to a high standard because they were aimed at army officers or sportsmen rather than the general public.

Zhukov (2000) observes how, since 1991 independence, Kyrgyz state facilities considered non-essential to state interests have been purchased by foreign firms, largely firms located in the Commonwealth of Independent States (CIS). This has been observed to be commonplace with respect to state tourism complexes in Kyrgyzstan and it applies to Lake Issyk-Kul (Allen, 2006). Although the sandy beaches of the north shore of the lake still attract high numbers of tourists – confirming claims about Issyk-Kul being the epicentre of the Kyrgyz tourism offering – this type of tourism is highly seasonal and enclave resort based. Post-Soviet privatization of the economy has resulted in many resort accommodation establishments being bought by individuals linked to the former body or organization to which the establishments previously belonged (during the Soviet era). This has resulted in establishments belonging to organizations based in a particular post-Soviet Republic being acquired by entities within that republic (Nusorov, 2001, as cited in Allen, 2006). For example, three of the largest north-shore resort accommodation establishments – the Karaganda, Hotel Kazakhstan and the Royal Beach – are now owned and operated by corporations based in Kazakhstan.

An insight into the nature of north-shore Lake Issyk-Kul tourism may be gleaned from Allen's (2006) data on the Karaganda establishment. In total, 330 visitors can be accommodated in this establishment; but occupancy levels range from 100 per cent in July and August to 50 per cent in June and September. Furthermore, out of the summer season the establishment averages approximately 50 guests per calendar month (an occupancy level of just 15 per cent), mainly visitors linked to government or business conference events. The characteristics of Karaganda clientele also provide an insight into the nature of north-shore Lake Issyk-Kul tourism – 80 to 90 per cent of guests are reportedly from Kazakhstan and Russia, with the remainder being from Uzbekistan and Kyrgyzstan. For the whole of 2003, there were fewer than 150 guests reported from international generating countries outside of the former USSR. This suggests that not only has Soviet era tourism shaped the type of tourism on offer in the north-shore area – mass, resort-style tourism centred on water-side and beach facilities – but it would also appear that 'Soviet era domestic tourism' continues to dominate native tourism patterns in present-day Kyrgyzstan.

Conclusions

This chapter suggests that a broader conceptual understanding of the term 'domestic tourism' is required in order to understand the shaping of domestic tourism in Kyrgyzstan. In the Soviet era it was accepted that intra-regional USSR travel was internal or domestic. In post-independence Kyrgyzstan, issues relating to citizenship and homeland are far from resolved (see Palmer, 2007). Kyrgyzstan possesses a multi-ethnic population and it is apparent that there persist ties between the republic and other former Soviet states – particularly neighbouring Central Asian republics. Nearly 20 years on from independence, tourists from these countries sit uneasily between international tourism defini-tions and traditionally accepted domestic tourism definitions. Technically, 80 per cent of international tourists to Kyrgyzstan comprise holiday-makers from CIS countries (Kyrgyz Destination Marketing Association, 2006) and interna-tional tourism now far outweighs Kyrgyz domestic tourism (Euromonitor International, 2007). With respect to the economic benefits of tourism, Kyrgyzstan is in a healthy position. The future of Kyrgyz tourism must, however, be questioned if the nation is to remain so heavily reliant on its Soviet era domestic tourism markets. Mamaraimov (2007, p1) recounts how disap-pointing product and service levels experienced at some of the north-shore Lake Issyk-Kul resort hotels have started to generate dissatisfaction from increasingly sophisticated Russian travellers: ' "We'd have been better off in Turkey with this kind of money", one tourist by name of Vladimir said. "Over here, they serve us unwashed cutlery. We came here in the hope to be able to fish some, but there is no fish here." '

Although it has been reported that the growing affluence of Kyrgyz people contributed to an increase in outgoing tourism expenditure in 2005 (Euromonitor International, 2007), overall levels of Kyrgyz domestic tourism are very low. It should not be forgotten that Kyrgyzstan ranks as one of the poorest countries in the world. Prices in the north-shore resorts of Lake Issyk-Kul are too high for many local Kyrgyz people. Mamaraimov (2007, p1) reports that 'a day in the Aurora (the most expensive resort) costs [US]$120, a day in other resorts and spas [US]$40 and more. Quality of service, however, leaves much to be desired. Resorts owned by Kazakh businessmen charge [US}$1000 a day and more.' As such, Kyrgyz domestic tourism (across all multi-ethnic groupings) is constrained by the internal economy.

Allen (2006) claims that the two different shore areas of Lake Issyk-Kul reflect the dichotomy facing Kyrgyz tourism. If we understand this dichotomy to involve a dilemma over attempting to maintain ties with Soviet era Central Asian neighbours versus becoming an independent nation within a wider inter-national community, then it might be recognized that such seemingly apparent contradictions characterize many of the socio-political transition strategies of the nation. The two distinct eras – 'pre-communism' and 'Soviet' – mean that Kyrgyzstan is a very interesting case study area in which to examine domestic tourism because the eras provide contrasting understandings of the term 'domestic'.

Future prospects

Within Kyrgyzstan, the site of Lake Issyk-Kul further provides a unique oppor-tunity to consider the legacies of domestic holiday-making relating to the pre-communist and Soviet eras. Despite strong contrasts between the nature of pre-communist community- or family-based *'jailoo'* subsistence-based tourism and Soviet era institutionalized and ideologically governed tourism, it is possi-ble to clearly identify the legacies of each era through modern tourism.

The two contrasting tourism development paths of the north and south shore might ultimately result in two very different tourism fortunes for the respective shorelines of Lake Issyk-Kul. There are informal reports that a tech-nical environmental carrying capacity level has been established for Lake Issyk-Kul. However, environmental specialists and experts believe that current carrying capacities are too high for Lake Issyk-Kul since it can allow a maxi-mum of 1 million tourists a year. Some Kyrgyz citizens have expressed concern over the future of the north-shore area, in particular, claiming that the lake is already in danger of becoming polluted and overcrowded (Asel, 2007). Interestingly, much concern surrounds mass tourism flow from neighbouring CIS countries ('Soviet era domestic tourism').

Tourism forms an important part of *Kyrgyzstan's Country Development Strategy* (2007–2010) and Lake Issyk-Kul remains a key tourism site. With respect to the future, it would appear that the lake will continue to be a major tourist destination. Research by UNESCO (2004) examining the impacts of tourism in one Issyk-Kul village revealed that a majority of local people living in the vicinity of the lake believe that Issyk-Kul tourism should be 'mass tourism'. This is a view that is generally supported by tourism officials on the basis that a limited number of tourists are not perceived to be able to bring enough income to local people to help raise their living conditions (UNESCO, 2004). But mass tourism requires huge infrastructural investment to safeguard the lake environment, and state infrastructural investment *per se* in Kyrgyzstan has been lacking since the country's independence. The country is still court-ing external investment; but external debt is a challenge to achieving economic reform. Between 1998 and 2000, total external debt in Kyrgyzstan was calcu-lated to be US$1694 million (EarthTrends, 2003) and was reported to exceed 100 per cent of the country's gross domestic product (GDP) (Helvetas, 2002). The heavy dependency on international assistance is demonstrated even further by facts such as '60 per cent of the country's 2001 budget was reserved for foreign debt repayments' (Helvetas, 2002, p7).

The political and economic challenges of Kyrgyzstan constrain any growth of domestic and outbound tourism. This chapter has considered the influence of historical domestic travel patterns in Kyrgyzstan (including transhumance practices alongside tourism) on tourism development. The legacies of the past (namely, the pre-communist and Soviet eras) appear limited in terms of modern Kyrgyz domestic tourism, but more notable in terms of Kyrgyzstan's international tourism development. Perhaps in time, more Kyrgyz residents will be able to afford to undertake domestic holidays and partake of the commercial tourism offerings that have developed as a result of pre-communist era and Soviet era domestic tourism.

References

Advantour (2008) *Issyk Kul*, www.advantour.com/kyrgyzstan/issyk-kul.htm, accessed 20 February 2008

Akmoldoeva, B. and Sommer, J. (2002) *Klavdiya Antipina: Ethnographer of the Kyrgyz*, Spring Hill Press, McKinleyville, CA

Allen, J. B. (2006) *What about the Locals?: The Impact of State Tourism Policy and Transnational Participation on Two Central Asian Mountain Communities*, PhD thesis, University of Texas, Austin, TX

Anon (1996) *Kyrgyzstan: Social Structure*, www.country-data.com/cgi-bin/query/r-7659.html, accessed 17 November 2007

Asel (2007) *Issyk-Kul: Chasing Short-Term Profit*, http://kyrgyzstan.neweurasia.net/2007/05/30/issyk-kul-chasing-short-term-profit/, accessed 15 September 2007

Bashiri, I. (1999) *Kyrgyzstan: An Overview*, www.angelfire.com/rnb/bashiri/Kyrgyzstan/Kyrgyz.html, accessed 20 February 2008

Beer, R. and Tinner, W. (2008) 'Four thousand years of vegetation and fire history in the spruce forests of northern Kyrgyzstan (Kungey Alatau, Central Asia)', *Vegetation History and Archaeobotany*, www.springerlink.com/content/5726h8w223m63637/?p=bfd511e3927444148f2532b2301b4d79&pi=4, accessed 20 May 2008

Butler, R. (1999) 'Tourism and migration: The changing role of second homes', Paper presented to the Association of American Geographers (AAG) Meeting, 23–27 March 1999, Honolulu

Cooper, C., Fletcher, J., Gilbert, D., Shepherd, R. and Wanhill, S. (1998) *Tourism Principles and Practice*, second edition, Pearson Education Ltd, Essex, UK

Daly, J. C. K. (2008) *Kazakhstan's Emerging Middle Class*, www.silkroadstudies.org/new/docs/Silkroadpapers/0803Daly.PDF, accessed 2 March 2008

EarthTrends (2003) *Economic Indicators – Kyrgyzstan*, www.earthtrends.wri.org, accessed 27 October 2004

Eckel, M. (2002) *Remote Kyrgyzstan Offers Pristine Mountains*, www.mydailycamera.com/livingarts/travel/26tkyrg.html, accessed 20 February 2008

Eckford, P. K. (1997) *International Tourism Potential in Issyk-Kul Oblast the Kyrgyz Republic: Report and Analysis*, WTO, Madrid, Spain

Euromonitor International (2007) *Travel and Tourism in Kyrgyzstan*, Euromonitor International, London

Gorsuch, A. E. and Koenker, D. P. (2006) *Turizm: The Russian and East European Tourist under Capitalism and Socialism*, Cornell University Press, Ithaca, NY

Hall, C. M. and Williams, A. M. (2002) *Tourism and Migration: New Relationships between Production and Consumption*, Kluwer Academic, Dordrecht/London

Hauser, M. (2004) *The Pamirs – 1:500 000: A Tourist Map of Gorno Badakhshan-Tajikistan and Background Information on the Region*, Pamir Archive, RWHL, Hinteregg, Switzerland

Helvetas (July 2002) *Country Programme Helvetas Kyrgyzstan 2002–2006*, Helvetas, Bishkek/Zurich

Hofer, M., Peeters, F., Aeschbach-Hertig, W., Brennwald, M., Holocher, J, Livingstone, D. M., Romanovski, V. and Kipfer, R. (July 2002) 'Rapid deep-water renewal in Lake Issyk-Kul (Kyrgyzstan) indicated by transient tracers', *Limnology and Oceanography*, vol 47, no 4, pp1210–1216

Kakeev, A. and Ploskikh, V. (2002) *Tsarina of the Mountains Kurmanjan and Her Times*, Ilim, Bishkek

Kareem (2005) *Kyrgyzstan (1)*, www.travelpod.com/travel-blog-entries/kareem/rtw-2005/1120646820/tpod.html, accessed 3 December 2007

KNAW Onderzoek Informatie (2007) *Project: Transhumount*, www.onderzoekinformatie.nl/nl/oi/nod/onderzoek/OND1324500, accessed 7 September 2008

Koenker, D. P. (2002) 'Good travel and bad: Creating the proletarian tourist', Paper presented at the workshop Observing and Making Meaning: Understanding the Soviet Union and Central Europe Through Travel, University of Toronto, 18–20 October 2002

Koenker, D. P. (2003) 'Travel to work, travel to play: On Russian tourism, travel, and leisure', *Slavic Review*, vol 62, no 4, winter, pp657–665

Koenker, D. P. (2007) *Republic of Labor: Russian Printers and Soviet Socialism, 1918–1930*, Cornell University Press, Ithaca, NY

Kyrgyz Destination Marketing Association (2006) 'Where does the tourism path lead?', *Kyrgyz Tourism Today: Quarterly Newsletter of the Destination Marketing Association Kyrgyz Tourism/DMA*, vol 1, November, pp1–8

Kyrgyzstan's Country Development Strategy (2007–2010), http://siteresources.worldbank.org/INTPRS1/Resources/Country-Papers-and-JSAs/cr07193.pdf, accessed 5 March 2008

Ling, C. (1998) 'Famed Kyrgyz Lake fights aftermath of chemical spill', www.hartford-hwp.com/archives/53/147.html, accessed 3 December 2007

Maillart, E. (2005) *Turkestan Solo: A Journey through Central Asia*, Tauris Parke Paperbacks, New York, NY

Mamaraimov, A. (2007) 'The Kyrgyz authorities cannot estimate travel to the country or capacities of this market', http://enews.ferghana.ru/article.php?id=2149, accessed10 April 2008

Nathan, J. (2002) 'Hot spot', *TIME Magazine*, 21 October, p1

Noack, P. C. (2005) 'Mass tourism in the late Soviet Union', www.uni-bielefeld.de/geschichte/osteuropa/fpnoack.html, accessed 11 December 2007

Palmer, N. J. (2006) 'Economic transition and the struggle for local control in ecotourism development: The case of Kyrgyzstan', *Journal of Ecotourism*, vol 5, no 1/2, pp40–61

Palmer, N. J. (2007) 'Ethnic equality, national identity and selective cultural representation in tourism promotion: Kyrgyzstan, Central Asia', *Journal of Sustainable Tourism*, vol 15, no 6, pp645–662

Saralaeva, L. (2003) 'Yeltsin set in stone in Kyrgyzstan', *IWPR'S Reporting Central Asia*, no 219, 23 July

Schmidt, M. (2005) 'Utilisation and management changes in South Kyrgyzstan's mountain forests', *Journal of Mountain Science*, vol 2, no 2, pp91–104

Sharipov, A. (2007) 'Kyrgyzstan: Role and place of ethnic minorities in conflicts between the opposition and the regime', *Central Asia News*, 2 May, pp2–5

Sweat, J. (2007) 'The city under the lake', *The Anthropogene*, 4 January, pp7–8

Thompson, K. J., Schofield, P., Foster, N. and Bakieva, G. (2006) 'Kyrgyzstan's "Manas" epos millennium celebrations: Post-colonial resurgence of Turkic culture and the marketing of cultural tourism in Kyrgyzstan', in D. Picard and M. Robinson (eds) *Festivals, Tourism and Social Change: Remaking Worlds*, Channel View Publications, Clevedon, pp172–190

UNESCO (United Nations Educational, Scientific and Cultural Organization) (2002) *Biosphere Reserve Information: Kyrgyzstan. Issyk Kul*, www.unesco.org/mabdb/br/brdir/directory/biores.asp?code=KIZ+02&mode=all, accessed 29 October 2007

UNESCO (2004) *Development of Cultural Eco-Tourism in the Mountain Regions of Central Asia and the Himalayas*, UNESCO Cultural Heritage Division, Bishkek

UNESCO (2008) 'Issyk-Kul as a cultural and natural landscape', *Tentative Lists Database*, Kyrgyz National Commission for UNESCO, Paris, France

UN–WTO (United Nations–World Tourism Organization) (1999) *Update of the Recommendations on Tourism Statistics*, UN–WTO, Series M no 83 (1994), Revised 20 December 1999, WTO, France, pp1–24

Van Veen, T. W. S. (1995) 'The Kyrgyz sheep herders at a crossroads', *Pastoral Development Network Paper* 38d, Overseas Development Institute, London, vol 14, pp1–35

World Bank (2008) *Kyrgyz Republic: Country Brief 2007*, http://web.worldbank.org/WBSITE/EXTERNAL/COUNTRIES/ECAEXT/KYRGYZEXTN/0,,contentMDK:20629311~menuPK:305768~pagePK:141137~piPK:141127~theSitePK:305761,00.html?gclid=CMaUtLyo05UCFQ6S1Qod-UHdhg, accessed 5 September 2008

Xhunga, M. (2006) *Credit Boosts Tourism at Kyrgyz Lake Resort*, 11 May, EBRD Kyrgyz Office, Bishkek

Zhukov, S. (2000) 'The economic development of Central Asia in the 1990s', in B. Rumer (ed) *Central Asia and the New Global Economy*, M. E. Sharpe, London, pp57–85

9

Indigenous People and Domestic Visitors of Taiwan

Geoffrey Wall and Janet Chang

Introduction

Tourists are in search of experiences that are different from those that they can readily acquire at home. In other words, they are in search of the 'other'. This chapter focuses on minority people as tourism attractions. No attempt is made here to distinguish between such words as indigenous, aboriginal or ethnic minority, although it is acknowledged that in some situations, such as rights to property, fine distinctions may have far-reaching implications. Indigenous peoples have often experienced the adverse consequences of colonization and have been oppressed and marginalized historically. They often continue to live in a disadvantaged situation with respect to the majority population who surround them. Because such people are different from mainstream society, they constitute the 'other' and they have tourism potential, as visitors may be attracted to witness aspects of their culture and lifestyles.

There is a large literature on the implications of tourism for such people. Most research has been done in the context of international tourism where differences in such attributes as race, ethnicity, religion, education and income are often particularly marked. However, it should not be assumed that the potentials and consequences of domestic and international tourism are identical. This contribution focuses on aspects of indigenous tourism where the primary clientele is domestic visitors.

Relationships between indigenous people and tourism

Six main perspectives can be identified on the relationships between indigenous people and tourism. They have been:

1   ignored;
2   seen as being in the way of development;
3   viewed as tourist attractions; and subsequently
4   viewed as being negatively affected by tourism;
5   increasingly viewed as potential beneficiaries of tourism; and
6   even viewed as potential decision-makers with respect to tourism.

These perspectives can be seen as a set of changes through time as more aboriginal people have become involved in tourism. They also reflect a changing situation regarding indigenous power and self-determination, although there are still few cases in which indigenous people have full control over the ways in which aspects of their culture are used for tourism. A seventh perspective might be the ways in which indigenous people themselves become tourists and whether or not they constitute a distinctive market segment; but little is known about this.

Until recent decades, indigenous people were largely ignored in the context of tourism. They tended to live in remote locations where there was limited tourism infrastructure and, consequently, few tourists. Tourism did not affect them greatly, either positively or negatively. In some cases, however, indigenous people found themselves in the way of tourism development. Perhaps national parks were established in places where they had hunted and fished for generations, and their hunting and gathering rights were curtailed and they were forcibly removed from their homelands. Although, globally, there is growing recognition of the importance of indigenous rights and land uses, there are still cases where land is expropriated to construct tourism facilities or to protect heritage sites. For example, a case of Li minority land being expropriated for the construction of a national tourism resort in Hainan, China, has been documented (Wang and Wall, 2005, 2007). This action was taken in the interests of the majority of the population, and although the amount of land expropriated was small, the forced move to new houses was only from one side of the road to the other, and the minority people were compensated, their lives were disrupted by government authority in the interest of outside investors and tourism development.

Most commonly, aspects of the cultural expressions of indigenous people, especially those that are colourful or spectacular, are commodified and made into tourist attractions. It seems that every indigenous person is expected to be able to dance and sing, and they are organized, often by outsiders, to entertain tourists (Yang et al, 2008). Their performances are literally staged and ethnic clothing becomes a work uniform as indigenous people dress to meet the tourists' expectations. Traditional ceremonies may be performed at times that are convenient to the tourists, and local products, such as textiles, carvings or foodstuffs, may become souvenirs. Sometimes these things are brought together and packaged for sale to, or as 'exhibits' for, the tourists in 'folk villages', which are small theme parks where the theme is minority culture (Xie and Wall, 2001), or in ecomuseums where minority people are encouraged to live in traditional ways and can be visited by tourists (Liu et al, 2005).

The adverse consequences of tourism for minority people have received a great deal of academic attention. The packaging of cultural expressions for tourism and the changes in meaning that this often entails have been widely recognized as one of the adverse consequences of cultural tourism. At the same time, however, it is widely recognized that, if done appropriately, indigenous people may benefit financially from sharing aspects of their culture with tourists for a price. Unfortunately, however, much of the money is usually appropriated by outsiders who are commonly not indigenous people themselves but who make the key decisions on what aspects of culture are to be presented and how this is done (Yang et al, 2008). Given this circumstance, it is not surprising that there is growing interest in finding ways for indigenous people to become more involved in the critical decisions that determine how aspects of their culture are to be shared with tourists and how the resulting benefits and costs are to be distributed.

This discussion provides an introduction to the complexities of indigenous tourism. Although it is not possible to explore all of the aspects introduced above, it is the broad context in which the following discussion will be placed. The focus of the discussion is the extent to which domestic tourists are novelty-seekers, looking to engage with the indigenous 'other', and the opportunities and complexities that arise as indigenous people celebrate their culture. Case study materials have been taken primarily from Taiwan, with occasional reference to mainland China. Initially, the long history of colonialism and the relatively recent evolution of tourism are introduced to explain how aspects of the culture of indigenous people were suppressed in Taiwan and are now being revived and appreciated. Then, using examples from the Atayal in Wulai, a town in the north of the island approximately a one-hour drive from Taipei, the colonial and tourism histories of certain aboriginal expressions are presented. Next, domestic tourist evaluations of the products available for purchase in Wulai are considered. The development of Danayigu Ecological Park by the Cou tribe is then discussed. Attention is next given to the marketing of indigenous products through an examination of an aboriginal festival in the Rukai tribal area. The motivations of visitors at aboriginal theme parks are considered and certain advertising strategies are evaluated. In all cases discussed in this chapter, domestic tourists dominate the market since international tourists currently constitute a small proportion of tourists in Taiwan.

Indigenous people and tourism in Taiwan

The study area

Historically, there has been an unbalanced relationship between indigenous people and non-indigenous people throughout the world. A majority of the contact between these groups has been characterized by the exploitation of indigenous people for the benefit of the dominating non-indigenous groups. As a result, indigenous people have struggled in their search for poverty reduction, cultural survival, self-determination, justice and equity (Butler and Hinch, 1996). The situations described above are particularly true of indigenous peoples in Taiwan.

Shaped like a tobacco leaf, Taiwan is located 160km off the south-east coast of China. It is a small island, 377km long and 142km wide (Cauquelin, 2004). More than two-thirds of Taiwan's surface is covered by mountains (Copper, 2003) and this is where the majority of indigenous people now live. First named Ihla Formosa by Portuguese mariners, Taiwan has been colonized by the Spanish (1626–1642), the Dutch (1624–1662), the Chinese Ming Dynasty loyalist Koxinga (1662–1683) and the Ching Dynasty (1663–1895), the Japanese (1895–1945), and the Republic of China (1945–present). The island's 439,000 aboriginal people are frequently overlooked in geopolitical assessments of Taiwan. Yet, at nearly 2 per cent of Taiwan's 22 million people, they compose a similar percentage of the national population as do the First Nations in Canada (3 per cent) and aborigines in Australia (1.8 per cent) (Munsterhjelm, 2002). As of January 2007, the number of officially recognized peoples in Taiwan stood at 13, including Atayal (Tayal), Saisiyat, Truku, Thao, Bunun, Kavalan, Tsou (Cou), Amis, Rukai, Puyuma, Paiwan, Yami and the Sakizaya. Today's official classification schemes were originally developed by Japanese government anthropologists a century ago as part of colonization efforts.

Household incomes of Taiwanese aboriginal people are less than 40 per cent of the national average and aboriginal unemployment is significantly higher than the national average (Munsterhjelm, 2002). Some attribute high aboriginal unemployment to the importation of nearly 300,000 'guest workers' from the Philippines, Thailand and Indonesia, who compete directly for jobs with aborigines. In rural areas, aboriginal farmers are typically small scale and are adversely affected by the agricultural sector's increasing openness to foreign agribusiness imports, especially since Taiwan became a member of the World Trade Organization in 2001. Taiwan is also undergoing rapid economic restructuring in which labour-intensive industries relocate to lower-cost areas such as the People's Republic of China and Vietnam. Additionally, environmental and economic devastation caused by the 21 September 1999 earthquake and numerous typhoons have created a situation in which Taiwanese aboriginal peoples are being squeezed from all sides. The Taiwanese government has encouraged tourism development in rural areas in response to these problems, and tourism has become an option for Taiwanese aboriginal peoples faced with responding to Taiwan's economic changes.

A Western-based economic rationale is that income generated through tourism can bring indigenous people increased economic independence, which will be accompanied by a higher degree of self-determination and cultural pride as poverty is decreased. Unlike many other forms of economic activity, such as the extraction of some types of forest resources from indigenous lands, appropriately planned and managed tourism is seen as possibly being a sustainable activity that is generally consistent with indigenous values about the sanctity of the land and people's relationship to it. From an economic perspective, indigenous people are seen to have a competitive tourism advantage because they possess unique cultural and physical resources. Therefore, a symbiotic relationship might be created to the extent that cultural survival and physical environmental preservation will contribute to economic success; and economic success will lead to cultural survival and physical environmental preservation (Butler and Hinch, 1996). This will require the achievement of a balance between economic viability, cultural integrity and social cohesion, and the maintenance of the physical environment.

The colonial legacy and tourism in Wulai

Cultural expressions come in both tangible and intangible forms, with associated stories and interpretations. Selected cultural expressions may be commodified as heritage and sold to tourists. In the process, their meaning and significance may be changed. The Atayal in Taiwan, parts of whose cultural activities were suppressed by colonial powers, and their attempts to reconstruct their culture within the context of tourism are examined next (Yoshimura and Wall, in press).

Wulai is located 27km south of Taipei City (see Figure 9.1). The indigenous people of Wulai are considered to be one of the subgroups of the Atayal. The 2004 census showed that Wulai had 767 households and 2192 residents, including 851 indigenous people and 1341 Han Chinese (Wulai Township Office, 2004). In Wulai, along the Nan Shih River, there is a natural hot spring that people come to enjoy and, at a walking distance, there is the tallest waterfall in Taiwan.

Figure 9.1 *Map of Taiwan showing location of Wulai*

Source: Yoshimura and Wall (in press)

The Wulai Atayal have experienced both colonialism and tourism development. During Japan's occupation (1895 to 1945), they were forced into village settlements and were required to abandon their most important socio-cultural activities: facial tattooing, headhunting and weaving. Prior to colonization, the Atayal men and women had their facial tattoos at the age of 15 to 16 when they were ready to get married. In order to get facial tattoos, men were required to become accomplished headhunters (Wiedfeldt, 2003). On the other hand, to get facial tattoos and, hence, to get married, women had to be accomplished weavers (see Figure 9.2) (Yamamoto, 1999, 2000). Banning these activities was a direct strike at the roots of Atayal culture. Not only was weaving banned, the Atayal lost most of their original textiles because many of them were taken to Japan; today, these textiles are preserved in a few Japanese museums, such as Tenri University Sankokan Museum.

After World War II was over in 1945, Japan's 50 years of occupation also ended. At the same time, nationalist China's colonization started. For the indigenous people of Taiwan, including the Atayal, this transition meant becoming more Chinese. After the mid-1960s, when tourists started visiting their village, the indigenous residents of Wulai generated most of their income

Figure 9.2 *Atayal woman with facial tattoo*

Source: photographed by M. Yoshimua at Shung Ye Museum of Formosan Aborigines, Taipei, 2006.

through international tourism, particularly from Japan (Hitchcock, 2003). It is ironic that the Japanese who banned facial tattoos returned as tourists to photograph elderly women who retained this feature. However, since the mid-1990s, the number of international tourists has declined, in part because of the opening-up of China as a competitive destination. Unlike many other parts of South-East Asia that have been approved as tourism destinations by the Chinese authorities, the political situation has meant that Taiwan has yet to benefit from the growing number of tourists emanating from mainland China. As a result, the market has become increasingly dominated by domestic visitors and Wulai's indigenous residents have gradually relinquished their tourism jobs.

In 1997, some indigenous women who had left their jobs in tourism started to engage in the revitalization of the Atayal weaving culture. However, these women now weave primarily for museums. Others, on the other hand, weave for domestic tourists, although they have little success in competition with less expensive Han Chinese factory-made woven products. Furthermore, cheaper, broadly similar products are produced by machine by majority Han entrepreneurs who undercut the hand-woven textiles that require more skill and time to make. This has greatly reduced the ability of Atayal weavers to create textiles as a commercially viable tourism product.

Atayal heritage has been commodified and has become a tourism attraction, albeit one among a number of tourist attractions in Wulai. Wulai's hot spring and waterfall are still important landscape features for tourist consumption; but most of the supporting businesses are now run by Han people. The fact that entrepreneurs from elsewhere run the businesses associated with the heritage of minorities is a common theme in the aboriginal tourism literature. In Wulai, tattoo-faced Atayal objects can be found in various artistic forms: murals, totem poles, tapestry, paintings, framed pictures, business cards and, of course, weaving. Textiles, which were once banned, have been revived and have become a part of the heritage tourism product of Wulai. Some indigenous weavers have attempted to sell their handmade weaving. However, as explained above, they have had little success in competing with the factory-made weaving brought in by Han Chinese entrepreneurs. The Wulai Atayal no longer attach the traditional meanings to their facial tattooing rituals, head-hunting and weaving. However, the Atayal reinvented their weaving tradition. Tourism was not the major catalyst for this; but it has played a part in influencing outcomes and meanings by creating a changing market for textiles. Textile products are now available in two main forms: a high-quality handmade product that is essentially a labour of love and, being relatively expensive, does not sell well to a domestic market; and a machine-made product made and sold by Han entrepreneurs who benefit financially from an appropriated and modified expression of Atayal culture, who sell their products to a predominantly Han domestic market.

Souvenir purchases and product evaluation in Wulai

The production and sale of handicrafts is one way in which indigenous peoples and tourists of different types interact. A study was undertaken to explore the perceived authenticity of Atayal woven handicrafts among tourists who visit Wulai (Chang et al, 2008). It involved the administration of a survey to domestic tourists in Wulai from 12 March to 6 May 2006, and 599 questionnaires were successfully completed, of which 132 were completed by tourists on package tours and 467 were on self-arranged visits, reflecting the dominance of the latter in the predominantly short-haul domestic travel market (Taiwan Tourism Bureau, 2004). The questionnaire comprised three parts:

1   tourist travel attributes;
2   the perceived authenticity of Atayal woven handicrafts; and
3   background information, particularly demographic characteristics.

A majority of respondents were single and female. Most (60 per cent) were between 20 and 39 years and were well educated (59 per cent had a college degree). Approximately one quarter (27 per cent) were employed in service industries or were students (25 per cent). Most (82 per cent) lived in the northern part of Taiwan, indicating again that Wulai is predominantly a short-haul, day-trip tourism destination. Wulai is more accessible to the core urbanized area (i.e. Taipei City) than other indigenous towns, and tourism developed earlier in Wulai and has become more commercialized than in other indigenous locations in Taiwan. It also has varied attractions that are not restricted to aboriginal culture. Slightly more than one third (37 per cent) of visitors came mainly for the hot springs and almost one quarter (23 per cent) were largely attracted by Atayal culture. In addition, almost one fifth (19 per cent) were interested in taking the cable car to the Yn Hsein Le Yuan theme park. Thus, there are a wide variety of reasons for tourists to go to Wulai in addition to the indigenous attractions and Wulai is best considered to be a general tourism attraction rather than a purely indigenous tourism destination.

Party composition was quite varied, involving a mix of family, relatives and friends. A slight majority reached Wulai by car (54 per cent) and substantial minorities came by coach (20 per cent) and public transport (14 per cent), reflecting the accessibility of the place to the city. With respect to expenditures, few spent less than TW$500 (approximately US$15.20), exclusive of transportation costs. Almost one third (30 per cent) spent between TW$1001 and TW$2000 (approximately US$30.30 to US$60.60) in Wulai and 40 per cent spent more than this, and occasionally much more. However, 28 per cent indicated that they spent nothing on souvenirs. The most common purchases were glutinous rice cakes (47 per cent) followed by rice wine (23 per cent). Of those purchasing souvenirs, 29 per cent indicated that they bought woven handicrafts. Approximately half (51 per cent) of these purchases were made from souvenir shops close to the survey location.

With respect to tourists' perceptions of the authenticity of products, tourists responded favourably to the traditional appearances of Atayal woven handicrafts. Factor analysis revealed that their perceptions of authenticity encompassed four dimensions: 'local flavour', 'traditional characteristics', 'utility and appearance', and 'market driven', the latter encapsulating non-traditional attributes introduced in response to market preferences. Of these, the 'utility and appearance' factor was rated the highest. This means that the domestic tourists who were interviewed put most weight on the practical use and appearance of the woven handicrafts. In contrast to the findings presented by Littrell et al (1993), tourists in this case did not perceive uniqueness as the most important attribute associated with authenticity. Rather, traditional colours, production methods and patterns were considered to be more important. According to the myths of the Atayal, the diamond shapes in the woven handicrafts represent the eyes of their ancestors, and red, white and black colours dominate. For tourists with even a rudimentary interest in learning about Atayal culture, this is something that is highly visible and easy to get acquainted with.

As in the work of Littrell et al (1993), no significant differences in perceived authenticity were found in association with gender or marital status. However, significant differences were found with age and education. Specifically, younger tourists tended to feel most strongly about the attributes of authenticity and were perhaps more sensitive to aspects of aboriginal cultures compared to their elders. In addition, those with college degrees were less concerned with attributes of authenticity, perhaps because they were less likely to participate in the package tours that were marketed partially through references to indigenous culture. Tourists from east and central Taiwan also placed more emphasis on authenticity than those from more proximate locations. This could be because more local visitors travel to Wulai for a wider variety of reasons and, through familiarity, may take Atayal culture for granted. However, it may also be explained by the fact that more indigenous tribes are located in east and central Taiwan than in the north (Hwang and Hwang, 2004); consequently, tourists from there may have more opportunities to experience indigenous cultures, including woven products.

With reference to travel mode, package tourists had greater concern for, and paid more attention to, authenticity than self-arranged tourists, for they were alerted to colourful aspects of Atayal culture in promotional materials. Nevertheless, the situation is likely little different from the domestic tourists studied by Xie and Wall (2003) in Hainan and Yang and Wall (in press) in Yunnan, who visited indigenous folk villages, largely on package tours, and did not have sufficient time to understand the complexities of the indigenous culture. In spite of this, the tourists had a satisfactory, if superficial, experience for they generally did not have much interest in gaining deep knowledge about indigenous history and customs.

The study that has just been summarized is one of very few that examines domestic tourists' perceptions of aspects of indigenous culture in a non-Western context. Domestic tourists are not a homogeneous group and the survey revealed that they held significant differences in perceptions in association with age, education and place of residence. Package tour visitors responded more positively than self-arranged tourists on matters concerning the authenticity of Atayal woven handicrafts.

As in all research, inevitably, more could be done. This research examined general perceptions of souvenirs rather than the evaluations of specific woven products. Therefore, variations in assessments of handicrafts of different types and from different sources were not uncovered. For instance, it is not known if tourists can distinguish between handcrafted woven goods, factory products, or even imitations or goods that look somewhat similar but are imported from mainland China. However, it would require a different research process to investigate these questions and the availability of sample objects to which to expose tourists.

Danayigu Ecological Park

Danayigu Ecological Park is one of the most well-known and successful aboriginal tourism attractions in Taiwan. It has been developed by the Cou tribe in Shanmei, a village in a mountain valley in Alishan County in Central Taiwan, 48km from Jiayi City. Shanmei has 189 households and the population is 668, almost all (99 per cent) of whom are Cou (Field survey, 2005; Chiou, 2003). A well-paved local road, Route 129, provides access to Jiayi City and connects with Xinmei and Chashan, which are nearby Cou villages. However, public transportation is not available and, although it attracts some international visitors, the main market is domestic tourists (Tao, 2006).

The Danayigu River flows through Shanmei, providing a focus for tourism. A former village head who had been exposed to ecotourism through a visit to South Africa saw the possibility of restoring the river and using it as a base for tourism and economic development. He thought that, if well protected, the fish stock would rejuvenate quickly and could be used as an attraction to solve the predicament of lack of funds for the development of scenic places, and that the development of an ecological park and Cou cultural traditions could be a good basis on which to build tourism (Interview, 2004). However, this was not an easy initiative to undertake and it took him several years to persuade the community that this could be a viable project from which all could benefit. In early 1987 he drafted *By-Laws for the Danayigu Self-Administered Conservation District* (Li, 2000) which were eventually accepted by the community. This was the first set of by-laws for indigenous self-administration in Taiwan (Gau, 2005). The purpose of the by-laws was to develop the tourism industry and to promote Shanmei economic growth by means of establishing Danayigu as a natural ecological park owned collectively by the Shanmei Cou. The highest authority of the park is the village assembly that authorizes, develops, operates and manages Danayigu. The by-laws also regulate both Shanmei Cou's and visitors' use of park resources and stipulate penalties if the regulations are violated. The statement was essentially a declaration of Shanmei Cou's regional autonomy. The Shanmei Cou had made Danayigu their communal homeland and property and, by way of communal resource management, it became a tourism destination.

A fish-stocking programme was undertaken and river patrols were instituted. After the river protection plan had been in place for two years, an area was then opened for permit-based fishing as a means of generating funds for the ecological park. During this period, the villagers worked hard to get the park ready, such as by constructing trails. They did this without external financial support. The park was formally opened to the public in 1995 and, in the following year, the park co-sponsored with the China Times Cultural Foundation the First Formosan Taiwan Gu Fish Festival. The event attracted more than 1000 visitors. 'It was on television and everyone felt that it was something fresh and interesting', said the former village head, smiling proudly at the memory. 'It was a big success!' (Liu, 2002).

Since then, the ecological park has evolved into an important tourism attraction, providing opportunities to experience a relatively natural landscape and cultural performances. It caters predominantly to a domestic clientele. Income is gained in many ways, such as an entrance fee, and from the sale of fish food, soft drinks, restaurant meals, agricultural products, souvenirs and provision of tourism services such as guides. Revenue of Shanmei in 2004 was TW$20,686,290 (US$827,452), including the income from Danayigu Ecological Park (80 per cent), government subsidies (5 per cent), interest (1 per cent), other (3 per cent) and the balance brought forward from 2003 (11 per cent) (Shanmei Community Development Association, 2005). The profits generated from Danayigu Park are used for community development, job creation and the provision of social services, including financial support for senior citizens and scholarships for students. Furthermore, taking advantage of proximity to a successful attraction, the existence of the park has enabled some community members to take their own initiatives, such as setting up bed-and-breakfast establishments.

Most importantly, the form of development that has been put in place has drawn heavily on Cou cultural attributes, including the sharing of resources, communal decision-making and the sharing of benefits. This case has been discussed in much greater detail by Tao (2006).

Marketing aboriginal products

If aboriginal cultural attractions are to be successful, their managers must know their market and use appropriate techniques to address that market. Three studies are now introduced that address these topics. The first concerns the motivations of domestic tourists who visit an aboriginal cultural festival. The second examines the extent to which domestic visitors to aboriginal attractions in Taiwan are novelty-seekers, and the third considers the advertising techniques that are most likely to be successful in attracting domestic visitors.

The Rukai Cultural Festival

The staging of festivals or events is very important from the perspective of destination marketing (Mules and Faulkner, 1996), and festivals are increasingly being used as instruments for promoting tourism and boosting the regional economy (Felsenstein and Fleischer, 2003). Getz (1993) and Formica and Uysal (1998) showed that the economic gains from festivals can be substantial because festivals provide interesting activities and spending venues for both local people and tourists. Much research, undertaken from a variety of perspectives, exists on festivals. However, very few studies related to aboriginal cultures have been published. The author undertook a study to profile tourists based on their motives and demographic characteristics (Chang, 2006). This was done in order to better understand the market for this aspect of cultural tourism: the motives of visitors have been found to be diverse and to vary from event to event, and little information on visitor motivations is reported in the limited number of studies that exist on aboriginal tourism events.

Wu-tai, located in the mountains of Ping-tung County (the most southern county in Taiwan), is the place of residence of the Rukai tribe. Wu-tai has a population of less than 3000 inhabitants, of whom more than 95 per cent are Rukai (Shiu et al, 2001). Wu-tai has a subtropical climate, mountains, traditional stone houses and attractive landscapes, and together with the Rukai culture, these features compose a base on which aboriginal tourism is developed. Approximately 20,000 tourists visit Wu-tai village yearly to see the natural scenery – in particular, Rukai houses, which are made out of a traditional stone with the appearance of black shale. The aboriginal cultural festival of the Rukai tribe is also called Rukai Day. In line with conventional customs, Rukai Day falls on 15 August each year. However, the Rukai cultural festival normally runs for three or four days and incorporates sports tournaments such as running. In fact, Rukai Day is the harvest festival of the Rukai tribe and sacrifices are offered to gods and ancestors after the millet harvest. This ceremony is recognized as being the peak of the festival and is the focal point for tourists as it includes entertaining performances, such as folk dances and folk singing. However, according to Rukai traditions, whoever participates in the festival, including tourists, must wear Rukai traditional outfits to gain admittance to the festival grounds, which are located in the Wu-tai Primary School. These outfits are sold in the local souvenir shops or stands.

A survey was undertaken in the village of Wu-tai on 15 to 17 August 2004 near the entrance of Wu-tai Primary School, where the annual aboriginal festival is held (Chang, 2006). The subjects of the survey were tourists who participated in the Rukai festival. In total, 365 questionnaires were distributed and 315 (86 per cent) usable questionnaires were obtained. Visitors were likely to be students (29 per cent), service industry employees (13 per cent) or business people (13 per cent) from the northern part of Taiwan, with a college level of education (63 per cent) and younger than 35 years of age (65 per cent), but approximately equally divided between males and females.

Factor analysis was used to identify the constructs underlying the 28 posited festival motivations. A three-factor solution provided the most distinctive and acceptable solution of the ten solutions that were analysed. The first factor was called *aboriginal cultural learners* since it emphasized festival participation and learning, as well as interaction with others. The second factor was called *change in routine*: people in this grouping stressed a desire for a break from their usual activities, and the third grouping was called *active culture explorers* and had the highest commitment to exploring aboriginal culture. No statistically significant demographic differences were found among the three groups, suggesting that, at least in this case, motivational variables may be more important than demographic variables in explaining differences among, and segmenting visitors to, aboriginal festivals. However, some further questions inevitably arise. For example, are tourists merely attracted by a superficial exposure to aboriginal activities, as may be obtained at a cultural festival, or are they really interested in experiencing aboriginal cultures and lifestyles in depth? Do they enjoy the diverse activities of the above-mentioned aboriginal tourism product and, if so, do they prefer an authentic experience or merely a product to be enjoyed? These questions merit further research. In the following section, the extent to which domestic tourists visiting aboriginal attractions in Taiwan are novelty-seekers is explored in greater depth.

Novelty-seeking

Tourists have different expectations for their travel activities. Some prefer to visit a familiar environment or to participate in customary activities, whereas others are interested in experiencing something different or the 'other'(Pearce, 1987). Motivations underpinning this kind of travel behaviour include individuals' needs for novelty, arousal or stimulation (Lee and Crompton, 1992). This may include travel abroad to witness other cultures. However, experiences of the 'other' may be gained domestically in places where there are peoples whose cultures and lifestyles differ from those of the majority population. Thus, the motivations of domestic tourists who visit aboriginal attractions were explored through administering a novelty-seeking survey to such visitors (Chang et al, 2006). The survey was conducted in January 2004 in both the Taiwan Indigenous People Cultural Park and the Formosan Aboriginal Cultural Village. The former is run by the government and is located in the south of Taiwan, and the latter is owned by a private entrepreneur and is in the centre of Taiwan. According to the Taiwan Tourism Bureau (2003), these two aboriginal cultural villages enjoyed the most visitors compared to other villages throughout the island – in fact, the two dominate the market.

In total, 350 questionnaires were distributed, 180 for the Taiwan Indigenous People Cultural Park and 170 for the Formosan Aboriginal Cultural Village, and 322 questionnaires (92 per cent) were returned that were valid and usable. Preliminary analyses indicated no significant differences in socio-economic characteristics, so they were combined and analysed as one data set. The demographic characteristics of the combined group of respondents were as follows: 54 per cent female, 66 per cent single, approximately half (49 per cent) aged between 20 and 29 years, with almost two-thirds (62 per cent) possessing a college degree. However, incomes were generally not high (41 per cent less than US$465 per month) since 38 per cent were students. Most were independent travellers (78 per cent) rather than on organized tours and almost half (46 per cent) lived in the south of the island. Thus, as is common to many cultural tourism sites globally, the clientele included a large proportion of single young adults, who were well educated, but not necessarily well paid, with a small preponderance of females.

Taiwanese tourists in this study generally displayed greater than neutral novelty-seeking scores. Given that most visitors to aboriginal cultural sites will be of a different culture than of those whom they are visiting, it is not surprising that many domestic tourists are attracted by the expectation of acquiring a novel experience. However, although the authenticity of the aboriginal culture was important, the natural scenery and well-managed environment appealed to the tourists the most. This suggests that visiting an attractive physical environment is also important, perhaps even more important to many of the respondents than visiting aboriginal culture. Unfortunately, it is not known which of the respondents came from urban or rural areas for this may have been a useful explanatory variable. In future studies, the relative importance of aboriginal culture and natural settings to different market segments may be worthy of investigation.

Some suggestions can be made to aboriginal cultural tourism operators based on the findings of this research. First, tourists value natural scenery highly among features of aboriginal tourism. Thus, the issue of the sustainable development of the village, which requires various stakeholders to be involved, should be addressed. Second, although the main objective of this research was not to evaluate tourists' satisfaction, it is noteworthy that aboriginal dances induced the most satisfactory responses. Thus, the interaction between employees and tourists could be further enhanced by providing well-planned and more diverse entertainment programmes in order to attract tourists' attention and upgrade tourists' impressions. In contrast to the tourists who spent more than 30 days in the Northern Territory of Australia (Ryan and Huyton, 2000), Taiwanese domestic visitors spent, on average, a half day in the aboriginal cultural village. Perhaps there is a potential to increase length of stay by enhancing the reasons for, and opportunities that can be undertaken at, the destination.

While some managing and staging is unavoidable, efforts should be made by the operator to maintain authenticity: visitors expect to experience authentic dances, shows, architecture and other cultural expressions when they visit aboriginal sites. Hence, as McIntosh (2004) points out, it is essential to establish and maintain an authentic experience, including a high-quality environment and interpretation, and guiding by well-trained aboriginal people. Finally, although the setting of this research was in cultural villages and not in real aboriginal homelands, one third of those surveyed were in the category of 'high novelty-seekers', displaying high interest in participating in aboriginal activities or making contact with aboriginal people. It shows that high novelty-seekers can be attracted to staged aboriginal cultural attractions and, in fact, constitute a substantial proportion of their markets.

Advertising experiments

If tourism enterprises are to be successful, then means must be found to engage with and attract a clientele. An exploration of aspects of advertising aboriginal attractions (Chang et al, 2005a, 2005b) is presented next.

There is considerable evidence to suggest that endorsers may be used to draw attention to, and enhance, the attractiveness of many types of products. An endorser (or spokesperson) refers to an in-advertisement presenter with special characteristics, such as physical attractiveness, fame or expertise, who is seen as the perceived source of the message in the context of creative advertising tactics (Rossiter and Percy, 1997). The advantages of using advertising endorsers include increasing product knowledge (Cutler and Javalgi, 1993; Mattila, 1999) and getting potential consumers' attention, as well as stimulating consumers' buying desire and, thus, penetrating the market. Furthermore, brand equity can be enhanced in a competitive market by using endorsers (Till and Shimp, 1998), and the implicit traits of endorsers, such as expertise and reputation, have a positive impact on advertising effectiveness. Endorsement advertising is widely adopted (Kahle and Homer, 1985). However, the practice of advertisement using aboriginal endorsers has not yet been widely acknowledged and undertaken.

In addition to endorsement, advertising appeal is an important factor in advertising effectiveness and consists of two main types: rational appeal and emotional appeal (Johar and Sirgy, 1991). The former stimulates customers through the content of information and logical reasoning in an advertisement. The latter influences consumers' attitudes and buying attention based on the image and emotions portrayed (Jeon et al, 1999). It is believed that types of advertising appeals should match types of products. In general, rational advertising appeals are often used for physical products, whereas services of an intangible nature often adopt emotional advertising appeals. Thus, it is worth exploring which type of appeal is most likely to be successful in attracting domestic tourists to aboriginal cultural villages. This was explored using an experimental approach in the context of visits to aboriginal folk villages in Taiwan.

As a first step, a series of brochures was designed that might be used to attract visitors to an aboriginal cultural village. The brochures were identical with the exception that photographs of different endorsers were substituted for each other; in one case, as a control, no endorser was included in the brochure. With respect to potential endorsers, three different types of individuals were used as endorsers: a celebrity, an aboriginal celebrity and an aboriginal employee (a dancer). Similarly, a rational and an emotive text were written and substituted for each other in the brochures. Thus, eight similar colourful brochures were created with different combinations of endorsers and messages. Sample brochure covers, one with an emotive message and no endorser, and the other with a rational message with an aboriginal employee endorser, are shown in Figure 9.3. The message is presented in Manadarin as is appropriate for a domestic Taiwanese clientele.

Figure 9.3 *Brochure covers for domestic tourists to Amis aboriginal cultural village*

Source: J. Chang and C. T. Tsai

Initially, the brochures were tested with a student sample of more than 600 students at a university in Taipei, using a 3 3 2 between-subjects factorial design: 461 completed questionnaires were obtained for six experimental groups, and 149 were gained for two control groups. The results of this study are presented in Chang et al (2005a). They revealed that an employee endorser (i.e. a dancer) stimulates a better response compared to a celebrity endorser. In addition, an emotional advertising appeal was more effective than using a rational advertising appeal in an aboriginal cultural village's brochure.

Following the successful completion of this study, it was replicated with a group of real tourists at an aboriginal village in Taiwan. The results of this investigation have been published in Chang et al (2005b). Again, it was found that an aboriginal employee achieved the most positive response, probably because of the impression of authenticity that the aboriginal dancer represents, no matter whether it is considered to be genuine or staged authenticity. Second, consistent with Jeon et al (1999), emotional advertising appeals were confirmed as being the appropriate type of appeal for a tourism product with a strong experiential content – for example, tourists experiencing folk dancing in an aboriginal cultural village. Therefore, emotional advertising appeals are recommended over rational appeals for use in the aboriginal cultural village's brochures.

For aboriginal practitioners, the findings can serve as a reference in adopting creative marketing tactics using employee endorsers and emotive messages. From a marketing standpoint, these results suggest that advertising which promotes authenticity, originality and expertise may be more successful in attracting tourists, rather than indirect claims to fame. More research is desired in order to determine the potential effectiveness of such advertising applications. The study is restricted in its analysis of domestic tourists to one aboriginal cultural village during the Taiwanese spring. Therefore, further research is encouraged in order to determine if the results can be generalized to a broader context in aboriginal tourism. Results are further constrained by lack of attention to tourists' prior experiences. This suggests that, for future research, it will be helpful to investigate whether or not tourists' prior experiences will moderate the effectiveness of endorsement and emotive advertising. An improved understanding of these relationships gained through experimental research will enable destination marketing managers to better allocate their resources in an effort to attract more tourists.

Conclusions

In much of the world, aboriginal people, through colonialism and, some would argue, through tourism as a form of neo-colonialism, have seen their cultures modified as they have interacted with more powerful majority groups. For example, the Atayal have seen their traditional cultural expressions suppressed, partially revived and expropriated by others as they have been forced to engage with outsiders in the form of colonists and tourists. Nevertheless, tourism, if developed appropriately, offers aboriginal people an opportunity to share aspects of their culture with others and to benefit from this economically. However, many tourists, although expressing a concern for authenticity, often have limited knowledge of aboriginal cultures, lack the time to obtain it, and can be satisfied, for good and ill, with staged presentations of indigenous culture. The market for aboriginal tourism is not homogeneous, as has been indicated through analyses of variations in the motivations of domestic visitors to aboriginal attractions in Taiwan. As for any product, the attributes of the market must be understood if means of accessing that market are to be developed appropriately. Through attention to the importance of novelty-seeking behaviour and aspects of advertising – namely, the use of endorsers and the content of messages – attention has been drawn to ways in which managers of aboriginal sites can market their product successfully in a differentiated domestic tourism market.

The very minority status of indigenous peoples ensures that they differ from mainstream society. However, while international tourists may be attracted to the exotic cultures of indigenous peoples, many members of the majority may look down on their indigenous peoples as poor, uneducated and inferior – an 'other' that is to be avoided rather than to be visited, appreciated and even celebrated. Yet, tourists seek novel experiences and some domestic tourists will undoubtedly be fascinated by the lifestyles and cultural expressions of their country's indigenous people. However, there may be limits to their willingness to be exposed to the 'other' so that interaction between the majority and the minority is managed to ensure that the comfort levels of both groups are not exceeded excessively. While high novelty-seekers interested in novel cultural experiences may be attracted to visit aboriginal cultures in locations distant from their homes, others, perhaps with limitations on the ability to travel internationally, may have satisfying exposure to other cultures closer to home. Regardless, the exposure of visitors to aboriginal cultures, although commonly providing satisfactory visitor experiences, is often fleeting, staged and lacking in interpretation, and so it may reinforce stereotypes rather than promote true cultural understanding.

Acknowledgements

This research was funded, in part, by research grants from the Social Sciences and Humanities Research Council of Canada held by Geoffrey Wall, and the

National Science Council of Taiwan (no 96-2415-H-034-006-SS2) and the Canadian Trade Office in Taipei (no 623-2-FRP2006-01) by Janet Chang.

References

Butler, R. and Hinch, T. (1996) *Tourism and Indigenous Peoples*, International Thomson Business Press, London

Cauquelin, J. (2004) *The Aborigines of Taiwan: The Puyuma: From Headhunting to the Modern World*, Routledge, London/New York

Chang, J. (2006) 'Segmenting tourists to aboriginal cultural festivals: an example in the Rukai tribal area, Taiwan', *Tourism Management*, vol 27, no 6, pp1224–1234

Chang, J., Wall, G. and Lai, C. Y. A. (2005a) 'The advertising effectiveness of aboriginal endorsers: an example from Taiwan', *Tourism Analysis*, vol 10, no 3, pp247–255

Chang, J., Wall, G. and Tsai, C. T. (2005b) 'Endorsement advertising in aboriginal tourism: an experiment in Taiwan', *International Journal of Tourism Research*, vol 7, no 6, pp347–356

Chang, J., Wall, G. and Chu, S. T. (2006) 'Novelty-seeking at aboriginal attractions', *Annals of Tourism Research*, vol 33, no 3, pp729–747

Chang, J., Wall, G. and Chang, C. L. (2008) 'Perception of the authenticity of Atayal woven handicrafts in Wulai, Taiwan', *Journal of Hospitality and Leisure Marketing*, vol 16, no 4, pp385–409

Chiou, T. L. (2003) *A Study of Alishan Saviki (Shanmei in Cou) Cou's Attitude toward Ecotourism Development*, MSc, National Taichung Teachers' College, Taichung, Taiwan (in Chinese)

Copper, J. F. (2003) *Taiwan: National-State or Province?*, fourth edition, Westview, Boulder, CO

Cutler, B. D. and Javalgi, R. (1993) 'Analysis of print ad features: services versus products', *Journal of Advertising Research*, vol 33, no 2, pp62–69

Felsenstein, D. and Fleischer, A. (2003) 'Local festivals and tourism promotion: The role of public assistance and visitor expenditure', *Journal of Travel Research*, vol 41, no 4, pp385–392

Formica, S. and Uysal, M. (1998) 'Market segmentation of an international cultural-historical event in Italy', *Journal of Travel Research*, vol 36, no 4, pp16–24

Gau, J. S. (2005) *Passing the Shady Valley: Danayigu Legend*, The Presbyterian Church in Taiwan, Taipei (in Chinese)

Getz, D. (1993) 'Festivals and special events', in M. A. Khan, M. D. Olsen and T. Var (eds) *Encyclopedia of Hospitality and Tourism*, Van Nostrand Reinhold, New York, NY, pp789–810

Hitchcock, M. (2003) 'Taiwan's ambiguous South-East Asian heritage', *Indonesia and the Malay World*, vol 31, no 89, pp69–79

Hwang, H. S. and Hwang, C. C. (2004) *Overall Examination of the Cultural Development of the Indigenous Peoples in Taiwan*, Yuan-Liou Publishing, Taipei, Taiwan (in Chinese).

Jeon, W., Franke, G. R., Huhmann, B. A. and Phelps, J. (1999) 'Appeals in Korean magazine advertising: a content analysis and cross-cultural comparison', *Asia Pacific Journal of Management*, vol 16, pp249–258

Johar, J. S. and Sirgy, M. J. (1991) 'Value-expressive versus utilitarian advertising appeals: When and why to use which appeal', *Journal of Advertising*, vol 10, no 3, pp23–33

Kahle, L. R. and Homer, P. M. (1985) 'Physical attractiveness of the celebrity endorser: A social adaptation perspective', *Journal of Consumer Research*, vol 11, no 2, pp54–961

Lee, T. and Crompton, J. (1992) 'Measuring novelty seeking in tourism', *Annals of Tourism Research*, vol 19, pp732–751

Li, C. R. (2000) *The Study of Cou's Management of the Fish Resources in the Danayigu Stream*, MSc, National Taichung Teachers' College, Taichung, Taiwan (in Chinese)

Littrell, M. A., Anderson, L. F. and Brown, P. J. (1993) 'What makes a craft souvenir authentic?', *Annals of Tourism Research*, vol 20, no 1, pp197–215

Liu, A. (2002) 'The Danayigu Ecological Park', *Sinorama Magazine*, January, www.sinorama.com.tw/en/show_issue.php3?id=200219101084E.T XT&page=1, accessed 16 February 2005

Liu, P., Liu, A. and Wall, G. (2005) 'Eco-museum conception and Chinese application: A case study in Miao villages, Suoga, Guizhou Province', *Resources and Environment in the Yangtze Basin*, vol 14, no 2, pp254–257

Mattila, A. S. (1999) 'Do emotional appeals work for services?', *International Journal of Service Industry Management*, vol 10, no 3, pp292–306

McIntosh, A. (2004) 'Tourists' appreciation of Maori culture in New Zealand', *Tourism Management*, vol 25, pp1–15

Mules, T. and Faulkner, B. (1996) 'An economic perspective on special events', *Tourism Economics*, vol 2, pp107–117

Munsterhjelm, M. (2002) 'The first nations of Taiwan: A special report on Taiwan's indigenous peoples', *Cultural Survival Quarterly*, summer, vol 26, no 2, pp53–55

Pearce, D. (1987) *Tourism Today: A Geographical Analysis*, John Wiley, New York, NY

Rossiter, J. and Percy, L. (1997) *Advertising Communications and Promotion Management*, Irwin/McGraw-Hill, New York, NY

Ryan, C. and Huyton, J. (2000) 'Who is interested in aboriginal tourism in the Northern Territory, Australia? A cluster analysis', *Journal of Sustainable Tourism*, vol 8, pp53–88

Shanmei Community Development Association (2005) *The Handbook of the Sixth Annual General Assembly of Shanmei Community Development Association of Alishan Township in Jiayi County – The Minutes of the Meeting*, January 2005, Shanmei Community Development Association, Shanmei (in Chinese)

Shiu, L., Hsiu, Y. and Hong, Z. (2001) *The Analysis of Aboriginal Agricultural Characteristics and Potentials in Aboriginal Townships in Taiwan*, Training Center of Aboriginal People's Productivity, National Chia-Yi University, Chia Yi, Taiwan

Taiwan Tourism Bureau (2003) *Annual Survey Report on R.O.C. Inbound Travelers*, Tourism Bureau, Taipei, Taiwan

Taiwan Tourism Bureau (2004) *Domestic Taiwanese Travel Report*, Ministry of Transportation, Taipei, Taiwan

Tao, T. (2006) *Tourism as a Livelihood Strategy in Indigenous Communities: Case Studies from Taiwan*, PhD thesis, University of Waterloo, Waterloo, Canada

Till, B. D. and Shimp, T. A. (1998) 'Endorsers in advertising: The case of negative celebrity information', *Journal of Advertising*, vol 27, no 1, pp67–82

Wang, Y. and Wall, G. (2005) 'Resorts and residents: Stress and conservatism in a displaced community', *Tourism Analysis*, vol 10, no 1, pp37–53

Wang, Y. and Wall, G. (2007) 'Administrative arrangements and displacement compensation in top-down tourism planning: a case from Hainan Province, China', *Tourism Management*, vol 28, no 1, pp70–82

Wiedfeldt, O. (2003) 'The Atayal of Taiwan: Basic economic, legal and social structures. Probing the causes for the stagnation of Atayal culture', in Shung Ye Taiwan

Aborigines Research Group in Japan (ed) *Studies of Taiwan Aborigines* (translated by E. Kaneko, H. Yamada Translations), Fukyo, Tokyo, pp4–47 (in Chinese)

Wulai Township Office (2004) *Population*, www.wulia.tpc.gov.tw/chinese/main01.html, accessed 10 July 2006

Xie, P. and Wall, G. (2001) 'Cultural tourism experiences in Hainan, China: The changing distribution of folk villages', *Tourism*, vol 49, no 4, pp319–326

Xie, P. and Wall, G. (2003) 'Authenticating visitor attractions based upon ethnicity', in A. Fyall, A. Leask and B. Garrod (eds) *Managing Visitor Attractions: New Directions*, Butterworth Heineman, Oxford, pp107–123

Yamamoto, Y. (1999) 'The prohibition of tattooing among the Atayal: History and analysis (1)', in Shung Ye Taiwan Aborigines Research Group in Japan (ed) *Studies of Taiwan Aborigines*, Fukyo, Tokyo, pp3–40

Yamamoto, Y. (2000) 'Interference by the bureau of aboriginal affairs and the elimination of tattooing: forbidding the Atayal to apply tattoos', in Shung Ye Taiwan Aborigines Research Group in Japan (ed) *Studies of Taiwan Aborigines*, Fukyo, Tokyo, pp49–70

Yang, L. and Wall, G. (in press) 'Authenticity in ethnic tourism: tourists' perspectives', *Current Issues in Tourism*, vol 35, no 3, pp751–771

Yang, L., Wall, G. and Smith, S. (2008) 'Ethnic tourism development: Chinese government perspectives', *Annals of Tourism Research*, vol 35, no 3, pp751–771

Yoshimura, M. and Wall, G. (in press) 'The reconstruction of Atayal identity in Wulai, Taiwan', in M. Parnwell and M. Hitchcock (eds), *Heritage Tourism in Southeast Asia*, NIAS Press (Nordic Institute of Asian Studies), Copenhagen

10

No, We Are Not 'Eco-Tourists': Hill-Walking and Eco-Tourism in Hong Kong

Chan Yuk Wah and Fung Yip Hing

Introduction

Although Hong Kong is internationally known as a finance and commercial city, it is a place full of nature. One specific topographical feature of Hong Kong is that it is dominated by hills and mountains. This chapter examines the development of domestic tourism in Hong Kong, with particular emphasis on nature tourism and eco-tourism. It elaborates on a popular native leisure activity called *haang saan* (*haang* means walk and *saan* means hill; a direct translation of the term is 'walking [on] the hill').[1] This term is used to include activities such as hiking, expedition and trail-walking. Not much has yet been written about this leisure pattern of the Hong Kong people. There are, indeed, scanty academic discussions about Hong Kong domestic tourism and holidaying patterns. The recent opening of a wetland park and its high-profile promotion as eco-tourism has aroused some interest in local eco-travels.

Interestingly, most of those who have engaged in *haang saan* for years rarely identify their activity as something related to eco-tourism. Many see it as weekend or day-off leisure activity. Contrary to this, the Hong Kong government has initiated the promotion of eco-tourism through the establishment of an artificially created facility called the Hong Kong Wetland Park (HKWP). The HKWP was the first officially established theme park to cater to recreational, educational and tourism purposes. It arouses awareness and interests in wetland ecosystems and their conservation. The park's designed ecosystems are very much a man-made simulation. Nevertheless, it has been well received by the Hong Kong public; as a consequence, it has become a well-known component of the formalization of 'eco-tourism development'.

Before its handover to China in 1997, Hong Kong had been a British colony since 1842. In the post-World War II decades, Hong Kong was a fast-growing economy, especially the light industrial sector. Since the early 1980s, its economic structure has been gradually transformed from an industrial economy to a service- and finance-oriented one. In the last three decades, Hong Kong citizens, leading a hectic and busy city life, have made outbound travel one of their favourite holiday-making activities (Zhang et al, 2003). Besides travelling abroad, Hong Kong workers and middle class alike are also increasingly fond of going to the countryside to enjoy nature. This trend has received an even greater push after the 2003 severe acute respiratory syndrome (SARS) epidemic and development of domestic eco-tourism.

The following sections explore two parallel paths of holiday-making eco-travel: hill-walking and wetland tourism. Hill-walking is perceived as a long-existing leisure activity of Hong Kong residents, which has been popular in the last two decades and gained more popularity after the SARS epidemic. In contrast, the wetland park made operational in 2006 has attracted masses of visitors from the local population, contributing to what scholars refer to as the phenomenon of 'mass eco-tourism' (Cheung, 2008). While the former is undoubtedly nature based, and yet rarely recognized as eco-tourism, the latter is, in fact, a recently developed artificial theme park widely promoted as an eco-tourism opportunity. Despite all the government's investments in the park, the HKWP does not seem to arouse the interest of the experienced hikers and trekkers. By comparing *haang saan* and wetland park tourism, this chapter contrasts two types of domestic eco-travel: an informal, self-organized and uncommodified leisure activity versus the officially controlled and promoted eco-park tourism.

Eco-tourism in different contexts

Eco-tourism, as a catchword describing the development of tourism and environmental conservation, has become a global tourism agenda since the 1990s. Similar to the rise of the environmental protection movement, eco-tourism has likewise originated from the West. Nevertheless, the notion has swiftly spread to other parts of the world and has thus been subject to much amendment under local improvization and local practices.

Since the late 1980s, eco-tourism has not only been endorsed by the World Tourism Organization (WTO) but has been the priority of a number of Western tourism organizations.[2] The 1992 United Nations Conference on Environment and Development in Rio de Janeiro, otherwise known as the Earth Summit, provided a new orientation for the eco-development of the travel and tourism industry. Consequently, Agenda 21, the global environmental agenda, endorsed sustainable guidelines and principles for the travel and

Figure 10.1 *Map of Hong Kong*

Source: www.yearbook.gov.hk/2007/en/pdf/Map_Eng.pdf

tourism industry. By the mid-1990s, many tourism service providers in the West had picked up this new trend of market demand, and named their products with all sorts of eco-labels (Font and Buckley, 2001).

The rapid spread of the term has much to do with the response of the tourism industry, which has capitalized on the public's environmental sentiment to produce new tourism products. However, while popularizing the term, the industry has also done much in watering down the meanings and missions of eco-tourism (Honey, 2002, p19). Green travel in many practical cases has become a marketing label and a mere strategy to devise a new market niche, rather than fulfilling the mission of conservation.

There has been a wide spectrum of definitions of the term eco-tourism. Popular understanding of the term often relates eco-tourism to nature and wildlife tourism. Scholars and conservation professionals, on the other hand, define it in a different light. They often require eco-tourists to be highly environmentally conscious and to contribute their travel expenditure to conservation projects. Academic discourses generate a number of criteria to define the term, and can be broadly clubbed together as responsibilities and travel morals (Cater and Lowman, 1994; Fennell, 1999, pp30–64; Honey, 2002, pp23–26; see also McLaren, 2003, pp102–103; Higham, 2007, p5):

- involving travel to natural destinations;
- minimizing impact to the hosting environment and communities;
- developing environmental awareness;
- bringing net benefits to the environment;
- providing direct financial benefits for conservation;
- providing financial benefits and empowerment for local people; and
- respecting local cultures (sensitive not only to the environment, but also to local culture – i.e. being less intrusive and exploitative than conventional tourism).

Indeed, nothing in it is new if eco-tourism merely means appreciation of nature and natural landscapes during travel. The recent trend of eco-tourism development entails a deeper understanding of the impacts of human activities (tourism included) on nature and culture, and a moral obligation to respect nature and support conservation and responsible travel. However, popular understanding of the term still varies tremendously. Even in the West, where the term originated, the content of eco-tourism has been evolving and has generated numerous discursive debates, involving the conflicts between conservation, tourism and economic development. Retrospectively, eco-tourism is recommended as an alternative kind of tourism with conservation purposes and an anti-development spirit. However, in practice, it has been employed as a tool for development. As Cochrane (2007, p289) has pointed out: 'Commercial organizations are unlikely to relinquish it as a marketing tool, while government agencies and NGOs see it as a useful way of trying to combine the objectives of economic development and environmental conservation.'

While eco-tourism is believed to entail some universal standards and principles, some researchers argue that eco-tourism is, in fact, a means of perpetuating Western power and economic interests (Hall, 1994; Mowforth and Munt, 2003; Cater, 2007). Cater (2007), for example, has contended that this alternative form of tourism is very much a Western construct. Hence, an outcome of Western-centric development, it has been viewed as the floodgates that have 'opened to eco-opportunistic Western exploitation' (Cater, 2007, p43) and should thus be 'more fundamentally contested in order to listen to different, distant, distanced, voices' (Cater, 2007, p63). Noting the untidy interpretations and practices of eco-tourism around the world, Higham (2007) argues that one major problem that exists in the development of eco-tourism is that many eco-tourism development initiatives have been poorly served by government agencies that are responsible for sustainable development. There are variously constructed 'natures', and eco-tourism has often been embedded in the national development trajectories of different developing countries (Lindberg et al, 1997; Nowaczek and Fennell, 2002; Weaver, 2002).

In Hong Kong, the upsurge of claims to eco-tourism development has to do with the government's awareness of the development constraints that the tourism industry began to face in the later half of the 1990s due to the emergence of many other Asian tourism destinations, as well as its awareness of Hong Kong's potentials in attracting inbound tourists to its countryside. By 1999, tourism-related departments such as the Hong Kong Tourist Association (HKTA)[3] and the Agricultural, Fishery and Conservation Department (AFCD) have begun to promote Hong Kong's countryside (HKTA, 2000). Most of the time, 'eco-tourism' is understood as something related to nature-based tourism in conjunction with some sort of environmental education. With the opening of the wetland park in 2006, the term 'eco-tourism' has been increasingly popularized and promoted locally as well as internationally. Cheung (2008, p259) explains how the population size of nature lovers has expanded in the last two decades from a handful of birdwatchers (mostly Westerners) to more localized eco-tourists. Cheung particularly emphasizes the big growth in mass eco-tourism with the establishment of the wetland park.

The upsurge in the popularity of the park has shaped a specific 'Hong Kong-style' ecotourism under the umbrella of a theme park. The dominant discourse on eco-tourism packaged in the context of the wetland park has brought many to understand eco-tourism as something purposefully designed and education oriented, constituting a localized character of eco-tourism and drawing a boundary between wetland park visitors and experienced hikers and trekkers.

Hiking and hill-walking

Trekking and mountaineering have been a major component of nature-based tourism (Gurung and De Coursey, 1994; Godde et al 2000). Hiking and hill-walking have been popular for more than two decades as weekend and day-off leisure activities in Hong Kong and are generally described as 'haang saan' or 'walking (on) the hill'. This term may be used to include activities such as hiking, expedition and trail-walking. Not much has yet been written about this leisure activity of the Hong Kong people. Before the 1980s, the number of hikers was very limited as the poor masses had to work hard to make ends meet. Since the 1980s, with the establishment and the opening of more nature trails by the government and the growth of the local-born working class, more young people made trail- and hill-walking their day-off activities. Since the SARS outbreak in 2003, a lot more Hong Kong people have become interested in hill-walking. This section examines the craze of hill-walking and its relationship to nature and eco-tourism.

Over the past decades, many of the hill-walking lovers have voluntarily and informally organized themselves into hikers' groups to explore different natural and remote parts of the countryside. According to the Hong Kong Federation of Countryside Activities (HKFCA),[4] there are now more than 300 hiking teams, some of which were established as early as in the 1930s. One of the earliest hiking groups, Yung Sheh Hikers, was established in 1932 and is still active in organizing regular hiking activities for their members. But a number of the early initiating groups have already dissolved, with new groups continuing to emerge. Catbus, established in 2005, is one of the more active new groups. Most of these hiking groups are only loosely associated with the HKFCA or the Hong Kong Hiking Association China (HKHAC).[5] The hiking groups organize and finance their own hiking activities independently. Some teams organize activities on a daily basis. The number of hikers joining each activity varies and may range from a few tens to over a hundred. The demand for physical strength and perseverance in these hiking activities and levels of danger involved in the trip also vary a lot.

A number of these hiker groups advertise their activities in a local newspaper, *Wen Wei Po*.[6] This daily publishes a list of the hiking activities every Tuesday. While some groups put their activity news in the monthly bulletins of the HKFCA and HKHAC, most of them, today, post their activities on their own websites or joint websites.[7] It is thus very convenient for hikers to check out what sort of activities would be available in the coming week(s) and make a selection from these based on their favourite routes and destinations.

Many of the hiking teams are operated by volunteers and do not have paid staff. Thus, there is either no charge for joining the activities or charges are minimal.[8] Different hiking teams have different orientations and interests for visiting the countryside and hill-walking. Some focus on the training of walking capacity, while others are motivated by the extraordinary landscapes. The major categories include physical-training trekking, exploring exciting scenery, exploring the coastline, exploring outlying islands and camping in wilderness. Through these activities and the sharing of interests and experiences on the websites, hikers often come across people with similar interests and build long-term friendships with other hikers.

There is usually no specific criterion for joining the teams. Anyone interested in a particular trip of a particular team on a particular day may show up at the designated assembly point at the specified time, bringing with him or her the essentials – namely, drinking water, food and basic personal gear (hat, sunglasses, gloves, etc.). The organizers or the team leaders are experienced hikers who design the route and take the lead in trekking. Before joining a tour, the most important thing for new hikers to consider is whether their physical capability allows them to trek on such a route.

Supposedly, all participants are responsible for their own safety (i.e. they must be honest about their physical capacity to be able to finish the designated route). Participants will endanger themselves as well as other co-hikers if they are oblivious of their own capability or deliberately lie about it. In the past, some team leaders had to return some participants early in the trip since it was discovered that these participants were obviously physically incapable of walking a particular route.

Notwithstanding this, most team leaders and other hikers are usually very friendly and willing to help each other whenever necessary. Within such a group there are usually hikers who can either offer first-aid treatment to those who become injured or set up guide ropes at dangerous places. Sometimes the team leaders and helpers provide interesting historical descriptions or folklore concerning the places of interest/visitation. Making jokes to encourage relaxation and sharing snacks with each other are basic behaviour codes of these hiking teams. Thus, in addition to obtaining physical training and enjoying the natural beauty of the landscapes, there is a lot of fun during the trips.

Many of the team leaders and their helpers are highly environmentally conscious. They require other hikers to carry away their own rubbish and do not allow them to leave waste behind in the countryside. They also instruct hikers not to pick flowers and other plants. Unfortunately, they are not able to prevent damage to the fragile ground surfaces, which have become more and more fragile due to the frequent steps of hikers. Such damage inevitably leads to increasing soil erosion along the trekking routes. Some team leaders are also critical of the 'official' ways of preserving the country parks. For example, several leaders criticized the government for building too many cement roads and staircases on the hills and mountains, transforming a wilderness area into a city space. The conservation-conscious hikers mentioned in this section do not, however, identify themselves as eco-tourists. To them, eco-tourism is the government's initiative for school-going kids to learn about nature.

The SARS effect on eco-travel

Besides creating an epidemic and resulting in a number of losses of life, the SARS outbreak in 2003 had a significant impact on the health consciousness and leisure patterns of Hong Kong residents. Because of the SARS threat, a weariness among the urban mass developed in regard to unhealthy urban life patterns in congested city spaces. Many became more health conscious and began to strive for a healthier lifestyle by being closer to nature and keeping a healthier pattern of eating and exercising. These were believed to be the ways of strengthening one's physique and would thus make people less vulnerable to attacks by viruses.

SARS was a kind of epidemic attacking those with weak immune systems. During the SARS outbreak, people felt vulnerable to diseases and viruses. For more than two months, the public was advised not to go to crowded places, such as restaurants, shopping arcades and busy streets. All people were required to wear face masks in public areas. Besides going to work, people stayed at home most of the time. Moreover, Hong Kong people had difficulty in travelling to other places during the epidemic as they were not welcomed overseas since Hong Kong was perceived as a contagious city.

Having being 'imprisoned' for over a month by the epidemic panic, many began to move towards the countryside and up the hills. Experienced hikers noticed that during the SARS period, the number of weekend hill-walkers increased substantially. The countryside was perceived as being a place of plants and fresh air, where people could obtain temporary relief from the life-threatening disease as well as from physical and mental 'imprisonment'. While the urban space represented a contagious, congested environment, the countryside was spacious, safe and clean. By landing on the hills and mountains, one got the chance to breathe in fresh air instead of the highly polluted air in the city, lessening the chance of contracting disease. Walking on the hills also allowed one to exercise in a more interesting way and to enjoy the companionship of friends, as life and friendship has become more valuable under the life-threatening risk of disease.

Today, the hills and mountains continue to receive crowds of visitors during weekends. '*Haang saan*' has been one of the major activities of local holiday-makers. The dichotomy between natural space and city space parallels that between healthiness and un-healthiness, fresh air and polluted air, congestion and relaxation, and working days and off days. '*Haang saan*' has become one of the major activities of local holiday-makers. Many, having developed a lifestyle of outings and expeditions during the last half decade, choose not to abandon such holidaying leisure patterns as long as the hills provide quality time for relaxation and 'freshness', which cleanses the weariness brought on by stressful urban living.

The following section elaborates on the conscious effort on the part of government of developing eco-tourism and how eco-tourism has been popularized as well as monopolized by 'official' interpretation.

Packaging nature: Theme park eco-tourism

Country parks

Over the past few decades, the Hong Kong government has played a major role in packaging Hong Kong's topography and natural landscape into walking trails, country parks and marine parks. Before the popularization of the concept of eco-tourism, a continued effort existed to bring the countryside under government control and management. During World War II, many of the hilly areas in Hong Kong were deforested. Afterwards, the colonial government undertook the role of reforestation by replanting and growing trees on the hillsides. During the 1970s, the then governor, Sir Fred MacLehose, placed more emphasis on managing the countryside. The first Countryside Ordinance was passed in 1976 and in the same year the first Country Park Committee was set up to assume responsibility for creating country parks. The first three country parks were established in Kam Shan, Shing Mun and Lion Rock Hill in 1977 (Yeung, 2007). By 1979, a total of 21 country parks and a number of walking trails were designed. There were also barbecue facilities in the country parks to allow visitors to enjoy bonfire picnicking. In 1995, the Marine Park Ordinance was passed to facilitate the establishment of marine parks.

Today, the AFCD is responsible for managing 23 country parks (which cover 40 per cent of Hong Kong's land area), 4 marine parks and 1 marine reserve. The number of country park visitors has continued to increase over the years, from 2.7 million in 1977 to 8.8 million in 1987, and to 12 million in 2006. During the 1980s, most of the visitors were young and were aged between 15 and 39. In 2006, the majority of visitors were older than 35. It was also found that barbecue lovers have decreased over the years (Yeung, 2007). Rather than sitting at fire places and eating roasted food, many have become more interested in walking on the hills to get exercise and breathe in fresh air.

Since 2000, the AFCD has placed a tremendous effort in publishing different series of books introducing the 'green side' of Hong Kong. In 2007, the AFCD and the Friends of Country Parks published a book entitled *Thirtieth Anniversary of Country Parks*. The book narrates the historical development of country parks and important events in a nostalgic and sentimental tone, especially apparent in its epilogue (Yeung, 2007):

> *For the past three decades, there are happy and sad memories in Hong Kong peoples' collective memories. However, it is also in these 30 years that Hong Kong has kept a green countryside. It has been loyally staying there waiting for us to return to its embrace where we can release ourselves from the troublesome world. This is the purpose of establishing the country parks – to set a boundary for protecting nature.*

With the opening of the HKWP in 2006, the AFCD came to play a major role in promoting eco-tourism in Hong Kong. The following section elaborates on this role and the major work of the HKWP.

Hong Kong Wetland Park

The Hong Kong Wetland Park (HKWP) was established on an ecological miti-gation area (EMA). It was originally created to compensate for the damage to marsh lands due to the development of a new residential area (Tin Shui Wai) in the New Territories. The feasibility plan of constructing the park was carried out by the Hong Kong government (represented by the AFCD) and the Hong Kong Tourism Board (the then Tourist Association) in 1998. The feasibility report confirmed that the expansion of the EMA into a wetland eco-tourism attraction would help to enhance the ecological function of the area and assist in the promotion of conservation, environmental education and tourism.

The HKWP was a development project costing over US$64 million and extending over 61ha of land. It has 60ha of wetland reserve and a visitor centre of 10,000m² in extent. Besides the HKWP, there is another well-known piece of wetland reserve named Mai Po Nature Reserve Zone. It comprises wetland marshes with fish and shrimp fields and is home to large populations of migra-tory birds. In 1995, after lengthy debates about the conservation of Mai Po between developers, the government, fishermen and environmental groups, Mai Po was eventually given to the World Wide Fund for Nature-Hong Kong for conservation management and research purposes. As a wetland zone of scientific research and educational significance, Mai Po is heavily regulated and the number of visitors is limited each year. Interested visitors need to reserve group tours a few months in advance.

By developing the HKWP, the government has been able to expand wetland and conservation education; the capacity to accommodate visitors has thus been enhanced. The original plan of the park was to receive 540,000 visi-tors a year. Unexpectedly, the first 12 months after the opening in May 2006 attracted 1.2 million visitors (HKWP, 2007). The park is known to have hosted as many as 21,000[9] visitors – the highest record – in a single day. In the first year of its opening, 90 per cent of the visitors were local Hong Kongers, while 6.5 per cent were tourists from mainland China and 3.5 per cent were overseas tourists.[10]

Different wetland ecosystems have been established within the park: streams, freshwater marshes, reed beds, mudflats and wet agricultural land. It is inhabited by a diverse species of fish, insects, amphibians, reptiles, birds and mammals. Besides native species, a number of foreign species also exist. Alien species, such as the mile-a-minute weed and the Nile tilapia, have frequently caused problems for the park since many have high reproductive rates and have been competing with native species for light, water and habitat. Some native species have fallen prey to the foreign species. One example is the golden apple snail from South America that often feeds on the eggs of other native freshwater snails. A great deal of effort is required on the part of park management staff to maintain a balance in the populations of different species. In a sense, the ecosystems of the park are the result of intentional installation and design, and high-calibre management.

Every Monday and Thursday, the park mainly receives tour groups from primary and secondary schools, of approximately 400 children. In the three years since its opening, it has received more than 400 study tour groups from different educational institutions (from kindergartens to universities).[11] School children are usually excited to see the crabs, mudskippers, colourful dragonflies and the only crocodile, named Pui Pui. Adult visitors are eager birdwatchers, although this activity is carried out at a distance from within a bird hide, where birds are observed through telescopes.

Besides maintaining simulated wetland ecosystems and providing recreation for the public, the HKWP also shoulders an educational mission, especially in teaching school children the ecological models of wetland habitats and wetland species, and environmental sensitivity.

The HKWP is undeniably a contrived park, artificially designed and heavily managed by the AFCD. However, its contrived nature does not thwart the interest of Hong Kong holiday-makers, especially families with parents and small children. Many of the visitors are aware of the 'unnatural' aspects of the park and are able to appreciate its well-intentioned educational aims. Some parents perceive their visit as a serious learning experience for their children. The author once observed a primary school child standing under the hot sun for 15 minute, copying down all of the complicated names of the plants written on a display board in the park. Such out-of-classroom learning feeds the appetite of many education-conscious Hong Kong parents. According to them, the park helps their children to learn something substantial about nature in a safe environment. It also addresses the pro-environmental sensibility of many middle-class parents who want their children to be closer to nature.

Prior to its opening, the HKWP had already launched a number of trips for volunteers and schools children to other wetlands in Hong Kong. The volunteer network that has been developing since 2001 has become an integral part of the public education aspect of the park. Over the years, it has received more than 3000 applications for volunteer training; at present, it has more than 1000 volunteer members. Although most of the members are working adults and students, families, as a whole, also volunteer. In this way, not only can the parents and children learn together at the park, the children are also provided with an opportunity to work as volunteers, passing on environmental knowledge to younger children. In this way, the HKWP has attracted a number of family members who spend their holidays and weekends in the park.

The eco-guides trained by the HKWP have, indeed, formed a strong and wide network among Hong Kong citizens to disseminate eco-messages to friends and co-workers. Many are nature lovers and are eager to learn more about plants and animals. Besides helping in the touring work, many see the park as a platform for them to discuss issues about wildlife and to meet people with similar interests.

Although the AFCD has been managing the Hong Kong countryside for decades, the opening of the HKWP has brought new meaning to its work in nature tourism, eco-tourism, conservation and environmental education. First, it plays a mediating role for Mai Po, allowing the latter to focus more on research work rather than catering to visitors. Second, it is the first large-scale governmental premises for promoting eco-tourism and conservation education. Third, at present, it is a successful model in compensating for the loss of, and damage to, natural lands as a result of development. Not only is the HKWP well aware of its promotional and educational tasks, it is also ambitious in joining international networks of wetland conservation. Currently, the HKWP networks with the Wetland Link International and Wetland Link International–Asia.

With the establishment of the wetland park in 2006, eco-tourism has been made a priority in the agenda of tourism promotion and development. The HKWP has successfully drawn the attention of the Hong Kong public. It has also won quite a number of international awards.[12] The active official promotion and interpretation of eco-tourism has made the public aware of the existence of a specific kind of eco-tourism. For Hong Kong, it is a new form of tourism and educational product packaged into a contrived theme park that is heavily managed, promoted and subsidized by the government.

Conclusions

The number of nature lovers and hill-walkers in Hong Kong has grown significantly in the last few decades. As elaborated upon in this chapter, SARS has had a direct impact on the health consciousness and leisure pattern of local people. Many have resorted to embracing nature as a way of overcoming the ills of a congested and contagious city space. People feel relaxed and are able to breathe in fresh air by 'walking the hill' (*haang saan*) after a stressful week at work. Not only is the hill a shelter to retreat from bustling city life and polluted air, it is also believed to be a sanctuary to resist the pressures and impacts brought about by political change (Yeung, 2007, p126):

> *Since the 1990s, many Hong Kong people had to worry about the changes of the 1997 handover, the following economic instability, and increasing number of social problems. To return to Nature became one way to escape from pressures and troubles.*

Many of the middle-class have developed hill-walking and expeditions as one of their major leisure activities and interests. For experienced hill-walkers, hill-walks bring them back 'home'. As one informant said: 'Going to the hill is like going back home.' The smell of nature provides them with a means for meditation. 'Walking the hill' is thus 'walking meditation', creating a spiritual cleansing effect. These experienced hill-walkers have, however, scarcely related to the concept of 'eco-tourism'. Eco-tourism is introduced as an educational and environment-friendly tourism through substantial official promotion, especially in the case of the HKWP. To experienced hikers, 'walking the hill' has been a long-term hobby, an interest developed well before the term 'eco-tourism' was widely known in Hong Kong. These hikers have been interested in hill-walking because of their love of nature, the excitement in overcoming difficult trekking routes and the opportunity to obtain healthy exercise during hill-walking.

The development of eco-tourism in Hong Kong takes on another approach. It has been promoted by the government to combine leisure, family, culture, and environmental and wildlife education. In contrast to eco-tourism projects elsewhere, which emphasize donations to conservation work, Hong Kong's eco-tourism is heavily subsidized by the government. Both the contrived wetland park and all other country parks are maintained with billions of dollars from public funds.

Some experienced hikers have commented that eco-tourism promoted by the HKWP is heavily loaded with 'unnatural' elements and is too much education oriented, making it mostly suitable for schoolchildren who wish to learn about the dragonflies, butterflies and birds. Nevertheless, parents are happy to watch their children memorize the difficult names of plants and animals in a relatively safe place. Eco-tourism, in Hong Kong, is thus a conceptual umbrella shrouding a contrived theme park with an overtone of education. It is not surprising that some of the experienced hikers refuse to consider themselves as eco-tourists. Whether it is the post-1997 political turmoil or the 2003 virus epidemic that drove the Hong Kongers to nature cannot be fully answered here. What is certain is that the number of people who would like to get closer to nature in their leisure time has increased, and instead of shopping, many now choose to socialize with friends and acquaintances in the tranquil embrace of hills and mountains. The subtle greening of Hong Kong people's leisure time has been paralleled by the high-profile official promotion of wetland eco-tourism. It will be interesting to trace the future evolution of these two forms of eco-travel.

Notes

1   Throughout this chapter we follow the Yale system of romanization of the Cantonese language. In Cantonese, both mountain and hill are called *saan*. In this chapter, *haang saan* is translated into hill-walking, as most *saan* in Hong Kong are hills rather than mountains.
2   Examples include the Travel Industry Association of America, the American Society of Travel Agents and the World Travel and Tourism Council (see Honey, 2002, pp19–20).
3   The HKTA was restructured and renamed as the Hong Kong Tourism Board in 2001.
4   It was established by a group of hikers and hill-walking lovers in 1989 under the Society Ordinance. All helpers and coordinators in the association are volunteers (see www.hkfca.org.hk).
5   See the HKHAC's activities at www.hkha-china.org.hk/index.html.
6   A local Chinese daily newspaper.
7   The websites such as www.hiking.com.hk and http://go2nature.net/forum/index.php are some examples. The websites of the HKFCA and HKHAC also provide space for this sort of advertisement.
8   Some trail-walking may include lunch at certain restaurants and entertainment at night after the walk. This type of walk usually involves charges per head.
9   Data from an official of the AFCD, interviewed on 19 May 2008.
10 Information provided by the AFCD, dated 29 May 2008.
11 Information provided by the AFCD, dated 29 May 2008.
12 The HKWP won the Awards for Excellence in 2007, awarded by Urban Land Institute. Besides this award, it has won 14 other architecture and design awards from the US, France and Poland since its opening (www.wetlandpark.com/).

References

Cater, E. (2007) 'Ecotourism as a Western construct', in J. Higham (ed) *Critical Issues in Ecotourism: Understanding a Complex Tourism Phenomenon*, Elsevier, Oxford, pp46–69

Cater, E. and Lowman, G. (eds) (1994) *Ecotourism: A Sustainable Option?*, John Wiley & Sons, New York, NY

Cheung, S. (2008) 'Wetland tourism in Hong Kong: From birdwatchers to mass ecotourists', in J. Cochrane (ed) *Asian Tourism: Growth and Change*, Elsevier, London, pp259–267

Cochrane, J. (2007) 'Ecotourism and biodiversity conservation in Asia: Institutional challenges and opportunities', in J. Higham (ed) *Critical Issues in Ecotourism: Understanding a Complex Tourism Phenomenon*, Elsevier, Oxford, pp287–307

Fennell, D. (1999) *Ecotourism: An Introduction*, Routledge, London

Font, X. and Buckley, R. C. (eds) (2001) *Tourism Ecolabelling: Certification and Promotion of Sustainable Management*, CABI Publishing, New York, NY

Godde, P. M., Price, M. F. and Zimmermann, F. M. (eds) (2000) *Tourism and Development in Hill Regions*, CABI Publishing, New York, NY

Gurung, C. P. and De Coursey, M. (1994) 'The Annapurna Conservation Area Project: A pioneering example of sustainable tourism?', in E. Cater and G. Lowman (eds) *Ecotourism: A Sustainable Option?*, John Wiley & Sons, London/Chichester, pp177–194

Hall, M. C. (1994) 'Ecotourism in Australia, New Zealand and the South Pacific: Appropriate tourism or a new reform of ecological imperialism?', in E. Cater and G. Lowman (eds) *Ecotourism: A Sustainable Option?*, John Wiley & Sons, London/Chichester, pp137–157

Higham, J. (2007) 'Ecotourism: Competing and conflicting schools of thought', in J. Higham (ed) *Critical Issues in Ecotourism: Understanding a Complex Tourism Phenomenon*, Elsevier, Oxford, pp1–19

HKTA (Hong Kong Tourist Association) (2000) *HKTA Annual Report 1999–2000*, HKTA, Hong Kong

HKWP (Hong Kong Wetland Park) (2007) 'Hong Kong Wetland Park will not sell group ticket without reserve', 9 February, Hong Kong Wetland Park, www.wetlandpark.com/en/visitor/press22.asp, accessed 19 January 2009

Honey, M. (2002) *Ecotourism and Sustainable Development: Who Owns Paradise?*, Island Press, Washington, DC

Lindberg, K., Goulding, C. and Huang, Z. (1997) 'Ecotourism in China: Selected issues and challenges', in M. Oppermann (ed) *Pacific Rim Tourism*, CABI Publishing, New York, pp128–143

McLaren, D. (2003) *Rethinking Tourism and Ecotravel*, Kumarian Press, Bloomfield, CT

Mowforth, M. and Munt, I. (2003) *Tourism and Sustainability: Development and New Tourism in the Third World*, second edition, Routledge, New York, NY

Nowaczek, A. and Fennell, D. (2002) 'Ecotourism in post-communist Poland: An examination of tourists, sustainability and institutions', *Tourism Geographies*, vol 4, no 4, pp372–395

Weaver, D. (2002) 'Asian ecotourism: Patterns and themes', *Tourism Geographies*, vol 4, pp153–172

Yeung, K. M. (2007) *Thirtieth Anniversary of Country Parks*, Friends of the Country Parks and Agricultural, Fishery and Conservation Department, Hong Kong

Zhang, H., Qu, H. and Tang, V. (2003) 'A case study of Hong Kong residents' outbound leisure travel', *Tourism Management*, vol 25, no 2, pp267–273

11

Crafting Filipino Leisure: Tourism Programmes in the Philippines

Maria Cherry Lyn S. Rodolfo

Introduction

Tourism is now widely recognized as a major vehicle to generate employment and reduce poverty in the Philippines, an archipelagic country of more than 7000 islands and inhabited by about 88.6 million people (National Statistics Office, 2007). The World Travel and Tourism Council (WTTC) estimated that travel and tourism contributed US$13 billion (597.9 billion Philippine pesos), or 9.1 per cent to the total Philippine gross domestic product (GDP), and employed 3.5 million, or 10.6 per cent of total employment (directly and indirectly) in 2007. The WTTC projected that the industry would generate US$25.7 billion (1522.1 billion Philippine pesos), or 8.7 per cent of GDP, and employ 4.1 million workers (9.7 per cent of national employment) by 2018 (WTTC, 2008).

Domestic tourism serves to realize these potentials amidst international tourism's seasonal demand and vulnerability to external events (i.e. economic recession, terrorism and health scares). The first household-based survey in 2005 revealed that at least 24 million Filipinos travelled as tourists (50 per cent) and same-day visitors during the first 6 months of the year. Their number was about 11 times the volume of international visitor arrivals during the same year.

The objective of this chapter is to explore the concept of domestic tourism in the Philippines and to examine the challenges to its sustainability. It presents the evolution of domestic tourism policies and uses the case of Puerto Galera in Oriental Mindoro to illustrate domestic tourism's impact on local communities and visitors.

Definition and measurement of domestic tourism

The Philippine Department of Tourism (DOT) defines domestic tourism as the tourism of resident visitors within the economic territory of the country of reference or within the political boundaries of the country of residence,[1] which is similar to the definition by the United Nations World Tourism Organization (WTO). Mena (2004) and Say (2006) proposed the following operational definition of domestic tourism to distinguish it from related concepts, such as domestic visitors[2] and excursionists[3]:

> *Any person regardless of nationality, resident of the Philippines and who travels to a place in the Philippines other than his usual place of environment[4] for a period of at least twenty-four (24) hours and not more than 365 days for any reason other than following an occupation remunerated at the place visited. Minimum distance of travel covered is between municipality and with purposes of trip as any of the following – pleasure (holidays, culture, active sports, visit to relatives and friends, other pleasure purposes); professional (meeting, official mission, business); other purposes (short-term studies, health, pilgrimage).*

There are two data sources on domestic tourism currently used by the industry. These are the *Report of Tourism Accommodation Establishments* and the 2005 *Household Survey on Domestic Visitors* (HSDV). The DOT-accredited establishments revealed at least 14 million domestic travellers, 6 times the 2.8 million foreign visitors in 2006. This figure hardly captured the real volume of domestic travellers because it excluded the visiting friends and relatives (VFR) market, who stayed at the homes of their friends and relatives.

Given that accreditation is voluntary, the DOT report does not count the guests of non-accredited establishments. The preferences and behaviour of domestic visitors – tourists and excursionists – should have been captured by the study on regional travel in the Philippines. Unfortunately, the last survey was conducted in 1997 due to the lack of funds. The national workshop on domestic tourism in 2003 became the platform for discussing the gaps in concepts and statistical collection and for eventually launching the drive for the conduct of the first household-based survey.

Together with census of accommodation units, the HSDV belongs to the advanced stage of data gathering in tourism given the resources required in implementing the methodology (Mena 2004). This HSDV should complement the accommodation and occupancy reports collected by the administrative municipal, provincial and regional tourism offices. These occupancy reports (including surveys of tourists at accommodation units and intercept surveys)

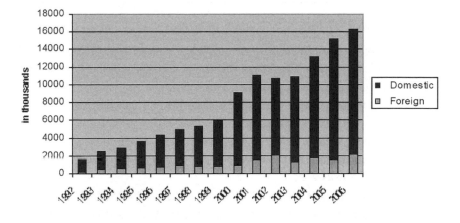

Figure 11.1 *Regional travellers in the Philippines*

Note: data include same-day visitors.

Source: data supplied by Department of Tourism

belong to the intermediary stage of data collection. The basic stage includes surveys of visitors at tourist sites. The HSDV (highlights in Box 11.1) aimed to provide baseline data on the extent and economic contribution of domestic tourism, to determine the profile and travel characteristics of domestic visitors, to gather data on the travel patterns of the Filipino households, and to gather data on second homes. Fabian and Say (2007) pointed out that the conduct of a household survey on domestic tourism was a necessary move as the Philippine statistical community faces the challenge of addressing the emerging requirements of data users for quality data on domestic tourism. Furthermore, with the Philippine Tourism Satellite Account already in place, there is a need to answer data constraints for its compilation. The challenge now is to institutionalize the survey and to conduct it on a regular basis to become truly relevant in understanding domestic tourism over time.

Domestic tourism development

The Aquino administration (1986 to 1992) marked the beginning of the revival programme in the Philippine tourism industry, specifically the domestic tourism market (Rieder, 1997) that was neglected during the 20-year rule of the late president Marcos. Its *Medium-Term Philippine Development Plan (MTPDP)* for the period of 1987 to 1992 aimed to build a tourism industry for the Filipinos and by the Filipino people and one that places heavy emphasis on

Box 11.1 *Each Filipino makes two trips and visits two places*

- *Volume of travel:* during the period of 1 April–30 September 2005, 43.5 per cent (23.7 million) of 54.6 million Filipinos over the age of 15 travelled within the country. The country's total population was 85 million during that year.
- *Number of trips:* in general, each individual made two trips and visited two places in the country at anytime in the past six months.
- *Gender and age profile:* of the 23.7 million Filipino travellers during the past six months, about 51 per cent or (12.1 million) were female. Three out of four travellers belonged to age group 15 to 44 years.
- *Purpose of visit:* Filipinos travel mainly to visit relatives or friends, as reported by more than half (55.6 per cent, or 13.2 million) of those who travelled. Three in every ten travelled for pleasure/relaxation, while about 13 per cent travelled for business purposes.
- *Length of stay:* 49 per cent, comprising 12.0 million domestic travellers, spent overnights in their places of destination. Four in every ten travellers stayed two to three nights in the place visited.
- *Accommodation used:* domestic travellers usually stayed in the houses of relatives or friends. Of those who travelled during the past six months, about 17 million indicated that they want to travel and visit other places in the next 12 months.
- *Utilization of travel packages:* almost 99 per cent, or 23.5 million domestic travellers, had independent domestic trips. These are the travellers who did not avail of travel package tours.
- *Expenditure pattern:* about 17.5 million of these independent travellers, spent about US$8 (400 Philippine pesos) for local transport either for themselves alone or including those of other family members, relatives or friends. Aside from transport fares, a large number of independent travellers spent, on average, US$8 (400 Philippine pesos) and US$22 (1100 Philippine pesos) on food and beverages, respectively. In addition, independent travellers reported an average spending of US$24 (1200 Philippine pesos) on accommodation and about US$64 (3200 Philippine pesos) on other expenses.
- *Frequently visited places:* the Philippines is an archipelago of more than 7100 islands, the biggest of which is Luzon, where the nation's capital of Manila is located. The most frequently visited place was the National Capital Region (NCR). Aside from the NCR, the top ten places visited were Cavite, Batangas, Laguna, Iloilo, Bulacan, Nueva Ecija, Pampanga, Cebu, Pangasinan and Albay (see Figure 11.2).
- *Frequently visited attractions:* the five attractions frequently visited by the domestic travellers were malls (23.6 per cent), parks (7.4 per cent), churches/shrines/cathedrals (7.3 per cent), beaches/resorts (2.2 per cent) and food chains/restaurants (1.0 per cent).
- *Host community information:* about 9 million households received visitors during the six-month reference period, representing 51.8 per cent of the total 17.4 million households in the country. Of these 9 million households who received visitors, 49.8 per cent received day visitors only, 19.2 per cent, or 1.7 million households, received overnight

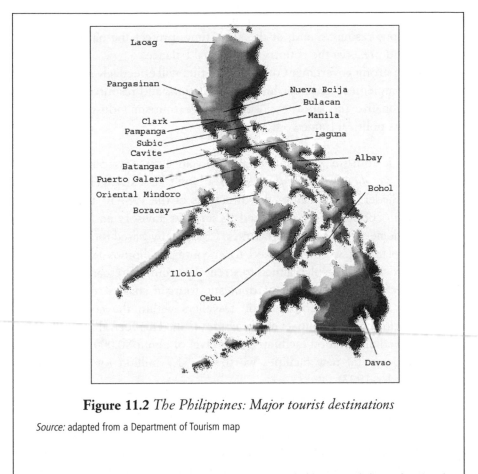

Figure 11.2 *The Philippines: Major tourist destinations*

Source: adapted from a Department of Tourism map

visitors only, while almost three in every ten households received day and overnight visitors. Almost 97 per cent of these households received local residents, while 2.7 per cent of the total households became hosts to foreign nationals and Philippine passport holders permanently residing abroad.

Source: DOT and National Statistics Office (2007)

sustainable development and its economic, social, environmental and institutional pillars:

a   Maximize the economic benefits that can be derived from the development of existing and potential Philippine tourism assets, which will benefit a wider base of the Filipino population.

b   Achieve a level of tourism development that is for and by the Filipino people, which will improve their quality of life; promote, conserve and preserve their heritage; and heighten their national identity and sense of unity.

c   Achieve a level of tourism development that will optimize the utilization of indigenous resources and, at the same time, protect the natural environment and preserve the country's ecological balance.

d   Provide strong government organization that will effectively and efficiently direct, implement and coordinate the functions and resources required to institutionalize the priority position of the tourism industry within the country's political framework.

The domestic tourism programme launched an awareness campaign called '*Huwag maging dayuhan sa sariling bayan*' ('Don't be a stranger in your own country') (Rieder, 1997). Under the directions of the 1987 to 1992 MTPDP, local tourism councils were organized to serve as advisory and coordinating bodies for domestic tourism programmes. Community-based tourism development and planning were supported to encourage Filipinos to directly and actively participate. The plan aimed to strengthen tourism research. One identified project was the conduct of domestic tourism studies to monitor the movements of foreign and domestic travellers within the country and to conduct socio-economic impact studies of tourism. This revival programme of the Aquino administration facilitated the travel of about 80,000 Filipinos and the development of new facilities worth US$51.7 million for the domestic market (Rieder, 1997).

The Ramos administration (1992 to 1998) ushered in a period of reforms that supported the implementation of the *20-Year Tourism Master Plan*, completed in 1991 under technical grant from the United Nations and the World Tourism Organization. The master plan was the first to set targets for domestic tourism volume and regional dispersion (see Tables 11.1 and 11.2). President Ramos pursued liberalization and deregulation of strategic sectors (domestic and international air transport, inter-island shipping, telecommunications and banking) that eventually paved the way for more seamless travel to and from the country and within the archipelago. The short-lived administration of President Joseph Estrada (1998 to 2001) focused on an intensive programme to develop and promote ecotourism programmes and to instil pride of place and country.

Apart from traditional programmes such as Lakbay-Aral, the DOT implemented the holiday economics programme that President Gloria Macapagal-Arroyo introduced during the last quarter of 2001 to promote domestic tourism amidst the decline in international arrivals, specifically from the US, the then number one foreign market of the Philippines prior to the terrorist attacks of 11 September 2001. The programme moved legal holidays from the actual date tied by law for its observance to dates (either Monday or Friday) that would promote longer weekends. In March 2002, the government issued Administrative Order No 32 to provide for the optional

Table 11.1 *Domestic and foreign tourism targets (1000 visitors and nights)*

Period	Short-term to 1993	Medium-term to 1996	Long-term to 2010
	Domestic markets		
Visitors*	2344	2685	5118
Nights	9000	10,310	19,653
	Foreign markets		
Visitors	1500	1710	5365
Nights	10,666	14,604	40,767
	Total		
Visitors	3844	4395	10,483
Nights	19,666	24,914	60,420

Note: * = estimated domestic visitors using commercial accommodation.

Source: UNDP/WTO (1991)

Table 11.2 *Distribution of target visitors within the Philippines (1000s)*

Location	Visitors	1993	1996	2010
Luzon	Domestic*	3117	3593	7037
	Foreign	1072	1158	2682
	Total	4189	4751	9719
Visayas	Domestic*	1341	1520	2815
	Foreign	344	417	1663
	Total	1685	1937	4478
Mindanao	Domestic*	1400	1593	1989
	Foreign	84	136	1019
	Total	1484	1729	3008
Total	Domestic*	5858	6706	11,841
	Foreign	1500	1711	53,665
	Total	7358	8417	17,206

Note: * = domestic visitors using commercial accommodation and estimated non-commercial accommodation.

Source: UNDP/WTO (1991)

adjustment or modification of work hours, giving way to a four-day work week in agencies under the executive branch of the government, including government-owned and controlled corporations and the local government units to spur domestic tourism among government personnel. This was implemented during the months of April and May 2002. In July 2007, a new law, Republic Act No 9492, was enacted and promulgated to provide predictability and consistency in the holiday economics programme to support and strengthen its merits (see Box 11.2).

Box 11.2 *Observance of holiday economics in the Philippines*

Republic Act No 9492 aims to rationalize the observance of national holidays in relation to the holiday economics programme. According to the law, unless otherwise modified by law and/or proclamation, the following regular holidays and special days will be observed in the country:

Regular holidays:

- New Year's Day – 1 January;
- Maundy Thursday – movable date;
- Good Friday – movable date;
- *Eidul Fitr* – movable date;
- *Araw ng Kagitingan* – Monday nearest 9 April;
- *Bataaan* and *Corregidor* Day;
- Labour Day – Monday nearest 1 May;
- Independence Day – Monday nearest 12 June;
- National Heroes Day – last Monday of August;
- Bonifacio Day – Monday nearest 30 November;
- Christmas Day – 25 December;
- Rizal Day – Monday nearest 30 December.

Nationwide special holidays:

- Ninoy Aquino Day – Monday nearest 21 August;
- All Saints Day – 1 November;
- Last day of the year – 31 December.

In the event that the holiday falls on a Wednesday, the holiday will be observed on the Monday of the week. If the holiday falls on a Sunday, the holiday will be observed on the Monday that follows, provided that for movable holidays, the president will issue a proclamation at least six months prior to the holiday concerned. However, the Eid-ul-Adha will be celebrated as a regional holiday in the Autonomous Region in Muslim Mindanao.

There are very limited studies that measure the impact of holiday economics since the time it was implemented by the government in 2001. The programme's merits are based on the fragmented reports of tourism suppliers who gain from the high occupancy rates and load factors. The government argues that holiday economics will stimulate tourism and overall consumption/spending[5] as the DOT promotes more destinations outside of the traditional ones, such as Cebu, Baguio and Boracay. Critics of the programme are not fully convinced of the merits of the programme for three reasons. First, prior to Republic Act No 9492, employers expressed concern about the impact of the programme on the productivity of the workers, the wage policies and the overall reliability of companies since they needed to adjust their production schedule to give way to last-minute holidays. According to instructions from the lawmakers, the DOT and the National Wages and Productivity Commission should come up with a study on the impact of the national law on holiday economics, and on productivity and domestic tourism by 2008.[6] Second, holiday economics does not really stimulate domestic travel because the majority of Filipinos have relatively low purchasing power compared to advanced economies. Low-income workers, in particular, who suffer from the high cost of foregone earnings, would tend to spend and consume less goods and services. Yarcia (2007) concluded that based on an empirical analysis of the holiday economics programme using the regression tool, the programme would not really boost employment and consumption. Third, an event would lose its historical significance if it was celebrated on some other day.

What is certain today is the growth in the volume of domestic passenger traffic due to the competition in transport services and marketing of more destinations outside of Manila, the nation's capital. The liberalization of the air transport industry in 1995 enabled the growth of domestic air traffic (from 4 million in 1995 to 11 million in 2007) and the introduction of more competitive fares. The Roll-On Roll-Off (RORO) programme by the Arroyo administration integrated more island destinations and reduced domestic travel costs, especially for Filipino students, young professionals and families, including those from the lower-income groups (Basilio, 2006). The challenging task was to ensure that infrastructure constraints – congestion in transport terminals, poor quality of roads, poor traffic management system, lack of lodging facilities and deterioration in destination quality – are addressed to make domestic tourism and local community life sustainable.

The case of Puerto Galera, the most popular resort destination in the Province of Oriental Mindoro and one of the favourite destinations among domestic visitors, is presented here to show the effects of tourism development on the quality of tourism experience and the quality of life of host communities. Using Butler's tourism area life-cycle model (1980), Galera, the white beach area in particular, is an example of a resort destination whose growth or maturity has already imposed severe constraints on its economic, social and environmental capacity.

Oriental Mindoro

The island province of Oriental Mindoro is one of the most popular destinations among domestic travellers because of the beaches in the municipality of Puerto Galera and its proximity to Manila and the catchment area south of

Metro Manila. Travellers can reach Mindoro after a three-hour drive from Metro Manila and either a 45-minute ferry ride to Calapan (and another one hour of land travel to Galera) or a one-hour boat ride direct to the beaches of Galera. The White Beach Resort in Galera has been perceived as a cheaper alternative to the popular island destinations of Boracay, Cebu and Bohol. Travellers enjoy activities such as swimming, scuba diving, snorkelling, kayaking, island hopping, wind surfing, parasailing and hiking. Galera acts as the core of tourism development, while the rest of the province (14 municipalities) serves as peripheral areas supplying manpower, food and other resources to Galera's tourism industry.

Domestic visitors account for 98 per cent of Galera's tourism market based on DOT statistics. The foreign market remains small at 2 per cent. From 2005 to 2006, Galera reported more than 3 million visitors – tourists and same-day visitors (see Table 11.3). However, interviews with local stakeholders revealed that the visitor count included Mindoro's returning residents from Batangas.

Table 11.3 *Visitor arrivals in Puerto Galera (2000–2006)*

Tourist	2000	2001	2002	2003	2004	2005	2006
Foreign travellers	38,857	21,986	39,474	27,101	26,892	42,832	74,195
Overseas Filipinos	56	781	–	–	4040	–	–
Domestic travellers	21,597	120,600	97,895	706,449	914,811	3,636,974	3,625,338
Total	60,510	143,367	137,369	733,550	945,743	3,679,806	3,699,533

Source: data supplied by Department of Tourism

During the consultations that formed part of the preparations for the Oriental Mindoro Investment Summit in 2006, the stakeholders raised issues related to the lack of information about the market behaviour and preferences that would aid them in product development.[7] In May 2007, given the lack of secondary information about the profile of visitors in Galera, a survey of tourist preferences and satisfaction was conducted. The respondents were asked to rate 25 travel attributes based on the level of importance in their choice of destinations and based on their satisfaction levels during the visit. The survey was conducted in six areas – namely, White Beach, Sabang, Coco Beach, La Laguna Beach, Aninuan and Balatero Pier (see Figure 11.3) during the period of 21 to 24 May 2007. A total of 260 valid responses were gathered from the white beach area. The respondents were approached while waiting for their boat ride back to the Port of Batangas. The rest (total of 40 responses) were collected from the other five areas. The 241 domestic visitors (59 were foreign visitors) accounted for about 80 per cent of total respondents. The white beach area is the most popular destination. It is a public area where facilities are clustered.

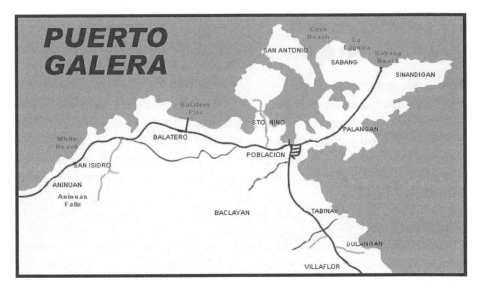

Figure 11.3 *Map of Puerto Galera*

Source: www.lakbaypilipinas.com

Age profile

Galera's market was quite young, with 66 per cent of the visitors belonging to the age group of 20 to 34. Another 15 per cent were 19 or younger. Only 12.1 per cent belonged to the category of 35 to 54. Domestic travellers were younger than foreigners. The majority of the local survey respondents were 20 to 24 (41.8 per cent) or 25 to 34 (29.7 per cent). On the other hand, most of the foreigners who responded to the survey were 25 to 34 (26.3 per cent) or 45 to 54 (24.6 per cent).

Civil status and place of origin

Most of the local visitors surveyed were single (77.5 per cent) and most of them (57 per cent) came from Metro Manila. About 21 per cent originated from the nearby provinces of Laguna, Batangas and Cavite.

Length of stay

The same-day visitors in Galera comprised 18 per cent of the total respondents. Fifty-seven per cent of domestic tourists stayed for an average of two to three days.

Purpose of visit

A high 68 per cent of the respondents visited Galera for holiday and leisure reasons, while 18 per cent represented the VFR market. The business market was found to be quite small at 3 per cent.

Travel companions
Fifty-four per cent of the respondents went to Galera with their friends. Another 38 per cent were joined by their families.

Economic impact
Domestic tourists spent an average of US$20 to US$25 per night on accommodation for an average stay of two nights. They also spent an average of US$5 to US$10 on food per day and another US$10 to US$20 on tourism activities during their entire stay. On the negative side, residents noted an increase in the cost of living, especially during the summer season, the peak of tourism activity in Puerto Galera.

Satisfaction ratings
Domestic visitors considered the absence of a language barrier as a positive attribute (mean rating = 4.179; highest is 5.0) during their stay in Galera. The hospitality and kindness of the local residents seemed to be highly appreciated by local travellers as well. They gave this attribute a high rating of 4.093. This was followed by natural and scenic attractions (4.039), climate (3.996), safety (3.938) and accessibility (3.889). Visitors were least satisfied with the 'domestic water service' (3.581), 'tourist information/assistance' (3.546), 'sports/recreation facilities' (3.542), 'shopping opportunities' (3.438) and the 'price of products' (3.356). Fast ferries and regular boats have relatively poor facilities, primarily because these were usually filled up beyond their capacity, thus making tourists concerned with their safety during the one-hour boat ride. There were also few tourist information booths in Puerto Galera and they were not always manned. Shopping opportunities were limited and stalls crowded the beachfront. The products that could also be found in most department stores in the metropolis were perceived to be quite expensive by domestic visitors.

Social and environmental impact
The volume of domestic visitors in the area has inflicted environmental and social costs on the local communities. Galera is an example of a lose–lose scenario in tourism development where both community and tourism suffer from the negative impacts of tourism (Boyd and Singh, 2003). The scenario focuses mainly on short-term economic gain and maximizing it as much as possible. In 2007, a survey of 200 households from the 13 communities (Aninuan, Baclayan, Balatero, Dulangan, Palangan, Poblacion, Sabang, San Antonio, San Isidro, Sinandigan, Sto Nino, Tabinay and Villaflor) of Galera (Rodolfo and Carlos, 2007) revealed three factors of perceived costs of tourism as an economic activity by the residents. Explaining 24.68 per cent of the total variance (an eigenvalue of 1.98), the primary factor, labelled as socio-environmental, consists of environmental degradation, loss of community character and waste. The second factor is more social in nature because it includes over-

crowding and noise. It explained 18.4 per cent of the variance and had an eigenvalue of 1.47. The last factor refers to the impact of tourism on standards of living (i.e. higher costs of living, particularly food), explaining 13.28 per cent of the variance and with an eigenvalue of 1.06. Fortes (1997) noted that there was already a high outflow of waste from tourist facilities as well as communities due to urbanization and the construction of commercial areas in coastal regions of the island. Moreover, the sea vessels used by tourists to get to the Island of Puerto Galera continuously discharge their wastes, such as combusted oil, solid wastes and other refuse, into the sea. As a result, the overall marine environment, particularly the coral reefs, sea grass beds and fish, suffers from pollution. Tourists have also complained about congestion along the shorelines due to the large volume of guests and vendors in the boats to and from the Port of Batangas. Other sources of dissatisfaction were the rubbish and dirty canals leading to the coastal waters (Rodolfo and Villareal, 2007). The loss of community character was related more to the social ill-effects of tourism, especially prostitution.

Support for tourism development

The attitudes and opinions of the residents provide good measures for determining the level of support of community towards tourism development (Wilton and Dillon, 2003). The household survey in 2007 showed that the residents still regarded tourism as highly beneficial to their community despite the evident social and environmental costs inflicted by the massive volume of visitors relative to the carrying capacity of the area. The level of support for tourism development was influenced by a number of factors, such as length of residency, distance of the household from the tourism area and education, among others. There were differences in perspectives about the impact of these variables on attitudes towards tourism development. Ap (1992) found that the people living farther away from tourist spots or resort areas of the region may have a negative perception of its impacts, while residents who were situated in tourist-dense areas were more inclined to have a positive outlook on tourism. Some authors thought otherwise as their studies revealed negative attitudes towards tourism from residents who have had more contact with tourists in such areas (Pizam et al, 1993). Moreover, Turner and Reisinger (2003) argued that the consequences of social contract between hosts and tourists depend largely on the social contract between individuals from different cultural backgrounds and the conditions under which they interact. Consequently, the varying cultural backgrounds of those involved in the social contract may influence their negative notions, attitudes and outlook towards each other, and can thus deter agreement between parties. According to Puczko and Ratz (2000), a number of residents would still support the development of a tourism industry even though local people had perceived tourism impacts as negative. They tend to oversee it since its economic benefits outweigh its costs. As a consequence, tourism development decision making has become an agent of the cost-benefit equation that involves the existence of trade-offs between economic and environmental impacts (Alampay, 2002).

In Puerto Galera, the residents are highly dependent on tourism (mainly domestic) for their source of livelihood, given that there are hardly any other major industries in the municipality that could provide better economic opportunities, particularly to those living along the coastal areas. Respondents explained that their daily activities have become more difficult to carry out, especially during the summer months when they have to accommodate guests, particularly groups of students or young professionals who could not find rooms. There were also concerns about the minimal economic benefits from tourism revenues due to significant outflows in terms of payments for food, beverage and other supplies that are sourced from outside the Province of Mindoro.

Those living farther away from the coastline were engaged mostly in fishing, micro-scale farming and retailing. Regression analysis showed that only one variable (i.e. distance from a tourist spot) was found to be statistically significant in influencing a person's perception of the overall effects of tourism in Puerto Galera. The negative coefficient implied an inverse relationship (i.e. those who lived farther away from the coastal area were less likely to attribute more positive effects of tourism on the community) (Rodolfo and Carlos, 2007).

Stakeholders continue to be challenged by the need to achieve sustainable coastal mass (domestic) tourism in Puerto Galera. The local government passed an ordinance to establish an environmental user fee of 50 Philippine pesos (US$1) per tourist to finance sewerage and treatment systems, as well as other coastal resource management projects. The provincial government continues to seek ways to disperse tourism activity from Puerto Galera to the areas in the other municipalities. Public–private partnership is growing stronger in the province, particularly in promoting the island to longer-staying tourists. Tour operators and the local tourism officers are developing packages that aim to promote other parts of Oriental Mindoro. The implementation of identified provincial infrastructure projects could significantly help to achieve this sustainability.

Conclusions

Domestic visitors serve as the backbone of overall tourism growth and development in the Philippines amidst international tourism's seasonal demand and vulnerability to external events. More than half of domestic visitors are tourists (primarily VFR) who spend at least one night in their destination based on the

2005 *Household Survey on Domestic Visitors*. The holiday economics programme aims to boost the domestic leisure segment, although its effectiveness as a national policy needs further evaluation. The HSDV is a major step towards addressing the emerging requirements of data users for quality data on domestic tourism, and the conduct of the next HSDV is becoming more urgent as stakeholders seek updated information on changes in domestic tourism patterns and travel characteristics by Filipino households.

Destinations and the quality of tourism experience tend to suffer as tourism becomes more mass based. Stagnant growth and decline are inevitable results when host communities do not accept these two realities and therefore fail to pursue appropriate measures to rejuvenate their destinations. Sustainability therefore requires at least two major tasks. The first is an improvement in the infrastructure and services to and from (and at) the host destination in order to keep satisfaction levels high, to sustain or expand the market, and to magnify the economic benefits. This can only be achieved if the second task is pursued. This revolves around initiatives (e.g. environmental tax and community participation) to minimize the negative costs of domestic tourism on the quality of life (economic, social and environmental) of residents and their future, and to generate greater support for tourism development even from those living farther from major tourist spots.

Notes

1   1993 System of National Accounts, *TSA Methodological Reference*; UN-EROSTAT-OECD, WTO (April 2000) and the *Recommendations on Tourism Statistics*: UN/WTO (1994).

2   The term *visitor* refers to any person travelling to a place other than that of his or her usual environment for less than 12 months and whose main purpose of travel is other than the exercise of an activity remunerated from within the place visited. This is a broader concept that encompasses domestic tourism and same-day visitors.

3   Visitor who does not spend the night in a collective or private accommodation in the place visited.

4   Usual environment – this corresponds to the geographical boundaries within which individuals displace themselves within their regular routine of life; it consists of the direct vicinity of their home and place of work or study and other places frequently visited.

5   In October 2003, the National Statistical Coordination Board released its study stating that if consumptions in tourism-related industries increased by 10 per cent as a result of extended weekends/holidays, the country could actually experience a 3.5 per cent growth in the level of GDP. The increase in tourism consumption will then lead to a 4.9 per cent rise in total consumer spending. Among the tourism-related industries, the levels of trade and food manufacture, which had a combined share to total gross value added of 23 per cent, will likely expand by 8.8 per cent and 5.5 per cent, respectively.

6   'Institutionalization of "holiday economics" proposed', *Committee News*, Publication of the Committee Affairs Department, vol 13, no 42, 16 March 2005.
7   Conducted with funding support from the University of Asia and the Pacific's Shell Petroleum Exploration Professorial Chair on Sustainable Development (May 2007).

References

Alampay, P. R. (2002) 'Sustainable tourism development in the Philippines', in *The Challenge of Sustainable Development for the Philippine Tourism Industry*, Makati City Manila, the Philippines, pp1–22

Ap, J. (1992) 'Residents' perceptions on tourism impacts', *Annals of Tourism Research*, vol 19, pp655–690

Boyd, S. and Singh, S. (2003) 'Destination communities: structures, resources and types', in *Tourism in Destination Communities*, CABI Publishing, Wallingford, UK, pp19–34

Butler, R. (1980) 'The concept of a tourist area cycle of evolution', *Canadian Geographer*, vol 24, pp5–12

Committee Affairs Department (2005) *Committee News*, vol 13, no 42, 16 March

DOT and National Statistics Office (2007) *2005 Household Survey on Domestic Visitors*, DOT and National Statistics Office, Manila

Fabian, E. and Say, M. (2007) 'Developing the survey instrument for the 2005 Household Survey on Domestic Visitors', Paper presented at the tenth National Convention on Statistics, Manila, the Philippines

Fortes, M. D. (1997) 'Puerto Galera: A lost biosphere reserve', in *South–South Co-Operation Programme on Environmentally Sound Socio-Economic Development in the Humid Tropics*, United Nations University Working Paper no 18, United Nations University, Paris

Mena, M. (2004) 'Developing the operational definition and measurement tools for domestic tourism in the Philippines', Paper presented at the ninth National Convention on Statistics, Manila, the Philippines

National Statistical Coordination Board (2003) 'Holiday economics can increase GDP by 3.5%', www.nscb.gov.ph, October, accessed 23 June 2007

National Statistics Office (2007) 'Philippines in figures', August, www.census.gov.ph/, accessed 20 December 2007

Pizam, A., King, B. and Milman, A. (1993) 'Social impacts of tourism: host perceptions', *Annals of Tourism Research*, vol 20, pp650–665

Puczko, L. and Ratz, T. (2000) 'Tourist and resident perceptions of the physical impacts of tourism at Lake Balaton, Hungary: Issues of sustainable tourism management', *Journal of Sustainable Tourism*, vol 8, no 6, pp458–479

Rieder, L. G. (1997) 'Philippines: The developments of Philippine tourism in the post-Marcos era', in F. Go and C. Jenkins (eds) *Tourism and Economic Development in Asia and Australasia*, Cassell, London, Chapter 12, pp222–236

Rodolfo, C. and Carlos, L. (2007) *Community Perceptions of Tourism Development: The Case of Puerto Galera*, University of Asia and the Pacific, Pasig City Manila, the Philippines

Rodolfo, C. and Villareal, A. F. (2007) *Demand and Supply Analysis of Puerto Galera Tourism*, University of Asia and the Pacific, Pasig City Manila, the Philippines

Say, M. (2006) *Concepts and Forms of Tourism: Philippine Experience, Agenda Item 9,* www.unstats.un.org/.../unsd_workshops/tourism/IWTS/Invitedper cent20presentations/IWTS_Item09(Philippines).ppt, accessed 20 September 2007

Turner, L. and Reisinger, Y. (2003) *Cross-Cultural Behavior in Tourism Concepts and Analysis*, Butterworth-Heinemann, Oxford

UNDP/WTO (1991) *Tourism Master Plan, Republic of the Philippines*, PH1/88/036, final report, WTO, Madrid

Wilton, J. and Dillon, T. (2003) *St Ignatius, Mt Resident Attitudes*, Exploring Tourism Development Potential, Community Tourism Assessment Program (CTAP) Research Report 2003–4, Institute for Tourism and Recreation Research, University of Montana, Missoula, MT

World Travel and Tourism Council (2008) *The 2008 Travel and Tourism Economic Research Report on the Tourism Satellite Accounts of the Philippines*, WTTC, London

Yarcia, D. (2007) 'Is holiday economics good for the tourism sector? The Philippine case', Paper presented at the tenth National Convention on Statistics (NCS), EDSA Shangri-La Hotel, 1–2 October 2007

12

Awaiting Attention: Profiling the Domestic Tourism Sector in Sri Lanka

Ranjith Ihalanayake

Introduction

Sri Lanka is an island off the south-eastern coast of India, situated 880km north of the equator, in the Indian Ocean, with a land area of 65,525km² (see Figure 12.1). Sri Lanka is a free, independent and sovereign nation with a population of 20.9 million (estimated). Its population comprises a number of ethnic groups, including Sinhalese (74 per cent); Tamils (18 per cent); and Moors, Malays, Burgers and others (8 per cent). The Sri Lankan economy is largely an agricultural one and rice is the main crop in which the country is self-sufficient. Traditionally, tea, rubber and coconut have been the main exports, even though they have been replaced, in recent years, by foreign exchange earnings from remittances from Sri Lankans employed abroad, tourism and other exports such as ready-made garments.

Sri Lanka has a long documented history, while its verbal history runs further back. The country's early civilization is dated to approximately 34,000 years ago and it is known that the island was colonized by the Balangoda people, a group of Mesolithic hunter-gathers who lived in caves. There are some signs suggesting that Sri Lanka had some sort of a trade link with countries such as Egypt, which had similar early civilizations. Moreover, it is well known that Sri Lanka was governed by an unbroken dynasty that paid great attention to the development of irrigation. However, since the second century BC, there have been several intermittent invasions, mainly in the northern part of the country by south Indian rulers, after which the capital was moved permanently from the north central to the western part of the country. According to *Mahavansa*, the written history of Sri Lanka, the early civilization and the Sri Lankan culture were heavily influenced by the arrival of the Aryans from north India. In 247 BC, Buddhism was introduced by Arahat Mahinda, the son of Emperor Asoka of India, which was the turning point of the great

Sri Lankan history. The introduction of Buddhism resulted in a new civilization with a cultural greatness. Recent excavations have shown that there have been several early settlements in places such as Anuradapura, Pollonnaruwa, Sigiriya and Dambulla that dated back to the period around 1500 BC.

In addition to the south Indian invasions, the country was colonized by the Portuguese, the Dutch and the British from 1505 to 1948. The impact of Western colonization has been very significant and has affected all aspects of Sri Lankan society, including the economy, the educational, political and legal systems, the culture, its religion and its infrastructure. Modern Sri Lankan society has been shaped, blended and polished by these historical changes. In much the same way, whatever Sri Lanka has inherited from its past is on offer to tourists/visitors today.

The current official tourism logo used by Tourism Sri Lanka – 'Sri Lanka: A land like no other' – is the best description one would give to the country considering what Sri Lanka can offer to the world tourism market. Sri Lanka is gifted with natural as well as man-made tourism attractions. The Sri Lankan tourism product consists of a wonderful collection of tourism attractions for almost all market segments. As noted earlier, it has a large collection of antiques and royal artefacts from the dynasty together with a splendid collection of natural attractions. However, as in many other developing countries, the Sri Lankan tourism sector has been conventionally dominated by international inbound tourism. The tourism sector, until recently, relied heavily on visitors from European countries. Sri Lanka's primary tourism product was designed for, and offered to, this particular segment of the market. The heavy reliance on one segment of the inbound market has made the industry very vulnerable, given the prevailing security situation in the country since the early 1980s. Owing to this, the tourism sector has suffered setbacks that could potentially continue in the future (Gamage et al, 1997/1998). In this context, it is quite appropriate to explore the ways and means whereby the largely unexploited domestic tourism sector may be utilized for the development of the sector, in particular, and the economy, in general. However, one major drawback in initiating the process of engaging the natives in tourism is the lack of empirical and theoretical research in this area. Therefore, this chapter serves as the first step towards exploring the domestic tourism sector in Sri Lanka.

The remainder of the chapter is set out as follows. The following section provides an overview of the Sri Lankan tourism sector, focusing on its historical developments. It also presents highlights of the international tourism sector since international tourism has become the major focus of Sri Lankan tourism authorities. The section on the 'Domestic tourism sector' is designed to portray the profile of the domestic tourism sector in Sri Lanka. In this section, existing sub-sectors within domestic tourism are explained, trends in visitor numbers are described, differences between the sectors are elaborated upon, and interrelationships among the various tourism sectors are defined. The final section presents the concluding remarks.

Tourism sector in Sri Lanka

Although the term 'tourism' might have sounded a little strange to early inhabitants, the activity could have been familiar, as Sri Lankans are fun-loving people who enjoy exploring the surrounding natural and man-made environment. In particular, there is a long tradition, among all Sri Lankans, of visiting places of religious significance. However, this activity has been labelled commonly as 'pilgrimage' among most Sri Lankans. Pilgrimage can be defined as a long journey or search of great moral significance, or a journey to a sacred place or shrine of importance to a person's beliefs and faith (Mustonen, 2005). Members of almost all religions in Sri Lanka, including Buddhists, Catholics, Hindus and Muslims, participate in some form of pilgrimages. There are hundreds of such places around the country that are associated with religious festivals throughout the year. These places and festivals attract thousands of people.

However, as far as Sri Lankan pilgrimages are concerned, they are unique. Certainly, there are more elements connected to it than mere pilgrimage. Pilgrims tend to visit and enjoy other natural and man-made attractions, together with the main activity. Therefore, the pilgrimage can constitute what is commonly known as domestic tourism. However, until very recently, very little attention has been paid to this important sector or activity by the government or the private-sector tourism authorities. There has not been much effort to exploit and develop even the most obvious opportunities in this sector. It is simply untouched and left alone to function without providing the necessary leadership to the sector in the areas of infrastructure, funding, and legal and regulatory systems. If such leadership is provided, all the stakeholders, including the tourism sector, the community and visitors, would benefit. The current situation in this sector is a result of the negligence by relevant authorities.

As noted above, the Sri Lankan tourism sector has been dominated by international inbound tourism. Most of the support, research (if any), funding and leadership, in general, have been directed at the international sector. However, Sri Lanka recognized the potential of the sector shortly after independence from British rule. The Ceylon Tourist Board, currently known as the Sri Lanka Tourist Board (Sri Lanka Tourism), was established in 1966 with a view to providing direction and leadership to this promising sector in developing the economy. Since then, the tourism sector, particularly international tourism, has been instrumental in generating foreign exchange, employment opportunities and household income to Sri Lankans, thus playing a vital role in economic development. Therefore, in order to understand how the Sri Lankan tourism sector operates, with its different systems and their interactions, it is important to have a brief look at the international tourism sector, focusing on its contribution to the economy, major tourism-generating markets and major visitor attractions among international visitors in Sri Lanka. This will help us to understand the reasons for the neglect of the domestic tourism sector and how these two tourism sectors interact.

Since its establishment, the Sri Lanka Tourist Board began monitoring the tourism sector, although activities were mainly focused on international tourism. Thus, unlike the domestic tourism sector, official tourism statistics are available for the international tourism sector (see Table 12.1). As depicted in Table 12.1, the international tourism sector achieved a steady growth during the late 1960s and early 1970s. During the next few decades, the sector grew even faster than before. This was the golden period for the Sri Lankan tourism sector. The main reason for this remarkable growth was the open economic policy adopted and implemented by the then government since 1977. However, this growth did not last long. Due to civil conflict that erupted in 1983, the tourism sector suffered a severe recession; as a result, international tourism arrivals dropped by more than 50 per cent during the period of 1983 to 1989.

Table 12.1 *Economic contribution of Sri Lankan tourism*

Year	Tourism arrivals		Tourism receipts		Tourism employment	
	Numbers	Growth (%)	US$ million	Growth (%)	Numbers	Growth (%)
1966	18,969	–	1.3	–	–	–
1970	46,247	144	3.6	177	12,078	–
1975	103,204	123	22.4	522	23,848	97
1980	321,780	212	110.7	394	47,900	101
1985	257,456	_20	82.2	_26	54,533	14
1990	297,888	16	132.0	61	59,914	10
1995	403,101	35	225.4	71	84,163	40
2000	400,414	_1	252.8	12	91,063	8
2005	549,308	37	362.3	43	125,004	37

Source: Sri Lanka Tourist Board (2005); WTO (2007)

Although the tourism sector recovered after 1990, when normalcy was restored, it could not enjoy a steady growth. This was mainly because the internal security situation was affected, from time to time, by various attacks of insurgents in the capital city. Among these attacks, the Central Bank bomb in 1996, the Galadari Hotel bomb in 1997, the suicide bomb attack to assassinate the former Sri Lankan president in 1998 and the attack at Katunayake

International Airport in 2001 were all detrimental. Since these attacks targeted key national, economic and tourism facilities, the international tourism sector plunged into chaos every time. Accordingly, Western countries such as the US, UK, Germany and Australia issued a travel warning to their citizens, jeopardizing tourism to Sri Lanka from such countries. In addition to the insurgency in the island nation, the most recent setback was the 2004 December tsunami. This struck a large part of the south, east and north-east coastal belt of the country and destroyed most of the established tourism facilities, including hotels, resorts, restaurants and other facilities. Against this background, Sri Lanka was unable to achieve sustainable growth in the international tourism sector that it would have otherwise achieved by now.

Table 12.2 *Sri Lankan tourism arrivals in the regional context*

Country	2002		2003		2004		2005	
	Numbers (thousands)	Regional share	Numbers (thousands)	Regional share	Numbers (thousands)	Regional share	Numbers (thousands)	Regional share
Bangladesh	207.25	5.13	244.51	5.77	271.27	4.77	207.66	3.43
Bhutan	5.6	0.14	6.26	0.14	9.25	0.16	13.63	0.23
India	2384.36	59.00	2726.21	58.81	3457.48	60.84	3918.61	64.76
Maldives	484.68	11.99	563.59	12.16	616.72	10.85	395.32	6.53
Nepal	275.47	6.82	338.13	7.29	385.30	6.78	375.40	6.2
Pakistan	498.06	12.32	500.92	10.81	647.99	11.40	798.26	13.19
Sri Lanka	393.17	9.73	500.64	10.80	566.20	9.96	549.31	9.08

Source: WTO (2007)

This interrupted growth in international tourism in Sri Lanka and its inability to fully capitalize on the sector is evident when Sri Lanka's regional position is analysed. As shown in Table 12.2, visitor numbers in Sri Lanka are relatively low compared to other South Asian destinations. Even countries such as the Maldives and Pakistan have surpassed Sri Lanka in terms of visitor arrivals. Gamage et al (1997/1998) argued that when Sri Lanka lost its international tourism market due to security disturbances, India and the Maldives gained: the Maldives and Goa, India, are substitute destinations offering similar tourism products. Since Sri Lanka continues to struggle with its internal security situation, which has been ongoing for the last two decades, the international tourism sector may never be a reliable option for economic growth. On the other hand, Sri Lanka has heavily relied on the Western European countries such as the UK, Germany, France, The Netherlands and Italy as the major tourism-generating markets. Thus, visitors from these countries are often blamed for tourism-related social problems, such as drug use, prostitution and paedophilia. Therefore, Sri Lanka must come out with a clear

Figure 12.1 *Map of Sri Lanka*

Source: Sri Lanka Tourist Board (2005)

vision in order to diversify its tourism industry, minimizing heavy reliance on international inbound tourism. Against this background, the potentials of the domestic tourism sector will become extremely important.

Domestic tourism sector

As noted earlier, domestic tourism activities in Sri Lanka existed for centuries and were connected closely with religious places, festivals and activities. Since domestic tourism was part of the main culture, not much attention was given to it. However, during the last two to three decades, there appear to have been some changes in the structure of the domestic tourism sector. Such changes can be attributed to several socio-economic transformations that occurred during this period. First, economic reforms and foreign exchange deregulation introduced under the open-market policy in 1977 altered the entire socio-economic landscape of Sri Lankan society and thus contributed to the change in tourism activities within the country. Second, as the international tourism sector becomes more and more vulnerable and unsteady, there appears to be a trend, at least among private-sector tourism entrepreneurs, to pay some attention to domestic tourism. Tourism operators have begun targeting and offering various tourism products to domestic visitors. This has been evident during recent years when international tourism numbers were down. In particular, local hotels began offering holiday packages at reduced prices to local visitors. Third, due to improvements in infrastructure (road systems, transport networks, etc.) and mass communication facilities (television, newspapers and radio), there has been an increased demand among many locals for travel and tourism.

These changes in the economy and in the wider Sri Lankan society were manifest in the domestic tourism sector, which now comprises two disparate sub-sectors – namely, the formal and the informal sectors. These sectors are recognized based on a number of demographic as well as socio-economic factors. Native tourists in these two sectors, formal and informal, may represent different classes of Sri Lankan society, as their income levels, professions, lifestyles and, more importantly, travel behaviour clearly reflect these differences. The tourism product that they might purchase – including the places which they visit, accommodation, lodging, food and transport services – and, overall, the total tourism experience that they have could very well be different. Therefore, it is important at this stage to explore and elaborate upon the differences between the two sectors in order to understand why they exist and, accordingly, to search for ways and means of improving upon the performance of the domestic tourism sector as a whole.

The formal sector

The formal domestic tourism sector has emerged as a recent phenomenon in Sri Lanka due to the socio-economic changes occurring in the country during the last few decades. This formal domestic tourism sector essentially constitutes the strong and newly emerging middle classes of Sri Lankan society. This class largely comprises professionals such as doctors, engineers, lawyers and university lecturers. These professionals, who hail from remote villages, were born to lower-class families of average Sri Lankans. However, they benefited immensely from free education and are now graduates of major Sri Lankan universities. The education that they received has given them a completely different lifestyle than their parents could ever have imagined. Their income levels are much higher than those of their parents, who mostly live on agriculture or other labour-intensive jobs. Unlike their parents, they live in modern houses in most of the busy suburbs or major cities, such as Colombo. They can also afford to have at least one vehicle and, in some cases, perhaps two.

Since their inception into the new so-called middle class, they are keen to try out and 'feel' the taste of the perks and privileges of their new society. In their search, it appears that they discovered tourism as a means of a leisure and recreation activity. There may be several reasons why tourism is attractive to this particular group. First, most of these professionals have a very hectic lifestyle in relation to their professional and their personal life. In most cases, unlike in traditional Sri Lankan families where the housewife is primarily engaged in rearing the children, the wife of the modern family is either in a similar profession or works for the public or private sector. Therefore, this lifestyle encourages them to search for alternative ways of engaging in leisure and recreation and, hence, tourism. Second, through tourism, the middle-class recreationists often have the opportunity to meet or make friends with the upper class, who essentially constitute the formal sector. There is a strong influence of the upper class in shaping the lifestyle of the middle class. Third, since each class has its own lifestyle, behaviour and aspirations, there is a strong inclination among the middle classes to 'follow' in the footsteps of the upper classes. Therefore, middle-class Sri Lankans are heavily influenced by people of the same class.

Although the formal domestic tourism sector is influenced and shaped by these factors, to the knowledge of the authors, there is no proper source of data on domestic tourism, including visitor numbers and tourism expenditure. As noted earlier, the domestic tourism sector, as a whole, is untouched in terms of research, funding, leadership and government support. Against this background, we have to rely on unconfirmed and unofficial data sources. As explained so far, because of the importance of the sector to Sri Lankan tourism and to the economy, even an estimation of its contribution may serve the purpose.

Table 12.3 *Domestic visitors in Sri Lanka: Gross estimate (2003–2006)*

	2003	Percentage	2004	Percentage	2005	Percentage	2006	Percentage
Visitors in formal sector (1000s)	1327	28.1	1381	31.7	1292	29.2	1302	28.2
Visitors in informal sector (1000s)	3391	71.9	2970	68.3	3118	70.8	3312	71.8
Total domestic visitors	4718	100	4351	100	4410	100	4614	100

Source: Shanta (1991, 2005); www.lib.uom.grltourstat

Table 12.3 presents an estimation of domestic visitor numbers in Sri Lanka for the period of 2003 to 2006. According to Table 12.3, domestic visitor numbers in the formal sector have shown a fluctuation during the period, although the magnitude is marginal. Overall, the formal sector accounts for little less than one third of the total domestic tourism sector. Even though the formal sector is relatively small compared to the informal sector, it has a great potential in terms of its economic contribution. Total domestic visitor numbers are far greater than those of international visitors in Sri Lanka.

The informal sector

As explained earlier, unlike the formal sector, the informal sector is not a recent group and has always comprised those residents to whom Sri Lankan culture has been an important aspect of their lives for centuries. It is, indeed, a part of the main Sri Lankan culture and is linked directly and strongly with traditional Sri Lankan pilgrimages. However, due to the negligence of the authorities to the needs and patterns of this segment, no records of the sector could be found to assess whether the sector possesses potential for 'tourism'.

Against this background, an estimation of visitor numbers in the informal sector could be used to shed light on this sector to address some of the existing issues. Table 12.3 shows that the informal sector manifests almost similar patterns as those of the formal sector. Fluctuations in volume can be linked to the unstable security situation coupled with the rising cost of living in the island nation. During the last couple of years, the inflation rate has been rising significantly, and for the last two years, the average annual change in inflation in Sri Lanka has been between 10 and 20 per cent (Central Bank of Sri Lanka, 2008). However, despite this, the domestic tourism sector is less vulnerable to such socio-political vagaries when compared with international tourism.

Table 12.3 shows that, on average, the informal sector has attracted little more than 3 million visitors a year. This is almost three times larger than those of the formal sector – in total, comprising approximately 4.5 million total domestic visitors per year. In comparison with the international tourism sector that had little more than 0.5 million visitors in 2005, the domestic tourism sector is about eight times larger. Overall, this implies that the domestic tourism sector's potential is promising and thus warrants due recognition.

Differences between the formal and informal

As it is apparent from the discussion so far, there are differences between the formal and informal sectors in terms of demographic factors, places visited and the way in which both groups experience the tourism concept. As noted earlier, visitors in the formal sector are the ones who constitute the upper and middle classes of Sri Lankan society, while the informal sector is formed by average working-class Sri Lankans who mainly live on agriculture, agriculture-related economic activities and other blue-collar jobs. Thus, their income levels are very low and most of them may be below the poverty line. This economic and social background has bred a lower living standard among them; therefore leisure and recreation are usually beyond their purview.

Religion is the main purpose of visits among the domestic visitors of the informal sector; thus, they generally visit places such as the Cultural Triangle (Kandy, Anuradhapura and Polonnaruwa), Kataragama (the Sacred City) and Adam's Peak Mountain (Sri Pada) during the special festive periods from May to August each year. While the visitors of the formal sector may visit more or less the same places, they could well be guided by different purposes such as leisure and holiday, business and education. Their touristic activities are not confined to the festive season only as they tend to take place during all school holidays, most weekends and other holidays, guaranteeing year-round tourism activities. Moreover, they might visit other attractions such as national parks, botanical gardens (such as Hakgala, Kandy and Nuwara Eliya), Colombo City and its main attractions, Dehiwala Zoological Gardens, the Pinnawala Elephant Orphanage and other natural attractions around the country. The most recent attraction of the formal sector has been sporting events. In particular, the international cricket tournaments that are organized in international stadiums located in Colombo, as well as in Asgiriya (Kandy), Dambulla and Galle, attract substantial numbers of domestic visitors from the formal sector. Of these stadiums, both Dambulla and Galle international stadiums are located in the north-central and southern provinces, respectively, where the majority of ordinary Sri Lankans live. International and national cricket tournaments in these stadiums can also provide a better opportunity for visitors in the formal and informal sectors to interact with each other.

Other than the places visited by visitors in the formal and informal sectors, additional differences are also visible between the two. Visitors in the former mainly travel in small groups, mostly in their private vehicles. In most cases, it could be a family or two travelling together in a much more conformable way. They always find accommodation/lodging in the formal sector (i.e. in hotels, guest houses, rest houses and so on). Since they are on holiday for leisure purposes, they could dine either in the hotel or elsewhere in other restaurants and thus spend more money in the region. In contrast, those accounted for in the informal sector tend to travel in much larger groups of 20 to 40 and, in some cases, even more, and in relatively less comfortable buses and vans that are used for public transport purposes. In the past, they even travelled in the back of lorries/trucks that were used for the transportation of goods. Since their visits mainly focus on religious activities, the enjoyment of the activity becomes secondary. Therefore, in most cases, visitors tend to become self-sufficient. For example, they bring required groceries, such as rice and vegetables, and prepare their meals wherever they stay. In most cases, they stay in halls that are designed for such large crowds. In these halls there are no beds and visitors sleep on the floor. While there are enough facilities for water, they have to share common toilets.

The accommodation facilities targeted at the informal sector are scarcely compatible with any standards and are provided in a casual way, while the same facilities are provided by the formal sector with proper standards. Thus, such facilities as accommodation for domestic tourism are provided through two different systems: the formal and informal. In most of the main cities such as Anuradapura, Pollonnaruwa, Kandy and Katharagama, where there are annual religious festivals, the existence of the informal accommodation system can be seen. For example, this system of informal accommodation is in operation in Katharagama where many visit throughout the year, in addition to during the festive season in July and August. Those who live in Katharagama town and the surrounding suburbs offer home-based accommodation facilities. While the owners limit their occupancy to one or two rooms, the rest of the house provides accommodation for groups of guests. Independent brokers operate in this area who approach visitors as soon as they arrive in the city and negotiate the price for a commission from owners. The price of such facilities varies vastly depending on the bargaining power of both the hosts and the guests.

Driven by these differences between domestic visitors in the formal and informal sectors, one last and important difference between the two is the economic contribution of each sub-sector of tourism. It is clear that the economic contribution of the latter group, particularly in the areas that they visit and in the economy, in general, appears to be minimal, while the former could make a substantial contribution in both. However, judging by the magnitude of the informal sector, it certainly has much to offer to the Sri Lankan economy.

Interrelationships between tourism sectors

While the different tourism sectors and systems discussed in this chapter possess varying demographic and socio-economic characteristics, one common factor is that they tend to rely on each other and, thus, are interdependent. As noted earlier, the international tourism sector is the main focus of the government and private-sector tourism authorities. Major resorts in southern coastal area, all five-star hotels and major tour operators rely heavily on international inbound visitors. More importantly, the economy tends to rely on international tourism for much-needed foreign exchange earnings. The foreign exchange earnings keep the economy moving during difficult times, such as in the present situation. Against this background, one might argue that the domestic tourism sector also relies on international tourism to a lesser extent. As shown in Table 12.1, the international tourism sector is instrumental in generating tens of thousands of indirect and direct employment opportunities in Sri Lanka. If there is a downturn in this sector, this could affect the local economy considerably, thus jeopardizing domestic tourism.

On the other hand, it could well be argued that the existence of domestic tourism, particularly tourism activities of the informal domestic sector, helps international tourism in two different ways: First, travelling for religious purposes, commonly known as pilgrimages, is an essential part of Sri Lankan culture. Such activities could protect and enhance the culture, which, in turn, is marketed as a major component of the Sri Lankan tourism product. Second, the long-term sustainability of Sri Lankan tourism depends, to a certain extent, on its ability to diversify the market. As explained so far, it is very clear that Sri Lankan tourism has the potential to diversify the sector by exploiting the domestic tourism sector. In this way, the tourism sector would be much more resilient to the local as well as international shocks that are very common in the present global context.

Conclusions

Sri Lanka is an island nation surrounded by the Indian Ocean that has inherited a long history of dynasty and foreign rule and has thus much to offer the world of tourism. However, during the last four decades since independence from British rule, Sri Lanka has mainly focused on international inbound tourism. Due to the security disturbances which occur from time to time since the early 1980s, the tourism sector has suffered a severe setback. Although the tourism sector recovered slowly, it could not enjoy steady growth. There is a common criticism about Sri Lankan tourism that it has been developed with a narrower perspective. Therefore, it is argued that if tourism, as a sector, is to make a worthwhile contribution, a much broader outlook is essential (Bruin and Nithiyanandam, 2000). Against this background, the importance and the potential of domestic tourism have been highlighted as a way of widening this perspective and, thus, diversifying the sector.

Until recently, the domestic tourism sector has been left unaddressed despite the fact that a strong and relatively new sub-sector emerged due to the socio-economic changes which occurred since the late 1970s. This was a recent phenomenon in domestic tourism and has added a new perspective to the landscape of domestic tourism, in addition to the traditional aspect of domestic tourism that is commonly known as pilgrimage. This implies that Sri Lankan domestic tourism comprises the new 'formal sector' and the conventional 'informal sector'. It is evident that the two sectors represent quite different demographic and socio-economic characteristics; thus, they experience tourism in their own unique ways. Of the differences between them, the differences in class and the way in which they experience tourism are crucial.

As much as there are differences among the sectors, it is evident that these sectors are also very much interdependent. The very existence of international tourism and domestic tourism sectors in the broader tourism sector, and the formal and informal sectors within the domestic tourism sector appear to help each other. For example, it is very clear that Sri Lanka is dependent on international tourism, and this is seen by many as a narrower perspective. However, if there is a downturn in international tourism, it could negatively affect the other tourism sectors. This has been evident in the past when the international tourism sector was affected by civil disturbances. On the other hand, although the informal sector makes minimal contribution to the economy, in general, and to the destinations, in particular, the tourism-related activities of this sector are essential elements of Sri Lankan culture. Culture is something that Sri Lanka is successful in marketing to international visitors as part of the total tourism product. Thus, the existence of the informal sector is not an impediment to Sri Lankan tourism, but an asset. In summary, it is clear that all the sub-sectors of Sri Lankan tourism depend on each other for their existence.

However, one major limitation of Sri Lankan tourism is its inability to fully capitalize on the domestic tourism sector. There are several reasons behind this, which may work as impediments to tourism development in Sri Lanka. First, the domestic tourism sector is given very little attention by both the government and the private-sector tourism authorities; thus, the sector lacks an established tourism system to cater to the current market. This includes essential tourism facilities such as accommodation, transportation and other services (i.e. visitor information). Although some facilities are available in various destinations, they are neither properly coordinated nor controlled. This provides the opportunity for some tourism providers to operate in an unprofessional/non-business-like manner, making the sector less attractive. Second, Sri Lanka has adopted a very fragmented approach towards domestic tourism, while a coordinated approach was adopted in international tourism. This has generated a disparity between sectors; thus, the full potential of the sector is not realized. Finally, very little research has been conducted in the area of domestic tourism, in particular, and in Sri Lankan tourism, in general. Against this background, an agenda for future research in domestic tourism is identified. First, as noted earlier, Sri Lankan tourism authorities collect, compile and maintain a very comprehensive database of major economic indicators of international tourism; but nothing is available in this nature about domestic tourism. Thus, a collection and compilation of economic data about domestic tourism is essential. Second, empirical research should be carried out to explore further characteristics, such as the differences between and interdependent nature of domestic tourism sectors. Finally, some attention should be paid to available tourism facilities for domestic visitors: it is important to establish whether such facilities meet visitors' expectations or whether they can be improved. In conclusion, this chapter holds that government and private-sector tourism authorities should invest in research in order to support policy formulation and to encourage the development of sustainable tourism. It should also be noted that the Sri Lankan tourism sector should address the above-noted limitations and should adopt a much broader view towards tourism, giving due recognition to the domestic tourism sector.

Acknowledgements

The author gratefully acknowledges the contribution made by M. Sunil Shantha, senior lecturer, Department of Social Sciences, Sabaragamuwa University of Sri Lanka, for providing valuable information, including data on domestic tourism in Sri Lanka.

References

Bruin, A. and Nithiyanandam, V. (2000) 'Tourism in Sri Lanka: "Paradise on Earth?"', in C. M. Hall and S. Page (eds) *Tourism in South and South East Asia: Issues and Cases*, Butterworth Heinemann, Melbourne, Australia, pp235–247

Central Bank of Sri Lanka (2008) *Annual Report 2007*, Central Bank of Sri Lanka, Colombo, Sri Lanka

Gamage, A., Shaw, R. N. and Ihalanayake, R. (1997/1998) 'Cost of political upheavals to tourism in Sri Lanka', *Asia Pacific Journal of Tourism Research*, vol 2, no 1, pp75–87

Mustonen, P. (2005) 'Volunteer tourism: Postmodern pilgrimage?', *Journal of Tourism and Cultural Change*, vol 3, no 3, pp160–177

Shanta, M. S. (1991) *The Problems and Prospects of Domestic Tourism Sector in Sri Lanka*, MSc thesis, University of Sri Jayewardenapura, Colombo, Sri Lanka

Shanta, M. S. (2005) 'Enhancing domestic tourism in Kataragama, Yala Sri Lanka', *Sabarahgamuwa University Journal*, vol 5, no 1, pp17–24

Sri Lanka Tourist Board (2005) *Annual Statistical Report*, Sri Lanka Tourist Board, Colombo, Sri Lanka

WTO (World Tourism Organization) (2007) *Yearbook of Tourism Statistics*, WTO, Madrid

13

Film-Induced Domestic Tourism in Singapore: The Case of Krrish

Audrey Yue

Introduction

Krrish is the first international Indian blockbuster film to be shot in Singapore under the Singapore Tourism Board's Film-in-Singapore subsidy scheme. Directed by Rakesh Roshan, the doyen of contemporary Bollywood cinema, *Krrish* is India's fourth-highest grossing film this decade and the third-highest grossing film of 2006. The story revolves around an Indian superhero, Krishna (played by Bollywood heart-throb Hrithik Roshan), who is born with magical powers, and traces his life as he meets Priya, a Singapore-based non-resident Indian, and follows her to Singapore. The film is the much-anticipated sequel to *Koi Mil Gaya* (2003). More than 60 per cent of the film was shot in Singapore over 60 days.

This chapter uses the exemplary case study of *Krrish* to examine the relationship between inter-Asian film co-production and film-induced domestic tourism in Singapore. It first establishes the current state of domestic tourism in the country and critically shows how Singapore's nascent creative film industry has contributed to the emergence of domestic tourism. By further examining the making of the film, the film text itself and its reception both in India and in Singapore, this chapter argues that the film's spectacle of modernity potentially enables both the local resident tourists and the global Indian visitors/audiences to partake in the shared experiences of post-colonial Asian modernity.

Domestic tourism in Singapore

The development of tourism in Singapore has shifted and changed since its post-colonial independence. In 1964, the government statutory organization,

Figure 13.1 *Map of Singapore*

Source: adapted from www.private-guides.com

the Singapore Tourist Promotion Board (STPB), was formed. It highlighted the centrality of international tourism to the country's economic and urban planning (Toh and Low, 1990). Although less than 100,000 tourists visited the country during this period, tourism was considered essential to a country lacking natural resources as it created opportunities for employment and urban modernization (Chang and Yeoh, 1999). During the 1970s, the STPB used the image of a multicultural garden state to promote the country in its Instant Asia campaign. Singapore was branded as an exotic tropical melting pot where many Asian cultures collide. As the economy grew and urban modernization took precedence in the 1980s, many local sites were demolished and tourism wavered in the wake of its loss. Singapore was deemed too sanitized and devoid of local 'flavours'. Tourism policy, together with heritage conservation and urban renewal policies, began to promote heritage tourism (Chang, 1997, 1999). Local significant sites such as Raffles Hotel, the Singapore River and Bugis Street, and ethnic 'enclaves' such as Chinatown, Little India and Kampong Glam, were rejuvenated in the hope of not only attracting more tourists but also instilling local consciousness. During the 1990s, the renamed

Singapore Tourism Board (STB) launched the New Asia Singapore campaign, which differentiated Singapore from its Asian neighbours by promoting the country as a new type of hybrid Asian city comprising the best of East/West, old/new and tradition/modernity (Chang and Yeoh, 1999; Henderson, 2000a). These themes were consolidated in 2004 with the Uniquely Singapore brand that encapsulated its status as a regional business hub and a post-modern global city (Yue, 2006, 2007). In 2007, more than 10 million tourists visited the country and tourism revenue totalled US$4.6 billion (STB, 2007a, 2007b).

Studies on tourism in Singapore concentrate on international tourism and focus predominantly on tourism management policies (Wong, 1996; Low and Toh, 1997; Khan, 1998; Tan et al, 2001), the spectacle of heritage (Teo and Huang, 1995; Chang, 1997, 1999; Leong, 1997; Henderson, 2000b; Savage et al, 2004), economic benefits (Khan et al, 1990; Toh and Low, 1990; Wong, 1996; Low and Toh, 1997), regional tourism (Chang, 1998; Henderson, 2001), branding and destination (Chang, 2000a; Henderson, 2000a, 2007), and global–local contestations of cultural identity (Chang et al, 1999; Chang, 2000b; Huang and Hong, 2007). Not surprisingly, none of these studies mention domestic tourism because unlike England, Canada, New Zealand and Australia where the domestic tourism industry is highly established as a consequence of industrialization and international tourism, domestic tourism, better considered a one-off or short-term recurring event, is a recent phenomenon in a small island city state such as Singapore. Domestic tourism was first explicitly promoted during the severe acute respiratory syndrome (SARS) crisis in 2003.

In the months of May and June 2003, at the height of the SARS crisis in Singapore, which literally stopped Asian tourism in its tracks, the STB launched a Step Out domestic tourism campaign to encourage local residents to 'step out of their homes, get back onto the streets and enjoy life' (STB, 2003). Events in this campaign include community street parties and charity concerts with blockbuster film screenings; mural painting competitions and music performances by local artists; arts and street festivals; shopping sales and tours; and discounts for entries to the zoo, bird park and aquarium. These activities were staged at local tourist attractions such as Fort Canning Park, Marina Bay, Raffles City, Orchard Road, Chinatown, Little India and Boat Quay, and coincided with annual tourist and cultural events such as the Great Singapore Sale and the Singapore Arts Festival. The STB subsidized sightseeing tour companies and venue fee entries, and provided incentive packages and seed funding for the private sector to participate. Health-compliant temperature checks were mandated and provided for staff and visitors daily, and SARS precaution signs were displayed prominently.

These activities were designed to stimulate the hard-hit tourism industry, which encouraged local residents to spend generously. Direct and indirect economic spin-offs were estimated to be around US$70 million (STB, 2003).

They were also designed to cultivate social responsibility and civic engagement. Public health awareness about the rationality and responsibility of managing the SARS crisis was integrated within the celebration of these events through themes and slogans such as 'Singapore Cares', 'The Courage Fund', 'Keep Our Spirit Alive' and 'Celebrate Life at the Bay'. These events were significant not because of their economic benefits or value-added public health; rather, by singling out the leisurely everyday practices – picnicking at Fort Canning Park, socializing and watching the sunset at the bay, strolling down Orchard Road, dining out in Boat Quay and shopping in Raffles City – which make up the everyday life of local residents, they show the similarity between touristic and everyday leisure. The STB reinforces this by emphasizing that these activities are selected 'because of their wide appeal to Singaporeans' (STB, 2003). This campaign reveals how Singaporeans, in their practices of everyday life, are, indeed, resident tourists and visitors in their home country. Rather than eschew the city–rural romanticism or native nostalgia highlighted in dominant domestic tourism studies, this trend of domestic tourism shows how tourist attractions and their attendant practices are, indeed, integrated as part of the fabric of everyday life for local residents. As Singapore's cultural geographer Terence Chang states, in 'a small island state of about 646km², most of its attractions function as leisure sites and cultural enclaves for Singaporeans' (Chang, 1999, p94).

Writing about heritage tourism in Singapore, Chang (1997) debunks the criticism by urban tourism studies such as Machlis and Burch (1983) and Greenwood (1989) that heritage tourism presents an inauthentic culture because it has become a commodity. This type of tourism harnesses the cultural, historical and ethical resources of a place as tourist attractions. Chang points to how local residents use heritage attractions as places of recreation and social interaction, and argues that heritage is also an important local resource to encourage the younger generation to return to their roots. He further shows how these attractions have become a place of multiple uses. On the cultural enclave of Little India, he writes that it is 'a popular tourist attraction, a place of residence for Singaporeans, a retail haunt for locals, a commercial enclave for Indian merchants, and a social centre for South Asian migrant workers' (Chang, 1999, p96). The use of Little India by different local and global non-local groups, and their conflicting claims to the space, shows how domestic tourism in Singapore is potentially a site of racial, spatial and identity contestation. For example, Indian merchants resent the Chinese shopkeepers because they feel they have more of a cultural right to the place; Chinese shopkeepers also feel that they can make claims to the place because they can afford the shop rentals. Both groups denigrate the South Asian migrant workers who congregate on the streets at nights and on the weekends.

Creative co-produced film economy in Singapore

In the wake of the Asian financial crisis of 1997, countries in Asia have sought to revitalize their economies through the development of creative industries. Creative industries combine the arts with business and services to enhance a nation's global competitiveness and to generate new economic wealth. They promote innovative cultural products that create jobs, bring profits and cultivate brand nationalism. The creative film industry in Singapore accelerated in 2002 when the government launched its *Creative Economy Cultural Development Strategy* (CECD) (Media Development Authority, 2002), which detailed expansion in the cultural industries of art, media and design. The film economy was already enjoying a revival in the mid-1990s with the international success of local films such as *Mee Pok Man* (1995), *12 Storeys* (1997) and *Bugis Street* (1997) that launched the film-making careers of Eric Khoo and Jack Neo and made them household names. During the early 2000s, local production companies such as the government-owned MediaCorp's Raintree Pictures began actively collaborating with regional film-makers in Asian blockbuster hits such as *2000 AD* (2000), *Infernal Affairs 2* (2003), *The Eye 1/2* (2002/2003) and *The Maid* (2005). Although these films were not shot in Singapore and do not use Singapore directors, they are co-produced by Singapore, utilizing local talent and benefiting from official film subsidy. The creative film industry gained momentum through the success of these regional inter-Asian film co-productions that have enabled local industries to nurture talent, create content and seek international partnership through venture capital. This type of industry does not organize film production as a traditional cultural industry developed for the prestige of national identity; it is considered more creative as a type of service industry that adds value to the national economy (Yue, 2007). The STB's Film-in-Singapore Scheme (FSS) evinces this.

Launched on the back of the new Uniquely Singapore tourism campaign, the FSS was introduced as a three-year US$7million plan in 2004 to attract international film and production companies to Singapore by creating a production-friendly environment to cater to their needs (STB, 2007c). The scheme subsidizes up to 50 per cent of the expenses incurred by international production companies during their shoot in Singapore. Working closely with other government agencies and bureaucracies, the STB also assists with on-ground logistic requirements and permit applications. The scheme aims to promote Singapore as an attractive destination for international tourists through film and television. This funding policy reveals the status of the current creative co-produced film commodity as a service that adds value to tourism.

Krrish is the first Indian blockbuster film, and the highest profile project, to be funded under the FSS. Other projects include collaborations with regional film and television industries, such as the Korean television series *Que Sera Sera*, the Indonesian television serial *Aiya*, the Chinese reality television idol-like franchise *Super Mates* and the music video of popular Thai singer Boy Peacemaker (*Anuwat Sakwaunsakpakdee*). The scheme has also supported local film and television productions, as well as international art-house films. The following case study of *Krrish* analyses the impact of film-induced tourism in Singapore and its relationship to domestic tourism.

Film-induced tourism: Domestic tourism and Krrish

Film-induced tourism is defined as tourist visits to a destination after the destination has been shown in the movies or on television. 'Movie-induced tourists' (Riley et al, 1998, p910) are people who seek out the scenic, historical and cultural properties of the movie location and view them as icons in their sightseeing. Film-induced tourism is a relatively recent field of study in travel and cultural media research. In vacation travel and tourism management research, the field comprises categorizing the forms and characteristics of movie tourism (Ritchie, 1984; Riley, 1994; Busby and Klug, 2001), and mapping visitation statistics after the release of films (Riley et al, 1998). In cultural media research, film-induced tourism falls broadly under the rubric of cultural tourism studies that examine the construction of the tourist gaze (Urry, 1990), the relationship between tourism and the image (Morgan and Pritchard, 1998), the effects on local communities and issues of sustainability (Goldsmith and O'Regan, 2004; Beeton, 2005). Together, the fields of tourism management and cultural media research focus on film celebrity and film marketing, psychology, sociology, economics, community development and urban cultural planning. They raise issues central to *Krrish*, especially in relation to how the film is constructed as a destination marketing tool within the context of international tourism, and its impact on domestic tourism and brand nationalism.

The making of *Krrish* and the subsequent release of the film are hallmark events that encouraged the special interests of Singapore's resident tourists and promoted the appeal of Singapore as a regional tourist destination to India and its diasporic audiences. Hallmark events are events that induce tourism (Ritchie, 1984). They are one-off or recurring events of short duration that are developed to promoting the appeal of a destination in the short and long term. For the domestic resident tourists, the making of the film is a media event that uses the glamour of stardom to re-imagine the city as a new and exciting place to be in or to visit, and in which to socialize and shop. For the international Indian and diasporic Indian audiences, the film location introduces the lifestyle practices of an affluent global city state that are similar to the experiences of modernity in their home countries. For both groups, *Krrish's* film-induced tourism enables them to partake in the shared experience of post-colonial Asian modernity.

Krrish was filmed in Singapore between 15 September 2005 and 10 November 2005. During the making of the film, Singapore's renowned Raffles Hotel's 103 suites were fully occupied by more than 100 members of the cast and crew from India and China, and the media in Singapore heavily reported the making of the film, covering topics such as the massive road closure of one of the main arterials in the central business district during peak hours, Hrithik Roshan's daily fitness regimes at a local gym, what he ate during training, and what was served during the prayer ritual ceremony that marked the beginning of the location shooting. Publicity shots around these media reports featured the new skylines of Singapore, from the rooftop of the refurbished and heritage-listed Lau Pa Sat hawker centre to the silhouette of the state-of-the-art concert theatre at the Esplanade Bay. Fans, predominantly young diasporic Indians, flocked to press conferences and fervently followed the cast around various shooting locations. Local residents, after seeing newspaper images showing local sites from a different perspective, revisited these hawker centres and shopping malls in droves. The cult of Indian celebrity is evident from newspaper headlines such as 'Catch Hrithik in action' (*The Straits Times*, 2005), 'One hunk of an alien has landed' (Loh, 2005), 'Alien goes home' (Yong, 2005) and 'Indian season begins; Bollywood star to film here, showcase Singapore' (Ramanivinita, 2005). These headlines promote the location shooting through the glamour of the Indian star and make Singapore suddenly more exciting and trendy because Indian superstars are staying in town. This excitement is augmented by the images that capture old landmarks from new camera angles, making Singapore suddenly more refreshing and intoxicating. As Singapore's foremost film blogger Stefan writes: 'It made Singapore look sexy' (Stefan, 2006).

The release of the film on 22 June 2006 sparked yet another media frenzy. It covered in detail the 30 locations used in the film, the film tourism scheme and advertised a highly discounted *Krrish* tour and an online contest for fans to attend the film's premiere in Singapore. These media discourses highlight not only the cult of celebrity; they also show how the placing of Singapore in the film is the ultimate in tourism product placement (Morgan and Pritchard, 1998) and how the country itself is constructed as a marketing destination tool. The relationship between the tourist attractions and the storyline further supports this.

When Priya is threatened with the loss of her job at a local television station after returning late from India, she hatches the idea of using the hero, Krrish, to make a television programme about an undiscovered man who has superpowers. The pitch is embraced by the station and Priya quickly invites Krrish to Singapore on the pretext of missing him and meeting her mother.

Krrish arrives in Singapore as a tourist and, befittingly, his itinerary is also organized to be touristic. After leaving the airport and settling in his condo-minium apartment, he saunters down the riverside of Boat Quay and Chinatown where he chances upon a *kung fu* busker, Kris, performing stunts to raise money for his disabled sister's operation. When Kris injures himself and the crowd begins to disperse, Krrish rushes in to complete the stunts and adds to Kris's coffers for the day. This opening scene, capturing the river city with its alfresco dining abutting high-rise office towers gleaming in steel and glass, establishes the location of the destination. It shows a post-modern and cosmopolitan city where the exoticism of tradition is comfortably juxtaposed alongside the excitement of modernity. The next day, Priya, on the pretext of asking Krrish to accompany her to work, whisks him to the zoo where the loca-tion shooting for the new programme featuring Krrish has already been prepared. At the zoo, Krrish is asked to compete in pole climbing with an orang-utan. This sequence captures another popular tourist attraction, the Singapore Zoological Gardens made world famous by its tropical celebrity apes. These two opening sequences show how tourist attractions are easily inte-grated within a storyline that revolves around the main protagonist as a tourist. This motif, combining the melodrama of the love story and the action thriller of the science fiction, continues throughout the story.

When Krrish refuses to participate in the zoo filming, Priya becomes annoyed and Krrish appeases her in a song-and-dance sequence staged at the country's latest water theme park, Wild Wild Wet. Shortly after, when Krrish's power is secretly discovered by Dr Arya, the megalomaniac scientist who exploited Krrish's mathematician father to invent a machine that can predict the future, the story scales into the frenetic pace of action. The search for Krrish moves from place to place, attraction to attraction. When Krrish is look-ing for Priya, who has been kidnapped by Dr Arya, the search, too, follows a similar pace. Krrish chases Dr Arya by the Singapore River and jumps from one traditional bumboat to another. He leaps from the historic clock tower of the Lau Pa Sat as he spots Dr Arya and scales down the majestic circumference of the Fountain of Wealth that centre-pieces the largest shopping centre in Singapore, Suntec City. These chases provide the rationale for the different locations in the action genre, and through them, the film consolidates the appeal of these attractions. These locations are especially highlighted by the STB in their special website of the film (STB, 2007d) and form the itinerary of the *Krrish* tour.

The three-day tour is promoted as a city tour of key film locations and aimed at international Indian visitors from Mumbai, Delhi, Chennai, Ahmedabad and Pune. It begins with a night tour, a river boat ride to the Lau Pa Sat to watch the making of *Krrish*, and the Fountain of Wealth to watch the screening of the film and the soundtrack. The second day orientates the visitor around the city, beginning with a cable-car ride to the Sentosa Island Underwater World, and ends with a fountain show back at the Singapore River by the Merlion. The final day's highlight is a morning at the zoo for a breakfast with the orang-utans. This itinerary, together with the tourism imaging examined above, promotes a similar ideology of post-colonial modernity for both the international Indian tourists and the local resident tourists.

Post-colonial modernity is the economic and cultural process of development and modernization experienced by countries in Asia after their independence from colonial rule. As an economic process, it is characterized by rapid development in infrastructure, commerce and marked improvement in the population's quality of life. As a cultural process, it is characterized by the pride of a new nationalism and the self-awareness of a new identity constructed by a country's success in breaking away from its former colonial government. Both India and Singapore have developed at an almost similar pace in the decades since their respective independence from British rule, and both countries have been hailed as exemplars of modernization in their respective Asian regions. This proximity, both economic and cultural, is captured by the film and its film-induced tourism.

Film-induced tourism has been argued as a feature that is characteristic of advanced post-modern and globalized countries (Iwashita and Butler, 2007). In Asia, the recent phenomenon of middle-aged female Japanese tourists visiting Korea as a result of the popularity of the Korean television series *Winter Sonata* has sparked a new wave of inter-Asian film-induced tourism (Kim et al, 2007). For the film-induced Indian tourists, the *Krrish* tour is arguably attainable only to the new Indian middle class. The tour promotes not the exotic spectacle of the city state, but the modernity of a lifestyle promised by the film and experienced in the city state: boat rides, shopping, movie-going, river-side strolls and eco-dining. The female protagonist (the non-resident-Indian Priya), an off-shore media specialist (representing the recent wave of information technology emigration) and the economic success that they bring all signal this new Indian modernity. Indeed, the tour has been promoted as a value-added incentive for the increasing outbound BTMICE (business travel meetings, incentives, conventions and exhibitions) Indian traveller (*Hindustan Times*, 2006b). The way in which the science fiction film captures the location resonates with these claims. Aerial shots of the cityscape showcase the futuristic skyline, with buildings framed from side angles to present their high-tech and shiny façades of steel, concrete and glass. Even the spiked dome roof of the concert hall is framed to resemble a giant science laboratory or a spaceship. To follow the *Krrish* movie trail is to partake in this shared experience of the modern, the new and the now.

Film tourism from India is not a new phenomenon. Since the mid-1990s, Yash Chopra has been shooting song and dance sequences in Scotland,

Switzerland, England and Australia. In 2006, it is estimated that about 150 to 200 people from Mumbai alone travelled abroad for shooting, and net expenditure by the industry on shooting abroad is US$25 million (*Hindustan Times*, 2006a). Inter-Asian film tourism, however, is a new phenomenon of the industry. Unlike earlier Bollywood films shot in Western locations that focus on the foreignness of snow-capped alps or the exoticism of colonial English architecture, inter-Asian film tourism, such as that of *Krrish*, uses the geographical proximity of the destination as an integral part of the plot. Singapore, keen to tap into India's media capital, has cleared the red tape that comes with location shooting. Praised by the director as an efficient country to film in (Rashid, 2006), Singapore is also relatively cheaper than New Zealand or France. Not coincidently, the success of *Krrish* is also part of Singapore's recently signed Comprehensive Economic Cooperation Agreement with New Delhi, which aims to cover nearly US$10 billion in trade annually. In these types of inter-Asian film co-productions, the commercial benefit of geographical proximity is also a way to promote economic and cultural proximity. *Krrish* highlights these shared experiences of post-colonial Asian modernity.

India's modernization and 'arrival' on the global scene is also echoed in the trans-national production of the film. The film, the country's most expensive Hindi film to date, is promoted as Bollywood's first science fiction film. Choreographed by Hong Kong's *kung fu* expert Ching Siu-tung and with special effects enhanced by an American team, the film is also touted as the first in Bollywood-branded entertainment. From scripting to screening, it has tightly integrated the synergies of media promotion, merchandizing and marketing with its brand tourism and brand associations. Reportedly worth US$117 million dollars (*Hindustan Times*, 2007), these media franchise strategies show how the industry has not only caught up with Hollywood; in harnessing the geographical proximity, as well as the shared experiences of post-colonial modernity, it is also producing a regional type of film that is more appealing to Asian audiences. Not surprisingly, when *Superman Returns* was also released in India around the same time as *Krrish*, it was the latter that broke domestic box office records. The modernization of the film industry is not only economic; it has also engendered a new sense of pride amongst Indian audiences as well as Singapore's resident tourists.

In Singapore, visitations from India have increased markedly since the release of the film, escalating from 2.53 million in 2005 to an expected annual growth of at least 20 per cent from 2006 (Dubey, 2006). The increased tourism has also been aided by the cheap airfares between the two countries when Singapore Airlines reduced its fares from India from US$430 to US$170 in 2005. Despite such economic benefits, what the film most significantly represents for the local resident tourists is the cultural experience of post-colonial modernity brought on by the economic success of modernization. Although the film has been criticized in Singapore by its indigenous film reviewers for not portraying the local population (see, for example, MLW, 2006), the tourism imaging described above serves to cultivate national pride in a symbolic way. As Hrithik Roshan states in an interview on why Singapore was chosen as a film location: 'That island had both the stunning structures and the infrastructure for the kind of film my father [Rakesh Roshan] wanted to make. We have many shots taken at great height' (cited in Sur, 2006). Roshan is obviously referring to the futuristic skyline offered by the city and its ability to be a credible backdrop to a science fiction film. This image connotes the modernity of the place and the experiences it proffers. Its discourse of pride is explicit in the aim of the film policy to promote the Uniquely Singapore brand through the Made-by-Singapore film genre.

The Made-by-Singapore film genre refers to films that have developed content for export through collaborations with foreign talent and partners (MDA, 2002). Stipulated by these guidelines, *Krrish* is, accordingly, a Made-by-Singapore film. This claim is not only evident in the Uniquely Singapore logo that accompanies the film on the homepage of its website and at the ending of the screening credits; it is also tagged in a headline from the country's official newspaper, *The Straits Times*, which describes Krrish as a 'Made-in-Singapore Bollywood superhero' (George, 2006). By branding the film as a nationally authentic product, this claim shows how policy governs creativity and, through it, develops products that have the potential to engineer new forms of nationalism. This practice of cultivating national pride can be considered as creative nationalism, the pride engendered by a nation imagined through the content of its creative industry. For *Krrish*, this new imagination is implicit in the synthetic portrayal of the country as a futuristic and hyper-advanced cityscape, and explicit through the intellectual property of the brand and the claims of its official media discourse. Although the creative authenticity of Uniquely Singapore is fabricated, this fabrication allows the film to be claimed as nationally authentic and potentially encouraging a Uniquely Singapore vision of nationhood to emerge.[1]

For the local resident tourists, the creative nationalism of the Uniquely Singapore brand is reflected in domestic travel patterns. On local Singapore blogs using Uniquely Singapore as a subject heading, the pride of the brand is now attached to the leisure experience of everyday life. One poster, Zainal (2008), is thrilled with how his status as a local Singaporean allows him discounts to tourist bus rides around the city. He describes these excursions as his 'adventures ... last holiday' and comments on how he cherishes this experience: 'I learned quite a number of interesting facts about the places, buildings, locations, et cetera about Singapore which I never knew before which truly makes Singapore, Uniquely Singapore!' Another poster, Jufferi bin Mohamad (2007), speaks of this pride through local cuisine, landmarks and shopping. Similarly, Renga (2007) also highlights food and the Singapore 'Singlish' slang as the unique traits of Singapore. Miss Kon (2007) discusses the friendly ambience of hawker centres, the scenic rides of public transportation and the carnivalesque celebrations along the shopping strip of Orchard Road and in Chinatown. From shopping and eating to street festivities, these postings encapsulate the creative nationalism of the Uniquely Singapore brand through the practices of everyday leisure. Even a local bus ride to enjoy local landmarks is also an event for relearning the place of one's roots.

Clearly, film-induced tourism in Singapore is a site of contestation between different nationalisms and populations. By collaborating with India in the making of *Krrish*, Singapore has used the hallmark event to cultivate domestic tourism. Not only are resident tourists enchanted by the spectacle of Bollywood and have begun to view their own local places with fresh eyes; it has also helped to cultivate new pride through creative nationalism, which, in turn, has also sparked off new forms of domestic tourism. For India, *Krrish* has also produced a new sense of pride in the globalization of its film industry as well as through the modernizing gazes of its audiences. In 2007, India moved up to become Singapore's third largest source market as a result of strong destination awareness and high disposable income (STB, 2007b). For these new Indian tourists, their touristic practices of shopping and family themed leisure (STB, 2007b) clearly echo the desires of modernity promoted by the film.

Conclusions

This chapter has discussed the nascent domestic tourism industry in Singapore as a hallmark event. It has shown how tourist attractions and activities in a small city state such as Singapore function as everyday places of interaction and socialization for the local resident tourist. Using the creative film industry and its co-production with India, it has also shown how *Krrish* is constructed as a film-induced tourist event for domestic resident tourists and global Indian tourists. During the making of the film in Singapore, the spectacle of Bollywood stardom makes the city glamorous and exciting. Local resident tourists, seduced by the media hype, revisit trusted old local places with renewed enthusiasm and vigour. For the diasporic Indian audience in Singapore, the film promotes the location as a modern destination that is culturally and economically similar to the new rich of India and the lifestyles of its middle-class diaspora. The success of the film as a media commodity franchise also reflects the new modernity of India, which has, in turn, increased visitations to Singapore. For Singapore, this ideology of shared post-colonial modernity is capitalized upon to fabricate a Uniquely Singapore authenticity that is harnessed for creative nationalism.

In the rush to generate economic wealth from tourism by 'catching up' with the new global creative industry, the film has inadvertently created Singapore as a place devoid of people and stereotyped by class and race. In the film, the Chinese busker Kris is exaggerated by his *kung fu* costume and skill, worthy only to be performing by the roadside or in the circus. A disabled Malay fan, Mohammed Zahid Mohammed Yassin, suffering from spinal bifida, is given a politically correct cameo appearance as a passer-by (Ng, 2005). There is no homage to the first generation of Indian migrants who populate the enclave of Little India and make up 7 per cent of the population, and no aware-ness of the plight of the tens of thousands of ghostly Indian migrant workers who risk their lives to take up the dirty jobs that no one wants in order that glit-tering skyscrapers like those that mark the film can be built. Their absences in the film resound through the cracks of these post-colonial futures; through these politics of domestic and film-induced tourism, *Krrish* has shown that building creative capacity, whether through economic, cultural, media or national capital, is also a process of creative destruction.

Note

1 See also Jones and Smith (2005) for a similar discussion on New Zealand and *The Lord of the Rings*.

References

Beeton, S. (2005) *Film-Induced Tourism*, Channel View Publications, Clevedon

Busby, G. and Klug, J. (2001) 'Movie-induced tourism: The challenge of measurement and other issues', *Journal of Vacation Marketing*, vol 7, no 4, pp316–332

Chang, T. C. (1997) 'Heritage as tourism commodity: Traversing the tourist–local divide', *Singapore Journal of Tropical Geography*, vol 18, no 1, pp46–68

Chang, T. C. (1998) 'Regionalism and tourism: Exploring integral links in Singapore', *Asia Pacific Viewpoint*, vol 39, no 1, pp73–94

Chang, T. C. (1999) 'Local uniqueness in the global village: Heritage tourism in Singapore', *Professional Geographer*, vol 51, no 1, pp91–103

Chang, T. C. (2000a) 'Theming cities, taming places: Insights from Singapore', *Geografiska Annaler*, vol 82B, no 1, pp35–54

Chang, T. C. (2000b) 'Singapore's little India: A tourist attraction as a contested land-scape', *Urban Studies*, vol 37, no 2, pp343–366

Chang, T. C., Milnes, S., Fallon, D. and Pohlmann, C. (1996) 'Urban heritage tourism: The global–local nexus', *Annals of Tourism Research*, vol 23, no 2, pp284–305

Chang, T. C. and Yeoh, B. (1999) 'New Asia – Singapore: Communicating local cultures through global tourism', *Geoforum*, vol 30, no 4, pp101–115

Dubey, B. (2006) 'Singapore goes ga-ga over *Krrish*', *The Times of India*, 22 June

George, S. (2006) 'Made-in-Singapore Bollywood superhero', *The Straits Times*, 9 June

Goldsmith, B. and O'Regan, T. (2004) 'Locomotives and stargates: Inner-city studio complexes in Sydney, Melbourne and Toronto', *International Journal of Cultural Policy*, vol 10, no 1, pp29–45

Greenwood, D. J. (1989) 'Culture by the pound: An anthropological perspective on tourism as cultural commodification', in V. Smith (ed) *Hosts and Guests: The Anthropology of Tourism*, University of Pennsylvania Press, Philadelphia, pp171–185

Henderson, J. (2000a) 'Attracting tourists to Singapore's Chinatown: A case study in conservation and promotion', *Tourism Management*, vol 21, no 6, pp 525–534

Henderson, J. (2000b) 'Selling places: The new Asia-Singapore brand', *The Journal of Tourism Studies*, vol 11, no 1, pp36–44

Henderson, J. (2001) 'Regionalisation and tourism: The Indonesia–Malaysia–Singapore growth triangle', *Current Issues in Tourism*, vol 4, no 2–4, pp78–93

Henderson, J. (2007) 'Uniquely Singapore? A case study in destination branding', *Journal of Vacation Marketing*, vol 13, no 3, pp261–274

Hindustan Times (2006a) 'Government apathy forcing filmmakers to foreign locales?', *Hindustan Times*, 29 June

Hindustan Times (2006b) 'Singapore in stiff competition with Dubai to woo tourists', *Hindustan Times*, 2 September

Hindustan Times (2007) 'A superhero for a brand!', *Hindustan Times*, 27 March

Huang, J. and Hong, L. (2007) 'Chinese diasporic culture and national identity: The taming of the Tiger Balm Gardens in Singapore', *Modern Asian Studies*, vol 41, no 1, pp41–76

Iwashita, C. and Butler, R. (2007) 'The influence of films and television on the destination image of Japanese tourists to the UK: Truth or consequences?', in *Proceedings of the 5th DeHaan Tourism Management Conference Culture, Tourism and the Media*, Nottingham University Business School, Nottingham, 12 December 2006, pp205–226

Jones, D. and Smith, K. (2005) 'Middle-earth meets New Zealand: Authenticity and location on the making of *The Lord of the Rings*', *Journal of Management Studies*, vol 42, no 5, pp923–945

Khan, H. (1998) 'The tourism explosion: Policy decisions facing Singapore', in D. Tyler, Y. Guerrier and M. Robertson (eds) *Managing Tourism in Cities*, John Wiley, New York, NY, pp65–88

Khan, H., Chou, F. S. and Wong, K. C. (1990) 'Tourism multiplier effects in Singapore', *Annals of Tourism Research*, vol 17, pp408–418

Kim, S. S., Agrusa, J., Lee, H. and Chon, K. (2007) 'Effects of Korean television dramas on the flow of Japanese tourists', *Tourism Management*, vol 28, no 5, pp1340–1353

Leong, L. W. (1997) 'Commodifying ethnicity: State and ethnic tourism in Singapore', in M. Picard and R. E. Wood (eds) *Tourism, Ethnicity and the State in Asian and Pacific Societies*, University of Hawaii Press, Honolulu, Hawaii, pp71–98

Loh, S. (2005) 'One hunk of an alien has landed', *The Straits Times*, 16 September

Low, L. and Toh, M. H. (1997) 'Singapore: Development of gateway tourism', in F. M. Go and C. L. Jenkins (eds) *Tourism and Economic Development in Asia and Australasia*, Cassell, London/Washington, pp237–254

Machlis, G. and Burch, W. (1983) 'Relations between strangers: Cycles of structure and meaning in tourist systems', *The Sociological Review*, vol 31, no 4, pp666–692

Media Development Authority (2002) *Creative Industries Development Strategy: Propelling Singapore's Creative Economy*, Ministry of Information, Communication and the Arts, Singapore

Miss Kon (2007) 'Uniquely Singapore', *Uh-huh. Get a Load of This*, 10 October, http://getaloadof-this.blogspot.com/2007/10/uniquely-singapore.html, accessed 25 February 2008

MLW (2006) 'A prosaic portrayal; Krrish makes Singapore look uninteresting', *Today*, 24 June

Mohamad, J. B. (2007) 'Uniquely Singapore', *Every Person Is Unique in His Own Way*, 27 October, http://juju5567.blogspot.com/2007/10/uniquely-singapore.html, accessed 25 February 2008

Morgan, N. and Pritchard, A. (1998) *Tourism Promotion and Power – Creating Images, Creating Identities*, John Wiley, Chichester, UK

Ramanivinita, V. (2005) 'Indian season begins: Bollywood star to film here, showcase Singapore', *Today*, 13 July

Rashid, A. (2006) 'Media and marketing: Singapore in Krrish', *DNA – Daily News and Analysis*, 4 November

Renga (2007) 'Uniquely Singapore', *Thoughts and Life*, 7 September, http://dosser-in-words.blogspot.com/2007/09/uniquely-singapore.html, accessed 25 February 2008

Riley, R. W. (1994) 'Movie-induced tourism', in A. V. Seaton (ed) *Tourism: The State of the Art*, John Wiley, West Sussex, UK, pp453–458

Riley, R., Baker, D. and Van Doren, C. (1998) 'Movie induced tourism', *Annals of Tourism Research*, vol 25, no 4, pp919–935

Ritchie, B. (1984) 'Assessing the impact of hallmark events: Conceptual and research issues', *Journal of Travel Research*, vol 23, no 1, pp2–11

Savage, V. R., Huang, S. and Chang, T. C. (2004) 'The Singapore River Thematic Zone: Sustainable tourism in an urban context', *The Geographical Journal*, vol 170, no 3, pp212–225

STB (Singapore Tourism Board) (2003) 'Singapore Tourism Board launches S$2 million domestic tourism drive to encourage Singaporeans and residents to "Step Out"!', http://app.stb.com.sg/asp/common/print.asp?id=200&type=2, accessed 26 August 2007

STB (2007a) 'Singapore welcomes its 10 millionth visitor', *Singapore Tourism Board: What's New*, http://app.stb.gov.sg/asp/common/print.asp?id=8023&type=2, accessed 10 January 2008

STB (2007b) 'Tourism sector performance for January–June 2007', *Singapore Tourism Board: What's New*, http://app.stb.gov.sg/asp/common/print.asp?id=7263&type=2, accessed 10 January 2008

STB (2007c) 'Film in Singapore! Scheme', *Singapore Tourism Board: Industry Assistance*, http://app.stb.gov.sg/asp/ina/ina04.asp, accessed 12 December

STB (2007d) '*Krrish*, a sequel to *Koi Mil Gaya*', *Uniquely Singapore website*, www.visitsingapore.com/publish/stbportal/en/home/micro_sites/in/krrish.html, accessed 21 October 2007

Stefan, S. (2006) '*Krrish*: Saturday, June 24, 2006', *A Nutshell Review*, http://anutshellreview.blogspot.com/2006/06/krrish.html, accessed 21 October 2007

Sur, R. (2006) 'Singapore helped me to connect with myself', *The Times of India*, 23 June

Tan, E. S., Yeoh, B. and Wang, J. (2001) *Tourism Management and Policy: Perspectives from Singapore*, World Scientific, NJ

Teo, P. and Huang, S. (1995) 'Tourism and heritage conservation in Singapore', *Annals of Tourism Research*, vol 22, no 3, pp589–515

The Straits Times (2005) 'Catch Hrithik in action', *The Straits Times*, 14 September

Toh, M. H. and Low, L. (1990) 'Economic impact of tourism in Singapore', *Annals of Tourism Research*, vol 22, no 3, pp246–269

Urry, J. (1990) *The Tourist Gaze: Leisure and Travel in Contemporary Societies*, Sage, London

Wong, P. P. (1996) 'Singapore: Tourism development of an island city-state', in D. G. Lockhart and D. Drakakis-Smith (eds) *Island Tourism: Trends and Prospects*, Pinter, New York, NY, pp249–267

Yong, H. (2005), 'Alien goes home', *The Straits Times*, 11 November

Yue, A. (2006) 'The regional culture of New Asia: Cultural governance and creative industries in Singapore', *International Journal of Cultural Policy*, vol 12, no 1, pp17–33

Yue, A. (2007) 'Hawking in the creative city: *Rice Rhapsody*, sexuality and the cultural politics of New Asia in Singapore', *Feminist Media Studies*, vol 7, no 4, pp365–380

Zainal (2008) 'Uniquely Singapore', *Shut Up and Stop Whining*, 24 January, http://naime.blogspot.com/2008/01/uniquely-singapore.html, accessed 25 February 2008

14

Cultivating Domestic Tourism with Global Advantage: Malaysia and Singapore Compared

Joan C. Henderson

Introduction

Malaysia and Singapore share a close and uneasy relationship in which they are bound by social, economic, political and historical ties. They are also connected physically by a causeway and bridge, with a constant flow of people and traffic crossing the borders for pleasure and business purposes. However, both nations exhibit marked differences in many respects, including geography, governance, stage of development and socio-cultural profiles. Since these contrasts have implications for leisure tourism, this chapter discusses domestic tourism activity within a wider framework of the multiple forces that have shaped demand and supply. Attention is also given to the effect of outbound movements on domestic trips through an exploration of recent trends and future prospects.

Analysis of the two cases and comparisons between them, based on data in the public domain, offers insights into the critical determinants of domestic holiday-taking and its underlying dynamics within a South-East Asian context. These cover factors such as geographical size and resources, tourist attraction inventory, disposable income, motivation and attitudes to leisure. Official policies and agendas and the role of the private sector in enabling and encouraging participation are additional considerations. Although the examples are distinctive, some of the observations have a more general applicability and their study improves understanding of this increasingly important aspect of the region's tourism, which has largely been neglected.

Background: Malaysia and Singapore

History and geography

Malaysia, once a collection of states ruled by independent sultans, and Singapore, the island at the southern tip of the Malaysian Peninsula, were formerly part of the British Empire. Administered as separate entities, the Federated States of Malaya gained independence in 1957, while Singapore was granted internal self-government in 1959. Sabah and Sarawak on the Island of Borneo and Singapore united with the peninsular states in 1963 to establish the Federation of Malaysia. However, Singapore was expelled from this federation due to internal disagreements in 1965. It became an independent republic and this course of events conferred a legacy of mutual mistrust (Turnbull, 1997; Harper, 1998).

Malaysia occupies 330,113km^2 and comprises 11 states on the Malaysian Peninsula, with 2 in Borneo, as shown in Figure 14.1. The peninsula is a land of forested mountain ranges running north to south and flanked by low-lying coastal plains that have seen large-scale clearance and cultivation in the west. Sabah and Sarawak have a similar topography and the country as a whole has an extensive coastline and more than 1000 offshore islands. Singapore consists of the major island and 55 much smaller islands which have a total surface area of 660km^2. The island is flat with a few low hills and most of the original jungle and swamps have been cleared for development. Stretches of the coastline have been reconfigured as part of a comprehensive planning exercise that dictates land use and seeks to maximize the commercial potential of the space available (Dale, 1999). However, land reclamation in Singapore is reaching its limits. Both Malaysia and Singapore have tropical climates, characterized by high temperatures and humidity throughout the year. Malaysia experiences the seasonal effect of the monsoon winds, which strike its eastern shores from November to March.

Politics and economics

Malaysia is a federal constitutional monarchy and its parliamentary government has been dominated by the Barisan National coalition led by the United Malays National Organization (UMNO) since the 1960s. Rulers have energetically pursued modernization and full development, presenting these goals as compatible with their dedication to Islam. Parti Islam SeMalaysia (PAS) is the main opposition party, and it claims to be the true defender of the Islamic faith. Although the party is driven by an agenda of turning Malaysia into a theocracy, it holds control of a single state in the more conservative north-east. The Government of Singapore is also synonymous with one party, the People's Action Party (PAP), which assumed office after the 1968 elections and has remained in power since. While the nominal system is that of a parlia-

Figure 14.1 *Present-day Malaysia and Singapore*

Source: Shalini Singh

mentary democracy, the PAP exercises control in a manner which inhibits the emergence of rivals; hence, any serious challenges to its authority seem unlikely in the medium term.

The longevity and nature of both regimes have permitted them to engage in long-term economic and physical planning. Consecutive five-year plans in Malaysia have transformed the economy so that the service sector accounts for about 47 per cent of gross domestic product (GDP), manufacturing and services having superseded agriculture and minerals (EIU, 2006). Average annual growth of between 5 and 7 per cent has been reported recently and national unemployment is running at less than 4 per cent (CIA, 2006). Prospects appear good with projections of real GDP growth of at least 5 per cent annually in the immediate future (EIU, 2007a). Singapore's economy is expected to expand by a similar degree (EIU, 2007b) and it too has seen transformation following independence. It is a highly industrialized regional and global financial hub where manufacturing represents almost 30 per cent of GDP. The growth rate was 7.9 per cent in 2006 (EIU, 2007c) when unemployment stood at 3.4 or 2.7 per cent if seasonally adjusted (Department of Statistics, 2007).

Malaysia's Vision 2020 was launched in 1991 with the objective that the nation would have attained developed nation status by 2020. It is deemed to have already reached medium human development status (UNDP, 2005) and GDP per capita in 2005 was US$4997 (EIU, 2006), but there are striking regional disparities. Western and southern states are more industrialized, urbanized and prosperous than those in the north and east, which remain predominantly rural. The affluence of a growing urban middle class concentrated in the capital of Kuala Lumpur and its environs contrasts with the deprivation in the eastern states of Terengganu and Kelantan, where 15.4 and 10.6 per cent of residents, respectively, live in poverty. The national figure for poverty in Malaysia, officially defined as a monthly household income of less than 661 ringgit (US$199), is 5.7 per cent (Economic Planning Unit, 2006a). On the other hand, poverty is not formally recorded in Singapore, and its citizens enjoy one of the highest standards of living in the region, with a GDP per capita in 2006 of US$29,473 (EIU, 2007b). It has a high human development ranking of 25 in the index, ahead of Malaysia (at 61) (UNDP, 2005), yet wealth is not evenly distributed and some residents face financial hardship.

Society and culture

Malaysia and Singapore are multi-ethnic societies. Malays comprise almost 60 per cent of the former's total population of 27 million. Other races are the Chinese (23.6 per cent) and Indians (7 per cent), alongside many aboriginal tribes in Borneo (EIU, 2006). The Chinese form about 75 per cent of Singapore's citizens and permanent residents, who number just more than 4 million, and the remainder are classed as Malays (13.7 per cent), Indians (8.7 per cent) and other (2.6 per cent) (Department of Statistics, 2006). Race is a sensitive matter in both countries, with tensions arising from Chinese pre-eminence in Singapore (Lai, 1995; Rahim, 1998) and their disproportionate share of wealth in Malaysia. *Bumiputera* (literally translated as sons of the soil and a word describing Malays and indigenous peoples) have been the subject of socio-economic affirmative action programmes in Malaysia, which have been criticized for their ineffectiveness and cultural and political marginalization of the non-Malays (Milne and Mauzy, 1998).

Religion is a complicating factor and Islam is integral to conceptions of Malay identity in both Singapore and Malaysia, and central to life in the latter. An uneasy ethnic pluralism has prevailed in Malaysia that is being tested by Islamic revivalism. The government is striving to sustain a balance between the secular and the religious in order to maintain the tradition of tolerance. Authorities in Singapore are very mindful of the dangers of religious and racial frictions, and community relations are carefully managed through policies that promote visions of harmonious multiculturalism, which are sometimes at odds with reality.

While there is a trend towards greater religious orthodoxy in Malaysia, modernization and associated consumerism are increasingly powerful influences. The new Malaysia is symbolized by Kuala Lumpur's skyline of residential and commercial buildings in which the Petronas Twin Towers, one of the tallest structures in the world, is a landmark. Coexistence of tradition and modernity can engender a curious hybrid culture epitomized by young Malay women, donning the traditional headscarf while wearing tight denim jeans, who throng the ubiquitous shopping malls where branded goods from around the globe are sold. Singapore's Malays can be observed in similar outfits and environments, and the society, in general, is a modern one of eager consumers. Most citizens enjoy a comfortable lifestyle, including spending on non-essentials such as 'recreation and other', which rose from 12 per cent of all household expenditure in 1973 to 18 per cent in 2003 (Department of Statistics, 2007).

There are, however, certain stresses accompanying life in the intensely urbanized and densely populated city state of Singapore, where private and public space is in short supply. Individuals are exposed to pressures at school and in the workplace, where personal advancement is saluted as the key to survival in a fiercely competitive world – a philosophy that is also espoused by the government (George, 2000). Malaysia's urban professionals endure similar burdens and some have expressed a strong desire to retreat to the perceived simplicity of *kampong* (village) life (Kahn, 1996).

Summarily, Malaysia and Singapore are thus unique historically, geographically, politically, economically and socio-culturally. Nevertheless, their histories and, perhaps, destinies, are linked and they share the experience of having undergone dramatic alteration in the years since their independence, the pace of which has been especially rapid in Singapore. One manifestation of the extent of 50 years of change is the emergence of a large and sophisticated tourism industry. The qualities discussed above all have implications for tourism policies, supply and demand, which is explored in the following sections, with particular reference to the domestic market after an introduction to tourism in both the countries.

Tourism and tourism resources in Malaysia and Singapore

Malaysia's tourism has evolved from a peripheral business of predominantly local orientation during the 1960s to a critical economic sector with a global reach (Ministry of Tourism, 2004). Most revenue is generated by inbound travellers and 17.6 million arrivals, and 36.3 billion ringgit (US$10.4 billion) receipts were recorded in 2006 (Tourism Malaysia, 2007a). The industry in Singapore has also seen growth, and again the emphasis is on international tourists, with 9.7 million in 2006 when receipts were S$12.4 billion (US$8.1 billion) (STB, 2007a). Outbound flows from both countries are substantial, but domestic markets are very different and resident travel is reviewed later.

Malaysia's coast and islands, with a rich marine life and coral reef ecosystems, are important tourism assets and there are beach destinations of assorted size and type. Rural tourism occurs away from the coast and former hill stations are popular venues. Mountain and rainforest landscapes, supporting a variety of flora and fauna and outdoor pursuits, are also core attractions and enable the practice of ecotourism in its many guises. Culture and heritage of a multiplicity of types, especially certain expressions of ethnic difference, are other attributes of tourist interest. More modern and purpose-built amenities of shopping malls and theme parks are unmistakable attractions, as are regular programmes of sporting events. The Genting Highlands is an inland resort that boasts the largest casino in the region and the only one in Malaysia, despite the fact that gambling is prohibited by Islam. Kuala Lumpur is associated with shopping, entertainment and cultural pursuits (Tourism Malaysia, 2007b).

Conventional tourism resources are not abundant in Singapore, but there have been persistent efforts to augment its attractions base. Promotional material draws attention to the clean and green environment and nature-related sites such as the zoo, night safari and botanic gardens. Sentosa is an offshore island designated as a leisure playground with beaches and a mixture of amusements. A few of the other islands, not reserved for industrial or military use, are open to the public, as are stretches of the coastline. The republic's multiculturalism and syntheses of East and West and old and new are also showcased, with its heritage illustrated by the ethnic enclaves such as Chinatown and Little India, and colonial buildings. Opportunities for fun are highlighted from shopping in the primary retail belt of Orchard Road to night clubbing by the revitalized riverside. Miscellaneous festivals and events are hosted and there has been a drive to portray Singapore as a city of culture and the arts (STB, 2007b).

Tourism policies and promotion

Malaysia

Tourism in Malaysia, whether domestic or international, is allocated a high priority by government because of its actual and possible contribution to income and employment. The industry is the most lucrative of all services and hailed as a key engine of development and as a means of diversifying the economy (EIU, 2006). In addition to anticipated financial rewards, officials are appreciative of tourism's function in articulating and reinforcing a unifying sense of national identity. The mitigation of damaging impacts, especially on the coast, is another reason for intervention. The capacity of tourists to offend Islamic principles was also a preoccupation of officials in the immediate post-independence era and led to the deterrence of certain groups, but this has now been overshadowed by economic imperatives. Cultural clashes are, however, a contentious matter for some states and there have been heated disputes with federal politicians about appropriate responses (Henderson, 2002).

Nevertheless, domestic tourism has been officially encouraged by both tiers of government for several years. For example, central funding of 100 million ringgit (US$29 million) was allocated during the mid-1960s to the construction of a series of budget hotels, designed to satisfy demand. The 1997 Asian financial crisis also precipitated action, and sums of money that could be taken out of the country were curtailed in a bid to stem foreign travel and economic leakages. Marketing campaigns were launched, the most prominent being Cuti Cuti Malaysia (which has no English translation), and civil servants were given alternate Saturdays off, so they had a full weekend for travelling. Special events received official sponsorship, and the national airline and other relevant parties were urged to devise domestic tours (Ministry of Tourism, 2004). Such measures are ongoing and Cuti Cuti Malaysia packages are lauded as instances of quality tourism, the official website advertising over 700 such products (Ministry of Tourism, 2007).

Tourism has come to occupy a place in national economic and physical plans which acknowledge the part to be played by the domestic industry. The *Ninth Malaysian Plan*, operational from 2006 until 2010, seeks to augment the overall role of tourism in the service and wider economies, and one way of achieving this is through an enhanced level of domestic tourism (Economic Planning Unit, 2006a, 2006b). The *Third Industrial Master Plan*, dating from 2006, and the *National Physical Plan* identify tourism as a growth area and tool in helping to overcome regional imbalance (FDTCPM, 2005). A mix of domestic and international tourism is advocated, and these themes, alongside a commitment to sustainable tourism development, are echoed in mandatory state structure plans.

The ascendancy of tourism was marked by the setting-up of a dedicated ministry in 2004, to which the National Tourism Organization of Tourism Malaysia reports. The focus of Tourism Malaysia is on inbound tourism, yet its latest strategy recognizes a statutory obligation to market Malaysia within the country. The goal is to 'develop and inculcate a wholesome Malaysian culture for domestic tourism' (Tourism Malaysia, 2004, p9), although there may be a danger that domestic tourism is fashioned to suit international tastes and patterns when economic development is the overriding political agenda.

Singapore

Tourism in Singapore is regarded as a core industry and vital to the government's economic diversification strategy, but the prime minister has spoken of the urgent 'need to remake the city and economy' if the potential is to be realized (*TTG Daily News*, 2005). The extant national economic plan cites leisure and business travel, education, healthcare and the creative industries as fundamental to the services sector, which is hoped will perform as a growth catalyst (Economic Review Committee, 2003). Motives underlying government involvement are principally economic, but tourism is also a channel for communicating conceptions of nationhood founded on ethnic harmony and a vehicle through which leaders can assert their competence to audiences at home and overseas (Hall and Oehlers, 2000).

Expansion of inbound tourism has been facilitated by official plans intended to broaden Singapore's appeal, centred on the creation and continuous improvement of attractions and international communications (Teo and Chang, 2000). A Tourism Development Fund aims to foster infrastructure and product development, strengthen industry capability and attract 'iconic' or major events (STB, 2005). Again, tourism tends to be defined in international terms, but there is awareness that innovation adds to the leisure choices of citizens and increases spending opportunities. The multi-million dollar redevelopment of Sentosa and upgrading of Orchard Road are instances of projects in progress that will be targeting locals. Two integrated resorts with casinos are due to open in 2009 and certain components must entice Singaporean customers if their operations are to be commercially viable.

The Singapore Tourism Board (STB) oversees tourism planning, development and marketing and has mutated into an economic development agency which is charged with turning the industry into a 'key driver of economic growth' (STB, 2004). While it does profess to involve the population in dimensions of policy-making and as brand ambassadors in some of its campaigns, there is very little domestic marketing of Singapore as an overnight destination. The board does sponsor entertainments such as the Food Festival and Great Singapore Sale, which are open to residents and partly rely on them, but the primary objective is to elevate Singapore's profile internationally and to lure visitors from abroad. Tourism developments are thus often more outwardly directed than inward, and domestic tourism may be subsumed by international tastes and trends, raising questions about the authenticity of aspects of national tourism.

Domestic tourism: A supply perspective

The attractions of each country previously summarized illuminate the modes of pleasure tourism and activities in which residents can engage. Domestic tourism also depends on a suitable stock of accommodation and a transport infrastructure and services which expedite access to sites and destinations. Assistance in arranging trips and the availability of packages from travel agents and tour operators are additional facilitators, and there must be knowledge of what is on offer, requiring marketing by private enterprises as well as official agencies. The work of formal organizations and destination marketers has already been commented on, while the other prerequisites are analysed below.

Malaysia

According to official statistics, in 2005, when average occupancy was 63.6 per cent, Malaysia had 2269 hotels with 155,356 rooms. Guests totalled more than 51 million, almost 30 million of whom were nationals (Tourism Malaysia, 2006). Hotels vary widely in quality and capacity. The capital city contains the highest proportion of hotels, many of which belong to chains and are of four- to five-star grade. International brands are less prominent elsewhere and there are accepted deficiencies in the physical stock and services (Ministry of Tourism, 2004). No figures are released, but advertising literature indicates that Malaysia has a spectrum of non-hotel accommodation which embraces village home stays, Sarawak longhouses, ecotourism lodges, and formal and informal camping sites. Some of the sizeable attractions such as national parks and theme parks incorporate accommodation and position themselves as complete destinations.

In the context of transport, external and internal accessibility is improving and the Malaysian government has invested in the country's communications. Road and rail systems are, however, more efficient along the western corridor and inadequacies in the north and east are acknowledged to have impeded both general and tourism development. Car ownership reflects improving living standards and 67 per cent of Malaysians possess a vehicle (Nielsen, 2007), but traffic congestion is also a serious problem in Kuala Lumpur and some state capitals. The relatively new and very modern international airport was built to cater to the projected pan-Asian rise in air traffic, with ambitious managers intending to outdo its rival – Changi (Singapore) – as a regional hub. Further provision for the burgeoning budget industry is planned (EIU, 2006), and Air Asia, headquartered in Malaysia, is a leading regional low-cost carrier which is constantly extending its routes within and outside the country.

Accommodation and transport suppliers, alongside Malaysia's travel agents and tour operators, have been asked by officials for some time to be more responsive to the needs of domestic tourists and there are signs of positive reactions. International and national hotel groups advertise short breaks at discounted prices and travel agents sell pre-packaged holidays or aid in booking independent services. However, the tour operation and travel agency business tends to be small scale and enterprises have insufficient finances for growth or sophisticated marketing. Choices and awareness are thus constrained, but there is likely to be widespread organization of travel on an independent and individual basis. Information technology is further empowering consumers, and popular forms of domestic tourism, such as camping and visiting friends and relatives, do not require costly sales and distribution networks.

Singapore

Owing to its size, Singapore's domestic tourism product range is much narrower and its attractions can generally all be enjoyed as day or half-day excursions. This factor renders overnight stays by domestic travellers almost unnecessary. Nonetheless, there are exceptions of camping and certain adventure sports. The National Parks Board permits free camping at designated spots in its five coastal parks, as well as on the Island of Pulau Ubin, which also has two outward-bound centres, with a third located in one of the mainland parks.

There were 254 formally registered hotels in 2006 which had a total of 33,518 rooms. These span larger properties managed by multinational chains through boutique hotels to small privately owned budget hostels. They are found primarily in the city, with a few by the coast, and occupancy averaged 85 per cent in 2006 (STB, 2007a, 2007c). Alternative accommodation includes holiday chalets and low-rise apartment blocks at a seaside suburb, which are government operated. These were initially intended for civil servants and military personnel, but can now be rented by the public. The question of whether to relax planning rules so that the handful of small farms surviving in a more rural zone can install overnight visitor accommodation facilities is still being debated.

There is no breakdown of guests by origin, but anecdotal evidence suggests that self-catering customers are almost all locals and that they are a very small market for hotel bedroom sales. An exception was during the 2003 outbreak of the severe acute respiratory syndrome (SARS) virus when overseas arrivals fell sharply and Singaporeans were reluctant to travel. Hoteliers looked to residents to earn some revenue and put together miscellaneous themed packages, an exercise which is occasionally repeated. Special deals are sometimes promoted to coincide with events such as the Great Singapore Sale and New Year's Day and National Day, where firework displays can be witnessed from selected downtown hotel premises.

Singapore is renowned for the efficiency of its public transport, which integrates buses and a light railway and serves most of the island. Private road travel is strictly regulated in order to minimize usage. As a consequence, the city is not blighted by the traffic gridlocks that are characteristic of most South-East Asian capitals. This is, indeed, commendable in view of the fact that the percentage of households owning a car has doubled since 1973 to reach 35 per cent (Department of Statistics, 2007). Internationally, Changi airport provides air connectivity and has a dedicated budget carrier terminal. Ferries sail to Indonesia and Malaysia, and the cruise centre is one of the busiest in the region. There is also a causeway carrying a road and railway line and a second road link between Singapore and Malaysia. Ease of movement and access is therefore not an obstacle to domestic travel and tourism. Owing to the transport infrastructure and the island's size, Singapore can be traversed by private car in about 40 minutes.

Travel agents, tour operators and transport companies evince the same lack of enthusiasm as hoteliers for arranging and marketing domestic holidays, and few, if any, can be found. Efforts are made by attractions that cannot depend solely on non-residents to boost local attendance, but there is usually no accommodation component, and little promotion of Singapore as an overnight destination to its citizens is undertaken by private businesses.

Domestic tourism: A demand perspective

Malaysia

Despite a paucity of data on domestic tourism in Malaysia, there are published figures which show that almost half of the 15 million trips made in 1998 were overnight stays and total spending was 2.4 billion ringgit (US$685 million). There has been expansion since then from 18.3 million trips in 2000 to 26.7 million trips in 2005, although average spending has remained low at 393 ringgit (US$112) in the latter year (Euromonitor, 2006a).

Domestic guests are estimated to comprise more than 50 per cent of all hotel customers and Table 14.1 discloses an uneven geographical spread. The pre-eminence of the West Coast and the Klang Valley where the capital is located is largely the result of the more developed, general and tourism-specific infrastructures of western states and their freedom from the monsoon.

Table 14.1 *Malaysia's domestic hotel guests by region (2003)*

Locality	Share (%)
Klang Valley	22.9
Penang	7.8
West Coast (excluding Penang)	27.2
East Coast	13.0
Highland resorts	6.8
Island resorts	8.9
Sabah	6.1
Sarawak	6.5

Source: Tourism Malaysia (2005)

An official survey of Malaysian domestic tourists reveals slight divergences by race, but concludes that there is a common pattern. The principal reason for travel is holidays and sightseeing, followed by business and seminar attendance. Most choose shorter holidays of between three and seven days and use three-star hotels. These decisions are mainly determined by costs. Malaysia is believed to be very safe and an excellent place for shopping, offering value for money and a good variety of goods. It seems that critical determinants of domestic travel, besides race, are region of residence, occupation, income and age. The younger generation, originating from prosperous districts and earning generous salaries, tend to be the most active travellers (Ministry of Tourism, 2004).

Findings correspond with a report which concludes that much of the Malaysian population takes part in domestic tourism, with behaviour influenced by demographics. School holidays are the peak season when families return to their hometown or elect to visit beaches, islands or theme parks for three to four days. Older travellers prefer to take tours, stay with their children in urban centres or join family vacations. Much tourism is generated by inhabitants seeking a respite from city life. Professionals, typically couples, take short breaks, usually to island locations, at least twice a year. The desire to shop is a strong motivator, though the younger generation is also drawn to theme parks, beaches, camping and backpacking (Euromonitor, 2006a).

Singapore

Statistics for domestic tourism involving an overnight stay in Singapore are not produced, which is indicative of its relative insignificance. Nevertheless, volumes of local visitors at attractions merit note and afford insights into the allocation of leisure time. Popular venues relate to shopping, nature, outdoor recreation and food and drink, and include Orchard Road, Sentosa, Chinatown, Boat and Clarke Quays, the Marina Square Shopping Complex and Jurong Bird Park (Euromonitor, 2006b). Road (53 per cent) and rail (36 per cent) travel were the leading methods of excursion transport in 2005, while seafaring made up 11 per cent of travel mode. Expenditure was S$360 million (US$236 million) that year, mostly attributable to leisure shopping (Euromonitor, 2006b).

Domestic and outbound compared

Malaysia

Domestic tourism in Malaysia is an outcome of supply-and-demand issues, which, in turn, are affected by the stance and actions of government and the industry. The supply has been shown to be plentiful and government to be supportive. Demand appears healthy, with a substantial proportion of the population having the means and motivation to undertake domestic trips. However, some of the forces at work in shaping domestic activity also apply to international travel. Enthusiasm for travel and holidaying has been stimulated by education, transport improvements, the increasing use of information technology and mounting wealth. These factors have meant new attitudes towards leisure and its consumption (Ministry of Tourism, 2004). Hence, when finances permit, Malaysians are inclined to undertake outbound trips, usually within the Asian region.

More than 30.5 million international trips were taken in 2000 and 30.8 million in 2005. International trips thus exceeded domestic trips, but the latter grew faster and at a steadier pace than the former (Euromonitor, 2006a). Expenditure is comparable and sums are surprisingly modest in both instances, a reminder that the amount covers day as well as longer trips. The statistics hint at how travel abroad can be more sensitive to internal and external events, demonstrated by the drop in 2003, which is attributable to the SARS epidemic and the onset of war in Iraq. Economic uncertainty and fluctuations in currency values are further impediments for Malaysians, and Islam imposes codes of conduct about diet and dress, as well as a strict prayer regime, which have implications for tourism.

The dynamics of outbound demand in Malaysia are such that most foreign holidays are taken within East Asia and long-distance travel is rare (Tourism Malaysia, 2006). Singapore is the preferred destination, preceding Indonesia, and authorities there logged 634,000 Malaysian visitors in 2006 (STB, 2007c), although land arrivals by road are sometimes excluded so that final figures for arrivals from Malaysia into Singapore are greater.

Singapore

The picture of domestic tourism is strikingly different in Singapore, where supply and demand and government and industry interest are extremely limited and there are few barriers to outbound travel. Prosperity has fuelled demand for international tourism and steps towards civil aviation deregulation, and the recent introduction of low-cost carriers has led to unprecedented opportunities. Favourable currency exchange rates, especially with immediate neighbours in the region, are yet another incentive. Cruising is also popular, and short voyages that offer gambling opportunities are particularly appealing since it is a banned activity in Singapore and the cruise companies exploit the advantage of sailing in international waters. The propensity of residents to travel is illustrated by the rise in departures from 10 million in 2000 to 15.8 million in 2005 when spending was S$6483 million (US$4251 million) (Euromonitor, 2006b).

While Singaporeans do undertake more long-haul journeys than Malaysians and are heavier spenders, most of their travel is also intra-regional. Malaysia and Indonesia are the most frequented destinations and attracted almost 10 and 2 million overnight trips, respectively, in 2005 (Euromonitor, 2006b). Geographic proximity partly accounts for the density of two-way tourist traffic between Malaysia and Singapore, but there are ties of kinship. There is a sizeable community of Malaysian Singapore permanent residents and members frequently return home or host visits from friends and relatives.

Future prospects

Looking ahead, impressive inbound and outbound tourism growth rates are forecast for the Asia Pacific region in the forthcoming decade (UNWTO, 2007). Malaysia and Singapore are set to adhere to this trend, although unexpected incidents may prove disruptive in the short term. The health of tourism and economies are closely aligned and any economic downturn will have adverse repercussions for demand for travel. It seems unlikely that Singaporeans will forego international trips, despite this element of unpredictability, but there may be exceptional years when domestic business gains from a drop in foreign travel.

With regard to Malaysia, projections are that there will be approximately 31.4 million domestic travellers by 2010 (Ministry of Tourism, 2004). Domestic tourism may therefore be threatened if foreign destinations are substituted for those at home or there could be enlargement of both markets, provided incomes are sufficiently high.

Conclusions

Tourism as a whole reflects conditions at the national scale. While contrasting as generators and attractors of tourists, Malaysia and Singapore display some similarities pertaining to tourism demand and the causes underpinning changes since independence. Economic progress has raised incomes and standards of living, stimulating travel and allowing for public expenditure on development and marketing, which has facilitated movement. The uninterrupted tenure of the governing regimes has also made possible the devising and implementation of specific pro-tourism strategies and long-term broader economic programmes in which tourism is one ingredient. Many individuals now possess the inclination, time and money to engage in tourism at home and abroad, and participation is made easier by the maturing of the tourism industry.

At the same time, there are obvious deviations between the two nations. Singapore's greater affluence and much smaller land mass have led to international travel dominating over domestic travel. Options for holiday-taking at home are severely restricted and the industry does not fully recognize or pursue this market, although circumstances at some time in the future may prompt initiatives to further develop domestic tourism by authorities and commercial enterprises. Malaysian residents have less disposable income and live in a large country with a wealth of tourism resources, predisposing them to a greater level of domestic travel. There may be a desire to enjoy overseas leisure trips, but holidays at home remain the most appealing and realistic choice for many. Patterns of foreign and domestic holiday-taking could be revised on the nation's progress towards full development, however, and the latter may become shorter and may alter in character with the primary holidays being taken abroad.

Markets are evolving and certain aspects of any expansion in domestic tourism are to be welcomed, not least the personal and social rewards of vacation travel. In addition, there are economic benefits that can accrue to destinations and are especially valuable in less prosperous rural communities. However, negative impacts cannot be overlooked. More residents on the move internally, in combination with greater numbers of inbound visitors, will have environmental, socio-cultural and economic consequences. This must be planned for if tourism is to be sustainable. The potential advantages are perhaps of greater importance in Malaysia, given comparative stages of economic development, and it is also more vulnerable to the damage that tourism can inflict on natural and cultural heritage. These are still of concern in Singapore where increasing reliance is being placed on an expanded service sector and authorities have also to confront the limits to growth which are inevitable because of physical constraints. Domestic tourism is thus one constituent of complex national leisure and tourism industries and is best understood in its broader context, within which policies to promote it must also be formulated if they are to be successful.

References

CIA (2006) *The World Fact Book*, www.odci.gov/cia/publications/factbook/geos/my.html, accessed 16 November 2006

Dale, O. (1999) *Urban Planning in Singapore: The Transformation of a City*, Oxford University Press, Kuala Lumpur, Malaysia

Department of Statistics (2006) *Key Statistics: People*, www.visitsingapore.com, accessed 23 February 2006

Department of Statistics (2007) *Singapore 2007 Statistical Highlights*, Ministry of Trade and Industry, Singapore

Economic Planning Unit (2006a) *Ninth Malaysia Plan 2006–2010*, www.epu.jpm.my, accessed 9 October 2006

Economic Planning Unit (2006b) *Eighth Malaysia Plan 2001–2005*, www.epu.jpm.my, accessed 9 October 2006

Economic Review Committee (2003) *Economic Review Committee: Executive Summary*, Ministry of Trade and Industry, Singapore

EIU (2006) *Malaysia Country Profile 2006*, Economist Intelligence Unit, London

EIU (2007a) *Malaysia Country Report 2007*, Economist Intelligence Unit, London

EIU (2007b) *Singapore Country Report 2007*, Economist Intelligence Unit, London

EIU (2007c) *Singapore Country Profile 2007*, Economist Intelligence Unit, London

Euromonitor (2006a) 'Consumer lifestyles: Malaysia', www.gmid.euromnitor.com.ezlibproxy1.ntu.edu.sg/Reports.aspx, accessed 13 April 2007

Euromonitor (2006b) 'Travel and tourism: Singapore', www.gmid.euromnitor.com.ezlibproxy1.ntu.edu.sg/Reports.aspx, accessed 13 April 2007

FDTCPM (Federal Department of Town and Country Planning Malaysia) (2005) *National Physical Plan*, Federal Department of Town and Country Planning Malaysia, Kuala Lumpur, Malaysia

George, C. (2000) *Singapore: The Air Conditioned Nation*, Landmark Books, Singapore

Hall, C. M. and Oehlers, A. (2000) 'Tourism and politics in South and Southeast Asia: Political instability and policy' in C. M. Hall and S. Page (eds) *Tourism in South and Southeast Asia: Issues and Cases*, Butterworth and Heinemann, Oxford, pp77–93

Harper, T. N. (1998) *The End of Empire and the Making of Malaysia*, Cambridge University Press, New York, NY

Henderson, J. C. (2002) 'Managing tourism and Islam in Peninsular Malaysia', *Tourism Management*, vol 24, pp447–456

Kahn, J. S. (1996) 'Growth, economic transformation, culture and the middle classes in Malaysia' in R. Robison and D. Goodman (eds) *The New Rich in Asia: Mobile Phones, McDonalds and Middle Class Revolution*, Routledge, London/New York, pp49–78

Lai, A. E. (1995) *Meanings of Multiethnicity: A Case Study of Ethnicity and Ethnic Relations in Singapore*, Oxford University Press, Oxford/Singapore

Milne, R. S. and Mauzy, D. K. (1998) *Malaysian Politics under Mahatir*, Routledge, London

Ministry of Tourism (2004) *Review of National Tourism Policy Main Report*, Ministry of Tourism, Kuala Lumpur, Malaysia

Ministry of Tourism (2007) 'Cuti Cuti Malaysia packages', www.virtualmalaysia.com, accessed 29 August 2007

Nielsen, A. C. (29 May 2007) 'Americans lead the world in car ownership, China and India fast catching up in absolute number of cars owned', www.acnielsen.com/news, accessed 28 August 2007

Rahim, L. Z. (1998) *The Singapore Dilemma: The Political and Educational Marginality of the Malay Community*, Oxford University Press, Kuala Lumpur, Malaysia

STB (Singapore Tourism Board) (2004) 'About STB', http://app.stb.gov.sg/asp/index.asp?, accessed 13 August 2004

STB (2005) 'Singapore sets out to triple tourism receipts to S$30 billion by 2015', Press release, 11 January

STB (2007a) 'Singapore hotels directory', www.visitsingapore.com, accessed 27 August 2007

STB (2007b) 'What to see: Uniquely Singapore', www.visitsingapore.com, accessed 14 September 2007

STB (2007c) 'Visitor arrival statistics', http://app.stb.com.sg/asp/tou/tou02.asp, accessed 24 August 2007

Teo, P. and Chang, T. C. (2000) 'Singapore: Tourism development in a planned context', in C. M. Hall and S. Page (eds) *Tourism in South and Southeast Asia: Issues and Cases*, Butterworth and Heinemann, Oxford, pp117–128

Tourism Malaysia (2004) *Promotional Plan 2005–2007*, Tourism Malaysia, Kuala Lumpur, Malaysia

Tourism Malaysia (2005) *Hotel Guests by Locality*, www.tourism.gov.my/statistic/hotel_guest_by_locality, accessed 7 November 2005

Tourism Malaysia (2006) *Tourism in Malaysia: Key Performance Indicators*, Tourism Malaysia, Kuala Lumpur, Malaysia

Tourism Malaysia (2007a) *Tourist Statistics*, www.tourism.gov.my/corporate/research.asp?page=facts_figures, accessed 22 August 2007

Tourism Malaysia (2007b) *Travel to Malaysia*, www.tourism.gov.my, accessed 14 September 2007

TTG Daily News (2005) 'Singapore to have two integrated resorts', *TTGTravelHub.Net Daily News*, 18 April

Turnbull, C. M. (1997) *A History of Singapore*, Oxford University Press, New York, NY

UNDP (United Nations Development Programme) (2005) *Human Development Report 2005*, United Nations Development Programme, New York

UNWTO (United Nations World Tourism Organization) (2007) *World Tourism Barometer*, United Nations World Tourism Organization, Madrid, Spain

15

Holiday-Making and the Leisure Space of the Macao People

Louis Tze Ngai Vong and Cindia Ching-Chi Lam

Macao background

Geographically speaking, Macao (People's Republic of China) is located on the south eastern coast of China in the Pearl River Delta region of Guangdong Province. However, one can hardly locate the city on a map as it barely occupies a total area of 29.2km² (Macao Statistics Census and Service, 2008). The entire city comprises a peninsula (known as the Macao Peninsular) and two islands – Taipa and Coloane. The northern end of the Macao Peninsular is a border gateway to mainland China. This border gateway connects Macao to the mainland territory of Gong Bei, a small county of Zhuhai City in the larger Guangdong Province.

Although Macao is a city of China, it enjoys a privileged status over the other mainland cities. In this sense, Macao is a special administrative region of the People's Republic of China in that it retains legislative, executive and judicial power that is independent of Beijing. This favourable arrangement is the result of a political reconciliation between China and Portugal at the end of the 20th century. When Macao was returned to China in the 1999, the different aspects of the city retained a rich Portuguese flavour, as is evident in its work ethic, architecture, cuisine, festivals and other cultural aspects. Furthermore, centuries of mixed-marriages between ethnic Chinese and Portuguese have also created a new ethnic group known as the Macanese, who are a living legacy of the history of Macao. Histo-culturally, the word 'Macanese' stands for the mixed-blood natives in Macao whose ancestors belonged to two specific races – Chinese and Portuguese. On the other hand, ethnic Chinese, who represent 94 per cent of the entire Macao population (Macao Government Tourist Office, 2008), are normally referred to as Macao Chinese. Although the Macanese are a living icon of Macao, they represent only a sliver of the entire population. Interestingly, however, it is this ethnic minority group with its

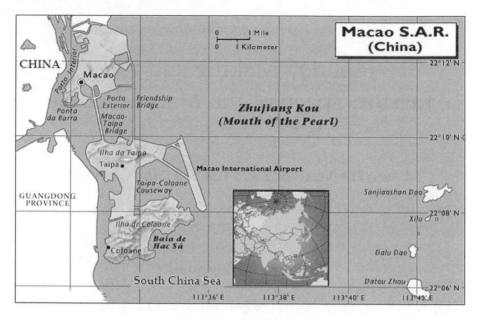

Figure 15.1 *Map of Macao*

Source: http://encarta.msn.com/map_701514358/macao_sar.html

Portuguese culture that gives a facelift to Macao to set itself apart from the rest of the mainland cities. It is under this geo-socio-political context that this chapter attempts to discuss the holiday-making and native leisure patterns and preferences of Macao people.

Leisure 'space' of the Macao people

Size matters. A population of half a million settled within such a small city makes Macao one of the most densely populated areas in the world. Such a reality limits Macao in providing sufficient leisure space for her residents (Vong, 2005). Modernization in the urban peninsular is driving Macao people to 'look outside' for recreational opportunities. Taipa Island and Coloane Island – both of which are connected by road bridges with the Macao Peninsular – are therefore the only places in Macao for the residents to take on recreational activities. Although urban life in the peninsular is busy, Coloane Island is relatively serene and preserves its semi-natural qualities for outdoor recreation. Recent years of rapid urbanization have transformed Taipa Island – an island once comprised of small villages – into a modernized residential district. Nonetheless, one can still trace the history of village life in Taipa,

Figure 15.2 *Holiday park in Taipa village*

Source: Cindia Ching-Chi Lam

which is what captures the interest of visitors. In this regard, Taipa village, a locally preserved heritage site on Taipa Island, exposes visitors to the island's aboriginal past. The landscape of the Taipa village is tightly packed, with traditional two-storey-high village houses that are built along narrow streets and alleys which intermingle with each other. Today, the descendants of this indigenous community still reside there.

Nature attractions and green holidays in Coloane

Holidaying on Coloane Island is a common pastime of the Macao people. The island, which is farthest away from the peninsular, is a popular place for outdoor recreation. It is also the only place in Macao where exotic beaches are located. These beaches attract as many domestic visitors as they attract foreign tourists during the summer season. The countryside also renders the contextual conditions for different kinds of outdoor recreational sports: examples include walking on the natural trails, hiking, rock-climbing, bicycling, canoeing and windsurfing. Nonetheless, recreational sports do not seem to be favoured by the Macao people. Instead, the most popular leisure choice year round is picnicking (Vong, 2006). In recent years, eco-tourism has become fashionable and residents seem to have rediscovered the beauty of the island's extended hiking trails. Perhaps walking along the countryside trails is the most direct approach to embrace nature. Alternatively, some choose to visit the different Coloane holiday parks, which have traditionally been popular places for family outings – today these parks have become even more popular. No matter what the residents' choices are, the island is resourceful in delivering natural attractions to Macao people.

Figure 15.3 *Picnicking in Coloane*

Source: Cindia Ching-Chi Lam

Enjoying a typical Macanese cuisine is another 'must-do' activity for those who stay in Coloane. Macanese cuisine is common in Macao; but it seems that taking the same dish at a different time in a different place means 'enjoying' something different. Since there are only a few popular Portuguese restaurants scattered throughout the island, it is not an easy task to reserve a table during peak seasons. This atypical provisioning makes eating out in Coloane a precious leisure experience for visitors. Just as a tourist brings back home authentic local souvenirs, Macao people love to return home bearing the famous Portuguese-style egg tarts from the original producer who began a legendary business on the island decades ago. In recent years, this local pastry has received widespread success in many East Asian countries and regions such as the Philippines, Japan, Thailand, Hong Kong and Taiwan. It is not an over-statement to claim that some visitors, both locals and tourists alike, come all the way to Coloane just for the egg tarts (Macao.com, 2008).

Cultural heritage serves as another attraction on the island. Coloane Island is a living testament to the dual existence of Chinese and Portuguese cultural legacy, evident in the historical buildings. For example, one can find a Catholic chapel and a Buddhist temple located in the same locality (though not very close to each other). Throughout time, these historic buildings – many of which bear traditional European architectural features – have been renovated for purposes that are very different from their original intentions – for exam-ple, as a public library or a public health centre. Although these resources are not particularly appealing to urban residents, their time-honoured architec-tural features do give a facelift to the island's landscape and serve as cultural assets on the island.

Although recreational opportunities are ample, it is very rare that urban residents will stay overnight on the island, unless for the purpose of camping. More often than not, urban residents simply drive their own vehicles to the island and return home the same day. Leisure travelling in Macao is, thus, luggage free. This is attributable to the size of the city. In this sense, holidaying in Macao is carried out in a very causal manner. The stereotyped image of visi-tors with backpacks seems irrelevant in the context of Macao.

Gong Bei as the rear garden of the Macao people

One of the busiest places in Macao is the border gate to Gong Bei. On a typi-cal day, there are thousands of people commuting between the two places. Gong Bei is a small territory of Zhuhai City in the Guangdong Province. Although Macao and Gong Bei are located in the same country and the people on either side of the border speak the same dialect (Cantonese), the two places maintain different currency systems. Hence, travel permits are required to 'cross the border' since the border gate functions as an immigration and custom checkpoint. Many Macao residents actually do daily shopping across the border due to price differentials and some even choose to reside in Gong Bei and commute to work in Macao on a daily basis. For these reasons, Macao people perceive going to Gong Bei as anything but outbound travel. The fact that many of the new immigrants in Macao are originally inhabitants from Guangdong Province makes social ties between Macao and Gong Bei so strong.

Macao people commute to Gong Bei for different reasons, and holidaying there is regarded as a major motive for travelling beyond the city limits (Vong, 2005). This is not to say that Gong Bei offers distinctive leisure opportunities that cannot be found in Macao. This is reflected in the leisure activities partic-ipated in by the Macao residents, which do not seem to differ significantly when they are in Gong Bei. There is a continuity of interests and leisure pursuits in this context. Perhaps the impetus driving Macao people to do so is the opportunity to take pleasure in a different context – a social environment that is different from their home town. In this sense, getting away or escaping from their familiar surroundings takes precedence over the choice of leisure activities in which they can participate. While in Gong Bei, Macao residents frequently visit shopping malls, bookstores, restaurants, supermarkets, karaoke centres, pubs and nightclubs. Interestingly, some of these leisure facilities explicitly target Macao visitors, instead of the locals (the Gong Bei residents), owing to the high volume of Macao commuters who cross over on a daily basis. For example, there is an underground shopping mall extending directly to the Gong Bei border gate. This is a two-level underground complex that holds hundreds of stores providing different kinds of goods and services, which include, but are not limited to, consumer electronics, books, food and bever-age outlets, clothing, personal care items and barber shops. Not surprisingly, this shopping centre, due to its enormous size, has become the primary attrac-tion for many Macao residents visiting Gong Bei.

Holidaying across the border is made even more regular and frequent by those Macao residents who can afford to purchase their own holiday villas or country houses. These residents actually use Gong Bei and its nearby regions as their rear gardens, akin to 'second homes'. During weekends and extended holidays, they escape from familiar Macao and journey to their villas in main-land China (Xinhua, 2001). This holiday-break phenomenon is on the rise as the economic and social ties between the two places become stronger. In a nutshell, the mindset of 'looking outside' for leisure has enabled Macao resi-dents to perceive Gong Bei as their pseudo-geographical territory. How should this phenomenon be coined? Also, should it be viewed as 'regional outbound' leisure travel for the simple reason that domestic visitors are issued travel permits by their national governing authority when they cross the border? Would this imply reconstructing our conventional understanding of outbound travel? If not, then would it be statistically prudent to consider the daily cross-ings of the Macao people within their motherland as outbound travel? Or should the socio-geopolitical uniqueness of Macao – under the political prin-ciple of one country, two systems – be accepted under the rubric of native leisure travel? While this chapter does not provide any shortcut answers to these questions, the phenomenon in Macao provides solid data for future research to address this issue appropriately. Suffice it to say that domestic travel in Macao takes a different form and requires unusual interpretations.

Macao as a rising Las Vegas in Asia

In the years to come, Macao people may not need to explore leisure elsewhere. The mindset of 'looking outside' for leisure may become obsolete as many residents begin to rediscover leisure in their hometown. This is due to the rapid development of Macao's gaming industry. In 2002, the Macao government liberalized the casino business and invited world-class gaming giants to establish their flagships in the city (Gough, 2006). The intention of the government is to position Macao as a magnificent gaming-entertainment centre in the Far East. The achievements in this regard have been remarkable in that just a few years after the announcement of the liberalization policy, both tourist arrivals and gaming revenue have reached record highs. Precisely, the gaming revenue generated in Macao has already surpassed that of the Las Vegas Strip in Nevada, US (Gough and Hu, 2007). Macau also become one of the 20 richest economies in the world by the year 2008 (*China Business*, 2008). Parallel to this achievement is the rapidly changing leisure landscape of the entire city. New colossal casinos and multifunctional entertainment complexes have become Macao's new landmarks in the city.

Notwithstanding the fact that these are tourism products, these brand-new entertainment facilities have enriched the leisure opportunity of Macao people insofar as expanding leisure opportunities in the city. For instance, in the Cotai Strip (the reclaimed land between Taipa and Coloane) stands Asia's largest multipurpose entertainment resort, which attracts as many tourists as it attracts local residents (*Macao Post Daily*, 2007). This, however, is only a snapshot of the entire project that is currently under way. In the face of this frenetic tourism boom, where different competitors are devising leisure experiences for their visitors, Macao residents will regularly see new-fangled leisure elements being added to their city. Owing to the advantage of being residents of Macao, the natives will have easy access to a repertoire of leisure opportunities, from which they may take their pick.

Fortunately, the city's cultural heritages have not faded in their tourist appeal. Instead, in 2005, these cultural assets were inscribed on the World Heritage List, which, consequently, serves as effective propaganda in diversifying this tourism city's offering (Bruning, 2005). Although Macao has been dubbed the Las Vegas in the Far East, this oriental city now has more to offer: her cultural heritage. Altogether, citizens are witnessing Macao transform into a preferred tourism destination, with a landscape comprising features of extravagant colossal casinos contrasted with time-honoured historical buildings.

Festivals as a distinct genre of holidaying

Major festivals are a veritable resource that enrich the leisure of Macao natives. In this sense, major festivals in Macao are usually celebrated as extended public holidays. Due to historical reasons, festivals in Macao commemorate multicultural coexistence. They honour and celebrate Chinese traditions as much as European significant occasions (Lam, 2006). Today, festivals are treasured by Macao people as major avenues for distinctive forms of leisure pursuits. In this sense, there are extraordinary festive pastimes that Macao people will participate in specifically during festive celebrations. For example, firecrackers and fireworks are symbols of the Lunar New Year, whereas riddle games remind people of the Mid-Autumn Festival. In addition, there are religious festivals that call for visits to sacred places by devout followers. By combining holiday-making with festive activities, Macao people are able to renew and relive their cultural traditions of sacred and secular relevance throughout their generations. From this perspective, holiday-making has been afforded with a cultural meaning and at the same time has become instrumental in preserving local rites and customs, ensuring continuity of social mores in current times of change, adaptation and assimilation. Hence, an exploration of local festivals becomes a useful enquiry for an understanding of the culturally distinct genre of holiday-making of the Macao people.

Lunar New Year

Perhaps the most significant festival for ethnic Chinese around the world, as for the Macao Chinese, is the Lunar New Year. This is a festival which lasts for 15 days during the first Lunar month of the traditional Chinese agricultural calendar (which usually coincides with February). Concisely, it is a festival to celebrate the beginning of a new year and is observed with a spirit of gratitude and a sense of renewal. During this festival, the whole family joins in to clean their home, prepare delicious food and wear new clothes. Families visit their relatives. Married couples give 'red packets' – palm-sized red envelops filled with money – to those they love, including, but not limited to, family members. The giving of red packets is an important festive practice. In Chinese culture, the colour 'red' conveys the idea of 'luck', 'joy', 'happiness' and 'richness'. Giving red packets is ideologically synonymous to forwarding intense joy and fortune. Alternatively, 'red' also means 'burning fire' in Chinese Feng Shui; therefore, such a practice can otherwise be interpreted as auspicious in the coming year.

More importantly, the Lunar New Year is the time when Chinese people value frivolity over serious work. Just as the colour 'red' is the designated colour of the Lunar New Year, firecrackers and fireworks are the object symbols of this Chinese celebration. Unlike other cities in China where fire-crackers and fireworks have been restricted by officials for fire precaution measures, Macao continues to enjoy this festive activity to the extent that burning firecrackers and fireworks (though not necessarily only practised in the Lunar New Year, but also at other significant occasions, such as Chinese-style wedding ceremonies) is a popular Chinese New Year practice. Locals customarily hold the belief that in order to bring good luck to the whole family in the coming year, people must burn firecrackers for incessant periods of time. Suffice it to say that there are different festive activities – besides burning fire-crackers – to be followed, just as there are taboos to be avoided, during the entire period of the Lunar New Year.

The overlap between holidaying and festivals is evident during the Lunar New Year. Customarily, the Lunar New Year is the time for family reunions. Many migrant workers in urban cities, therefore, long to get together with their family members who reside in rural villages or small towns. Because of this, an enormous number of home-going migrant workers leverage on the extended holidays and flock back to their hometown for the New Year reunion. Macao is no exception to this rule. With more than 20 per cent of the entire working population made up of import labour (mostly from mainland China), holidaying 'back home' is a distinct feature of this festival in Macao, just as it is a common phenomenon in the other major cities in China.

Mid-Autumn Festival

The Mid-Autumn Festival is another well-known Chinese celebration that is associated with a distinctive form of leisure celebration. Also referred to as the Moon Festival, it originates from agricultural practice when farmers would rejoice together to celebrate the abundance of the summer's harvest. Just as moon cakes – which are round pastries made from lotus-seed paste and whole salty egg yolk – are the festival's symbolic food, candle lanterns and riddle games are the definitive leisure choices. In this sense, children play lanterns with their friends and adults challenge each other with riddle games. More recently, Macao people have turned to 'burning wax' as another fashionable pastime. This is essentially an outdoor activity, usually in a public park, where people engage in burning candles and shape the melted wax into interesting forms and artefacts. This 'creative' leisure activity has, however, received much criticism for its inherent hazards to physical safety (burn injuries) and air quality (environmental pollution) during the festival.

The Dragon Festivals

Locally, the celebration of the Dragon Boat Festival is yet another illustration of the cultural embedding of leisure pursuit. This festival commemorates an honest minister in ancient times who is said to have committed suicide by drowning himself in a river. To mourn over his death, the villagers occasionally threw rice dumplings into the river – to feed his ghost – and beat drums to commemorate this decent man. Today, this festival is best known by its dragon boat competition, which is also the highlight feature in Macao (Glenn and Osti, 2006; Moreira, 2006). Interestingly, the dragon boat competition of modern times has inherited a distinct feature of the past: drum-beating. While villagers beat their drums to commemorate their beloved minister, the drummer – who is a member of the crew on the dragon boat – beats the drum rhythmically to synchronize the strokes of the paddlers. Unlike the other festive leisure that is short lived, dragon boat racing has gained popularity in Macao as a year-round and favourite team sport. In recent years, this custom-turned sport has received international recognition as a major sporting event (Sofield and Silvan, 2003). For example, every year, Macao hosts the International Dragon Boat Race to celebrate the Dragon Boat Festival. Interestingly, during this time, another international dragon boat tournament is hosted in Hong Kong, although there is no connection whatsoever between these two events.

Whilst the Dragon Boat Festival is celebrated as a national festival, there is yet another 'dragon' festival that is celebrated locally and on a much smaller scale. This is the Drunken Dragon Festival. The Drunken Dragon Festival aims to worship a celestial dragon that sacrificed itself to protect mankind from plague. Mythically speaking, there are many versions of the legend. The most popular is that in ancient times, there was a plague-contaminated village whose villagers killed a dragon-incarnated serpent and threw its body into the river. The villagers then drank the river water and were miraculously cured. Today, in celebration of this festival, worshippers, dressed in special costumes, take part in a parade where they dance – in a specific dance format – and drink wine until they all get drunk in the parade. This is practised with the belief that by dancing in a drunken state, the 'worshippers' are able to replicate the motion of a dragon, which is mythically believed to sway and swing its body as it moves!

A-Ma Festival

A case in point that illustrates how religious worship overlaps with leisure travel in Macao is the A-Ma Festival. This festival celebrates the birthday of a goddess, A-Ma, who is extremely popular among the inhabitants along the coastal line of the South China Sea. Histo-culturally, it is said that A-Ma was a mortal turned goddess. While alive and residing in Fujian Province, she was able to make omens. After her death, it was believed that she had incarnated as a goddess and protected mortals from harm. To worship A-Ma, people have built temples in her name. In this regard, Macao owns one of the oldest temples of A-Ma, known as A-Ma Temple (the temple has a history of more than 500 years and is situated in Macao Peninsular). Every year, during this festival, which may last for a few days, the devout followers in Macao self-organize festive activities to celebrate this occasion. For example, they queue up in the temple to burn incense and candles to pray for good luck and fortune. The most eye-catching festive activity, however, is an A-Ma-themed Chinese opera held in the vicinity of the A-Ma Temple. The opera, with performers well dressed in opera costumes, is performed in a temporary bamboo-shed theatre in the open space in front of the A Ma Temple. Interestingly, however, the opera is dedicated to one, and only one, audience: the A-Ma Goddess.

On the other hand, the Macao government has also built the world's tallest A-Ma statue at the highest hill point of Coloane Island. Incidentally, the local devout followers, with the support of the government, have renovated the surrounding mountainous areas, in the vicinity of A-Ma statue, into a place for group worship, known as the A-Ma Cultural Village (*People's Daily*, 2001a). Since then, large-scale festive activities, including, but not limited to, dedication ceremonies, A-Ma-themed cultural dances and processions of an A-Ma statue have been formally held (Iu, 2006; *People's Daily*, 2001b). Put simply, this act of up-scaling a traditional festival into a quasi-governmental fiesta attracts inbound religious tourists. Most likely, the government's intention is to use the popularity of A-Ma Goddess in the region where Macao is situated in order to endorse religious tourism in Macao. With this in mind, Macao is working hard to portray the city as a place of historical significance for A-Ma Goddess and to dub the historic A Ma Temple and the newly acclaimed A-Ma cultural village as desired areas for local and overseas pious followers to take their spiritual pilgrimage.

Due to the need for tourism development, Macao has repackaged, if not reinvented, one of the oldest festivals in the city into a regional tourism event. This process of rejuvenation has carefully preserved the rituals and mores that are cherished by pious followers, but which may not necessarily be comprehensible to the lay public (the 'A-Ma-themed opera' is a good example). On the other hand, it has also incorporated prevalent and explicable forms of celebration, such as dances, parades and exhibitions, in order to increase public awareness, as well as the leisure appeals of the festival, in such a way as to make it easy for the general public to comprehend and, therefore, to participate in this festival.

Portuguese folk dance

The City of Macao claims much pride as the historical meeting point of the East with the West accruing from its occupancy by the Portuguese. The socio-cultural inheritance, thus gained, endows this oriental port town with some Western religio-cultural traditions that continue to be upheld even today. As a consequence of Portuguese influence, major Judeo-Christian observances, such as Christmas, Easter, the calendared New Year and St Valentine's Day, also hold significance in Macao. During some occasions, however, these festivals are celebrated with an exquisite Portuguese flavour, primarily the cheering Portuguese folk dance. While the original folk dance of Portugal is typically a traditional country dance of the local farmers, as they celebrate a full harvest, the Portuguese folk dance in Macao essentially resonates with the joy and happiness of community life in that it recognizes Portuguese rights in this oriental city. There are dancing clubs in Macao that endorse and teach Portuguese folk dance. Whenever an opportunity arises and circumstances permit, these amateur dancers perform in different festivals or special occasions, reliving and perpetuating the traditional Portuguese rite. Unfortunately, Portuguese folk dance is loosing its appeal among the younger generation. Perhaps in the years to come, one will be able to derive pleasure from this traditional rite only as an audience, rather than as active participants. Nevertheless, the Portuguese folk dance is now presented as a shining icon of Macao by its tourism bureau.

Conclusions

Political history has created this ex-Portuguese colony, geographically and culturally, as the meeting place between East and West. Such historical influences have given this Chinese city a tremendously rich and visible heritage of dual culture. Today, a returned territory of China, Macao is re-creating itself as an integrated, but exotic, 'other' within the People's Republic of China. To be exotic, Macao prides itself as the only gambling paradise in communist China, while the city vigorously promotes its shinning heritage assets to the outside world. Macao thus is unique within mainland China and wins the privileged status of being a special administrative region of the People's Republic of China. It is this politically exceptional status of Macao that has come to challenge our understanding of, and definition of, domestic tourism in Macao. Macao residents who are now nationals of the People's Republic of China are legally required to use travel permits to travel 'domestically' for whatever purpose. In explanation of such an anomaly, one can interpret this as a symbol of 'one country, two systems', rather than a technical hurdle that discourages the inland travelling of Macao people.

Finally, insofar as domestic leisure and travel are stigmatized as less appealing in comparison to outbound international travel, it is pragmatic and prudent for policy-makers to devise effective policies to rejuvenate the former. One possible approach is to integrate holiday-making with traditional festival, strengthening the meaning of domestic holiday-making in the local context. The Macao experience illustrates the significance of local rites and custom (e.g. the A-Ma Festival) to the Macao people and ethnic Chinese alike. These leisure pursuits not only provide opportunities to rejuvenate a sense of place and belonging within locals, but affirm a distinctive local appeal in a global context.

References

Bruning, H. (2005) 'Competitive heritage', *Macao Post Daily*, 21 July, p2

China Business (2008) 'Macau's rotten basket of riches', 8 April, www.atimes.com/atimes/China_Business/JD04Cb01.html, accessed 31 August 2008

Glenn, J. M. and Osti, L. (2006) 'Cultural authenticity in sport events: The case of the dragon boat races', in *Proceedings of the Cauthe 2006 Conference – 'To the City and Beyond'*, Melbourne, Australia, pp1066–1080

Gough, N. (2006) 'Wynn, Adelson and company are changing the face of the enclave in the hope of replicating their success in the US gaming hub', *South China Morning Post*, 16 September, pB3

Gough, N. and Hu, F. Y. (2007) 'Macao casinos tipped to outdo Nevada', *South China Morning Post*, 29 August, pA3

Iu, E. (2006) 'A Ma cultural village hosts 4th Macao Cultural and Tourism Festival', *Macau Post Daily*, 31 October, p4

Lam, C. C. (2006) 'Influence of and to festivals with tourism development: A case study of Macao', in A. Aktas (ed) *Turk-Kazakh International Tourism Conference*, Akdeniz University, Turkey, pp311–315

Macao Government Tourist Office (2008) *Travel Info: About Macau*, www.macau-tourism.gov.mo/en/info/info.php, accessed 25 August 2008

Macao Post Daily (2007) 'Venetian Cotai to open on August 28', *Macao Post Daily*, 14 June, p1

Macao Statistics Census and Service (2008) *Environment Statistics*, www.dsec.gov.mo/index.asp?src=/english/pub/e_amb_pub.html, accessed 25 August 2008

Macao.com (2008) *Dining: Lord Stow's Bakery*, www.macao.com/index.php?option=com_restaurants&Itemid=231&task=show_details&id=23, accessed 15 December 2007

Moreira, P. (2006) 'Dragons on the water: The influence of culture in the competitive advantage of tourism destinations', in J. Ali-Knight and D. Chambers (eds) *Case Studies in Festival and Event Marketing and Cultural Tourism*, LSA, Eastbourne, pp79–71

People's Daily (2001a) 'Macao to build A-Ma cultural village', *People's Daily*, 3 May, http://english.peopledaily.com.cn/english/200105/03/eng20010503_69174.html, accessed 20 December 2007

People's Daily (2001b) 'Macao schedules A-Ma cultural festival', *People's Daily*, 4 May, http://english.peopledaily.com.cn/english/200105/04/eng20010504_69236.html, accessed 20 December 2007

Sofield, T. H. B. and Silvan, A. (2003) 'From cultural festival to international sport –
The Hong Kong Dragon Boat Races', *Journal of Sport Tourism*, vol 8, no 1, pp9–20

Vong, T. N. (2005) 'Leisure satisfaction and quality of life in Macao, China', *Leisure Studies*, vol 24, no 2, pp195–207

Vong, T. N. (2006) 'Leisure participation in Macao SAR: An exploratory study', *Journal of Macau Studies*, vol 33, pp138–145

Xinhua (2001) 'Macao residents stream to China inland for visit', 16 April, http://english.peopledaily.com.cn/english/200104/16/eng20010416_67802.html, accessed 8 December 2007

16

Epilogue: Domestic Tourism in Asia – Contexts and Directions

John K. Walton

I am grateful to Shalini Singh for inviting me to provide a contextual commentary on this interesting volume. I have learned a great deal from the process. As an international historian with a particular interest in domestic tourism and its destinations, mainly in the UK and Spain, but also in countries across Western Europe, together with the US and parts of Latin America, I have found the widespread neglect in tourism studies both of domestic tourism and of informed historical perspectives to be impoverishing and distorting. In the Asian context, especially, the present initiative appears long overdue, although, inevitably in the present state of research, it contributes more to remedying the first problem than the second. A recent overview of tourism development in South-East Asia provides a good illustration of the current status of domestic tourism studies in the region: the author points out, in passing, that domestic tourism is significant in (especially) Indonesia, Thailand, the Philippines and Malaysia, only to move on without apology to focus on the international tourism that dominates the agenda (Wong Poh Poh, 2003; see also Chon, 2000).

It is clear that across Asia, domestic tourism is very important in a variety of settings, challenges existing assumptions, priorities and labels among policy-makers and tourism academics, and (because of this) is difficult to 'find' for research purposes. Indeed, it often falls outside the dominant assumptions of what actually constitutes 'tourism' in an academic sense, which makes it effectively invisible in and to the relevant literatures. It has a very important informal sector, and is dominated by small businesses that do not generate the accessible, deceptively user-friendly and (often) suspect statistics associated with international tourism and the making and recording of government tourism policies. Moreover, it takes forms which are often hybrid or alien when viewed through the expectations of dominant tourism ideology, which tends to perpetuate its invisibility, especially when individuals or families have complex and often seasonal domestic economies that may include tourism without depending on it or being dominated by it. Participatory and grassroots activities involving pilgrimage and popular festivals are recurrent themes, as is visiting family and friends; and effective research in the field therefore demands qualitative research skills, especially those of anthropology and ethnography (and, ideally, oral history), together with empathetic recognition of the power of agency among the participants, whether service providers, consumers or just members of the 'host' population who flit in and out of the tourist economy, or merely help to construct its ambience by just being the responsive object of the tourist gaze.

These circumstances also help to explain the lack of a properly researched historical dimension to provide a context for Asian developments. The core academic business of tourism studies, especially as expressed through economics and business studies, focuses almost exclusively on the modern international activities of big business, often in a very present-minded, policy-orientated instrumental way, and a recurrent theme in these chapters is the absence of historical context, except in terms of the 'usable' history deployed by heritage, festival and events tourism, and by some kinds of theme parks. This is in sharp contrast to the extensive body of work on domestic tourism and its histories in Western Europe (especially the UK), the US, Australia and, for example, Argentina (Walton, 1981, 2000; Aron, 1999; Baranowski and Furlough, 2001; Berghoff, 2002; Pastoriza, 2002; White, 2005). But the cases of Mexico or Turkey, where recent explosive initiatives in international tourism have dominated the research agenda, are more representative of developments across the globe (Clancy, 2001; Burak, 2004). It is much more difficult to get a grip on trends and traditions if your historical roots are shallow, and the dominant emphasis on recent developments in international, 'McDonaldized', 'mass' package tourism has tended to obscure conventionally defined traditions, including their trends and practices. The scope for using international tourism as an agency for 'modernization' and development, and as a positive contributor to the balance of payments, has influenced priorities in the commission and production of academic outputs, the generation of funding opportunities and the construction of careers. As part of this process, the emergent academic discipline of tourism studies has tended to define its concerns in such a way as to exclude everything that cannot be categorized as modern, 'mass' and international as somehow 'not tourism', and policy-makers have colluded in and reinforced this, contributing to the development of academic cultures in which studies of tourism policy, especially when using official statistics, marginalize the domestic and the 'traditional' (Walton, 2005, pp1–18). In this respect, the editor of this book has identified a very significant set of problems, which are articulated convincingly in her introduction.

So this book is overdue and welcome, tentative though some of its chapters must be, and dominated by local ethnographic case studies or broad national overviews, with little sense of regional scales of interpretation at intermediate levels within countries. Geographical coverage is necessarily patchy, limited by what was on offer in response to the call for chapters. Of the South-East Asian countries singled out by Wong Poh Poh as having domestic tourism activities on a significant scale, only Malaysia and the Philippines feature here: Thailand is an important absentee, as is Indonesia. Nor is Turkey included, despite the spectacular recent development of 'mass' tourism in this gateway state between Europe and Asia. India is represented by an ambitious overview; but there is only one chapter each on China and Japan, each of which deals with a rather specialized aspect of tourism within these extensive and highly complex societies, and South Korea is absent. So are Pakistan and, perhaps less surprisingly, Bangladesh. On the other hand, several small island and peninsula locations (Hong Kong, Macao, Singapore) are represented despite the limited scope for genuine domestic tourism within their relatively narrow geographical confines, although the chapter authors make every effort to engage with the issues. There is, in the most literal sense, little room for domestic tourism beyond the local day trip to take root in these places, as the overwhelming preponderance of international visitors in Singapore's Bollywood tourism, or the extreme contrasts revealed by the comparative study of Singapore and Malaysia, underline. Hong Kong may be big enough (and have sufficient green space) to play host to hill-walkers and a nature park, but there are limits to the scale and scope of these developments for internal markets, interesting though some of the issues that are raised may be. But Kyrgyzstan and Mongolia are unexpected and interesting additions to the list, bringing in distinctive dimensions from post-communist Central Asia, alongside the post-communist or transitional cultures of Vietnam, China and, in a sense, Cambodia (depending on how we label the Khmer Rouge, who challenge all existing categories by the pathological enormity of their abuses). A stronger focus on the periods of maximum socialist influence in Vietnam, the People's Republic of China or parts of India, for example, and of their legacy, might have encouraged interesting comparisons with developments in Eastern Europe before the fall of the Berlin Wall or, indeed, with Cuba (Schwarz, 1997; Ghodsee, 2005; Gorsuch and Kuenker, 2006) The main focus of Ghodsee's work on the Black Sea is on gender and local workforces in tourism, and it is worth noting that both these important themes are also marginal to the present book.

Other apparent imbalances demand attention. The predominant approach adopts the orthodox assumptions about neo-classical economics, the pursuit of growth, and the descriptive accumulation of statistics that dominate much of tourism studies, although several chapters are led by anthropological and sociological perspectives, and there is a single (and highly original) Marxist contribution, focusing on contemporary pilgrimage or pagoda tourism in

Vietnam. The general lack of historical context is disappointing, if under-standable: it would have been interesting and useful, for example, to have learned more about the colonial domestic tourism legacy in Cambodia or the Philippines, or in parts of India or the People's Republic of China, where current domestic tourism has older multicultural antecedents, whatever may have happened to these in Cambodia as a result of the Khmer Rouge trauma and its aftermath. From an external perspective, there seems to be remarkably little in this book on Asian Islamic cultures and tourism, which reflects in part (but only in part) the geographical absences mentioned above: there seems to be very little published research on this theme in this setting. Pilgrimage, in particular, and religion, in general, are recurrent foci of attention; but there is little or nothing on religious conflict in relation to tourist sites and journeys, or the impact of caste systems, or of ethnic divisions; although the chapter on Han tourism in Tibetan areas of the People's Republic of China is the most obvious exception here. This lacuna reflects a general lack of engagement with internal conflicts of all kinds within the countries and communities that are analysed here, whether in India, Sri Lanka or the Philippines. This absence is surpris-ing, not least because internal political violence is always particularly damaging to tourism, whether domestic or international, and there is the potential for interesting and revealing analysis along these lines. From a European perspec-tive, and in the light of the enormous importance of Asian developments in this field, there is also surprisingly little on domestic beach tourism in those coun-tries that have coastlines, apart from a solitary Philippines case study of an individual, and very popular, resort. Similarly, we hear little about tourism in mountainous regions, apart from certain aspects of pilgrimage (although the only extended discussion of hill-walking concerns Hong Kong), or about spa tourism, apart from intriguing Mongolian variations on the theme. Domestic tourism to capital cities, another big European theme, is also scarcely discussed, although the impact of internal demand from macrocephalous capitals on the development of rural tourism is highlighted in Kyrgyzstan and Mongolia. The absence of material on domestic demand for, and enjoyment of, sports tourism (participant as well as spectator, and including winter sports and, of course, the increasingly inevitable golf tourism, with all the problems that golf courses pose for sustainability) is also interesting and, perhaps, reveal-ing about the predominance of international over domestic markets in these (and other) fields in Asian tourism. The same may apply to the low profile of sex tourism in these pages, and the passing allusions to the impact of (espe-cially) US forces' 'rest and recreation' activities in World War II, the Vietnam War and the Cold War would merit further research in contemporary history (with an extension to cover the role of the Japanese armed forces, from at least the early 1930s to the end of World War II) as we seek to understand the pres-ent and future through the past. More pertinently in this context, it is difficult to imagine that the demand for sexual services in tourist settings has ever come entirely from international tourists (Howell, 2003). And what of battlefield or 'dark' tourism, which is so important to domestic as well as international markets in parts of Europe and the US (Lennon and Foley, 2000)?

The main focus of the present collection is on traffic flows and tourist experiences; but within that framework there is surprisingly little development of arguments around transport and other kinds of infrastructural provision, apart from recreations and attractions. The relative (and changing) importance of bus and rail as opposed to air travel for domestic tourism, not forgetting ferries (and their hazards) in the Philippines and other archipelagos, deserves deeper analysis in terms of fare structures and travel experiences, on which there is an extensive European literature. Accommodation for domestic tourists is mentioned in passing in some of the chapters, but never constitutes a theme, and the same applies to public health and provisioning, except where their absence generates problems of amenity and sustainability. Sustainability itself is also a theme that flits in and out of this collection, mainly in the background (although it is, in a sense, central to the Hong Kong contribution, and surfaces in other chapters), without ever retaining an extended position at the front of the stage. Problems of sea, lake and river pollution are mentioned in chapter after chapter, along with the degradation of other aspects of attractive environments, and a widespread belief in the incorruptibility of holy waters that has a counterpart in the enduring European willingness to regard the purifying powers of the sea as inexhaustible (Hassan, 2003). Above all, it would be good to have more on conflicts over access to, and use of, desirable spaces, especially beaches, examining privatization, commodification, social exclusion and regulation, and the ways in which developments in international tourism impact upon domestic markets, practices and access. The chapter on Hong Kong, for example, tells us very interesting things about the development of mountain walking and attitudes to it on the part of the participants, without exploring the property ownership framework and the culture of access to mountains within which this takes place. The importance of such issues in European and North American contexts has become apparent (Taylor, 1997; Shaffer, 2002). Such venues and themes are so important in writings on Western domestic tourist cultures, extending, for example, right across Eastern Europe, and on, for instance, Argentina and Mexico, that we are entitled to ask whether these absences from the book reflect a lack of interest in such destinations among domestic tourists in Asia, which would suggest that this kind of tourism, where it exists, is mainly based on imported colonial preferences or on the later rise of international mass tourism, drawing on Western markets and models; or whether they are an accidental consequence of the spread of papers on offer for this particular venture. Colonial hill stations in India or Vietnam, or beach resorts in India, adapted and hybridized for post-colonial

domestic markets, are of immense potential interest to the researcher, following on, for example, from work already done on Indian hill stations
(Panter-Downes, 1985, Kennedy, 1996). After all, no book of these dimensions
can hope to offer a representative survey of all the varieties of domestic tourism
across a continent, and the editor rightly makes no such claim. This is an exercise in opening out an enormous field of enquiry, rather than an attempt at
definitive coverage.

What are the themes that do emerge? In the first place, and central to the
agenda of the book, there is the question of what exactly constitutes 'domestic
tourism' in these variegated settings. Singapore, Hong Kong, and (especially)
Macao are so compact that it is difficult to envisage 'domestic tourism' as
extending beyond the day, half-day or evening outing, in which case it is hard
to differentiate it from the broader concept of 'leisure'. Taiwan is big enough
to offer more scope; but its domestic package tourists seem to be far
outweighed by outsiders. Comparing Singapore with Malaysia is problematic
from this point of view, as like is not being set alongside like in this respect.
Meanwhile, Han tourism to predominantly ethnic Tibetan areas of China (or,
indeed, potentially to Tibet itself) poses questions about the definition of
'domestic tourism' within complex polities which contain disputed territories
or 'nations without a state', as Vasantkumar points out in Chapter 6 while
emphasizing the sheer complexity of 'domestic' tourism in such a multilingual
and multicultural nation. These questions have been treated in European
discussions of the relationship between tourism and 'national identity', and
comparable issues arise in the Basque country, which crosses the political
boundary between Spain and France, or in the Baltic states during the era of
Soviet domination. Over and above all this, the varying levels of international
tourism in different Asian countries and tourist settings will themselves affect
the extent, nature and direction of domestic tourism.

More positively, the relationship between pilgrimage and tourism is a
theme that recurs continuously, inviting comparison with other parts of the
globe (Gladstone, 2005). Some would argue, of course, that all tourism is a
form of pilgrimage, directed at sites and experiences that are sacred as objects
of the desiring, celebrating or commemorative gaze, even if the rituals
observed are those of families or friendship groups, celebrating their own
anniversaries or shared experiences at conventional resorts or camping
grounds, rather than those of formally constituted religious organizations.
Most accounts of 'pilgrimage' in the US, which is short of deep-rooted historic
sacred sites of a traditional kind (apart from the sacred places of the Native
Americans), are really about this kind of secular ritual, although we might
interpret, for example, recurring sporting events or party conventions in those
terms. Campo's categories of pilgrimage in a US context, viewed in relation to
organized religion, civil religion and cultural religion, and embracing

Graceland, Gettysburg and Mount Rushmore, as well as Catholic, Hindu or Mormon sites, are helpful here (Campo, 1998; Cross and Walton, 2005, Chapter 5). The Disney empire might also have been included. But religious pilgrimage as such, to shrines and other holy places, is surely identifiable as a distinctive category, although some of the traditions associated with it are of relatively modern invention or creation, as in the Western European cases of Lourdes (France) or Knock (Ireland), where the relevant apparitions of the Virgin Mary are of relatively recent vintage (1858 and 1879, respectively) as pilgrimage sites go, and the tourism flows may be international as well as domestic (Kaufman, 2005). The modern foundation of the Vietnamese Zen pagoda as pilgrimage destination, which is examined by Alneng (see Chapter 2), built as recently as 1994, is remarkable in international context. Pilgrimage tourism can spread throughout the year or be highly seasonal, associated with particular calendar festivals and even single days. In the latter case, it becomes less visible or amenable to the researcher's gaze because of the informal and ephemeral characteristics associated with such events. The problems that this poses for the researcher are certainly not confined to Asia; but it is instructive to see these and other pilgrimage-related issues recurring in chapter after chapter of this book, and to note the sheer magnitude of this phenomenon across the continent (Miyazaki and Williams, 2001; Timothy and Olsen, 2006).

But the importance of the informal sector – whether involving visiting family and friends, or the use of 'unofficial' accommodation, catering and, indeed, entertainment – is confined neither to pilgrimage nor to Asia. It was, and remains, a feature of British resorts from their earliest years, as accommodation had to be sought in private houses at peak periods and many businesses were seasonal and family run, and were advertised by word of mouth. Subsequently, taxation and regulatory regimes were systematically evaded in the informal commercial sector of small seasonal enterprises, even in Spain during the Franco dictatorship or the Soviet Union at the height of state pretensions to complete control. Subletting rooms during the tourist season and entertaining family and friends merged into each other, with a sliding scale of commodification; and it is hardly surprising to find similar arrangements in Sri Lanka or India in the early 21st century, when they remain alive and well in the most established of domestic tourism cultures in other parts of the world (Walton, 1978; Gorsuch and Koenker, 2006). But the concept of the informal sector in domestic tourism extends much further, to food stalls, entertainers in local bars or at festivals, and so on; and where there is also international tourism, it becomes increasingly difficult, and potentially distorting, to isolate the two. Here as elsewhere, 'domestic tourism' is a necessary and useful category, not least in encouraging a corrective redirection of the gaze, but also a difficult one.

Two of the most interesting chapters in this book deal with 'heritage tourism' in Japan and Taiwan (see Chapters 3 and 9), promoted by imaginative local leaders from within villages with ailing economies, and aiming mainly at domestic markets. There are interesting potential comparisons here with developments in Western Europe and the US over the last century, seeking to sustain and communicate the living memory of the ways of life of the immediate and further past through the recreation of crafts and cultures, and the case of Asuke is particularly reminiscent of the development of the Beamish open-air museum in north-east of England, which borrowed and adapted from Scandinavian precedents under a charismatic curator and rode the industrial heritage wave, which began to break in England during the 1970s, presenting its version of the recent past to an overwhelmingly regional market (Cross and Walton, 2005, Chapter 6). Comparisons with and cross-references to the Japanese *onsen* traditional spa culture, and the extent to which it and other aspects of Japanese domestic tourism have adapted to new trends, would be very interesting (Miyazaki and Williams, 2001).

It will be clear that there will be endless scope for developing the Asian domestic tourism theme from the stimulating chapters that can be found in this collection, and in scattered locations elsewhere. One of the interesting things to emerge from some of the chapters in this volume is the development of ambitious government initiatives in the gathering of statistics to inform domestic as well as international tourism policy, although the case study of Puerto Galera in the Philippines demonstrates the enduring practical limits of such initiatives (see Chapter 11). The statistics of domestic tourism in the informal sector are likely to remain intractable almost by definition. But this should not engender defeatism. The ways forward lie through the imaginative use of case studies and local or regional sources. The approaches through ethnography and anthropology that have proved so fruitful in some of the chapters in this book can be supplemented and enriched in various ways: through archives where they exist and are accessible, newspapers, tourist guides and travel literature (often read 'against the grain'), trade directories, novels, film and television representation, art, architecture and 'heritage', planning records, censuses, taxation records, records of crime, and governance and urban regulation. All of these sources will present their own problems of coverage and interpretation, as those of us who have researched on domestic tourism in Europe, the US, Australia and Argentina have already found. But they can be made to generate deeper understanding of the issues, processes and conflicts at stake; and if they also lead the participants into approaches that are grounded in the past as well as the present, so much the better.

References

Aron, C. (1999) *Working at Play*, Oxford University Press, New York, NY

Baranowski, S. and Furlough, E. (eds) (2001) *Being Elsewhere: Tourism, Consumer Culture and Identity in Modern Europe and North America*, University of Michigan Press, Ann Arbor, MI

Berghoff, H. et al (eds) (2002) *The Making of Modern Tourism: The Cultural History of the British Experience, 1600–2000*, Palgrave, London

Burak, S. et al (2004) 'Impact of urbanization and tourism on coastal environments', *Ocean and Coastal Management*, vol 47, pp515–527

Campo, J. E. (1998) 'American pilgrimage landscapes', *Annals of the American Academy of Political and Social Science*, vol 558, pp40–56

Chon, K. (ed) (2000) *Tourism in Southeast Asia*, Haworth Press, New York, NY

Clancy, M. (2001) *Exporting Paradise: Tourism and Development in Mexico*, Pergamon, Oxford

Cross, G. and Walton, J. K. (2005) *The Playful Crowd: Pleasure Places in the Twentieth Century*, Columbia University Press, New York, NY

Ghodsee, K. (2005) *The Red Riviera: Gender, Tourism and Post-socialism on the Black Sea*, Duke University Press, Durham, NC

Gladstone, D. L. (2005) *From Pilgrimage to Package Tour*, Routledge, London

Gorsuch, A. E. and Koenker, D. P. (eds) (2006) *Turizm: The Russian and East European Tourist under Communism*, Cornell University Press, Ithaca, NY

Hassan, J. (2003) *The Seaside, Health and the Environment in England and Wales since 1800*, Ashgate, Aldershot, UK

Howell, P. (2003) 'Race, space and the regulation of prostitution in colonial Hong Kong', *Urban History*, vol 31, pp229–248

Kaufman, S. K. (2005) *Consuming Visions: Mass Culture and the Lourdes Shrine*, Cornell University Press, Ithaca, NY

Kennedy, D. (1996) *The Magic Mountains: Hill Stations of the British Raj*, University of California Press, Berkeley, CA

Lennon, J. J. and Foley, M. (eds) (2000) *Dark Tourism*, Continuum, London

Miyazaki, F., and Williams, D. (2001) 'The intersection of the local and the translocal at a sacred site', *Japanese Journal of Religious Studies*, vol 28, pp399–440

Panter-Downes, M. (1985) *Ooty Preserved: A Victorian Hill Station*, Century, London

Pastoriza, E. (2003) 'El ocio peronista: la conquista de las vacaciones: El turismo social en la Argentina', in *Fiesta, Juego y Ocio*, Editorial Universidad, Salamanca, Spain, pp383–420

Poh Poh, W. (2003) 'Tourism development in southeast Asia', in L. Sien Chia (ed) *Southeast Asia Transformed*, Institute for South East Asian Studies, Singapore

Ryan, C. (ed) (2007) *Battlefield Tourism*, Elsevier, London

Schwartz, R. (1997) *Pleasure Island*, University of Nebraska Press, Lincoln, Nebraska

Shaffer, M. S. (2002) *See America First: Tourism and National Identity 1880–1940*, Smithsonian Institute, Washington, DC

Taylor, H. (1997) *A Claim on the Countryside*, Keele University Press, Edinburgh

Timothy, D. J. and Olsen, D. H. (eds) (2006) *Tourism, Religion and Spiritual Journeys*, Routledge, London

Walton, J. K. (1978) *The Blackpool Landlady: A Social History*, Manchester University Press, Manchester

Walton, J. K. (1981) 'The demand for working-class seaside holidays in Victorian England', *Economic History Review*, vol 34, pp249–265

Walton, J. K. (2000) *The British Seaside: Holidays and Resorts in the Twentieth Century*, Manchester University Press, Manchester

Walton, J. K. (ed) (2005) *Histories of Tourism*, Channel View, Clevedon

White, R. (2005) *On Holidays: a History of Getting Away in Australia*, Pluto Press, North Melbourne

Index